S0-BNG-805

Moral Problems in American Life

Moral Problems in American Life

New Perspectives on Cultural History

Edited by

KAREN HALTTUNEN and
LEWIS PERRY

CORNELL UNIVERSITY PRESS

Ithaca and London

Copyright © 1998 by Cornell University

All rights reserved. Except for brief quotations in a review, this book, or parts thereof, must not be reproduced in any form without permission in writing from the publisher. For information, address Cornell University Press, Sage House, 512 East State Street, Ithaca, New York 14850.

First published 1998 by Cornell University Press

First printing, Cornell Paperbacks, 1998

Printed in the United States of America

Library of Congress Cataloging-in-Publication Data

Moral problems in American life : new perspectives on
  cultural history / edited by Karen Halttunen and Lewis
  Perry.
      p.   cm.
    Includes bibliographical references and index.
    ISBN 0-8014-3270-7 (alk. paper). — ISBN 0-8014-8350-6
  (pbk. : alk. paper)
      1. United States—Moral conditions.   2. United
  States—Social conditions.   I. Halttunen, Karen, 1951–   .
  II. Perry, Lewis.
  HN57.M67   1998
  306'.0973—dc21   98-8356

Cornell University Press strives to use environmentally
responsible suppliers and materials to the fullest extent
possible in the publishing of its books. Such materials
include vegetable-based, low-VOC inks and acid-free
papers that are recycled, totally chlorine-free, or partly
composed of nonwood fibers.

Cloth printing   10   9   8   7   6   5   4   3   2   1
Paperback printing   10   9   8   7   6   5   4   3   2   1

For Our Teacher,
David Brion Davis

NON-RETURNABLE

Contents

Contents

Illustrations

Moral Problems in American Life

Introduction

KAREN HALTTUNEN AND LEWIS PERRY

This volume surveys the moral landscape of the American past, from the early-eighteenth-century emergence of Anglo-American moral reform societies through the response of military chaplains serving in Vietnam to the antiwar movement. Its purpose is to illuminate the moral dimensions of the American historical experience and to demonstrate what can be achieved through a historically informed moral inquiry. The fourteen essays included here examine a wide range of difficult moral questions that have engaged past generations of Americans and persist into the present. What constitutes a moral community, and how is it to be shaped under modern conditions of a pluralistic, mass society? What role should religion, public education, and the family play in making the moral community? What is the impact of economic, racial, and sexual inequalities on the vision of a virtuous nation? How should a moral community respond to social viciousness, crime, and mental disorders? What are the moral implications of artistic expression, school curricula, sexual behaviors, and the popular media? At what point does obedience to a higher moral law mandate civil disobedience, and what are the proper limits to such disobedience within a democracy? When is a society morally justified in waging war, whether within its own boundaries or in the territories of other peoples?

The primary concern in all these essays is less with moral abstractions and manifestos than with how moral problems have been defined and addressed within the stream of everyday experience. We thus approach the subject of moral problems in American life primarily through close attention to a range of cultural practices that link private experience with public commitment. The essays that follow include studies of moral reform

movements such as the Anglo-American "reformation of manners," abolitionism, and Progressive efforts to enforce right-handedness in schoolchildren. They examine religious practices such as Jewish liturgical prayers,
the spiritual direction of the children of interfaith marriages, and wartime
pastoral care in the armed services. They study specific historical variants
on the social institutions of marriage, public schools, labor unions, and
mental hospitals and penitentiaries. They scrutinize the enduring moral
authority of such key texts as the Bible and the U.S. Constitution and of
influential bodies of thought including classical liberal theory, Darwinian
science, Progressive educational ideas, and history itself, both popular and
academic. They decode the moral meanings embedded in a variety of expressive forms: abolitionist iconography, personal correspondence, sit-ins
and boycotts, poetry recitation, bohemian sexual confessionalism, avant-
garde art, and documentary film.

Despite their wide range of subject matter, these essays are united in an
effort to recapture the moral complexities of lived experience in the past,
with particular attention to the specific historical contexts of older systems
of moral understanding. The authors of these essays join in exploring a
problem-oriented history, attentive to the dilemmas, conflicts, ironies, and
contingencies of moral experience that emerge clearly from the close study
of the moral meanings embedded—often deliberately, sometimes unintentionally—in daily practices. The primary intent of this volume is thus
neither to search through the past for fixed moral certainties nor to fault
past Americans for failing to achieve the moral insights of our own contemporary culture. It is rather to shed light on the moral challenges and
dilemmas confronted by past Americans, the costs they incurred in taking
on their commitments, the moral binds in which their positions sometimes placed them, and the occasions when their creativity illuminated
the rigidity of the culture in which they acted. We are attentive to the
ironic ends to which the best moral efforts sometimes led our subjects: to
moral communities that thrived on the identification and stigmatization
of outsiders, moral commitments that ensued in violence, moral choices
that curtailed others' freedom of choice, moral movements rooted in self-
deception, and moral experiments aimed at liberation that renewed subjugation. And we are attentive as well to the complex ways in which moral
boundaries are redrawn, as the ethical meanings of various practices—
government-sponsored lotteries, the corporal punishment of those with
mental disorders, the husband's assumed rights of proprietorship in his
wife—undergo change over time.

The first section of the volume, "Problems of Moral Community," sets
forth some of the collection's recurring concerns with the problems of
shaping moral community in a modern society. In "Original Themes of
Voluntary Moralism: The Anglo-American Reformation of Manners," Joel

Bernard examines the eighteenth-century emergence of societies "for the reformation of manners," which sought to stamp out such immoral practices as prostitution, sabbath breaking, profanity, gambling, and drunkenness—offenses that had previously been punished by the established church. In response to the English Toleration Act of 1689, which legalized religious dissent, and to the growing anonymity of London life, these societies gathered together men of various religious persuasions under the banner of a shared morality, in a network of voluntary associations that was soon extended to the British North American colonies. Despite the overall failure of a metropolitan reform model to stamp out vicious conduct in far-flung colonial societies, the movement's effort to establish moral commonality among theologically diverse strangers in a collective effort to bring about a moral society established a model for subsequent Anglo-American moral activism in an increasingly pluralistic, mass society.

In "Gothic Mystery and the Birth of the Asylum: The Cultural Construction of Deviance in Early-Nineteenth-Century America," Karen Halttunen pursues this problem of moral community into the early nineteenth century. Her primary concern is with popular representations of social deviance within the prevailing Gothic idiom of mystery, which shaped a wide range of popular genres including Gothic fiction, true-crime literature, "mysteries of the city" fiction, urban sensationalism, and social-reform literature. The cult of mystery imaginatively relegated socially vicious and aberrant persons to a moral underworld where they engaged in unspeakable practices hidden from the gaze of the morally respectable. Through a close reading of the popular genre of the asylum exposé—accounts of life in prisons and mental hospitals written by professed former inmates—she argues that the pervasive cult of mystery was a cultural corollary to the new social practice of concealing the most extreme social deviants (that is, serious criminal offenders and those labeled insane) behind the walls of institutions designed to hide these transgressors against moral community from the sight of the respectable.

The third essay in this section, Jonathan A. Glickstein's "The World's 'Dirty Work' and the Wages That 'Sweeten' It: Labor's 'Extrinsic Rewards' in Antebellum Society," addresses the moral problem of economic inequality by examining the cultural construction of manual labor and its purported rewards in the antebellum period. Monetary wages, according to such theorists as the Reverend Henry Ward Beecher, redeemed and dignified the world's dirty work by promoting economic self-help and independence and by providing avenues to a higher standard of living. In the face of the moral challenge issued by the critics of "wage slavery"—including northern labor radicals and southern proslavery Malthusians—defenders of the wage-labor system articulated the idea of American exceptionalism, arguing that the economic laws of supply and demand offered unique benefits to American workers, who lived in conditions of labor scarcity and land abundance. The consequences of this doctrine of American exceptionalism, Glickstein observes, have been a moralistic view of poverty, a deep-rooted disapproval of those who failed to discipline themselves to "dirty work" and rise from poverty through individual effort.

In "Deviance, Dominance, and the Construction of Handedness in Turn-of-the-Century Anglo-America," Tamara Plakins Thornton returns to the question of deviance in the moral community. She examines the enlistment of Progressive Era scientific authority to transform older religious superstitions about left-handedness into a systematic assault against this trait as a genetic marker for other forms of deviance. Correlated with criminal behavior, mental disorder, mental retardation, epilepsy, homosexuality, and psychopathic tendencies and linked to women, children, blacks, the lower classes, and those considered to be savages, left-handedness emerged as a kind of composite race of the socially inferior and undesirable. The most extreme solution proposed was eugenics; less extreme, the educational enforcement of right-handedness. Thornton demonstrates that left-handedness functioned as a symbolic surrogate for deviance in general, a uniquely flexible opportunity to theorize about marginality and inferiority within such major political contexts as British imperialism and American immigration. Along with Halttunen's essay, Thornton's raises the larger question that has been explored by sociologists of deviance: is it essential to the existence of moral communities to identify certain types and classes of persons as moral outsiders, against whose negative image—whether profane, mentally ill, or left-handed—the moral community must define itself?

The volume's second part, "Race and the Problem of Slavery," addresses one of the deepest and most enduring moral problems in American life: black chattel slavery and its legacy for American race relations since emancipation. The first two essays in this section explore the distinctive contributions of black abolitionists to ongoing dialogues concerning both racial and sexual inequality. In "Black Abolitionists and the Origins of Civil Disobedience," Lewis Perry examines the practice of civil disobedience—sit-ins, tax resistance, boycotts, and aid to fugitive slaves—by black abolitionists in the decades before the Civil War. He argues that, as nominally free persons denied such rights of citizenship as suffrage, property rights, and civil rights, black abolitionists conducted a remarkably searching exploration of the limits of obligation under American republican government. While some chose nonresistant forms of civil disobedience (especially to protest the segregation of public transportation), insisting that they were in fact citizens and that their civility and good character validated their claims to full participation in a republican government, others emphasized the highly problematic nature of *submissive* disobedience for

4

blacks and claimed their right of violent self-defense (especially in response to the Fugitive Slave Law), on the grounds that they had not yet been granted full citizenship. Both strategies, Perry argues, addressed the same critical dilemma: though in the short run African Americans' freedom could come only from defying the law, in the longer run their protection had to come from extending the law's reach.

In the second essay of this section, "'The Right to Possess All the Faculties That God Has Given': Possessive Individualism, Slave Women, and Abolitionist Thought," Amy Dru Stanley analyzes the abolitionist discourse of possessive individualism from the vantage point of enslaved and freed women. Her focus is on the complex ideological functions of the abolitionist image of the enslaved and suffering female body as the central symbol of the wrongful self-dispossession of the slave. Stanley argues that black women abolitionists enlisted this symbol to disrupt rather than to validate the conventional categories of sex difference customarily associated with classical-liberal belief and held uncritically by most white abolitionists: the assumption that only freed*men* would become sovereign, self-owning individuals and masters of households with proprietary rights to their dependent wives and children, whereas freedwomen would be delivered into a state of legal coverture in marriage. Black women abolitionists used the symbolic power of the debased female body to lay claim to personal sovereignty as a universal right; many black freedwomen followed suit after emancipation by taking legal action to challenge their husbands' proprietorship over them.

In "Worrying about the Civil War," Edward L. Ayers addresses the contemporary popularity of the Civil War in American culture and assesses the dominant narrative of the war as shaped by James McPherson's Pulitzer Prize–winning *Battle Cry of Freedom* (1988) and Ken Burns's 1990 documentary for the Public Broadcasting Service (PBS). Together, they have told a reassuring story of the nation's rebirth, treating the Civil War as a conflict both necessary and good that resulted in the end of slavery and a strengthened American nationalism. This treatment of the war, Ayers observes, ignores a tradition of skepticism that peaked in the 1920s and 1930s when revisionist historians such as Charles and Mary Beard and Avery Craven challenged the notion that the Civil War had been a highminded crusade against slavery. Such revisionism declined after World War II, especially after the emergence of the civil rights movement, which generated a renewed admiration for abolitionist activism (though Robert Penn Warren and Edmund Wilson revived the revisionist position during the Civil War centennial). Despite the work of various scholarly dissenters, the present understanding of the war continues to "paper over the complicated moral issues raised by a war that left hundreds of thousands of people dead." Ayers reminds us that the Civil War was neither morally purposeful nor economically inevitable, and he calls for a new revisionism that addresses the Civil War as a moral problem, a highly contingent and morally complex episode in American history.

In "Caste, Class, and Equal Citizenship," William E. Forbath joins Ayers in examining the moral significance of the Civil War for twentieth-century Americans. He tracks the constitutional legacy of the Reconstruction amendments, which, in their efforts to protect the rights of former slaves, introduced the language of equal citizenship into the Constitution, enlarging the conception of citizenship rights to include economic justice. That language was picked up by a wide range of groups—industrial workers and farmers, women and African Americans, Gilded Age and Progressive reformers—who shaped the "social citizenship" tradition of constitutional thought, which found important similarities between caste and class inequalities. New Dealers shaped this tradition into the conviction that political democracy in the modern industrial economy was doomed without economic democracy for working men and women. But when the federal government, in an effort to maintain the support of the Solid South (itself a legacy of the failures of Reconstruction), condoned Jim Crow and the disenfranchisement of southern blacks, it not only denied African Americans the full assistance of New Deal programs but also severely damaged the social citizenship tradition. In our own times, Forbath argues, this tradition should be revived to provide a basis for a common identity and cooperation among groups of hard-hit Americans that today's liberal-rights talk, with its emphasis on racial, ethnic, and sexual difference, tends to separate.

The essays in the third part, "Religion and Moral Community," focus on problems of religious difference in American life. In "Jewish Prayers for the U.S. Government: A Study in the Liturgy of Politics and the Politics of Liturgy," Jonathan D. Sarna examines the history of Jewish prayers for the U.S. government, from the American Revolution to the present, as a reflection of Judaism's changing relationship to American culture as a whole. Throughout their long history in the diaspora, Jews have uttered special prayers "for the welfare of the government," which by the eighteenth century made specific reference to the dominion of kings. Even after the American Revolution, American Jews clung to the traditional form of the Hanoten Teshua but gradually permitted some innovations of language in the vernacular sections of their liturgy. Then in 1830, the Charleston Reform Movement replaced the traditional prayer with an English-language prayer glorifying America as the model for all nations, and in 1846, Rabbi Max Lilienthal, a German immigrant, offered his own Hebrew prayer appropriating biblical depictions of Israel to the United States. Over the next 150 years, hundreds of prayer books testified to the Americanization of Judaism by offering a variety of identifiably American prayers for the gov-

ernment, including blessings for this country as guarantor of Jewish liberty
and, after 1948, placing the new state of Israel second behind the United
States in their concerns. Liturgical texts, Sarna demonstrates, talk history.

In "Interfaith Families in Victorian America," Anne C. Rose explores another area of American life where religious pluralism has shaped moral
problems. The religious commitments of interfaith families, she reveals,
developed as a series of moral choices that sought to negotiate between
the claims of family harmony and the free exercise of religious conscience.
Through a close examination of nineteen interfaith marriages—involving
men and women of Protestant, Catholic, and Jewish backgrounds—she
finds that intermarriage tended to be as much a consequence as a cause of
diminished religious loyalty: most interfaith partners were children of parents who had made their own unconventional religious choices. At the
same time, she reveals that intermarriage was not necessarily the result
of religious indifference or an agent of secularization; interfaith families
provided arenas where religious doctrines and practices were subject to
self-reflective interpretation and debate and often produced pious children who identified themselves with a single religious community. Over
time, Rose argues, interfaith marriage contributed to the privatization of
religious belief in American culture. Interfaith families thus encountered
spiritual dilemmas and opportunities that have continued to shape American religious communities throughout the twentieth century.

In the last essay of this section, "Prophetic Ministry and the Military
Chaplaincy during the Vietnam Era," Anne C. Loveland examines the
moral challenges posed to Vietnam War chaplains by theological radicals
calling for a "prophetic ministry" committed to social change and by the
growing antiwar movement. Critics of the military chaplaincy initially criticized the chaplains' dual roles as military officers and as clergy and their
presumed tendency to resolve all vocational conflicts in favor of the military role. That concern grew as religious groups came to question the
morality of U.S. intervention and charge the chaplains with complicity in
an unjust war, especially after they raised no outcry against the My Lai massacre and the bombing of Cambodia. In reality, the chaplains overwhelmingly supported the war and defended their vocation, seeing the prophetic
role as inappropriate to combat and embracing instead a primarily pastoral role of offering comfort and assurance to fighting men. Over the
course of the war—in response less to outsiders' radical criticism than
to problems within the armed forces—the chaplaincy developed a new,
institutional ministry aimed at humanizing the military system: by establishing the Personal Response program to improve servicemen's understanding of and sympathy for the Vietnamese people and by addressing
drug and alcohol abuse, marriage and family problems, and various disciplinary issues. Nevertheless, many chaplains resisted this departure from

their spiritual ministry to individuals, and during the 1970s tensions developed between chaplains who remained committed to the traditional pastoral role and chaplains who adopted the newer, prophetic one.

The final section of the volume, "Redrawing Moral Boundaries in Modern America," explores a major moral watershed in various areas of American life in the late nineteenth and early twentieth centuries. In "Listen, My Children: Modes and Functions of Poetry Reading in American Schools, 1880–1950," Joan Shelley Rubin explores the moral dimensions of poetry reading in American public schools from the late-Victorian period into the post–World War II era. Arguing that the history of reading must be distinguished from literary history, she demonstrates the importance of looking not only at what was published and canonized in any given period—for example, the "new poets" emerging in the second decade of the twentieth century—but also at what was used and how. To challenge the notion that poetry lost its cultural power in the late nineteenth century, she reveals that schoolchildren continued to read and recite the poetry of the past—Longfellow, Bryant, Tennyson, Wordsworth—well into the twentieth century. But the rationale for their poetry reading shifted, from the Victorian belief that memorizing high-minded poetry promoted morality, aesthetic sensitivity (closely linked to the moral sense), and sometimes patriotism, to the Progressive conviction that poetry should be faithful to children's own experience. Instead of decoding the text, schoolchildren were increasingly encouraged to embrace and even submit to it, in a cultural practice linked to the larger middle-class pursuit of intense experience for its own sake.

Christine Stansell's essay, "Talking about Sex: Early-Twentieth-Century Radicals and Moral Confessions," joins Rubin's in exploring the dramatic reconfiguration of moral problems wrought by modernity in the early twentieth century. Stansell examines sexual emancipationism among the Left intelligentsia, who linked free love to political radicalism, especially an identification with the working classes and an opposition to capitalism, and saw it as a means of achieving full democratic equality between the sexes. In the bohemias of Chicago and New York in the second decade of the twentieth century, Stansell shows, free-love feminism generated an ethic of confessionalism in which practitioners announced their sexual arrangements—in conversation, circulated correspondence, books, memoirs, and plays—as a form of political manifesto, which found utopian possibilities in sexual disclosure. To be modern was to tell all in sex talk that staked free-lovers' claims to personal authenticity and commitment to revolution by associating free love with the struggle for a just world. But despite its claims to radical freedom of expression, this ethic of confessionalism actually encouraged men to talk and women to listen, discouraging women from giving voice to their own vulnerabilities under sexual arrangements that often left them stranded and hurt, emotionally and materially, by husbands and lovers. Through the practice of confessionalism, Stansell argues, radical sexual heterodoxy unintentionally generated a modernization of patriarchal forms.

In the last essay of the volume, "'What If History Was a Gambler?'" T. J. Jackson Lears explores a historical watershed in American ideas about chance around the turn of the century. The belief that the individual can master fate through will and conscious choice has been a fundamental dogma of Western liberal thought, which dominated American thinking about luck through the nineteenth century. The faith in human mastery, which rested on a predominantly mechanical understanding of scientific causality, was best evidenced in arguments against gambling as a loss of self-control. But in the late nineteenth century, the faith in human mastery began to decline, as widening inequalities undermined the cultural power of the work ethic and its standard slogans about the self-made man; a new discourse of masculinity celebrated manly risk taking; and qualities of "childlike" or "primitive" spontaneity and vitality came to be valued. After the turn of the century, a shift from mechanical to probabilistic ideas of scientific causality lent a new legitimacy to the role of chance in human affairs. Surrealists, dadaists, and other avant-garde artists expressed a growing skepticism about the possibilities for human control through managerial strategies. Lears's essay closes with an examination of Ralph Ellison's *Invisible Man* (1952), whose protagonist comes to accept arbitrary fate as the beginning of wisdom, as he asks, "What if history was a gambler?"

The essays in this volume address some of the most difficult moral issues with which Americans have engaged throughout their history. Some of the cultural devices explored here—the civil prosecution of profane language, the symbolic use of the convent to address social deviance, the eugenic effort to eradicate left-handedness—have fallen into disuse. But many of the moral problems treated here continue to trouble and divide Americans in the lively contemporary debates about "values" in American civilization. To a degree frequently lamented by participants on various sides of our contemporary "culture wars," these debates are characterized by polarization and a narrowly sectarian partisanship, often resulting in mutual misunderstanding and deadlock, in which combatants label their own positions as "moral" and the opposition as "immoral" and sometimes resort to deadly violence. In many of these battles, partisans resort to history to confirm their own moral positions, treating the past as a storehouse filled with old-fashioned moral certainties and the ideal-type traditional institutions that once sustained them.

The essays in this volume point to the limitations of such uses of history. There has been no easy moral certainty for any generation of Americans and no historical period when church or state, family or public school, proved an unproblematic source of moral training and moral truth. American history is filled with moments of grave moral doubt and institutional crisis, with deadly internecine conflicts over fundamental values, with moral dilemmas and paradoxes and double binds. Within a problem-oriented history of moral experience in American life, the myth of simple solutions collapses. It is our hope that this volume will work against easy claims to moral certainty, challenging those who insist on their own definitive ownership of any single moral perspective torn from its own complex contemporary situatedness in the American past.

There are, of course, pitfalls for this problem-oriented approach. The view of moral discourse as historically contingent and open-ended can lead to moral middle-of-the-roadism or paralysis. But as T. J. Jackson Lears observes, the acceptance of the role of chance in human affairs does not necessarily mandate ethical or political quiescence. The steady effort to understand past moral decisions within their own historical context—and to respect past positions with all their moral blinders and unintended consequences—need not conceal from us the demonstrable moral gains made by our predecessors. Our historical subjects did not succeed in abolishing slavery, affirming married women's rights of self-proprietorship, and introducing an educational curriculum more attentive to the experience of children without striking strong moral commitments—whatever the limitations of their positions and their practical arrangements for implementing them. Our approach to historically informed moral inquiry, in short, does not stop with the identification of conformity and self-deception. It also seeks to identify moments of creativity and new departures in moral thought and action.

In preparing this volume, the editors have relied on the generous support and assistance of a number of people. We are grateful for the initial encouragement of Toni Davis and for the editorial advice of Sean Wilentz and Richard Wightman Fox. At Cornell University Press, Peter Agree has proved a staunch supporter of this project, and the two anonymous readers for the Press have contributed significantly to the shape and quality of the collection.

Most important, all the volume's contributors owe a profound debt to our teacher and mentor, David Brion Davis, whose vast body of scholarship has provided the intellectual and moral model for the historical work represented in this volume. In "John Woolman's Prophecy," the epilogue to *The Problem of Slavery in Western Culture,* Professor Davis identified a mid-eighteenth-century "turning point in the history of Western culture" that marks the starting point for the essays assembled here: "To both religious and secular writers the period brought an almost explosive consciousness of man's freedom to shape the world in accordance with his own will and reason. And as the dogmas and restraints of the past lost their compelling force, there was a heightened concern for discovering laws and principles that would enable human society to be something more than an endless contest of greed and power. This quest for moral assurance led inevitably to examinations of inequality, sovereignty, and servitude."[1] In the sequel volume, *The Problem of Slavery in the Age of Revolution,* Professor Davis explored the contexts and consequences of "a profound transformation in moral perception" that led to growing recognition of the "full horror of a social evil to which mankind had been blind for centuries." But in this volume, as throughout his work, Davis refused to idealize the heroism of an antislavery tradition, to dismiss abolitionists as irresponsible misfits, or to discredit their beliefs by pointing to their ulterior motives.

"Speaking only for myself," he stated the implications of his approach to historical understanding: "I am prepared to believe that nothing in history is absolute or clear-cut; that truth is always framed in ambiguity; that good and evil are always colored by human ambivalence; that all liberations are won at a cost; that all choice involves negation. I also think that history is filled with moral ironies, and that one can point to ironies but never prove them." Nonetheless, Davis affirmed, "we are the beneficiaries of past struggles, of the new and often temporary sensitivities of a collective conscience," of courageous declarations "in new contexts and to new audiences, 'How long? Not long.'"[2]

It is our shared experience that David Brion Davis tries to instill in all his students his own powerfully ethical understanding of the moral significance of historical practice. The hallmark of Davis's scholarship is the conviction that, if the positivistic goal of "value-free" scholarship is both nonviable and undesirable, the history of values must not succumb to simplistic moral formulation or narrow partisanship but should attempt to recapture the complexities and painful ambiguities always at work in the most compelling moral controversies of any era. In his afterword to this volume, Richard Wightman Fox offers a biographical tribute to David Brion Davis as scholar and teacher. Here, we dedicate this volume to him with profound gratitude for his immeasurable and ongoing influence on our lives and our own intellectual journeys through the moral landscape of American life.

[1] David Brion Davis, *The Problem of Slavery in Western Culture* (Ithaca, 1966), 485.

[2] David Brion Davis, *The Problem of Slavery in the Age of Revolution, 1770–1823* (Ithaca, 1975), 11, 16. The "complex change in moral vision" that preceded the "eruption of antislavery thought" continues to stand as a major theme in Davis's work; see, for example, "At the Heart of Slavery," *New York Review of Books,* October 17, 1996, 54.

PROBLEMS OF MORAL COMMUNITY

"A Black List of the Names, or Reputed Names, of Seven Hundred Fifty Two Lewd and Scandalous Persons, who, by the Endeavours of a Society set up for the promoting a Reformation of Manners in the City of London, and Suburbs thereof, have been Legally Prosecuted and Convicted . . ." (1698). Reproduced by permission of the Houghton Library, Harvard University.

CHAPTER ONE

Original Themes of Voluntary Moralism:
The Anglo-American Reformation of Manners

JOEL BERNARD

In late 1690, several "Officers and Inhabitants" of the densely populated Tower Hamlets, a commercial district of East London along the Thames, met to form an association to deal with a recent outbreak of crime and vice. The new society's members pledged "to consult and resolve upon the best methods for putting the laws in execution against houses of lewdness and debauchery, and also against drunkenness, swearing and cursing, and profanation of the Lord's Day." To this end, they undertook to participate in policing the parish—informing against moral violations and accompanying constables on their rounds. Supporters soon discovered a novel advantage of voluntary organization: it facilitated cooperation between members of both the Church of England and dissenting denominations. Mindful of England's recent bitter denominational strife, Anglican minister Josiah Woodward remarked approvingly that "lesser Differences in Matters of Religion did not in the least divide them in prosecuting these things which they saw were directly contrary to all Religion."[1]

Fourteen years later, an anonymous *Account of the Progress of the Reformation of Manners in England, Scotland, and Ireland, and Other Parts of Europe and America* trumpeted the success of what had become an international

---

[1] [Edward Stephens], *The Beginning and Progress of a Needful and Hopeful Reformation in England* . . . (London, 1691), 4; Josiah Woodward, *An Account of the Rise and Progress of the Religious Societies in the City of London, &c. and of the Endeavours for Reformation of Manners Which have been made therein,* 2d ed. (London, 1698), 74–75.

movement for moral reform. Its burgeoning influence in England was apparent in a flurry of royal proclamations and court orders enjoining stricter punishment of "prophaneness and immorality" and a sharp rise of legal prosecutions for immoral behavior. Its main innovation, however, was the formation of voluntary societies "for the reformation of manners." Looking beyond their diverse religious beliefs and social positions, zealous citizens formed moral enforcement associations in imitation of the Tower Hamlets society. Within little more than a decade, reformation societies had created a national network for moral propaganda: pressuring petty law officers and magistrates to enforce existing laws and parliamentarians to pass stricter laws against immorality; printing sample oaths, articles of association, and warrant forms for constables and justices of the peace; and circulating "dissuasives" to immorality addressed to ordinary men and women.[2]

A local reformation of manners begun in London had become an international Protestant movement, with voluntary moral societies in Dublin and Edinburgh as well as in Switzerland, the German States, and the Low Countries. From the New World, too, issued the responsive echo of moral reformation. "A Gentleman" from New England, the author of the *Account* reported, "informs us . . . that great Care hath been . . . taken of late for the Punishment of Vice and Profaneness by the Methods that are here used; and . . . That several Societies are formed in Boston, and he thinks that in a little time he shall acquaint us of others set up in other parts of that Country." That same year, the General Assembly of Connecticut recommended that the colony's ministers "in imitation of our nation . . . excite and stirre up their good people to perticular societies in order to indevour a reformation of what provoking evils are to be found amongst us"—in other words, form societies for the reformation of manners.[3]

---

[2] [Walter Yates], *An Account of the Progress of the Reformation of Manners . . .* (London, 1704), esp. 8–14; this is the expanded second edition of *An Account of the Societies for Reformation of Manners in London and Westminster, and Other Parts of the Kingdom* (London, 1699). See also *A Help to a National Reformation*, 5th ed. (London, 1705), 72–82 (oaths), 105–8 ("A Speciman of an Agreement . . ."), and 109–22 (dissuasives). For full accounts of the movement, see G. V. Portus, *Caritas Anglicana . . .* (London, 1912); A. G. Craig, "The Movement for the Reformation of Manners, 1688–1715" (Ph.D. diss., Edinburgh University, 1980); Tina Beth Isaacs, "Moral Crime, Moral Reform, and the State in Early Eighteenth-Century England: A Study of Piety and Politics" (Ph.D. diss., University of Rochester, 1979). For more specific studies, see Robert B. Shoemaker, *Prosecution and Punishment: Petty Crime and the Law in London and Rural Middlesex, c. 1660–1725* (Cambridge, 1991), 238–72, and Shoemaker, "Reforming the City: The Reformation of Manners Campaign in London, 1690–1738," in Lee Davison et al., eds., *Stilling the Grumbling Hive: The Response to Social and Economic Problems in England, 1689–1750* (New York, 1992), 99–120.

[3] [Yates], *An Account of the Progress of the Reformation of Manners*, 9; J. Hammond Trumball et al., eds., *The Public Records of the Colony of Connecticut* (Hartford, 1850–90), 4:468.

Societies for the reformation of manners were a novel eighteenth-century response to the perennial problem of immorality. Within a century and a half, such voluntary organizations would become the dominant expression of Anglo-American social activism, gathering men and women of all classes and denominations (or no religious affiliation at all) in support of shared moral concerns such as temperance, pacifism, abolitionism, and women's rights. On his visit to the United States in the 1830s, Alexis de Tocqueville's initial surprise at the importance of these civil associations registered the contrast between the vitality of public life in Anglo-American culture and its crabbed character on the European continent, where voluntary organizations were still either illegal or suspect. The mundane character of Anglo-American reform societies in the nineteenth century provided no hint of their novelty almost a hundred and fifty years before.[4]

English societies for the reformation of manners emerged at a time when traditional moral controls were buffeted by far-reaching social change. For centuries, religious rituals and institutions had borne primary responsibility for articulating and resolving moral problems through the pastoral functions of churches or the discipline of ecclesiastical courts. Although temporal authority had contested the powers of the Anglican establishment for centuries, until the Toleration Act of 1689 English law still presumed that all Englishmen were members of the Church of England. The moral authority of the establishment was manifest not only in legally mandated attendance in parish churches or diocesan cathedrals but also in ecclesiastical courts with wide purview over the expression of belief and over public and private behavior. Officers of the spiritual arm punished violations of religious ordinances, doctrinal lapses, and immoral behavior without discrimination—heresy, nonattendance at church, and Sabbath breaking, together with fornication, drunkenness, and profanity. During the century after the Reformation, legal reform gradually eroded the Anglican Church's control over lay behavior, as plaintiffs sought the sterner sanctions of civil justice, and as puritans denounced the moral laxness and partiality of ecclesiastical judges. A series of parliamentary statutes provided new temporal sanctions and enlisted the vigilance of

[4] Alexis de Tocqueville, *Journey to America*, ed. J. P. Mayer (New Haven, 1960), 212–16, 252–53, and Tocqueville, *Democracy in America*, ed. Phillips Bradley (New York, 1960), 2:106–10, 115–20. For the contrast with France, see Maurice Agulhon, *The Republic in the Village*, trans. Janet Lloyd (Cambridge, 1982), esp. 124–50. Although not intended as a contribution to the discussion of the "bourgeois public sphere," my account of the rise of voluntary moral associations touches on the general issues raised in Jürgen Habermas's *The Structural Transformation of the Public Sphere* (Cambridge, Mass., 1989).

civil magistrates and officers for formerly religious offenses such as heresy (1533), absence from church (1558), bastardy (1575), drunkenness (1606), swearing (1623), and Sabbath breaking (1625).[5]

The introduction of more specific sanctions against immorality, and the provision of secular authority to enforce them, fitfully occupied Parliament for more than a century. Compared with the arcane procedures and largely unwritten sanctions of religious courts, parliamentary statutes administered by justices of the peace and constables promised, at least, greater efficiency. Yet, by the late seventeenth century it had become apparent that the fundamental weakness of moral control lay not in the ambiguous source of its statutory authority but in the antiquated mechanisms for enforcing it. Even the new jurisdiction of secular laws and courts could not overcome the inefficiencies of parish-centered policing by a part-time force of citizen constables. These local officers still performed adequately in small communities where defendants could be located socially and punished appropriately. But the social map of rural England supplied poor guidance in a great metropolis such as London, whose population by the late seventeenth century had swelled to over a half million—a figure not equaled by any other city in the Anglo-American world until mid-nineteenth-century New York.

In late-seventeenth-century London, the idealized religious and social solidarity of parishes had given way to a plethora of different denominations and a highly transient population squeezed together in tenements along streets and alleys. In parishes containing tens of thousands of inhabitants with only a tenuous personal connection, parochial policing

---

[5] On the structure and powers of ecclesiastical courts and the transfer of morality to civil courts, see Edmund Gibson, *Codex Juris Ecclesiastici Anglicani; or, the Statutes, Constitutions, Canons, Rubrics, and Articles of the Church of England* . . . (1713; 2d ed., Oxford, 1761), 2:1000–1017, 1076–96; Richard Burn, *Ecclesiastical Law* (London, 1763), 1:409–26; William Blackstone, *Commentaries on the Laws of England* (Oxford, 1765–70), 3:61–68, 87–103; 4:41–65; William Searle Holdsworth, *A History of English Law* (London, 1903–72), 1:614–21. The largest numbers of defendants before disciplinary ecclesiastical courts were summoned for fornication, adultery, and premarital sex, usually followed by defamation, church nonattendance, nonreceipt of communion, violations of saints' days, and working on the Sabbath. See Ralph Houlbrooke, *Church Courts and the People during the English Reformation, 1520–1570* (Oxford, 1979), app. 3, 278–81; Martin Ingram, *Church Courts, Sex, and Marriage in England, 1570–1640* (Cambridge, 1987), table 2, p. 68; and Richard M. Wunderli, *London Church Courts and Society on the Eve of the Reformation* (Cambridge, Mass., 1981), 138–39. On the duties of ecclesiastical officials and parish constables, see Richard Burn, *The Justice of the Peace and Parish Officer* (London, 1755), 1:217–25; Ingram, *Church Courts, Sex, and Marriage*, 325–26; Sidney A. Peyton, comp., *The Churchwardens' Presentments in the Oxfordshire Peculiars of Dorchester, Thame, and Banbury* ([Oxford], 1928), lxix–lxxii; and Joan R. Kent, *The English Village Constable, 1580–1642: A Social and Administrative Study* (Oxford, 1986), esp. 190–200.

proved manifestly inadequate. In the metropolis, it was difficult enough for a constable to seek out a justice of the peace to write a warrant for an offense such as swearing, then carry it back to serve on an offender whose name and address he did not know; it was even more impractical to carry the stranger to a magistrate, which might involve a journey of a mile or two on foot. By day or night, one might walk the streets of the city and hear the oaths of carters and watermen, observe the stagger of drunks, and be accosted by beggars and prostitutes. On Sundays in certain neighborhoods, tradesmen and costers pursued a brisk illegal business, their wares exposed beside cellars to allow for hasty removal at the approach of a constable, while barbers on their way to appointments shouldered their basins through the streets, and tipplers convened rowdy congregations in alehouses.[6]

All the contrasts of opulence and poverty, of civility and lawlessness, were heightened by the swelling population and sprawling geography of the City and its liberties. Later in the century, Adam Smith, a prescient observer, discerned in London the early outlines of a mass society in which unknown individuals interacted casually and randomly every day. The great defect of the decline of the personal relations of village society, he believed, was the alienation from traditional moral standards of the new rootless laborer in the city. "While he remains in a country village," wrote Smith, "his conduct may be attended to, and he may be obliged to attend to it himself. In this situation, and in this situation only, he may have what is called a character to lose. But as soon as he comes into a great city, he is sunk in obscurity and darkness. His conduct is observed and attended to by nobody, and he is therefore very likely to neglect it himself, and to abandon himself to every sort of low profligacy and vice."[7]

The long-term decline of the moral authority of the Anglican establishment was most clearly manifested in the aftermath of the Glorious Revolution. The freedom of worship granted by the Toleration Act in 1689 acknowledged this problem and tried to resolve it by ending repression and legalizing Protestant dissent. But even a jealously worded definition of toleration ratified the widening gap between the liberty of Protestant religious belief and the enforcement of moral behavior: one the (limited)

---

[6] Thomas B. Macaulay, *The History of England from the Accession of James the Second* (London, 1858), 1:362–86. Gregory King's 1695 population estimate for "London and the Bills of Mortality" was 529,920: "Natural and Political Observations and Conclusions upon the State and Condition of England," in *Two Tracts, by Gregory King . . .* , ed. George E. Barnett (Baltimore, 1936), 419.

[7] Adam Smith, *An Inquiry into the Nature and Causes of the Wealth of Nations*, ed. Edwin Cannen (1776; reprint, New York, 1937), 747.

province of individual conscience, the other of secular legal jurisdiction.[8] The distinction was implicit in a public letter from William III to the Bishop of London shortly afterward, voicing concerns about rampant immorality, pledging to "Endeavour a General Reformation in the Lives and Manners of all our Subjects," and directing the circulation of printed abstracts of the laws enforcing morality. Within the next decade, other royal letters and proclamations followed, censuring the neglect of parish law officers and bidding justices of the peace to execute the laws against immorality energetically. Magistrates issued well-publicized charges to parish officers and grand juries to redouble their efforts to apprehend offenders. The example of the Tower Hamlets society spurred pious gentlemen to form other societies "for the reformation of manners." They, in turn, recruited informers from satellite societies of tradesmen and constables throughout London. Within a few years, the city's twenty or so reformation societies had blossomed into a national movement with local associations in most sizable English towns.[9]

Because voluntary moral associations were first formed so soon after the Toleration Act, their potential effectiveness lay in the new possibilities offered for a united front on a source of common religious concerns. The articles of the main London society, run by Anglican gentlemen, disclaimed controversial goals, promising never to "medle with Affaires of Church or State." A few years later, the coordinators wrote to the city's dissenting ministers, explicitly providing the original rationale for ecumenical moral activism. They acknowledged that most of the "many hundreds" of convictions for immorality already obtained depended on the zeal of forty or fifty informers "all except one or 2 in the communion of the Church of England." They asked "the reverend Non conformists Ministers" whether they would "prevaile with any considerable number of the members of their congregation . . . to take notice of the breaches of the Lawes & to give

---

[8] On the Toleration Act and its legal consequences, see Burn, *Justice of the Peace and Parish Officer*, 1:257–63; Michael R. Watts, *The Dissenters: From the Reformation to the French Revolution* (Oxford, 1978), 249–62; Shoemaker, *Prosecution and Punishment*, 133; Gibson, *Codex Juris Ecclesiastici*, 2:965–66, 1074–75; Peyton, *Churchwardens' Presentments*, xlvi–xlvii, lxii; William Hale, comp., *A Series of Precedents and Proceedings . . . of Ecclesiastical Courts in the Diocese of London* (London, 1847), esp. lx.

[9] "His Majesty's Letter to the Lord Bishop of London, 1689" [1690] is reprinted in Edward Cardwell, ed., *Documentary Annals of the Reformed Church of England . . .* (Oxford, 1839), 2:326–29. See also Tony Claydon, *William III and the Godly Revolution* (Cambridge, 1996), esp. 110–21. For the details of the spread of reformation societies, see *Proposals for a National Reformation of Manners, Offered to the Consideration of Our Magistrates and Clergy* (London, 1694); [Stephens], *Beginning and Progress of a Needful and Hopeful Reformation*, 4; Woodward, *Account of the Rise and Progress of the Religious Societies*, 65–120, esp. 83; [Yates], *An Account of the Societies for Reformation of Manners*, 9–10.

informations against Offenders." Shortly afterward, separate reforming societies of dissenters sprang up.[10]

Organized cooperation between members of different Protestant communions marked a historically important innovation and ultimately became the hallmark of Anglo-American moral reform. All the London reformation societies assembled for quarterly meetings, alternately in Salters Hall, to hear dissenting clergymen, and at St. Mary-le-Bow, to hear ministers of the Church of England. Still, old usages changed slowly; most of the formalities of social distinction continued to be observed. Gentlemen usually met separately from tradesmen, justices of the peace from constables or informers, Anglicans from dissenters. The movement was aptly characterized by one speaker as "divers Societies, some consisting of Persons of inferior, and others of higher Rank," but the advantages of even this moral ecumenicism at a distance were prominently featured in reformation sermons and tracts. In a sermon at Salters Hall, Presbyterian minister John Shower claimed that despite "different sentiments about Matters of Faith and Worship, all sorts of Christians . . . do yet agree that these Instances of Immorality do properly come under the Cognizance of the Civil Magistrate." All denominations accepted a magistrate's power to punish immorality, wrote Anglican Walter Yates, because "unrestrained Vice and Prophaneness are as fatal to *Publick Societies,* as they are destructive to *Private Persons.*" His *Account of the Societies for Reformation of Manners* bore the endorsement of forty-five noblemen, Anglican bishops, and judges and closed with an address, "To the Men of Religion and Virtue of all Ranks, Orders and Denominations, without distinction."[11]

Nonetheless, voluntary societies often roused unintended social and religious tensions. The gentlemen and ministers who wrote reformatory tracts or preached sermons and who supplied guidance to other societies were not the same men who scoured the city for immorality. Nor, for their part, were members of the fast-riding, hard-drinking, loud-swearing gentry among those snagged by informers' dragnets, though they probably

---

[10] "An Agreement of Divers Gentlemen & Citizens in & About London for Promoting the Execution of the Lawes Made Against Profaness [*sic*] and Debauchery (1693)" and "A Copy of the Paper Offered to the Dissenting Ministers being Instructions to the Informers & the Rules & Methods that are Observed by Them," in Leon Radzinowicz, *A History of English Criminal Law and Its Administration* (London, 1948–1986), 2:431 and 2:434–38, respectively; quotations from 2:431, 435. See also "An Agreement of Divers Constables & Other Officers of London," in ibid., 2:432–33.

[11] [Yates], *An Account of the Societies for Reformation of Manners,* 147; John Shower, *A Sermon Preach'd to the Societies for Reformation of Manners in the Cities of London and Westminster . . .* (London, 1698), 21–23; quotation from page 22. Thomas Reynolds, *A Sermon Preach'd to the Societies for Reformation of Manners in the Cities of London and Westminster . . .* (London, 1700), 55.

sat on the bench pronouncing judgment on those who were. Revealing glimpses of the social background of those prosecuted are provided by the so-called Black Lists or Black Rolls—black-letter broadsides naming male-factors and their crimes—and by London societies' tallies of annual prose-cutions. In the representative year of 1708, societies prosecuted about thirty-three hundred persons, the majority for "Lewdness" or "Exercising trades on the Sabbath," two offenses that never accounted for less than three-quarters of the total. As a result, the social profile of defendants fit two distinct (and distinctly gendered) types: female prostitutes and male petty tradesmen. Although gentlemen and higher-status tradesmen or craftsmen were occasionally prosecuted for Sabbath breaking or swearing, the more usual encounter took place between a constable and a street-walker or between an informer who was a skilled craftsman and a victualler, servant, or laborer who was his social inferior. These inequities made informers a source of popular opprobrium and of occasional violence. Daniel Defoe complained on behalf of "the Plebeii," of "the Partiality of this Reforming Rigor," and of the injustice of setting the poor drunkard or swearer in the stocks or sending the whore to the house of correction while winking at the same vices among the gentry. He memorably dubbed the laws against immorality "Cobweb Laws, in which the small Flies are catch'd, and the great ones break through."[12]

Though it was true that the poor formed the vast majority of those pros-ecuted, the social status of defendants revealed much less about reform-ers' intentions than about English judicial procedure and the public visi-bility of those who fell afoul of the law. Any voluntary movement with public moral aims operated within an unreformed legal system sharply constrained by class privilege and cumbersome, expensive procedures. As long as the judicial system required complainants and law officers to pay court costs of prosecuting most crimes against morality and to accept the burden of attending court sessions without compensation, it more or less

---

[12] [Daniel Defoe], *Poor Man's Plea to all the Proclamations, Declarations, Acts of Parliament, &c. . . . for a Reformation of Manners*, 2d ed. (London, 1698), 6–9; quotations from pages 6, 9. "A Black Roll containing the Real or Reputed Names and Crimes of Several Hundred Persons that have been Prosecuted by the Society this last year (1693–94). . . ," in *Proposals for a National Reformation of Manners*, 34–35; "A Black List of the Names, or Reputed Names, of Seven Hundred Fifty Two Lewd and Scandalous Persons . . ." (1698) [printed as the frontispiece to this essay], and "The Eleventh Black List, of the Names, or Reputed Names, of Eight Hundred and Thirty Lewd and Scandalous Persons . . ." (1706), both in Houghton Library, Harvard University. For figures on prosecutions, see also Portus, *Caritas Anglicana*, 178, 183. Extant broadsides and annual accounts are tallied in Portus, *Caritas Anglicana*, App. 5, 251–54 (and the foldout, facing p. 254), and app. 3, 238–39. See also Shoemaker, *Prosecution and Punishment*, table 9.1, p. 245, and 251–52 for the social status of plaintiffs and defendants.

dictated the bottom-heavy results it got. As reformers quickly discovered, prosecuting malefactors by indictment before a grand jury convened in a courthouse was prohibitively expensive; they therefore chose the cheaper mode of prosecuting immoral behavior in the streets, before a single justice sitting in his own parlor who summarily fined defendants or remanded them to the house of correction. Even so, not all misdemeanors subject to summary judgment proved equally easy to police. Policing transient offenses such as drunkenness or swearing proved more difficult than apprehending prostitutes and Sabbath-breaking tradesmen who were obliged to frequent well-known public places to seek clients or to carry goods or tools of their trade on Sunday. These individuals provided the easiest targets for informers and constables and therefore bore the brunt of the reformation of manners.[13]

Societies for the reformation of manners unwittingly raised a problem—the equitable legal application of moral ideals—that had always existed as a sectarian reproach to worldly establishments but whose incongruity was heightened by the voluntary commitment to ecumenical moral reform. The societies often acknowledged and sometimes attempted to overcome these inequities of prosecution. They circulated sample copies of correctly endorsed warrants, pointedly including hypothetical offenders of high rank: drunkard "J. G. Esq.," fined five shillings, and profane swearer "Sir A. B. K[nigh]t" (a repeat offender), fined twenty. And they insisted, as well, that "No Men's Quality ought to Shelter them from Punishment," going so far as to claim that punishing immoral men of authority performed a greater service than punishing poor men without influence. Yet whatever their intentions, the de facto distinction between the chargeable public vice of the poor and the largely immune private vices of the gentry reified situationally and spatially a class distinction affirmed more discretely by traditional policing. In every confrontation between informer and malefactor, prudent self-interest vied with moral conscience. Like a hunter approaching an unknown quarry, an informer had to size up a potential defendant's social standing relative to his own. If mistaken, he might find himself sued, forced to make a humiliating public retraction, or even physically assaulted. The dissenting minister John Shower, to his credit, acknowledged this as a real dilemma of conscience as well as calculation. There were, as he characterized them, "Persons of that Quality and Figure, Character and Interest in the World that you dare not meddle with them": employers of journeymen, customers of tradesmen, landlords of tenants, and masters of servants—all the latter depending on the former

---

[13] Shoemaker, *Prosecution and Punishment,* 140, 164–65, 167, 218, 246–47, 250.

for "Favour and Good Opinion." Shower weakly counseled "a little Courage and Resolution, with Wisdom and Prudence," then beat a retreat: "But in some cases, as matters now stand, where it would be likely to do more hurt than good, I think you may forbear: And believe, and hope that the Punishment of meaner Persons, will so far influence the Greater Sort, as to bring them to be more private, and less Scandalous in their Crimes." In practice, this was what generally happened anyway as vigilant constables and informers haunted the streets, marketplaces, and fairs where common people socialized.[14]

Reformation societies set out a global field of endeavor for zealous advocates of piety and morality. Their expansion throughout England also inspired fresh efforts by a reawakened Anglican Church to address the religious needs of the British Isles and the American colonies. In 1699, Anglicans created the Society for the Promotion of Christian Knowledge (SPCK) to proselytize the British Isles; two years later, the Society for the Propagation of the Gospel in Foreign Parts (SPG) spun off to support missions in the colonies. Although the broad aims of these missionary organizations were compatible with the reformation of manners, their specifically denominational goals also competed with those of dissenting sects. One of the first missionaries of the SPG to America, the former Quaker George Keith, landed in Boston, where he engaged in a noisy public dispute with Puritan ministers. Then he ordered an entire printing of the *Account of the Societies for Reformation of Manners,* "for the promotion of a Reformation, by these Methods, in those Parts of the World."[15]

Although the moral character of the American colonies differed one from another, all were provinces, not metropolitan societies like London. Transplanting an English reformation of manners to an institutionally underdeveloped colonial frontier posed distinct challenges for Anglican

---

[14] [Yates], *An Account of the Societies for Reformation of Manners,* 44–45. The sample warrants are in *Help to a National Reformation,* 98, 99. Shower, *Sermon Preach'd to the Societies for Reformation of Manners,* 44–45. The distinction between public and private vice is made, for example, in White Kennett, *A Sermon Preached at Bow-Church, London, Before the Societies for Reformation of Manners . . .* (London, 1702), 24.

[15] [Yates], *Account of the Progress of the Reformation of Manners,* 9. On the origins of the SPCK and SPG, see [John Hooke], *A Short Account of the Several Societies, Set Up of Late Years for Carrying on the Reformation of Manners, and for the Propagation of Christian Knowledge* (London, 1700); W. O. B. Allen and Edmund McClure, *Two Hundred Years: The History of the Society for Promoting Christian Knowledge, 1698–1898* (1898; reprint, New York, 1970); Edmund McClure, ed., *A Chapter in English Church History; being the Minutes of the S.P.C.K. for the years 1698–1704* (London, 1888); *An Account of the Society for Propagating the Gospel in Foreign Parts* (London, 1706); *A Collection of Papers Printed by Order of the Society for the Propagation of the Gospel in Foreign Parts* (London, 1715), 73; H. P. Thompson, *Into All Lands: The History of the Society for the Propagation of the Gospel in Foreign Parts, 1701–1950* (London, 1951), esp. 3–34.

missionaries, who had to start from scratch and to manage with little local support. It was true that royal governors arrived with identically worded instructions to "take care that drunkenness and debauchery, swearing and blasphemy be severely punished" and issued proclamations for the reformation of manners in imitation of royal ones. Urged by their governors, colonial assemblies obediently passed omnibus laws against immorality. But neither colonial governors nor legislators demonstrated much will or ability to enforce them. For while in theory the moralizing interests of the Church of England and colonial governors were identical, by temperament colonial bureaucrats were no more inclined to moral zeal than the English country squires who they were or aspired to be. Officials at the apex of colonial society were usually either proud aristocrats habituated to genteel dissipations or military men accustomed to the rough-and-tumble morals of garrison life. On one occasion, the governor of Maryland threatened to challenge the commissary of the Bishop of London to a duel. And while the proclamation against immorality issued in 1704 by Lieutenant Governor John Evans of Pennsylvania may have enhanced his career prospects at Westminster, its local credibility probably suffered from his recent involvement in a Philadelphia tavern affray during which he "fell to beating" a constable who attempted to intervene.[16]

Virginia's response to the English reformation of manners was characteristic: formal obedience in a region entirely unsuited—topographically or socially—to consistent moral oversight. The colony's Anglican establishment was in disarray; ecclesiastical courts never functioned. Contemporaries described ministers "of immoral lives or weak parts and mean learning" preaching without surplices, bibles, or communion cups in poorly adorned churches decaying on untended glebes. In 1690, Lieutenant Governor Francis Nicholson ordered the colony's churches and chapels to post King William's letter to the Bishop of London enjoining moral reformation, warning local officials that they would "answer for their neglect therein at their perill." During the next fifteen years, the House of Burgesses passed a series of laws punishing immorality. But churchwardens rarely presented offenders in county courts as the law required, and even if they had, rural courthouses adjacent to taverns provided an inappropriately uproarious venue in which to prosecute immoral behavior. In Henrico County, spiteful grand jurymen occasionally presented each other for swearing, drunkenness, or fighting "in my own sight" or "by his own con-

---

[16] Leonard Woods Labaree, ed., *Royal Instructions to British Colonial Governors, 1670–1776* (New York, 1935), 2:503; H. P. Thompson, *Thomas Bray* (London, 1954), 78; "Minutes of the Provincial Council of Pennsylvania," in *Colonial Records of Pennsylvania* (Harrisburg, 1851–1853), 2:162 (Evans's proclamation); John Fanning Watson, *Annals of Philadelphia and Pennsylvania . . .* ([Philadelphia], 1855), 2:481 (Evans's affray).

fession." Drunkenness and swearing were more usually punished when someone entered the courtroom drunk, and then only after he disturbed the deliberations or insulted the participants. The impossibility of supervising the morals of such a dispersed rural population led itinerant Scots-Presbyterian minister Francis Makemie to warn the SPG that if it wished to further a reformation of manners in the southern colonies, it should first promote the settlement of towns.[17]

Although the culture of the Virginia gentry was probably no better or worse than its counterparts in other British borderlands, it lacked even the semblance of a moral counterweight offered by a secure religious establishment. For most purposes, perfunctory formalism sufficed, causing Planter William Byrd to remark that Virginians "thought their being Members of the Established Church sufficient to Sanctifie very loose and Profligate Morals." But there were deeper reasons for the unresponsiveness of the southern gentry to moral restraints, ones that went to the heart of their primary social concern: the discipline of labor. Because a large proportion of the lower orders in the southern colonies were bound servants or slaves, moral transgressions assumed a different cast than in England, where free labor and annually contracted servitude were more usual. On one side, the exaggerated authority bestowed on colonial masters undermined many of the moral inhibitions of English employers, particularly those regarding sexual exploitation and violence. On the other side, the conditions of bound labor discouraged initiative and encouraged irresponsibility. Promiscuity and drunkenness may well have been weapons of weakness on the part of servants, but they also threatened the economic interests of the master, who was, in this regard, as unhappily bound to his laborers as they to him. The fewer inhibitions of masters and the greater provocation of servants resulted in a familial style of moral justice, mostly at the mas-

---

[17] H. R. McIlwaine, ed., *Executive Journals of the Council of Colonial Virginia* (Richmond, 1925–1930), 1:120, 214, 267–68, 2:35–37; Nicholas Trott, *The Laws of the British Plantations in America, Relating to the Church and Clergy, Religion and Learning* (London, 1721). On the early Virginia church, see Henry Hartwell, James Blair, and Edward Chilton, *The Present State of Virginia and the College*, ed. Hunter Dickinson Farish (1697; reprint, Williamsburg, 1940); Robert Beverley, *The History and Present State of Virginia*, ed. Louis B. Wright (1705; reprint, Chapel Hill, N.C., 1947), 261–64; Hugh Jones, *The Present State of Virginia. . .*, ed. Richard L. Morton, (1724; reprint, Chapel Hill, N.C., 1956), 95–101, 117–28 (quotation on 118). See [Francis Makemie], *A Plain and Friendly Perswasive to the Inhabitants of Virginia and Maryland for Promoting Towns and Colonization* (1705; reprint, [Boston, 1942]), 11. Characteristic presentments are found in "Henrico County Record Book No. 1, Deeds and Wills, 1677– 1692," 32–33, 274, 294, 312–13, 336, 371–72, 402 (microfilm transcript in Virginia State Library, Archives, Richmond); and in Beverley Fleet, ed., *Virginia Colonial Abstracts*, vol. 11 (Richmond, 1941), 11, 68, and vol. 25 (Richmond, 1945), 27. For the character of the colonial Anglican clergy, see the papers of the Bishop of London in William Wilson Manross, comp., *The Fulham Papers in the Lambeth Palace Library . . .* (Oxford, 1965).

ter's whim and largely outside formal legal jurisdiction. Long sufferance alternated with explosive rage. When the slaves of Byrd or, later, Landon Carter got drunk, the masters vented annoyance in their diaries—and summarily punished them by whipping or tying them "neck and heels" in the cellar.[18]

The practical difficulties of transplanting a metropolitan moral reformation to remote transatlantic provinces were greatly magnified in those colonies without religious establishments, where SPG missionaries first needed to address the weakness of Anglican institutions. The dearth of clerical livings in England and the poverty of those in the colonies meant that missionaries were often recruited among the incompetent, the immoral, or simply the poorly connected. As a result, they not infrequently succumbed to local manners rather than reforming them. In North Carolina, for example, an early attempt to form parish vestries failed. "At the first that met," reported missionary John Urmston, "[they] were very disordered with drink. They quarreled and could scarce be kept from fighting. . . . In another precinct the Vestry met at an Ordinary where rum was the chief of their business." Nine years later, Urmston himself was fined for drunkenness in court. Thomas Crawford and Francis Le Jau were other SPG missionaries who labored unsuccessfully in impoverished, unhealthy backwaters lacking even rudimentary support for Anglican worship. In 1705, Crawford arrived in Dover Hundred in Kent County, Delaware, in response to a petition complaining of "the increase of Sin and Crime." He found most of the inhabitants ignorant of Anglicanism and too poor even to buy prayer books. Crawford conducted services and formed a society for the reformation of manners, using the London society's *Account*. His society secured the support of a local justice of the peace and managed to prosecute some of the "Irreligious and openly profane." But after a few years, the society met infrequently and transacted "little or no business." In 1709, Crawford reappeared in London, too poor to buy clothes and accused of bigamy. His colonial mission had lasted four years; his replacement soon departed, and the parish church stood empty for years.[19]

---

[18] William Byrd, "History of the Dividing Line between Virginia and North Carolina . . . ," in The Writings of Colonel William Byrd. . . , ed. John Spencer Bassett (1901; New York, 1970), 11; *The Secret Diary of William Byrd of Westover, 1709–1712*, ed. Louis B. Wright and Marion Tinling (Richmond, 1941), 53, 56, 337; *The Diary of Colonel Landon Carter, 1752–1778*, ed. Jack P. Greene (Charlottesville, 1965), 2:940–41. For the morals of the similarly situated Anglo-Irish gentry, see Constantia Maxwell, *Country and Town in Ireland under the Georges* (Dundalk, Ireland, 1949), esp. 17–65.

[19] John Urmston to SPG (1711), in William L. Saunders and Walter Clark, comps., *The Colonial and State Records of North Carolina* (Raleigh, 1886–1914), 1:769, and 2:401 (1720). For the missionary efforts of the SPG in North America, see Thompson, *Into All Lands*, 46–91. On Crawford, see his letters in "Records of the Society for the Propagation of the

Francis Le Jau's pastorate in Goosecreek, South Carolina, lasted longer but was no more successful. Dispersed settlement hindered regular meeting; his parishioners were poor and his house and church remained unfinished; his glebe lands were uncultivated. The "Libertinism and Wicked Morals" of some of the leading men, he complained, were "too open and scandalous," and the planters' barbarous treatment of Indians and Negroes appalled the devout Le Jau. Although he wrote that "a Society for Reformation of Manners would do wonders in some places hard by me," forming one was impractical in the face of genteel indifference. "The Evil cannot be stop't for want of authority to repress it," he lamented, "and we of the Clergy have hardly the liberty to speak and our Chief Men are little inclin'd to compel men to be less scandalous." He eventually found a few parishioners willing to enter a society, but it apparently never functioned. Le Jau sickened and died, and his moral initiative passed with him.[20]

In most of England's transatlantic colonies, the weakness of ecclesiastical institutions, the dispersion of the population, the dominance of the gentry, and the familial discipline of servitude inhibited early efforts by Anglican missionaries to form voluntary moral societies, providing formidable barriers even to enforcing existing laws against immorality. Taken together, all these difficulties provided one practical definition of the primitive moral condition of colonial societies: materialistic, worldly, profane. In one region alone the reformation of manners achieved relative success. New England's well-populated, highly literate, compactly settled villages, overseen by an articulate and independent clergy, satisfied virtually every precondition for the effective enforcement of morality. English calls for a reformation of manners struck a responsive chord to the Puritan jeremiad's highly charged images of moral declension. In 1690, "according to order," Boston printer Cuthbert Potter distributed seven hundred copies of King William's letter on reformation, and about the same time the governor and General Court of Massachusetts, citing "a long *Series* of Afflictions and Calamities" connected with the warfare against the

---

Gospel. Letterbooks relating to the American Colonial Church" (henceforth called "SPG Records"; references in some volumes paginated, in others numbered by document), ser. A, vol. 2, nos. 97, 115, 160–62 (quotation from 162), vol. 4, pp. 250–55 (quotation from 254), vol. 5, nos. 46, 47 (microfilm, Widener Library, Harvard University); W. S. Perry, ed., *Historical Collections Relating to the American Colonial Church*, vol. 5, *Delaware* (Hartford, 1878), 1–4, 16–19; Nelson Waite Rightmyer, *The Anglican Church in Delaware* (Philadelphia, 1947), 44–49.

[20] Francis Le Jau's correspondence is scattered through the "SPG Records," ser. A, vols. 2–12, esp. vol. 4, p. 296; vol. 5, nos. 130–32, 252, and vol. 6, no. 103. A selection of these letters is in Frank J. Klingberg, ed., *The Carolina Chronicle of Dr. Francis Le Jau, 1706–1717* (Berkeley, 1956).

French and Indians, called for "a speedy REFORMATION of our *Provoking Evils*" and stricter enforcement of "all Laws of this Colony against *Vice*, and all sorts of *Debauchery* and *Prophaneness.*"[21]

Boston, with about sixty-seven hundred inhabitants in 1700, exemplified the possibilities of maintaining order among a relatively compact, homogeneous population.[22] Situated on a peninsula joined to the mainland by a narrow neck, the dwellings of its inhabitants crowded between the shoreline and three hills, the town offered an ideal setting for moral oversight. But even more immediate reasons than topography or fidelity to the original errand existed for a rapprochement between the traditions of Puritanism and reforming Anglicanism. Signs of the steady erosion of provincial Puritanism were already apparent in the growing number of government functionaries and native-born converts worshiping at King's Chapel, in the controversial "midway" Anglo-Puritanism of the new Brattle Street Church, and in the open—often boisterous—celebrations of royal anniversaries and Anglican holy days that scandalized pious Puritans. After the imposition of royal government in 1691, the larger political and religious convergence of metropolitan England and colonial Massachusetts promoted the Puritan embrace of ecumenical methods to express traditional motives.

The movement for a reformation of manners in Massachusetts arrived under the auspices not of royal functionaries or Anglican missionaries but of members of the Puritan establishment itself. It channeled a hesitant Puritan ecumenicism, poised between parochial defensiveness and provincial emulation, offering a colonial counterpart to the same impulse in London: as a means of bridging religious differences. Puritan piety and Anglican reformatory zeal provided the middle ground of this compromise. In furthering this goal, Puritanism provided one support lacking in Anglicanism. For while Canon 73 of the Church of England explicitly forbade ministers from holding private "conventicles," the Massachusetts Body of Liberties explicitly sanctioned "private meetings for edification in religion amongst Christians of all sortes of people," a permission that invited voluntary ecumenical association.[23]

[21] Worthington C. Ford, comp., "Broadsides, Ballads, etc., Printed in Massachusetts, 1639–1800," in *Collections of the Massachusetts Historical Society* (Boston, 1922), 75:22; "By the Governor and General Court of the Colony of the Massachusetts Bay, in New England," in Cotton Mather, *The Present State of New England* . . . (Boston, 1690), 47–52 (quotation from, 47–48).

[22] Evarts B. Greene and Virginia D. Harrington, *American Population before the Federal Census of 1790* (New York, 1932), 22 n.

[23] William H. Whitmore, comp., *The Colonial Laws of Massachusetts . . . Containing also the Body of Liberties of 1641* (Boston, 1889), 57. See, by contrast, [Church of England], *Constitution and Canons Ecclesiastical, 1604* (Oxford, 1923).

Founded in 1702, New England's societies "for the suppression of disorders" were the creation of the Reverend Cotton Mather, who offered an enlightened justification of moral activism wholly devoid of theology. He appealed to the *"Good Man"* who *"Loves to do Good,"* a man who *"Sublimated"* his *"Natural Affection to Society* . . . to Associate for the Interests of Religion"—a vision of secular moralism that Benjamin Franklin would first parody and then emulate. Mather's *Methods and Motives of Societies to Suppress Disorders,* printed anonymously the following year, described the successes of the English reformation societies, emphasizing their cross-class and interdenominational potential: "Virtuous men of divers Qualities, and Perswasions. *Noblemen, Clergymen, Gentlemen, united with Persons of Inferior Station. Dissenters united with Conformists."* His first society in Boston enlisted "about a dozen or fourteen good Men, whereof some are *Justices,"* who agreed to meet periodically to discuss "What and where Disorders do arise, in the *Town,* and how may such Disorders be prevented." A few years later, participants included members from three churches, and auxiliary societies had formed in the North and South Ends. Like their London counterparts, these societies circulated tracts and abstracts of the laws against immorality—directing special efforts to sailors, soldiers, Indians, and settlers of the colony's frontier plantations. But Boston's provincial reformers relied mainly on private admonition rather than legal prosecution, carrying out their work with "Prudence & Silence & Modesty." Mather's moral concerns ranged haphazardly from finding truant children and reproving their profane language to preparing a list of "wicked houses" in Boston and sending admonitions to the young men who frequented them. By 1711, however, the societies were "languishing and near expired." Three years later they had been dissolved, and Mather was lamenting some "unworthy and improper Members."[24]

The exemplary figure in the convergence of Puritanism and reforming Anglicanism was merchant Edward Bromfield, an English emigrant who had risen to membership in the governor's council. A man "of steady zeal against every vice" and a fellow communicant of Puritan diarist Samuel Sewall, he eventually converted to Anglicanism and was buried in King's Chapel. Bromfield's complex local and transatlantic connections involved membership in Boston's South Church and ties of marriage with the Puri-

[24] [Cotton Mather], *Methods and Motives of Societies to Suppress Disorders* [Boston, 1703], 4–5; Mather, *Bonifacius: An Essay upon the Good.* . . , ed. David Levin (1710; reprint, Cambridge, 1966), 132–37; Worthington Chauncey Ford, ed., *The Diary of Cotton Mather* (New York, 1912), 1:418–19, 500, 516–17, 523, 531, 2:2, 27, 42, 131, 160, 206–207, 229, 235, 275–76, 283; Edward Bromfield to Thomas Bromfield, October 9, 1704, in "SPG Records," ser. A, vol. 2, no. 29. See also Richard P. Gildrie, *The Profane, the Civil, and the Godly: The Reformation of Manners in Orthodox New England, 1679–1749* (University Park, Pa., 1994), esp. 185–209.

tan ministry, as well as a brother, Thomas, in England, who was one of the founding members of the SPG. Excerpts of Edward's letters to England found their way anonymously into the widely circulated tract *A Help to a National Reformation*. "Our Imitation of the pious zeal of Godly Men in Old-England," Edward acknowledged, "is a sufficient Testimony of our Approbation of what is doing there. . . . We are beholden to you (under God) for what good has been done by our Societies in this Country, and should be glad and earnestly desire further directives from you, what Progress to take in Reformation and Propagating the Gospel of our Lord Jesus." The same tract went on to quote "A Reverend Divine of New England" (probably Mather), who exclaimed, "In some Towns of this Country, the Ministers, who furnish themselves with a *Society* for the *Suppression of Disorders,* hardly find any notorious Disorders to be suppressed."[25]

Cautious ecumenicism offered an important motive for Puritan-led moral reformation, particularly among cosmopolitan ministers and magistrates such as Mather and Bromfield. But in New England villages unaffected by Anglicanism, a deeper reason was offered by the continuing search for a wider basis of Puritan moral authority. In the small, religiously homogeneous towns outside Boston, members of the "visible" church represented only a small fraction of the population. As in England, all townspeople were required to attend services on Sunday, but in New England where church membership was voluntary, no one who heard the sermon was a birth member of the establishment. Consequently, a rural New England reformation of manners aimed to unite church members with willing nonmembers in a pledge of individual or familial moral oversight. In effect, rural New Englanders tailored a London model to fit Puritan devotional preferences for fasting, formal covenants, family prayers, and prayer groups, especially youthful ones.

The quasi-reformation society formed by Bromfield's brother-in-law, the Reverend Samuel Danforth of Taunton, typified the relatively placid course of these clerically led rural reformations. One of the larger towns in Bristol County, south of Boston, Taunton had a population of about a thousand. According to Bromfield's account, after reading of the English

[25] See Bromfield to Thomas Bromfield, October 9, 1704, and Bromfield to SPG Sec., February 24, 170[8] (quoted), both in "SPG Records," ser. A, vol. 2, no. 29, and vol. 3, p. 178, respectively. The former was excerpted as a letter from "A Gentleman in New England" in *Help to a National Reformation*, 11–12. Bromfield is probably the "Gentleman from New England" whose letter of November 20, 1705, is also excerpted in *Help*, 14–16 (quotation from 16) and whose letter of April 10, 1702, is cited in [Yates], *Account of the Progress of the Reformation of Manners*, 9. See also "A Reverend Divine of New England" to ——, November 23, 1705, in *Help to a National Reformation*, 13–14 (quoted), and Daniel Denison Slade, *The Bromfields* (Boston, 1872), 4–6. For Thomas Bromfield and the SPG, see James S. M. Anderson, *The History of the Church of England in the Colonies and Foreign Dependencies of the British Empire* (London, 1856), 3:154–58.

reformation societies, Danforth gathered several of the town's inhabitants "noted for their piety" to fast and pray and to "consult what might be done to promote a Reformation of Disorders." Their "Exhortations and Reproofs" convinced most families in the town to hold morning and evening prayers and gave rise to a devotional society among young people that "[put] an End to . . . their former disorderly and profane Meetings to Drink, &c."[26]

In early 1705, members of Taunton's church publicly renewed its covenant, first engaged in 1676 during King Philip's War. Adding some new sins to the original list, they pledged "to Endeavour a *Suppression* of *Open Vice* in our selves and others, according to our *Capacities,* and that our *Houses* shall not be Houses of Resort for unlawful Tipling or other *Disorders.*" Danforth recorded that this "reformation covenant" was read at the Sunday morning service, with only church members standing, "as an outward Sign of their inward Consent to the *rest* of the *Inhabitants.*" In the afternoon it was read again. This time, "every one that stood up, brought his Name ready writ in a Paper and put into the Box, that it might be put on Church Record. . . . We gave Liberty to all Men and Women Kind, from *sixteen Years old and upwards* to act with us; and had *three hundred Names* given in. . . . We have *a hundred more* that will yet bind themselves in the *Covenant*"—in all, about 40 percent of the town's population and a large majority of its adult inhabitants.[27]

Puritan reformation covenants were not entirely new, but their renewed use in the wider context of a transatlantic reformation of manners gave them added meaning. They supplied a new voluntary engagement—a contract—between the signer and his or her community, a majority of whom were not church members. Taunton's reformation covenant was bound with a printed sermon by Danforth—"the more Easily Lodged with them, as a Perpetual Monitor of the Methods to *Encourage* Piety, whereto they have with great Solemnity Engaged themselves." Other churches printed their reformation covenants as broadsides, to be carried home by their signatories and perhaps glued over the mantelpiece as was common in England. One from Hatfield closed with the injunction, "Dearly Beloved, What you have formerly transacted, is now thus put into your Hands, to help your memories." Its admonitions stood as a visible, volun-

---

[26] "A Gentleman from New England" to ——, November 20, 1705, in *Help to a National Reformation,* 14–16. See also E. Bromfield to T. Bromfield, October 9, 1704; John Joseph May, comp., *Danforth Genealogy* (Boston, 1902), 34–35; and Slade, *The Bromfields,* 4–6. In 1690, Taunton had 196 militia, or a total population of 1,000; see Greene and Harrington, *American Population,* 21.

[27] Samuel Danforth to ——, March 5, 1705, in Thomas Prince, comp., *The Christian History, Containing Accounts of the Revival and Propagation of Religion in Great-Britain & America, For the Year 1743* (Boston, 1744), 111.

tary commitment to community unity, one wider than either full church membership or the quasi membership of the halfway covenant—a moral engagement offered to all men and women willing to lead upright lives.[28]

As in England and other colonies, concern with immorality in New England culminated in new laws: in a Massachusetts act "against Intemperance, Immorality, and Prophaneness, and For Reformation of Manners" and in Connecticut's act "for the better Detecting and more effectual Punishment of Prophaneness and Immorality." Each differed in emphasis—taverns in the former case, church attendance in the latter—but both attacked the single most persistent problem of Anglo-American moral control: the low morale of petty law officers. The Massachusetts law generated unintended consequences. After it gave officers broader responsibilities for seeking out illegal taverns, record numbers of Boston's citizens began to refuse election, choosing instead to pay a ten-pound fine. In 1714, when the law against immorality, with its injunction to zeal, was read as required at the town meeting, three of seven elected selectmen and four of eight constables refused office; the next year, six of fourteen elected constables refused. The year following, nineteen unwilling citizens paid fines or offered acceptable excuses before the full complement of eight constables could be sworn, and instead of taking a single afternoon in March, the election process dragged on until June, as absentees were elected, notified, and in their turn declined, requiring new elections at subsequent meetings. In 1717, the law was again read—and twenty-five men refused election before the eight positions could be filled.[29]

Refusal to serve in town offices may have been a lowly form of resistance to elite demands for moral order, but it was more likely some compound of self-interest and conscientious scruple against taking an oath that invited personal conflict. Instead of merely lamenting the lack of zeal among elected officers, however, Massachusetts's magistrates mobilized to do something about it. Their sense of moral purpose resulted in new practices—part substantive effort, part display of official power—that demonstrated a resolve to suppress vice. The 1712 law created a new town office, the "informer," whose duty it was to bring immorality and public nuisances to official cognizance. A few years later, a meeting of provincial magistrates

[28] Samuel Danforth, *Piety Encouraged* (Boston, 1705), title page (quoted) and 23–25. See also "A Covenant for Reformation, Assented to in Hatfield . . . 1709 [altered to 1705 in MS handwriting]" (broadside, n.p.) and "A Covenant for Reformation Assented to in Long-Meadow, in Springfield . . . 1728" (broadside, n.p.).

[29] A. C. Goodell et al., eds., *Acts and Resolves . . . of the Province of Massachusetts Bay* (Boston, 1869–1922), 1:679–82; Trumball et al., eds., *Public Records of the Colony of Connecticut*, 5:323–24. *A Report [Eighth] of the Record Commissioners . . . Containing the Boston Records from 1700 to 1728* (Boston, 1883), 98–102, 108–10, 116–26, and *passim*.

and town officials created two special watches to put some spine in petty officers. The first was an all-day Sabbath watch during the summer and autumn to prevent "Loose vain persons negrose &c." from "unnecessarily Travilling or walking to and from Boston and Roxbury, with neglect of attending worship of God in either place." Constables and other citizens manned the gates at Boston Neck, carrying before magistrates any passersby whose explanations were unsatisfactory or who were "refractory" or "rude." Similar resolve was displayed in a second agreement between officers of the province and Boston to undertake a special night watch "to Inspect the Order of the Town."[30] Its spirit was succinctly conveyed by a participant, sixty-three-year-old councillor and judge of the superior court Samuel Sewall: "Monday, August 8 [1715]. Set out at 11. at night on Horseback with Tho. Wallis to inspect the order of the Town. Constable Eady, Mr. Allen, Salter, Herishor Simson, Howell, Mr. John Marion [a selectman]. Dissipated the players at Nine Pins at Mount-Whoredom [later, Mount Vernon]. Benjamin Davis, Chairmaker, and Jacob Hasy were two of them. Reproved Thomas Messenger for entertaining them. As came home between 2 and three took up Peter Griffis the notorious Burglar, and committed him to Prison. Generally, the Town was peaceable and in good order."[31]

Boston's special watches of magistrates and petty officers demonstrated the determination of men such as Sewall and Bromfield to carry forward personally the reformation of manners. But they also supplemented other innovations to increase the direct involvement of magistrates in moral oversight. Like watches, for example, special annual "visitations"—one directed to families, the other to schools—either imitated English models or extended the logic of English practices. In the first instance, magistrates agreed to devote one day every year to a "Walk" or visitation of the town's families "in Order to prevent & redress [suppress] disorders." Mixed groups of high and petty officials—councillors, judges, justices of the peace, selectmen, constables, tithingmen, and overseers of the poor— divided into eight (eventually twelve) parties, one for each ward. The walk began at nine or ten in the morning and concluded at five with a meeting of the visitants in the Town House (after 1742, Faneuil Hall) to discuss their findings. The first visitation in 1707 enlisted the province's lead-

[30] A Report [Eleventh] of the Record Commissioners . . . Containing the Records of Boston Selectmen, 1701 to 1715 (Boston, 1885), 54, 123, 169–70 (quoted), 171 (quoted), 191, 212, 231; A Report [Thirteenth] of the Record Commissioners . . . Containing the Records of Boston Selectmen, 1716 to 1736 (Boston, 1885), 113, 271–72 (quoted); A Report [Fifteenth] of the Record Commissioners . . . Containing the Records of Boston Selectmen, 1737 to 1742 (Boston, 1886), 354 (quoted), and succeeding volumes.

[31] The Diary of Samuel Sewall, 1674–1729, ed. M. Halsey Thomas (New York, 1973), 2:795.

ing officials—Sewall, Bromfield, the attorney general, the Speaker of the House, prominent Anglican Sir Charles Hobby, as well as other justices of the peace and judges of the superior court.[32]

The name given these day-long official parades through Boston—"visitations"—invoked the periodic oversight by Anglican prelates of the religious and moral order of their English dioceses. Characteristically, Boston's secular version went even further, bringing the majesty of the law to the doorstep of every one of the town's families. The impression that visitations were meant to convey was suggested by the annual litany in the selectmen's minutes, descending by rank, of "Esquires of the Council," "Esquire Justices," selectmen, overseers of the poor, and, at the bottom, constables, all of whom paraded once a year in groups down every street of the town, inquiring of "disorderly Persons, New-comers," and "the circumstances of the Poor & Education of thir Children."[33]

Boston's annual visitations functioned as provincial substitutes for metropolitan rituals, responding to similar practical concerns. Like reformation societies, ritual innovation constituted one basis for Anglo-American unity. This was equally true of the Bay Province's increasingly formalized concern with schooling—one explicitly characterized as moral control. The 1712 act for reformation of manners claimed that "the well educating and instructing of children and youth in families and schools are a necessary means to propagate religion and good manners" and required that no schoolmaster instruct children without selectmen's approval. Two years earlier, Boston's town meeting had voted "for the promoting of Diligence and Good Literature" to initiate school visitations "Agreeably to the Usage in England"—presumably the occasional visitations of bishops or the annual exercises of English charity schools sponsored by the SPCK. Boston's school exercises generally took place in the summer, complementing the family visitations in February. The town chose several gentlemen "of Liberal Education" to inspect with ministers and selectmen the proficiency of the schoolmaster and his scholars. As in England, this involved exercises performed by students before a group of distinguished visitors, followed by prayer and "Instructions of Piety" from one of the ministers. Initially only selectmen, ministers, and a few invited guests participated, but the number of visitors increased as provincial pride blossomed. By midcentury, the list of dignitaries included the governor and lieutenant governor, members of the council, town representatives, selectmen, overseers

---

[32] *Records of Boston Selectmen, 1701 to 1715,* 55–56 (quoted), 62–63, 67–68, 88–89, 104, 144–45, 177–78; *Records of Boston Selectmen, 1716 to 1736,* 7, 15, 122–23, 146–47, 181, 195, 204, 212–13, 225–26, 237, 265–66, 284–85.
[33] *Records of Boston Selectmen, 1701 to 1715,* 221.

of the poor, diverse royal officials such as the collector of customs, prominent ministers, other leading citizens, and occasionally visitors from colonies as far away as Nova Scotia, South Carolina, and Surinam.[34]

Like societies for the suppression of disorders, the visitations and watches of Boston's magistrates reflected at once the idealized harmonies and practical divergences between life in England's provinces and its metropolis. Colonial reformers with similar concerns imitated English practices but often got different results. Sewall's matter-of-fact account of late-night encounters with miscreants whose names he knew—"You go to jail, and you go to bed"—was the stuff of village life in England, Old or New. It was distinctively Puritan only because his tone of authority was so morally righteous and unapologetic. (William Byrd's exercise of authority over his slaves was similarly unapologetic, but not remotely "moral." He punished his slaves' misbehavior not because it offended his expansive moral sensibility but because it troubled his ease.) Yet despite palpable differences in moral tone among England's American colonies, none of these provincial expressions resembled those of the impersonal, increasingly perilous environment of London, where petty law officers often feared for their lives— and where at least two reforming constables were killed by unruly soldiers. Whatever the results of moral reformation elsewhere, no one familiar with manners in the mother country doubted that New England's distinctive religious culture made it work there. An English visitor in 1740 remarked that Boston's observance of the Sabbath was "the strictest kept that ever I yet saw anywhere"—so strict that authorities would not even tolerate strolling by the waterside or on the Common. It was a "rare thing," he wrote, "to meet with any drunken people, or to hear an oath sworn, in their streets."[35]

In very different settings on both sides of the Atlantic during the eighteenth century, Anglo-American reformers sought to find a common ground of Protestant unity: between Anglicans and dissenters in England, between colonists and inhabitants of the mother country, between Anglicans and Puritans in Boston, or between the members and nonmembers

[34] Goodell et al., *Acts and Resolves*, 1:681–82. For school visitations, see *Boston Records from 1700 to 1728*, 65 (quoted), 109, 117, 129; *Records of Boston Selectmen, 1716 to 1736*, 134, 153, 165, 176; and the annual lists in other volumes of selectmen's minutes through the 1790s. For a list of dignitaries, see *A Report [Twenty-Third] of the Record Commissioners . . . Containing the Selectmen's Minutes from 1769 through 1775* (Boston, 1893), 132–33. On SPCK charity schools, see Allen and McClure, *Two Hundred Years*, 135–65.

[35] Thomas Bennett, "Boston in 1740," in *Proceedings of the Massachusetts Historical Society, 1860–1862* (Boston, 1862), 115, 117. For the two English constable martyrs, see Josiah Woodward, *A Sermon Preached . . . at the Funeral of Mr. John Cooper, A Constable, who was barbarously Murther'd at May-Fair . . .* (London, 1702), and Thomas Bray, *The Good Fight of Faith . . . At the Funeral of Mr. John Dent, who was barbarously murder'd in the doing his duty . . .* (London, 1709).

of New England's village churches. From the perspective of these original participants, moral voluntarism offered a different, yet reassuringly familiar, path to the re-creation of a community of interest threatened by religious, social, or geographical diversity. Institutionalized moral reformation produced a middle ground in the widening space between religious establishments and dissent. As London's zealous citizens and constables navigated the turbulent new world of urban anonymity, New England's ministers led their village congregations in the reaffirmation of tradition through prayer circles and reformation covenants, while magistrates and legislators everywhere in the colonies deferred ceremoniously to metropolitan authority. Thus, when Samuel Sewall attended the opening of Boston's new Town House in 1713, Cotton Mather supplied the invocation, and the new grand jury was charged "to enforce the Queen's Proclamation, and especially against Travailing on the Lord's Day"—the same charge delivered in quarter courts throughout England. Three years later a new monarch reigned, so in the printed version of Benjamin Colman's *Sermon for the Reformation of Manners,* a note followed the text: "Here the Royal Proclamation of the KING, and that of the *Government* were read."[36]

The transatlantic reformation of manners had all but exhausted its energy by the time the London society printed its final account in 1738, claiming to have initiated one hundred thousand prosecutions. But the artifacts of innovation remained, in printed tracts and sermons, accounts of reformation societies, royal proclamations, and parliamentary statutes. Dispersed throughout England, they also circulated in the transatlantic commerce of print and could be found in the American private libraries of Virginia planter Robert Carter and Boston clergyman Thomas Prince. A reference work such as Ephraim Chambers's *Cyclopaedia: or, an Universal Dictionary of Arts and Sciences* (London, 1738), for example, included under the definition of "Society" a subentry for "Society for Reformation of Manners," and John Gillies' *Historical Collections Relating to Remarkable Periods of the Success of the Gospel, and Eminent Instruments Employed in Promoting It* (Glasgow, 1754) provided an excerpt from the *Account of the Progress of the Reformation of Manners* issued a half century earlier. Both Chambers's and Gillies' books were cited in newspaper announcements of the formation of a New York City Society for the Reformation of Manners in 1769. Even though the moral challenges posed by colonial backwaters were not yet equal to those of Adam Smith's Glasgow or those of London, and metropolitan solutions remained less appropriate, these reminders kept

[36] *Diary of Samuel Sewall,* 2:713; Benjamin Colman, *A Sermon for the Reformation of Manners. Being designed as a Sutable Exhortation to Enforce the Reading of the King's Royal Proclamation for the Encouragement of Piety and Vertue, and for the Preventing and Punishing of Vice, Prophaneness, and Immorality* (Boston, 1716), 26.

in circulation a form of ideological currency to be husbanded or spent in the future.[37]

Subsequent Anglo-American voluntary movements have continued the effort of the eighteenth century to bridge the gaps opened by legitimate differences of belief, gathering shifting constituencies in order to "meddle" in the widening interstices of posttoleration church and state. From a modern retrospect, however, the dominant current of reform has not been the rise of secular moralism but of secular voluntarism of a liberal cast. The long history of popular resistance to moral coercion suggests that the moralist impulse has always contended with notions of entitlement to self-expression and privacy. The decline of spiritual establishments has dramatically expanded the scope of these rights, and voluntarism has been the vehicle of their expression. Since the Age of Revolution, the debate over morality has shifted increasingly to the socially liberating claims of class, race, and gender—a moralism of equal entitlement almost wholly distinct from, if not necessarily opposed to, a moralism of Christian self-control. Voluntarism has become a means to new social ends. While the newer "liberties" to which many individuals lay claim are not identical to moral "license," they are close enough analogues so that the boundaries between self-expression and moral coercion are continually contested.

Recent libertarian controversies over pornography, abortion, and gay rights exemplify pointed challenges to secularized Christian moralism. In contrast to their eighteenth-century precursors, the historical significance of these latter-day debates lies mainly in their narrower scope. Today, ecclesiastical jurisdiction over community morals is a quaint historical footnote; not even temporal courts presume to punish Sabbath breaking, profanity, blasphemy, fornication, and adultery. Consequently, organized

---

[37] Louis B. Wright, "The 'Gentleman's Library' in Early Virginia: The Literary Interests of the First Carters," *Huntington Library Quarterly* 1 (1937/38): 61; Ephraim Chambers, *Cyclopaedia: or, an Universal Dictionary of Arts and Sciences,* vol. 2 (London, 1738), s.v. "Society"; John Gillies, *Historical Collections Relating to Remarkable Periods of the Success of the Gospel, and Eminent Instruments Employed in Promoting It* (Glasgow, 1754), 1:423. For the Society for the Reformation of Manners and Suppression of Vice in the city of New York, see *New York Gazette, or Weekly Post-Boy,* September 25, October 2, 1769, and *New York Chronicle,* September 7–14, 1769. For Thomas Prince, see *The Christian History,* 111. William the Third's 1698 proclamation "for Preventing and Punishing Immorality and Prophaneness" initiated a custom, practiced by every British sovereign through Victoria, of issuing within the first year of accession identically titled royal proclamations "for the Encouragement of Piety and Virtue, and for the Preventing and Punishing of Vice, Prophaneness, and Immorality." See Robert Steele, ed., *A Bibliography of Royal Proclamations of the Tudor and Stuart Sovereigns and of Others . . .* (Oxford, 1910), 1:507 (1698, William III), 514 (1702, Queen Anne). For the successor proclamations, see James Ludovic Lindsay, *Bibliotheca Lindesiana: Handlist of Proclamations, 1714–1910* (Aberdeen, Scotland, 1893), 3 (1715, George I), 32 (1727, George II), 97 (1760, George III), 276 (1820, George IV), 301 (1830, William IV), and 333 (1837, Victoria).

moralism fights what appears to be a losing battle, disputing smaller and smaller pieces of the terrain of contemporary social "manners." The legacy of the eighteenth-century reformation of manners is, thus, the infinite modern varieties of voluntary social activism—all long since freed from establishments of church or state.

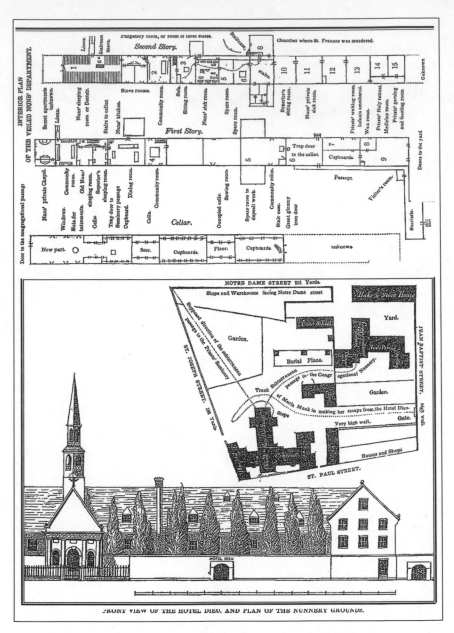

The architecture of evil: three views of Maria Monk's Hotel Dieu Nunnery in Montreal. Frontispiece to Maria Monk, *Awful Disclosures of the Hotel Dieu Nunnery of Montreal* (New York, 1836). Courtesy of the American Antiquarian Society.

CHAPTER TWO

Gothic Mystery and the Birth of the Asylum: The Cultural Construction of Deviance in Early-Nineteenth-Century America

KAREN HALTTUNEN

In January 1836, a book that was to become one of the publishing sensations of the nineteenth century first came before the American reading public. Maria Monk's *Awful Disclosures of the Hotel Dieu Nunnery of Montreal* purported to tell the story of a young Protestant girl, educated in the convent, who embraced the Catholic faith and took the veil only to discover that her vow to "obey the priests in all things" meant "to live in the practice of criminal intercourse with them." Aided and abetted by her Protestant clerical advisers in New York City, Maria Monk described the seduction and rape of young novices by priests, the quick baptism and killing of infants born to these unholy unions, and the torture and murder of those nuns who resisted the rules of the perverse order. Much of the account is elaborately spatial in nature, laying out both narratively and through visual maps and diagrams the floor plans of the multileveled structure, with special attention to its "secret recesses": its torture chambers, dungeon cells, secret doors and trapdoors, burial pits for dead infants, and subterranean passageways through which the lustful priests gained access to their female prey. In the architecture of this fantastic nunnery, "the chambers of pollution are above" and "the dungeons of torture and death are below." The *Awful Disclosures* sold some three hundred thousand copies before the Civil War and went through numerous reprintings over the course of the nineteenth century, well earning its historical reputation as the *"Uncle Tom's Cabin* of Know-Nothingism."[1]

In its relentless attention to the "impenetrable secrecy, which is the cement of the gloomy superstructure" and to "the mystery of iniquity" practiced within, *Awful Disclosures* enlisted a set of literary conventions widely practiced in nineteenth-century American popular print: the cult of mystery.[2] Like countless other texts of the period, *Awful Disclosures* undertook to expose the secret evils that lay buried beneath the deceptively serene surface of nineteenth-century social life, taking its readers on an imaginative guided tour of a subterranean world of moral perversity. Originating in late-eighteenth-century Gothic fiction, the cult of mystery soon evolved into a pervasive cultural idiom for understanding the nature of social deviance, one that was enlisted by true-crime writers, urban novelists and journalists, and social reformers bent on eradicating a range of identified moral evils including intemperance, gambling, prostitution, violent crime, Mormonism and Catholicism, and slavery. But the cult of mystery was also enlisted by a small group of social deviants themselves: the inmates or former inmates of two newly invented reform institutions, the penitentiary and the mental hospital. The Gothic exposés of asylum life that achieved great popularity in the mid–nineteenth century suggest an important historical connection between the popular cult of mystery and the emergence of a new form of social discipline centered on the asylum, with its privatization of punishment for moral and mental deviance. The "mystery of iniquity" captured a peculiarly nineteenth-century approach to understanding and addressing what were perceived to be the greatest "moral problems" of the era.

The literary origins of the cult of mystery lay in eighteenth-century Gothic fiction, which made its first appearance in Horace Walpole's *The Castle of Otranto* in 1764 and which quickly became one of the most popular fictional modes of the period. The Gothic literary imagination centered on the haunted castle, with its dark winding passageways, trapdoors with rings, secret doors hidden behind tapestries, veiled apparitions, and sub-

---

[1] Maria Monk, *Awful Disclosures of the Hotel Dieu Nunnery of Montreal,* intro. Ray Allen Billington (Hamden, Conn., 1962) (facsimile of 1836 ed.), 56, 74, 344; Billington, introduction to *Awful Disclosures,* n.p. See also Ray Allen Billington, *The Protestant Crusade, 1800–1860: A Study of the Origins of American Nativism* (Chicago, 1964), 99–108, and Jenny Franchot, *Roads to Rome: The Antebellum Protestant Encounter with Catholicism* (Berkeley, 1994), chap. 7.

[2] Monk, *Awful Disclosures,* 327, 353.

terranean vaults—all presided over by a gloomy tyrant, brooding over some secret crime buried in his past. Titles such as *The Mysteries of Udolpho* (1794), *The Mysterious Monk* (1796), and *The Mysterious Warning* (1796) pointed clearly to Gothic fiction's primary attention to the matter of mystery. The formula shaped hundreds of popular works printed in England in the last decades of the eighteenth century and survived into the nineteenth century in such forms as the "shilling shocker" and the sensation novel. From the 1780s on, Americans imported Gothic fiction in volume for distribution through bookshops and circulating libraries, and the genre exerted a significant influence over Charles Brockden Brown, Washington Irving, Nathaniel Hawthorne, and Edgar Allan Poe.[3]

In the work of Poe, the Gothic cult of mystery assumed a specialized form for whose invention literary historians usually grant him full credit: the murder mystery. It is true that many of the major conventions of detective fiction were at work for the first time in "The Murders in the Rue Morgue," published in 1841. But the "peculiar distortion of more usual narrative conventions" that characterizes detective fiction—which begins with a corpse, then moves into the past through an investigation whose purpose is to uncover the sequence of events that resulted in that corpse, and only at last reconstructs the crime in its proper chronology[4]—actually appeared over half a century earlier in the nonfictional literature about murder in America. The first murder mystery narrative in American print concerned the actual murder in 1783 of Eunice Bolles by Hannah Ocuish in New London, Connecticut; significantly, the narrative strategy of this account conformed to the lines of the "whodunit" even in the absence of a single detective intelligence brought to bear on the case. As I have argued elsewhere, the nonfictional "murder mystery" narrative emerged in the late eighteenth century as a by-product of the new legal discourse of the crime—embodied in the popularity of printed murder-trial transcripts— that was replacing the earlier religious discourse, which had focused on the printed execution sermon preached for the condemned murderer. Thus, by the end of the eighteenth century, American readers were be-

---

[3] Eino Railo, *The Haunted Castle: A Study of the Elements of English Romanticism* (London, 1927); Edith Birkhead, *The Tale of Terror: A Study of the Gothic Romance* (London, 1921); Devendra P. Varma, *The Gothic Flame* (London, 1957); Donald A. Ringe, *American Gothic: Imagination and Reason in Nineteenth-Century Fiction* (Lexington, Ky., 1982); Eve Kosofsky Sedgwick, *The Coherence of Gothic Conventions* (New York, 1980).

[4] Howard Haycraft, *Murder for Pleasure: The Life and Times of the Detective Story* (New York, 1941), 12; Frank Kermode, "Novel and Narrative," in Glenn W. Most and William W. Stowe, eds., *The Poetics of Murder: Detective Fiction and Literary Theory* (New York, 1983), 180.

ginning to understand the crime of murder in a new way that focused on its "shades of mystery."[5]

Once Gothic fiction had introduced American readers to imaginary worlds of mysterious crime, and true-crime writers had applied the convention to actual murder cases, "mysteries of the city" fiction began to pour off the American press in imitation of Eugène Sue's *Les Mystères de Paris* (1842–43). The torrent of American imitations included not only *The Mysteries and Miseries of New York* and *The Mysteries and Miseries of New Orleans* but also *Mysteries of Lowell* and *The Mysteries of Manchester*. These works typically offered lurid depictions of the seamy side of urban life: drunkenness and debauchery, gambling and prostitution, thievery, rape, and murder. The most popular of these was George Lippard's *The Quaker City; or, The Monks of Monk Hall* (1845), the single best-selling novel in America before *Uncle Tom's Cabin*. It told the story of Monk Hall, a towering pile of masonry (reputedly a former nunnery or monastery), where the wealthiest and most outwardly respectable Philadelphians gather nightly to carouse, consume brandy and opium, and deflower virgins. Monk Hall is "a place hard to find, abounding in mysteries, and darkened by hideous crimes committed within its walls." It has three stories aboveground and three below, filled with secret passageways and trapdoors leading ever downward to the Pit—"a hideous cavern, hidden far below the red brick surface of broad-brimmed Quakertown"—where the Hall's master, the monstrous pimp Devil-Bug, stows his murder victims.[6] Throughout *Quaker City* and related works by such authors as Joseph Holt Ingraham, E. Z. C.

[5] Henry Channing, *God Admonishing his People of their Duty, as Parents and Masters . . .* (New London, 1786). *Strictures on the Case of Ephraim K. Avery . . .* (Providence, 1833), 5; Karen Halttunen, "Divine Providence and Dr. Parkman's Jawbone: The Cultural Construction of Murder as Mystery," *Ideas from the National Humanities Center* 4 (1996): 4–21. For examples of the murder-mystery narrative strategy, see *An Account of the Apprehension, Trial, Conviction, and Condemnation of Manuel Philip Garcia and José Garcia Castillano . . .* (Norfolk, 1821), 5; and *The Most Important Testimony adduced on the Trial of John Francis Knapp, and Joseph Jenkins Knapp . . .* (Providence, 1830), iv. For accounts of crimes that included particularly mysterious dimensions, see *Mystery developed; or, Russell Colvin, (supposed to be murdered,) in full life: and Stephen and Jesse Boorn, (his convicted murderers,) rescued from ignominious death by wonderful discoveries . . .* (Hartford, 1820); *The life and confessions of Mrs. Henrietta Robinson, the veiled murderess! . . .* (Boston, 1855); *Confession of Adam Horn, alias Andrew Hellman . . .* (Baltimore, 1843), p. vi; Amy Gilman Srebnick, *The Mysterious Death of Mary Rogers: Sex and Culture in Nineteenth-Century New York* (New York, 1995).

[6] Ned Buntline [Edward Zane C. Judson], *The Mysteries and Miseries of New York: A Story of Real Life* (New York, 1848); Buntline, *The Mysteries and Miseries of New Orleans* (New York, [Osgood Bradbury], 1851); *Mysteries of Lowell. By the Author of "The Mysteries of Boston"* (Boston, 1844); [Chandler Eastman Potter?], *The Mysteries of Manchester: A Tale* (Manchester, N.H., and Boston, 1844). George Lippard, *The Quaker City; or The Monks of Monk Hall: A Romance of Philadelphia Life, Mystery, and Crime*, ed. and intro. David S. Reynolds (Amherst, 1995), 60, 305.

Judson (Ned Buntline), and Osgood Bradbury, the ruling assumption was that the sometimes lovely facade of the visible city concealed a depraved hidden city of dark "mysteries" and crimes.[7]

The same assumption about a mysterious hidden city guided nonfictional urban sensationalism, whose master practitioner was city reporter George G. Foster. As he exclaimed in *New York in Slices: By an Experienced Carver* (1849), "Wall Street! Who shall fathom the depth and rottenness of thy mysteries?" That work's sequel, *New York by Gas-Light* (1850), drew readers into a guided tour of the city at night, exploring its vicious subterranean regions—oyster cellars, underground coffeehouses, underground dance halls (complete with trapdoors)—accessible only through dark labyrinthine passageways (sometimes equipped with trick doors). "NEW YORK BY GAS-LIGHT! What a task have we undertaken! To penetrate beneath the thick veil of night and lay bare the fearful mysteries of darkness in the metropolis . . . all the sad realities that go to make up the lower stratum—the under-ground story—of life in New York!" In his careful mapping of "the moral geography" of New York, Foster identified the Five Points neighborhood as "the very type and physical semblance, in fact, of hell itself." But in exercising his "Asmodean privilege"—a reference to the demon Asmodeus, whose particular form of mischief was to lift the roofs off city structures to expose the evils practiced below—Foster suggested that the entire city rested on a dark subterranean world of vice and crime. His mapping of the city's moral and social life aimed at helping contemporaries come to terms with the sprawling, new nineteenth-century metropolis, which, in leaving behind the eighteenth-century walking city, was proving increasingly resistant to comprehension, more and more "mysterious."[8]

This characteristically Gothic movement to expose secret evils was also at work in the reformist opposition to Mormonism, Masonry, and Catholicism. The literature of "countersubversion" (so called by David Brion Davis because the reformers in question proclaimed their enemies to be fundamentally subversive of the American republic) represented these groups as dangerous secret societies established on mysterious rituals involving outrageously evil practices such as rape, murder, and incest. The *Awful Dis-*

---

[7] See David S. Reynolds, *Beneath the American Renaissance: The Subversive Imagination in the Age of Emerson and Melville* (New York, 1988); Michael Denning, *Mechanic Accents: Dime Novels and Working-Class Culture in Nineteenth-Century America* (London, 1987); Janis P. Stout, *Sodoms in Eden: The City in American Fiction before 1860* (Westport, Conn., 1976).

[8] Foster quoted in Reynolds, *Beneath the American Renaissance*, 295; *"New York by Gas-Light" and Other Sketches by George G. Foster*, ed. and intro. Stuart M. Blumin (Berkeley, 1990), 69, 120, 72.

closures of Maria Monk was only the best-known example of this genre, whose other anti-Catholic examples included Rebecca Reed's *Six Months in a Convent* (1835) and the anonymous *Female Convents* (1834). The anti-Mormon works focused pruriently on the practice of polygamy, describing how diabolical Mormon patriarchs tortured and raped recalcitrant women; anti-Masonic tracts exposed the Masonic practice of disemboweling victims or slitting their throats, all under the veil of secrecy of the fraternal order.[9]

Similar works of reform literature exposed the mysteries of a secret criminal underworld, secret houses of sexual assignation, and secret gambling "hells." Reformed gambler Jonathan H. Green's *Secret Band of Brothers* (1847), for example, purported to reveal "the true and secret history of a daring and powerful secret association," a fraternity of crime headed by two hundred Grand Masters, men of apparent respectability who commanded an army of low-life criminals and grew wealthy on their evil activities. The popular literature of various social reform movements drew on the Gothic image of the haunted house to convey to their readers the power of the evils they would expose: Henry Ward Beecher's attack on prostitution in "The Strange Woman" represented the brothel as a haunted house whose walls ran red with blood; his sister Harriet Beecher Stowe's most famous antislavery polemic depicted the plantation house of Simon Legree as a crumbling ruin haunted by his guilt as slaveholder. Similarly, in his popular temperance tract, "Deacon Giles' Distillery," George Cheever narrated the nightly visitation of the liquor factory by demons from hell.[10]

From Gothic fiction through true-crime literature, "mysteries of the city" fiction, nonfictional urban sensationalism, and a variety of social-reform genres, the Gothic cult of mystery emerged as a compelling idiom for addressing a range of presumed moral evils in early-nineteenth-century America. Throughout these many Gothic literary productions ran a persistent fascination with the subterranean: "Track the subterranean ramifications of this evil [intemperance], and you will see how the whole nation, the whole empire, is undermined." In the cult of mystery, criminals dwell

[9] Reynolds, *Beneath the American Renaissance*, 64; Franchot, *Roads to Rome*, chap. 7; David Brion Davis, "Some Themes of Countersubversion: An Analysis of Anti-Masonic, Anti-Catholic, and Anti-Mormon Literature," in Davis, ed., *The Fear of Conspiracy: Images of Un-American Subversion from the Revolution to the Present* (Ithaca, 1971), 9–22.

[10] Jonathan H. Green, *Secret Band of Brothers* (1847; Hicksville, N.Y., 1980), x (originally the title page); Karen Halttunen, "Gothic Imagination and Social Reform: The Haunted Houses of Lyman Beecher, Henry Ward Beecher, and Harriet Beecher Stowe," in Eric J. Sundquist, ed., *New Essays on "Uncle Tom's Cabin"* (Cambridge, 1986), 107–34; George Barrell Cheever, *The Dream: or, the True History of Deacon Giles' Distillery, and Deacon Jones' Brewery* (New York; 1848).

in a literal underground of "deep cellars" with secret passageways, trap-doors, and private dungeons; the poor live in cellars teeming with vice; and brothels are customarily likened to "the burning, galling, diseasing, outer-workshops of the bottomless pit." Monk Hall is a multistoried struc-ture with a series of vertically stacked trapdoors leading to its lowest and most evil pit, below which runs a foul stream. And one "mysteries of the city" novel depicted a full-scale "hell of this great city! I mean *the subter-ranean streets of N. York!*" whose entrance lay through a cemetery vault, a world of sewers and caves whose inhabitants commit every outrage known to humankind, including necrophagy. (In one of the novel's more horrific scenes, a madam disposes of a murder victim by ripping back the rich car-pet of her luxurious brothel parlor to expose a trapdoor, beneath which the sound of running water can be heard; shoving the corpse through the door, she explains that the sewer line will carry it to the dark city below whose inhabitants will consume it by morning.) [11]

The cult of mystery revealed two fundamental assumptions about the nature of evil in nineteenth-century popular literary culture. First, evil was regarded as essentially mysterious, hidden, occult; characteristically, moral-reformer John McDowall condemned the commerce in pornographic lit-erature and prints as "this mystery of secret iniquity." At the same time, evil was seen as something that must be exposed, unveiled, brought to light; temperance reformer John Gough wrote, "I wish I could lift the curtain that conceals from their view the secrets of this awful charnel-house." The typical narrative movement of Gothic mystery—the move to unveil—con-veys a powerful cultural imperative to expose the evils that lie buried be-low the surface of life, an imperative that helps explain the highly spatial, often architectural, component of the Gothic understanding of evil. The Gothic literature of social exposé frequently offered readers detailed ver-bal tours of the secret institutions being unveiled: "Come with me," wrote Gough, "and I will show you a scene I once witnessed [an urban slum]." Some works—including the *Awful Disclosures of Maria Monk* and a number of nonfictional murder narratives—even provided readers with maps and floor plans to assist their imaginative exploration of hidden evil.[12]

[11] John B. Gough, *Sunlight and Shadow, or, Gleanings from my Life Work* (Hartford, 1881), 292; Buntline, *Mysteries and Miseries of New York,* 5:108; *Memoir and Select Remains of the Late Rev. John R. M'Dowall, the Martyr of the Seventh Commandment in the Nineteenth Century* (New York, 1838), 266; Charles E. Averill, *The Secrets of the Twin Cities; or, the Great Metropolis Un-masked* (Boston, 1849), 102.

[12] M'Dowall, *Memoir,* 271; John B. Gough, *Platform Echoes: or, Leaves from my Note-book of Forty Years* (Hartford, 1885), 227; Gough, *Sunlight and Shadow,* 105. For a discussion of maps and

What is most striking about the cult of mystery is the steady movement of the Gothic sensibility outward from the realm of literary fantasy into a pseudosociological description of a wide range of social phenomena. How are we to explain the evolution of the conventions of Gothic mystery into an idiom for understanding the nature of social evil in nineteenth-century American culture? Some answers to this question are suggested by yet another expression of this nineteenth-century Gothic sociology: exposés of that new social institution, the asylum, particularly the prison and the mental hospital. Purportedly nonfictional works such as *Secrets of the Mount-Pleasant State Prison, Revealed and Exposed* and *Astounding Disclosures! Three Years in a Mad-house* offered to expose to the reader the dark secrets of these modern repositories of the morally nonconforming; related fictional works, with titles such as *The Mysteries of Bedlam* (whose author claimed to be a former attendant) professed the same purpose: "to expose the horrors of madhouses, with their mysteries."[13] A close reading of these works suggests an important historical connection between the popular cult of mystery and the new social practices surrounding newly constructed categories of criminal and mental deviance, into which moral outsiders were cast.

The "mysteries" of the prison and the mental institution rested, according to this literature, on the deliberate secrecy of their arrangements. Routinely, the asylum exposés promised to reveal the "hidden life" of these institutions, their "secret workings," the fair exteriors of which, they warned, were deliberately calculated to deceive the public about their concealed realities. As mental patient Isaac Hunt explained, "Secrecy always implies guilt; the more corrupt inside, the fairer the outside in order to deceive." Asylums were "dens of cruelty and oppression, whose walls but seldom give out a note of the fearful deeds working within." Lydia Smith, another former mental patient, challenged outsiders "to see through the flimsy guise which covers the slimy serpent" of the hospital.[14]

Most asylum exposés were purportedly written by former inmates: as the author of one such work asserted, "A true narrative of State Prison Life can

---

floor plans in murder literature, see Halttunen, "Divine Providence and Dr. Parkman's Jawbone," 15–17.

[13] James R. Brice, *Secrets of the Mount-Pleasant State Prison, Revealed and Exposed* . . . (Albany, 1839); Isaac H. Hunt, *Astounding Disclosures! Three Years in a Mad-house. By a Victim. Written by Himself* . . . ([Skowhegan?], 1852); *The Mysteries of Bedlam; or, Annals of the Madhouse* . . . (Philadelphia, n.d.), 41.

[14] Elizabeth Parsons Ward Packard, quoted in Jeffrey L. Geller and Maxine Harris, eds., *Women of the Asylum: Voices from behind the Walls, 1840–1945* (New York, 1994), 61; Tirzah F. Shedd, *Women of the Asylum*, 83; Hunt, *Astounding Disclosures*, 75, 43; Lydia Smith, quoted in Geller and Harris, *Women of the Asylum*, 133.

be written only by a convict, in a convict's cell." Narrators dramatized their writing of such exposés by explaining that they did so under difficult conditions—"writing in an arched cell four by seven, with seven feet solid masonry, and three sets heavy iron gratings, between me and God's free sunlight"—and with no certainty that their writings would ever see the light of day: "Whether my brown manuscript be doomed to rot within these walls and this damp cell, to be found and burned, or finally, overcoming all the difficulties under which it is written and kept, find its way to the outer world; still I am determined to write." Some claimed to write despite direct prohibitions against revealing any of the secrets of their incarceration: "But that I am forbid / To tell the secrets of my prison-house, / I could a tale unfold, whose lightest word / Would harrow up thy soul." Others charged that the authorities had deliberately extended their institutionalization to prevent such exposure; Hunt reported that he had been held at the Maine Mental Hospital only "because Dr. [James] Bates is afraid, if he discharges me, that I shall reveal the terrible secrets of this Institution to the world!"[15]

But in defiance of all efforts to suppress their exposés, asylum inmates and former inmates such as Hunt went forward with their revelations of the "terrible secrets" of the institutions that had incarcerated them. The central convention of their literary revelations was the imaginative guided tour of the prison or mental institution. The invitation of Smith to her readers was typical: "But come, let us go together a little further behind the scenes, behind the bolted doors and barred windows, back to the dens of misery." Former convict James R. Brice offered a detailed description in *Secrets of the Mount-Pleasant State Prison,* including Sing-Sing's dimensions and construction materials, the number of stories and rooms and their layout, the structure's ventilation system, and its doors and locks, stairways, galleries, and furnishings. Hunt's *Astounding Disclosures!* explicitly invited readers to "go with me in your imagination to visit the hospital. . . . In the first place we will go round to the south end of the old south wing, and go up three or four stone steps and look in through the guard grates."[16]

The typical movement of such guided tours was one of *descent* into the terrible lower depths of the institution. In the significantly titled *Mysteries of the Tombs, A Journal of Thirty Days Imprisonment in the New York City Prison,* author George Wilkes invited his readers, "Let us now escape from this

---

[15] [J. A. Banker], *An Illustrated History and Description of State Prison Life, by One Who Has Been There* (Toledo, 1871), pp. 11, 13, 14; John M. Brewer, *Prison Life!* ([Baltimore?], [1862?]), pamphlet heading; Hunt, *Astounding Disclosures,* 13.

[16] Smith, quoted in Geller and Harris, *Women of the Asylum,* 133; Brice, *Secrets of the Mount-Pleasant State Prison,* passim; Hunt, *Astounding Disclosures,* 83.

pandemonium [of the courtroom] and descend through the magistrate's court or police office, to the lower regions of the sepulchre." Mental patient Sophie Olsen reported having to descend "three long flights of stairs" to reach "this charnel house of human woe," the Fifth Ward of the Illinois State Hospital for the Insane at Jacksonville.[17] The asylum of popular nonfiction was a classically Gothic structure with its "subterranean passageways from building to building, where they can take their victims from cell to cell without the outside passers-by ever seeing them, or hearing their sighs or groans, or beholding their tears, caused by the horrid cruelties practiced upon them by those fiends in human form."[18] And just as the characters of Gothic fiction tended to lose themselves in an architectural plan that they could never quite make out, so did the occupants of the asylum. As the anonymous author of *Mysteries of Bedlam* reported, "It was a long time before I myself, the *Discharged* [officer of the institution], had access at all to the worst kinds of cells and dormitories of the establishment . . . [including the] damp, dark, and nauseous vault" into which the pauper insane were cast. Hunt identified the south wing of the Maine Hospital as "forbidden ground," informing his readers that, even on this imaginary tour, they could only peer through the grates.[19] The Gothic propensity for casting evil in architectural terms was nowhere more pronounced than in the asylum exposé.

Asylum exposé narrators, many of whom claimed to be innocent prisoners or sane mental inmates, often dwelled on the sheer horror of living among those who were truly criminal or mentally ill. Granville Clark's *Seventeen Years in Prison* complained of having been forced to live amid the "soul sickning [*sic*] deformities" of human nature "in its most revolting form." George Wilkes reported on the "filthiest animal degradation" of the inmates of the Tombs. The female narrator of *Confessions of a Maniac,* who claimed to have been driven mad by intemperance, dramatically

[17] George Wilkes, *The Mysteries of the Tombs, A Journal of Thirty Days Imprisonment in the New York City Prison; for Libel* (New York, 1844), 11; Sophie Olsen, quoted in Geller and Harris, *Women of the Asylum,* 70.

[18] Hunt, *Astounding Disclosures,* 78. Hunt was responding to Elizabeth Stone's narrative of her incarceration at McLean, which he included in his own volume. He preceded this description by offering an analogy between McLean Mental Hospital and the Ursuline convent at Charlestown, Massachusetts, that was destroyed by a mob in 1834.

[19] *Mysteries of Bedlam,* 37; Hunt, *Astounding Disclosures,* 83. Once again, this convention was present in Monk's *Awful Disclosures.* Of one particular room in the Hotel Dieu Nunnery, she explained that "beyond this room we were never allowed to go; and I cannot speak from personal knowledge of what came next" (77). In all three of Montreal's convents, she reported, "there are certain apartments into which strangers can gain admittance, but others from which they are always excluded" (23).

intoned, "I am here, within the walls of this dungeon, a companion to the gibbering idiot, and the raving madman." Hunt described the "demented or imbecile" inmates of his hospital as "disgusting and loathsome objects" who "know nothing more than swine." Even more graphically, Olsen reported, "Beside me, sitting, or rather crouching on the same bench, were a few silent and very filthy women, with their one garment indecently torn, and a puddle of unfragrant water on the floor under their feet."[20] Distancing themselves from the people around them and appealing to the presumed fastidiousness of morally respectable readers, the authors of these works claimed to "expose" the horrors of moral and mental abnormality.

But more commonly, asylum exposés focused on the terrible tortures allegedly practiced within the secret confines of the hospital or prison. A poetry anthology titled *The Prison Bard* included this verse on the "Death of Charles T. Torrey": "No voice of pity sounded in his ear, / Nor looks of sympathy his eyes did meet; / But walls, and grates, and cells, and iron doors, / And whips, and chains, and fellow suff'rers' roars!" James Brice included in his guided tour this architectural feature of the prison: "In the west hall, north of the arch, is the Flogging Post. . . . Reader, if you could but once witness a state prison flogging. The victim is stripped naked and beaten with a cruel instrument of torture called a cat, from his neck to his heels, until as raw as a piece of beef." The *Illustrated History and Description of State Prison* reported prisoners who were whipped, worked, and starved to death. At the Maine Mental Hospital, Hunt reported such abuses as the punitive use of bed straps and leather muffs; patients struck, kicked, whipped, and showered to near drowning, and the use of "fiendish drugs" as a form of mental and physical torture; he cited several deaths from such ill-treatment, one by roasting alive. Referring to the hospital as the "Calcutta black hole," he quoted the wife of a patient as saying, "I would sooner see my husband buried alive than sent to the hospital and suffer as I have seen insane persons suffer there." Even the relatively benign account *Life in Sing Sing State Prison*, written by the prison chaplain, reported on that institution's "reign of terror"; the even more upbeat *Memorials of Prison Life*, also by a prison chaplain, graphically described the punitive practice of showering, saying that "no one, without experience, knows any

---

[20] Granville Clark, *Seventeen Years in Prison. With Adventures and Anecdotes* (Doylestown, Pa., 1851), 14; Wilkes, *Mysteries of the Tombs*, 33; Sarah Stickney Ellis, *Confessions of a Maniac* (New York, 1843; bound with *The Dangers of Dining Out, or, Hints to Those Who Would Make Home Happy*), 128; Hunt, *Astounding Disclosures*, 83; Olsen, quoted in Geller and Harris, *Women of the Asylum*, 71.

thing of the torture of this infliction," which most prisoners regarded "with inexpressible horror."[21]

To convey the full horrors of such practices, a number of accounts likened these asylums to the most notorious of premodern European prisons. In a work titled *Two Years and Four Months in a Lunatic Asylum,* the Reverend Hiram Chase wrote, "Could the beams of these prison houses speak out, and could the stones cry out of the walls of some of those upper back halls in the asylum at Utica, the revelations of the woes and sufferings of humanity would so shock and astonish the outward world, that instead of classing this institution with the *humane* and *benevolent* institutions of the country, it would be classed with those ancient bastiles which have furnished a history of the most cruel and bloody tragedies ever acted under the sun!" Elizabeth Stone agreed: "*Charlestown McLean Asylum* is nothing but a *bastile*—a place to imprison and torture christians." Most commonly, asylum exposés likened these institutions to the Spanish Inquisition; according to Brice, the prison code at Sing-Sing, "if exposed and published to the world, would astonish the the [*sic*] reader, and surpass the inquisition of Spain."[22] His words were echoed by patient Elizabeth Packard, who wrote that "Insane Asylums are the 'inquisitions' of the American government," and by Ada Metcalf, who called them "Inquisitorial Prisons."[23]

Like the haunted castle of Gothic fiction, the Gothic asylum was presided over by an evil tyrant: "Not even the Spanish Inquisition ever produced the superior of Dr. Ray, as a horrid, barbarous, cruel and vindictive Inquisitor!" wrote Hunt. And Dr. Bell, who headed the McLean Hospital where Elizabeth Stone had been confined, was "as much an inquisitor as ever was Torquemada." After his incarceration at the Utica Mental Hospital, the Reverend Hiram Chase echoed this view, charging that "the sole power over

[21] George Thompson, *The Prison Bard: or Poems on Various Subjects. Written in Prison* (Hartford, 1848), 213; Brice, *Secrets of the Mount-Pleasant State Prison,* 32, 69; [Banker], *Illustrated History and Description of State Prison,* chap. 15; Hunt, *Astounding Disclosures,* 58, 38, 37; Rev. John Luckey, *Life in Sing Sing State Prison, as seen in a Twelve Years' Chaplaincy* (New York, 1860), passim; James Bradley Finley, *Memorials of Prison Life,* ed. Rev. B. F. Tefft ([Cincinnati, 1850]; reprinted, New York, 1974), 26.

[22] Rev. Hiram Chase, *Two Years and Four Months in a Lunatic Asylum . . .* (Saratoga, 1868), 31; Elizabeth Stone, quoted in Hunt, *Astounding Disclosures,* 77; Brice, *Secrets of the Mount-Pleasant State Prison,* 68.

[23] Packard and Ada Metcalf, both quoted in Geller and Harris, *Women of the Asylum,* 63 and 131, respectively. See also Hunt, *Astounding Disclosures,* 57, 59. This recurring motif of the Inquisition pointed to a popular interest in that institution's history in nineteenth-century America, evident in such works as B. F. Ells, *A History of the Romish Inquisition* (Hanover, Ind., 1835); Cyrus Mason, *A History of the Holy Catholic Inquisition: Compiled from Various Authors* (Philadelphia, 1835); and Giacinto Achilli, *Dealings with the Inquisition; or, Papal Rome, Her Priests, and Her Jesuits: With Important Disclosures* (New York, 1851).

the patient is vested in one man, whose word is law, and whose commands are as imperious as the Sultan's of Turkey." Chase found in his doctor "positive and decided marks of tyranny in his organization: A dark countenance, low built, short neck, a low forehead, not broad, and eyebrows nearly or quite meeting." Many former asylum inmates regarded such tyrannical authority as a direct violation of American political principles. "By this power every free-born citizen of the United States can be deprived of their liberty and happiness," observed Stone after her commitment to McLean, whereas Elizabeth Packard labeled as "Treason against the principles of our Government to treat opinions as Insanity, and to imprison for it, as our present laws allow." As usual, Hunt elaborated this position most exhaustively: the "madhouse" threatened "this great and mighty Republic, this boasted land of liberty, the home of the exile from the tyrannical governments of the earth"; hospital government was an "absolute Monarchy, with a tyrant at its head."[24]

With their repeated analogies between the nineteenth-century asylum and the bastille or the Spanish Inquisition, their references to their keepers as Inquisitors and tyrants, and their charges of antirepublican monarchy and despotism, writers of asylum exposés clearly demonstrated their participation in the movements of "countersubversion" identified and analyzed by David Brion Davis. Any claims made by the new prisons and hospitals to liberal benevolence and humanitarianism, these authors charged, were false. Behind their innocently ordinary stone facades and beneath their more visible upper regions lay a place "the most like hell, in my judgment, so far as we have any knowledge of what hell is, of any other place on earth."[25] Like the Masons, the Mormons, and the Romanists, the keepers of these new institutions were engaged in a concerted effort to subvert and undermine the principles of republican government, by unjustly depriving American citizens of their liberty, confining them against their will, burying them away from the freedom-loving public eye, and submitting them to unspeakable tortures and even death.

On one important level, the asylum exposés were part of an ongoing reform effort, which cited remnants of premodern practices of incarceration and corporal punishment within the new "rehabilitative" institutions in an effort to bring their practices into line with the purportedly perfectionist goals behind these institutions. The humanitarian revolution of the eighteenth century had mandated new penal methods focused on the

---

[24] Hunt, *Astounding Disclosures*, 78; Chase, *Two Years and Four Months*, 9, 45; Stone quotation from Hunt, *Astounding Disclosures*, 73; Packard, quoted in Geller and Harris, *Women of the Asylum*, 66; Hunt, *Astounding Disclosures*, 3, 67.

[25] Chase, *Two Years and Four Months*, 91.

mind rather than the body of the criminal offender and a new "moral treatment" of those with mental disorders that eschewed heroic treatments and corporal punishments in favor of gently environmental healing and the inculcation of habits of self-government. But in reality, nineteenth-century prisons and mental hospitals quickly relapsed into outdated practices of severe corporal punishment. And false imprisonment on grounds of insanity was probably not unknown, as suggested by the case of Elizabeth Packard, who was committed to an asylum by her clergyman-husband for arguing questions of dogma but managed to get out and secure a formal declaration of her sanity and then lobby for legislative reform of the institutional commitment of the mentally ill. From this perspective, the asylum exposés represented a significant call for continued reform efforts on behalf of imprisoned criminals and individuals with mental disorders.[26]

But I would like to take a different approach that recognizes the larger cultural pattern at work within the asylum exposés—the Gothic cult of mystery, which assumed the occult, "mysterious" nature of evil with respect to a wide range of social phenomena. The Gothic cult of mystery captured the imaginative response to the privatization of punishment in the new asylum, the relegation of once highly visible transgressors to a largely invisible ("secret," "mysterious," "subterranean") existence behind the walls of prisons and hospitals. In the early modern period, criminal malefactors had been publicly displayed before the collected people in "the spectacle of punishment," a theatrical ritual involving full public confrontation with and acknowledgment of the sinner.[27] By contrast, the modern practice of hiding deviants in the asylum generated a prurient curiosity about them and the secret place where they ended up. However much these social institutions reflected a new official faith in the perfectibility of human nature, at the same time they actively shaped a new Gothic understanding of human evil as hidden and ultimately uneradicable. Ironically, the medieval image of the haunted castle readily lent itself to the imaginative treatment of the modern total institution. The "Gothic" imagination was concerned

[26] See, for example, Karen Halttunen, "Humanitarianism and the Pornography of Pain in Anglo-American Culture," *American Historical Review* 100 (April 1995): 303–34; David J. Rothman, *The Discovery of the Asylum: Social Order and Disorder in the New Republic* (Boston, 1971); Louis P. Masur, *Rites of Execution: Capital Punishment and the Transformation of American Culture, 1776–1865* (New York, 1989); Mary Ann Jimenez, *Changing Faces of Madness: Early American Attitudes and Treatment of the Insane* (Hanover, N.H., 1987); Michael Meranze, *Laboratories of Virtue: Punishment, Revolution, and Authority in Philadelphia, 1760–1835* (Chapel Hill, 1996); Barbara Sapinsley, *The Private War of Mrs. Packard* (New York, 1991).

[27] See Michel Foucault, *Discipline and Punish: The Birth of the Prison*, trans. Alan Sheridan (London, 1977); and Pieter Spierenburg, *The Spectacle of Suffering: Executions and the Evolution of Repression; from a Preindustrial Metropolis to the European Experience* (Cambridge, 1984).

primarily not with the medieval past but with the liberal-humanitarian present. In addressing the modern asylum as a place where social deviance was hidden from public view—and capitalizing on the prurient popular curiosity that resulted from that hiddenness by offering guided tours of the new social realm of evil—the asylum exposés enlisted the Gothic mode to express a peculiarly modern sensibility about human evil.

But that sensibility operated within a considerably wider realm than just the asylum exposé. The broader explanation for the emergence of the popular cult of mystery lies in the relationship between the privatization of punishment in the asylum and a larger revolution in social discipline that marked the emergence of modern bourgeois culture. The social "deviants" selected for incarceration in the asylum were those persons deemed unacceptable within an emerging bourgeois ethos of civilized self-restraint, the demands of which, as Max Weber and Norbert Elias, among others, have demonstrated, steadily escalated into the modern period. That ethos gradually replaced the social praxes of the premodern culture of shame—centering on public and corporal punishment—with those of a modern culture of guilt—centering on the private internalization of values through "character formation."[28] Under modern liberal social discipline, every man became his own warden, every woman her own keeper, within what Weber called the "iron cage" of industrial capitalism. Alice James once characterized her own nervous mental state in terms that suggest much about the bourgeois condition in nineteenth-century America: "It used to seem to me that the only difference between me and the insane was that I had not only all the horrors and suffering of insanity, but the duties of doctor, nurse, and strait-jacket imposed upon me too." Her unusually painful experience of middle-class behavioral norms as a form of internal imprisonment sheds light on the symbolic resonance of prisons and mental hospitals in nineteenth-century literature, for as Mario Praz has observed, the Gothic prison expressed the psychic condition of anxiety with no possibility of escape.[29]

If the social privatization of punishment in the asylum meant that the notoriously deviant were hidden from the sight of the properly self-

---

[28] Max Weber, *The Protestant Ethic and the Spirit of Capitalism*, trans. Talcott Parsons, intro. Anthony Giddens (London, 1991); Norbert Elias, *The Civilizing Process: The History of Manners*, trans. Edmund Jephcott (New York, 1978); Myra C. Glenn, *Campaigns against Corporal Punishment: Prisoners, Sailors, Women, and Children in Antebellum America* (Albany, 1984); Jay Fliegelman, *Prodigals and Pilgrims: The American Revolution against Patriarchal Authority, 1750–1800* (Cambridge, 1988); Steven Mintz and Susan Kellogg, *Domestic Revolutions: A Social History of American Family Life* (New York, 1988).

[29] Alice James, *The Diary of Alice James*, ed. and intro. Leon Edel (Harmondsworth, 1982), 149; Weber, *Protestant Ethic*, 181; Mario Praz, introduction to *Three Gothic Novels* (Harmondsworth, 1968), 20.

restrained, the psychic privatization of bourgeois social discipline meant that the deviant impulses within each individual were buried from acknowledgment. Middle-class culture was haunted by the fear that human nature was not really perfectible, that respectability was a mere sham, the outward show of "confidence men" and "painted women." As Nathaniel Hawthorne wrote in his sketch "The Haunted Mind," "In the depths of every heart, there is a tomb and a dungeon, though the lights, the music, and revelry above may cause us to forget their existence, and the buried ones, or prisoners whom they hide."[30] The psychic process to which Hawthorne referred was what Sigmund Freud at the end of the century would label "repression." But what Freud, in his scientific essentialism, failed to recognize was that the psychic process of repression itself had a history. The Gothic imagination, as Henri Ellenberger has suggested in his monumental study *The Discovery of the Unconscious,* made a significant historical contribution to twentieth-century depth psychology.[31] But where Ellenberger addresses the *discovery* of the unconscious, I would suggest the role of the Gothic in the actual *creation* of the modern bourgeois unconscious, as a by-product of the cultural history of repression in the late eighteenth and early nineteenth centuries, a history shaped by the emergence of modern liberal social discipline with its historically new strictures on human conduct and feeling.

The slow revolution in social discipline that replaced corporal punishment with the internalized operations of guilt, and public punishment with the private practices of the aptly named "penitentiary"—all in the context of a growing privatization of middle-class daily life—generated a diffuse fascination with things hidden and mysterious, with that which did not meet the eye. The Gothic sense that evil had somehow been buried, gone underground, helps explain the symbolic power of the underworld in nineteenth-century culture. Whereas premodern Christianity tended to relegate evil to a supernatural underworld locus in hell, nineteenth-century Americans located it imaginatively in a semifantastic, semisociological underworld peopled by gamblers and prostitutes, Mormons and Catholics, slaveholders and rum sellers, the very poor and the very rich, the criminal and the insane. Eventually, this nineteenth-century underworld would evolve into the depth psychology of the unconscious, which is the prevailing twentieth-century model for understanding what was once

---

[30] Karen Halttunen, *Confidence Men and Painted Women: A Study of Middle-Class Culture in America, 1830–1870* (New Haven, 1982); Nathaniel Hawthorne, "The Haunted Mind," in *Nathaniel Hawthorne: Tales and Sketches,* ed. Roy Harvey Pearce (New York, 1982), 201–2.

[31] See Henri F. Ellenberger, *The Discovery of the Unconscious: The History and Evolution of Dynamic Psychiatry* (New York, 1970), chap. 3.

understood as human evil.[32] That ultimate development was obscurely anticipated by the anonymous author of *The Mysteries of Bedlam,* who wrote, "Were the deep ocean dried, and all its secrets opened to one's scrutiny, less varied, less monstrous would its discoveries probably be, than those which would be obtained from the unveiling of one distempered spirit."[33]

[32] For a provocative study of this evolution in Western thought, see James Hillman, *The Dream and the Underworld* (New York, 1979).

[33] *Mysteries of Bedlam,* 92.

The world's "dirty work": an oppressed seamstress being browbeaten in a New York sweat-
shop. Henry Ward Beecher regarded such ill-treatment as a temporary aberration in the
northern system of dignified "free labor." Library of Congress.

CHAPTER THREE

The World's "Dirty Work" and the Wages That "Sweeten" It: Labor's "Extrinsic Rewards" in Antebellum Society

JONATHAN A. GLICKSTEIN

How much economic and social inequality a society should tolerate and why such inequalities develop are not merely matters of economic and social conditions, or even ones of political power. They are also profoundly moral matters because they raise the question of which members of the society, in consequence of the extant inequalities, are enjoying undeserved benefits and which ones are bearing undeserved burdens. As one scholar has put the issue, "How a group or society distributes available resources among members reflects not only power and authority relations but also the moral basis of the group, its consensus about distributive justice, and its implicit priorities."[1] Those who have been most at odds with prevailing occupational hierarchies and their modes and patterns of resource distribution, from the utopian socialists of the early nineteenth century to left / liberal academic philosophers of today, are those who have most insistently conceptualized economic and social inequalities as moral problems, matters of social injustice. Yet the contrasting tradition of support extended by neoclassical economic and other thinkers to the distributive processes and outcomes of free market capitalism—to its structure of incentives and occupational rewards—has consistently, if oftentimes more implicitly, embodied its own economic ethics.

I am particularly grateful to Ann Plane and Mary Furner for comments on earlier drafts of this essay. Financial assistance was provided by a University of California President's Research Fellowship in the Humanities.
[1] Hanna Papanek, "To Each Less Than She Needs, from Each More Than She Can Do," in Irene Tinker, ed., *Persistent Inequalities* (New York, 1990), 163.

The view that work was, or should be, a "blessing" for those who performed it was most extensively developed by the privileged classes of nineteenth-century Western societies. At least in part, these classes' heightened emphasis on work's natural, intrinsic moral benefits and intellectual satisfactions was a complex and paradoxical response to the work performed by the laboring classes themselves. The celebration of work by some of the more intellectual and socially alert elements of the middle and upper classes—elements that included Marx on the left and Carlyle on the right—was stimulated by the very regimentation and trivialization, as well as by the impending redundancy, of growing numbers of manual labor employments under early capitalist industrialization and mechanization.

This philosophical and even agonized insistence on the creative and other intrinsically fulfilling attributes of work blended into the animus against the early-nineteenth-century's purported commodification of social relationships—the tyranny of the "cash nexus." Among clergy and other public moralists in England and the United States, it developed into dramatic warnings against justifying work primarily in terms of its monetary, or extrinsic, value. Such warnings now appear, for the most part, to have been an early expression of concern over the "'crisis of legitimation'" in capitalism, the degree to which capitalist societies seemed to be eroding the "moral basis of their own social order," and thereby inviting social conflict, through their pecuniary and calculative tendencies.[2] Last but hardly least, the one-sided emphasis of many of these same, as well as other, nineteenth-century commentators on the morally uplifting and disciplinary effects of various forms of menial labor in itself signaled an exploitative mentality insofar as it reflected pervasive and convenient assumptions that members of certain social groups—notably blacks, Irish immigrants, and women—were most naturally suited for and would derive the greatest intrinsic "rewards" from such labor.

The early- to mid-nineteenth-century insistence on work's intrinsic value and satisfactions, either existing or potential, thus had diverse and even contradictory dimensions and impetuses, only some of which have been mentioned here. But this insistence was often quite overwhelmed by the contrary inclination, exhibited in both working-class and middle-class circles, to accentuate the importance of manual labor's strictly extrinsic, or material, inducements and rewards. At the same time, the obvious "fact" that wage-earning manual laborers and other ordinary people typically needed to work to survive and may thus themselves have "naturally" attached a practical value to their occupations obscures as much as it illuminates, if only because the particular arrangements of private enterprise

[2] Adrian Ellis and Krishan Kumar, preface to Ellis and Kumar, eds., *Dilemmas of Liberal Democracies* (London, 1983), x.

and social stratification that fostered such a need were themselves cultural constructions and by no means the only arrangements capable of developing. Of relevance here is the commonplace observation that "if we had a different system than capitalism, or a system not based on private property, we would have a different distribution of income."[3] To this we might add a variation in the form of a question, one that speaks more directly to my subject here: Would manual labor carry the same instrumental value if the prevailing arrangements were somehow such that those who performed this manual labor actually employed the "capitalists" (that is, those who provided the plants and other productive resources)? Bizarre as this scenario might appear, it should at least suggest that the considerable emphasis on manual labor's material inducements and rewards in antebellum America and the ideological representations of those inducements and rewards generally were not a given but require further investigation.

Consider the extended newspaper debate that the conservative Whig Henry J. Raymond conducted with Horace Greeley over the merits of establishing Fourierist communities in the United States. In that debate Raymond made a good many arguments designed to puncture the era's bubble of utopian enthusiasm. But none was more basic than the one he used to dismiss the claim that the phalanx would effectively employ a variety of expedients to bring out the intrinsic "attractiveness" of hard labor. To this claim Raymond responded:

> Working by music, plowing in uniform, conferring nominal and empty honors, &c., might do for children, but to urge it as a means of making hard labor attractive, is nonsense. The only thing that can make labor attractive to the mass of men is the stimulus of reward, the hope of recompense, and above all, the certainty of possessing and enjoying that recompense, whatever it may be. So far as these motives operate, they make labor attractive. Men now toil first to obtain a subsistence; and then to acquire the means of comfort for themselves and their children.[4]

In his unequivocal privileging of work's instrumental value over its intrinsic appeal, Raymond, of course, was speaking preeminently of manual labor, and of legally free labor at that. His remarks well represented those pervasive American, and especially middle-class, social attitudes that generally failed to deviate from traditional Old World attitudes and failed to provide a ringing affirmation of physical labor's intrinsic dignity. Recognition that hard and dirty work remained such whether it was performed in the United States or in the Old World spurred commentators across a wide

[3] Duncan Kennedy, *Sexy Dressing, Etc.* (Cambridge, Mass., 1993), 97.
[4] Raymond's reply in *Courier and Enquirer*, April 16, repr. in Horace Greeley and Henry J. Raymond, *Association Discussed* (New York, 1847), 70.

ideological spectrum to frame and debate the question of American manual labor's dignity in terms of its extrinsic rewards. The characteristic tendency of the more zealous exponents of American exceptionalism was to claim that manual labor could not be "drudgery" in the United States precisely because of the material and advancement rewards to be gained thereby.

Yet historians disagree over the bearing that manual labor's material rewards had on its social status during the nineteenth century. Reflecting the growing attention to the eighteenth-century Anglo-American "consumer revolution," one scholarly view holds that in the wake of the American Revolution, consumer and "entrepreneurial" impulses perceptibly raised the "worth" of productive manual labor, obliterating centuries-old attitudes that had disdained it as "ungentlemanly."[5] A contrasting view emphasizes the stigma that republican and producerist traditions, extolling a condition of economic independence, continued to attach to wage-earning manual labor during this same period. Only toward the end of the nineteenth century did organized labor and its leaders themselves begin to accept permanent wage labor and to assert its dignity in terms of its instrumental value or the wage earner's capacity to meet consumer needs and wants.[6]

Both these views slight the complexity and diversity of mid-nineteenth-century ideological constructions. On the one hand, the acquisitive values of post-Revolution liberal capitalism did not so much eradicate as transmute the age-old attitudes of disdain for manual labor. During a period in which small producing elements—independent artisans and farmers as well as wage earners—experienced increasing inequality vis-à-vis upper-middle-class occupational groups, these liberal-capitalist "success" values unmistakably suggested that the dignity of manual labor still ultimately resided in its escapability into other and "better" occupations, ones whose profit-making potential was less limited and more quickly fulfilled; the talented and deserving members of American society did not finish the "race of life" working with their hands. On the other hand, the persistent antebellum references, within as well as outside the working classes, to the abysmal wages and living standards of Europe's "pauper laborers" reveals that an American propensity to construct wage labor's respectability around its capacity to acquire market rewards was developing well before the end of the century. There is, moreover, the additional case of unmar-

---

[5] Gordon S. Wood, "Inventing American Capitalism," *New York Review of Books,* June 9, 1994, 48–49.

[6] Lawrence B. Glickman, *A Living Wage* (Ithaca, 1997). Glickman perceptively treats the ways that the late-nineteenth-century "living wage" discourse was discriminatory with respect to female and nonwhite wage earners, although he slights the pre–Civil War ideological antecedents that I refer to in the main text.

ried female wage-earners, such as the first generation of New England factory women, whose newly acquired discretionary spending power assumed special symbolic meaning as a signifier of unprecedented economic independence and freedom from paternalistic controls.[7]

The antebellum era's ideological constructions of labor's extrinsic rewards were broadly defined by an ongoing series of debates, both transatlantic and interclass in nature, which turned on the existing and the proper mix of incentives that drove legally free labor, including its more unskilled and more "repugnant" kinds. Were these incentives, at least in the United States, primarily of a "positive" nature? Did they consist of a free worker's hopes and prospects for actual economic and social improvement and the stimulating operation on him or her, in bourgeois parlance, of "higher wants"?[8] Or were the prevailing incentives for needed manual industry, even in America and in the northern states specifically, of a "negative" kind? Were they dominated by the free laborer's imperative merely to avoid starvation, reflecting the so-called utility of poverty? These debates most frequently and directly addressed the material inducements and rewards obtaining for the growing population of free waged laborers in the antebellum North. But they were also invariably informed by perceptions of one or more of the alternative possibilities, including freehold farming, black chattel slave labor, and even various forms of the most literally "dirty" work—the self-employed casual labor concentrated in the major cities. Consider as one contribution to these debates the following remarks from Boston's *Chronotype* in 1846:

> Labor for nothing is not very pleasant. . . . The mind wants a motive, future enjoyment, victory, praise, something to work for. . . . Let this motive be strong enough and any kind of labor becomes delightful. . . . It is the principle of property which seems to have been designed by our Creator to sweeten labor. . . . When I become a more civilized man and for some great object work on an extensive plan, the expected result sweetens every blow of the toil. . . .
>
> We may set it down as a settled principle that the right of individual property, the hope of some benefit to be gained, is absolutely necessary to secure happy industry, and of course the greatest amount of industry. The fear of the whip or of starvation cannot do it. . . .
>
> Now who can deny that there is a tendency in civilized society, with all its glorious achievements and improvements, to separate into two classes, the extremely rich and luxurious who cast off labor and betake themselves to

[7] For discussion of these issues, see Jonathan A. Glickstein, *Concepts of Free Labor in Antebellum America* (New Haven, 1991), esp. chap. 1.

[8] Relevant discussions of gender issues include Thomas Dublin, *Transforming Women's Work: New England Lives in the Industrial Revolution* (Ithaca, 1994), and Jean Matthews, "Race, Sex, and the Dimensions of Liberty in Antebellum America," *Journal of the Early Republic* 6 (Fall 1986): 283–84 especially.

mere consumption, and the extremely poor whose labor brings them from day to day only the provender absolutely necessary to keep the machine in motion. . . .

Surely it is worth while to investigate the causes of such an evil tendency, especially in a new country, and inquire whether it may not be counteracted. Is there no plan by which the hope of humanity—that is, the hope of always growing richer and happier, may be given as the motive to every human laborer?[9]

Every one of these remarks has a rich history. Moreover, the idealistic materialism that infused them, a materialism that encompassed but extended beyond an ethos of rational, maximizing self-interest, ran throughout antebellum culture, notwithstanding the fact that the *Chronotype* at this time was one of the leading promoters of utopian Fourierism. In our own, more postmodern age, when "settled principles" are few and far between, both the idealism and the certitude of the *Chronotype* may seem quaint. But meriting note here are the related axioms around which this idealism and certitude gathered: that economic improvement and the hope of such improvement, centered on the acquisition of "property," constituted the most efficacious of all labor incentives; that such extrinsic "sweeteners" of labor were most vital of all to "more civilized" individuals, those who had developed their ambition and wants to a particular if undefined point; and that both the negative lash of hunger which drove the "wage slave" and the slaveholder's lash which motivated the formal, chattel slave were poor substitutes for the divinely inspired "principle of property." Accompanying these more widely held axioms was the special conviction that animated both middle-class labor reformers and radicals of the *Chronotype*'s ilk and some of the more thoroughly working-class movements of the period, though it was not confined to either of these: the conviction that however ethically and economically superior, however more "civilized" they might be, positive labor incentives were in fact disappearing from the United States—that the free laboring population of this "new country" was by midcentury experiencing a "Europeanizing," absolute impoverishment.

Recent scholarship has thrown into doubt the empirical validity of most, if not all, of the "principles" affirmed in the *Chronotype* piece. But it is the ideological constructions themselves that are the primary interest here. Can we probe more deeply into the intellectual framework within which this and other contributions to the antebellum debates over labor's extrinsic incentives were situated?

In 1843 Philadelphia's *Public Ledger* editorialized how little had changed in England for all the economic development it had undergone in "mod-

[9] "The Philosophy of Labor. No. 2," *Chronotype* (Boston), July 20, 1846.

ern times." England's present commercial and manufacturing system, the *Public Ledger* observed, followed the feudal practice of concentrating wealth and exalting its "nonproductive" owners "upon the degradation" of the laboring population. As to modern English political economy, it merited similar indictment for its governing feudal assumptions: "All its precepts, all its recommendations, are for the benefit of capital; and it treats labor, not as something endowed by God with the right to comfort, to happiness, equal to that of the capitalist, but as an *expense* incidental to capital, which the capitalist cannot avoid entirely, but should *reduce* as much as possible."[10]

The *Public Ledger*'s criticisms of English political economy had for decades been the particular stuff of labor activist and "radical" political economy in both England and the United States. But the *Public Ledger* was a mainstream journal, and as with its encomiums elsewhere to its own country's exceptionally egalitarian conditions and practices, the paper's dismissal of "the modern school of political economy" for legitimating injustices within English society was also within the American mainstream, whatever the extent to which America's college professors had continued to teach from the "English classics." A definitive examination of so pervasive and open-ended a phenomenon must remain a will-o'-the-wisp. Yet the ideological construction of manual labor's extrinsic rewards in antebellum America can to a remarkable extent be characterized as a dynamic process in which the inherited conceptual framework of British classical economics collided and intertwined with, and was always selectively interpreted by, a mythology of American economic exceptionalism that was itself undergoing continuous change in the face of different pressures and challenges.

Our own dominant perception of British classical economy likely remains that of a set of gloomy propositions predicated on a society of increasingly scarce resources. In 1776 Adam Smith introduced a "high-wage," optimistic economic growth scenario, one that markedly challenged earlier "utility of poverty" mercantilist notions which had insisted that the wants of the lower classes are intrinsically limited, that these classes would not, on their own initiative, extend their industriousness and their productivity beyond the fulfillment of bare subsistent needs. But Smith's scenario itself, in turn, came to be significantly modified and reversed by Thomas Malthus and David Ricardo. As reactions against the radical perfectionist doctrines of their era and as alarmist responses to the rising poor-relief costs and other immediate problems of England during the early Industrial Revolution, the most compelling paradigms of Malthus and

---

[10] "Capital and Labor," *Public Ledger* (Philadelphia), October 20, 1843.

Ricardo bleakly characterized the insuperable, "natural" laws of societies as tendencies toward overpopulation and diminishing returns. Rather than maintaining a level of wages and earnings that would permit saving and actual improvement in their economic and social condition, the great majority of the British working classes would be overwhelmingly stimulated by the negative incentive of providing the barest necessaries for themselves and their families. Nor, according to Malthus and Ricardo, should this most primordial, this most natural of labor incentives and market forces—the hunger that was "Nature's penalty" for laziness and inactivity—be interfered with and blunted by destructive governmental poor laws. In sustaining a population of dependent paupers, those laws imposed only still further downward pressure on the wages of the independent, "virtuous" laboring poor by drawing from a "wages fund" that at any one time was fixed and limited in size.[11]

Such were some of the most severe and dismal principles of the Malthusian-Ricardian classical economic paradigms. But scholars have also long noted and argued over the tempering of those principles by Malthus and Ricardo in other parts of their writings. Rather than merely inserting the "utility of poverty" notions of pre-Smithian mercantilist thinkers into their free market vision, Malthus and Ricardo did acknowledge a bourgeois potential in the laboring population—the capacity of workers, through education and refinement, to develop a taste for comforts and conveniences that would encourage them to practice "moral restraint" and keep down their numbers. While retaining to the end an insistence on the demoralizing, labor incentive–destroying effects of poor relief, Malthus and Ricardo expressed the recognition and hope that workers might gradually develop a welcome dependence on a level of wages above "subsistence" in the bare physiological sense of that term. Therefore, rising real wages could themselves, as Adam Smith had earlier suggested, serve as both an accompaniment of and a stimulus to improved worker habits and increased industriousness and productivity.[12]

---

[11] A. W. Coats, "The Classical Economists and the Labourer," in Coats, ed., *The Classical Economists and Economic Policy* (London, 1971), 144–79; Gertrude Himmelfarb, *The Idea of Poverty* (New York, 1984), 23–176; J. R. Poynter, *Society and Pauperism* (London, 1969); and Edgar S. Furniss, *The Position of the Laborer in a System of Nationalism* (New York, 1957).

[12] Malthus softened his arguments in, above all, the revised editions that followed his famous *Essay on the Principle of Population* (London, 1798). It was in fact the third edition (London, 1821) of his key work, *Principles of Political Economy and Taxation*, that Ricardo added to his seemingly gloomy principles (such as those predictive of the "stationary state") his more pessimistic conclusions regarding technological unemployment. Even the most optimistic passages in Malthus and Ricardo convey little expectation that more than a small proportion of British laborers would ever convert the bourgeois tastes and elevated "social" (or "relative") subsistence that they managed to acquire into upward mobility out of the working classes. See Coats, "Classical Economists"; Richard B. Simons, "T. R. Malthus on British Society," *Journal of the History of Ideas* 16 (January 1955): 67–72; Samuel Hollander, "On Malthus's Population Principle and Social Reform," *History of Political Economy* 18 (Summer 1986):

For empirical and more strictly ideological reasons, this mellowing of the original Malthus-Ricardo economy of scarcity was carried a good deal further by later British classical economists such as J. Ramsay McCulloch, Nassau Senior, and John Stuart Mill. Not only did British population, wage, and other data from the 1820s and 1830s appear to discredit the bleakest, "inevitable misery" predictions made by Malthus and Ricardo, but their successors also recognized, in a period of continuing labor unrest, that such doctrines were too gloomy to win the allegiance of workers. Nor could McCulloch and others remain comfortable with such core components of the initial paradigms as Ricardo's labor theory of value and his doctrine of the inverse relationship between wages and capitalist profits, in view of the labor exploitation theories that Robert Owen, his followers, and other radicals were all too freely drawing from such material.[13]

From at least the time Marx dissected "bourgeois" political economy as a system of capitalist apologetics for the misery of the British laboring classes during the Industrial Revolution, historians have recognized that the "wages fund" and other so-called natural laws of high political economy were themselves ideological constructions. Whether or not they indeed amounted to learned rationalizations for misery, classical economic principles sought to universalize market-oriented rationality and the bourgeois sense of the rectitude of competitive individualism. Yet the entrance of such formal economic ideas into both the British and the American "public domains" of thought, where they underwent interpretation and reinterpretation, still furthered their metastasis as ideologies even as their technical content was diluted. The mere "transmission" of economic principles in this period significantly wrought their "transformation."[14]

In the antebellum United States a basic part of this ideological work consisted of the tendency of commentators such as the *Public Ledger* to slight or ignore completely the mellowing of British political economy referred to above.[15] That tendency—its own form of historical "memory"—

187–236; Maxine Berg, *The Machinery Question and the Making of Political Economy, 1815–1848* (Cambridge, 1980), 43–74; and Edwin Cannan, *A History of the Theories of Production and Distribution in English Political Economy from 1776 to 1848* (1893; New York, 1967).

[13] Mark Blaug, *Ricardian Economics* (New Haven, 1958); Mark Blaug, *Economic History and the History of Economics* (New York, 1986), 91–114; Ronald L. Meek, *Economics and Ideology and Other Essays* (London, 1967), 51–73; Noel W. Thompson, *The People's Science* (Cambridge, 1984); Gregory Claeys, *Machinery, Money, and the Millennium* (Cambridge, 1987); R. M. Hartwell and S. Engerman, "Models of Immiseration: The Theoretical Basis of Pessimism," in Arthur J. Taylor, ed., *The Standard of Living in Britain in the Industrial Revolution* (London, 1975), 189–213; Ellen Frankel Paul, *Moral Revolution and Economic Science* (Westport, 1979); Maxine Berg, "Progress and Providence in Early Nineteenth-Century Political Economy," *Social History* 15 (October 1990): 367–75.

[14] Maurice F. Neufeld, "Realms of Thought and Organized Labor in the Age of Jackson," *Labor History* 10 (Winter 1969): 31–32.

[15] This slighting and ignoring was a significant tendency, particularly among journalists, politicians, and others within the reasonably informed general public. Among American

was particularly marked among the many who formed their impressions of the British paradigms secondhand or through popularized versions. We can attribute the American slighting in part to the intrinsic power, the salience, and the notoriety of the bleakest elements of the early Malthusian-Ricardian scenario, which even in Britain overshadowed for years all that came later. But we should also stress that the particular attention paid in the United States to the original harsh scenario best suited the ideological needs of a host of commentators there, including politicians, poor law officials, and labor leaders. Indeed, it is striking how British classical economics could be similarly interpreted—that is, agreement reached as to its central principles—by antebellum Americans who were trying to meet diverse, frequently conflicting ideological needs, individuals who often occupied widely different positions on the issue of American economic exceptionalism. We can identify several prominent configurations, or patterns of responses, for purposes of illustration.

There were, first, the most unequivocal American economic exceptionalists, generally commentators of a moderate and conservative bent affiliated with the Whig Party, who rejected out of hand the "fatalistic" and "dismal" Malthusian-Ricardian economy of scarcity and subsistence as completely inapplicable to the expansive, "go-ahead" American conditions. The Whig polemicist Calvin Colton epitomized this tendency to define and celebrate American "free labor" entirely in terms of the positive labor incentives and generous extrinsic rewards that it ostensibly enjoyed. In its optimism and complacency, Colton and this configuration generally were guilty of many facile generalizations, as well as exclusions and silences bearing on gender and race, that social historians have exposed in recent years. Morever, Colton's persistent boasting of the pervasive "freedom wages" in the United States was, for all its chauvinism, a simultaneous admission of the fragility of American economic exceptionalism. With other Whigs he conducted an ongoing campaign for the high protective tariffs that he deemed essential to preventing the American wage advantage from actually being actually destroyed by direct competition with European "pauper" laborers.[16]

In addition, Colton and like-minded Whigs, elaborating the *Public Ledger* editorial quoted above, conveniently fastened on the most harsh and "heartless" classical economic "inevitable misery" paradigms as product and symbol of the Old World's entrenched and corrupt class structure. Al-

---

academics and writers of economic treatises, slighting of the mellowing those advances represented was of a more characteristically deliberate nature; they commonly dismissed the contributions of a McCulloch or Senior as inappreciable alterations of the original dismal scenarios.

[16] Calvin Colton, *The Rights of Labor* (New York, 1846), 3–10.

though other configurations exhibited this same general tendency, the distinction of this moderate-conservative Whig configuration was to launch a "counterhegemonic" attack on British and other European societies for the purpose of celebrating and legitimating capitalist hegemony within the Unites States itself. Lastly, in the hands of the American political economist Henry C. Carey, these counterhegemonic diatribes against Europe were most fully taken to the point where the "dismal science" of Malthus and Ricardo was dismissed not because it was singularly inapplicable to the land-abundant, labor-scarce, high-wage United States but because it was wrong for all societies. Intrinsically and hopelessly flawed in its doctrine of overpopulation and other pessimistic principles, the classical economy-of-scarcity paradigm was to be thrown out along with the monopolistic and exploitative Old World arrangements that it sought to legitimate.[17]

A second general configuration, also Whiggish and also bolstering the mythology of American economic exceptionalism, highlighted those elements of the severe classical economic paradigm in which it in fact found great merit. The dominant elements in this configuration were the almshouse officials and other middle- and upper-middle-class Americans alarmed over the growing poverty and pauperism in their own nation's urban centers. It was less a matter of such officials and like-minded commentators finding any particular validity in, say, Malthus's famed ratios or Ricardo's doctrine of rent. Rather, they embraced as universal and over-powering truths the more general axioms of middle-class, free market competitive morality that underlay classical economics: admonitions that the laboring poor must take responsibility for their own condition; that they could and should, with some assistance from the more enlightened classes above them, internalize the bourgeois values of self-discipline, self-direction, and acquisitiveness; and that compulsory outdoor relief for at least the able-bodied members of the laboring population, by insulating that population from the salutary prodding of "physical want," or "Nature's penalty" for indolence, inevitably served to debilitate laborers morally and to increase the numbers of dependent poor. "Similar moral causes produce similar effects everywhere," warned George Arnold, minister-at-large to the poor in New York City, in the 1830s regarding the spread of pauperism there. And a like-minded writer for the *American Quarterly Review* bemoaned the same apparent anomaly: the increase of pauperism in a country where labor was relatively scarce, where wages were high, and where it was "impossible to imagine a state of civil society in which it would be more difficult for the Poor Laws to produce their ill effects."[18]

[17] Henry C. Carey, *Principles of Social Science*, 3 vols. (Philadelphia, 1858).
[18] George Arnold, *Third Semi-Annual Report as Minister—At-Large in New York City, 1833* (New York, 1834), 8–9; "Poor Laws," *American Quarterly Review* 4 (Sept 1833): 82.

Nothing is more interesting in this configuration than its efforts to sustain a mythology of American exceptionalism—the belief in the unique pervasiveness of generous positive labor incentives for free labor in the United States—while also insisting that the operation of negative labor incentives remained just as vital there as in any other nation. New York's *Journal of Commerce* suggested in 1848 that the "Communist" plans afoot in France to remedy inequalities of property would prove just as demoralizing and destructive in the United States, for here as everywhere "the fear of poverty and the ambition to become rich are the great stimulants to production. . . . The love of riches may impel men to labor who are secure of a provision for their wants; but no man will work, without the stimulant of want."[19]

Like the first configuration, this second configuration illustrated how the belief that America offered uniquely abundant economic rewards and opportunities "to become rich" encouraged a pronounced disapproval, even contempt, for those who failed to discipline themselves, to exploit these opportunities, and to rise out of poverty in time. A moralistic view of American poverty and pauperism followed readily from the conviction that the United States singularly lacked the unjust laws and institutions and the closed class structure that acted to "repress the ambition of the lower classes" in Old World societies.[20]

Occasionally accompanying this attitude, however, was a less moralistic note of ambivalence. Drawing on some recent lectures by the prominent Unitarian clergyman and Whig-Republican Henry W. Bellows, New York's *Evangelist* observed in 1858 that "there is a poverty which invigorates both body and mind, which teaches the virtues of frugality and economy, and which leads to hardy industry. But, on the other hand, there is a poverty which unmans and crushes, and which sinks into the hopeless abyss of Pauperism."[21] The *Evangelist* was articulating the very uncertainty regarding poverty's actual efficacy as a labor incentive that Malthus himself had expressed years before when he noted that once poverty had "passed certain limits," it "almost ceases to operate" as a "spur to industry." Along with "the hope of bettering our condition," Malthus continued, it is "the fear of want, rather than want itself, that is the best stimulus to industry."[22] Under what circumstances, and for which individuals, do poverty and hunger in-

---

[19] *Journal of Commerce* (New York), quoted in "Wealth and Want," *New-York Tribune,* October 14, 1848.

[20] Quote from Junius H. Hatch, *New York Assembly Journal,* March 26, 1822, 878.

[21] "Pauperism and Crime," *Evangelist* (New York), March 4, 1858. The gendered nature of these remarks enjoyed a long tradition in Anglo-American poor law thought and policy in the implication that the resulting condition of pauper dependency was a particularly unnatural and unfortunate one for males.

[22] T. R. Malthus, *An Essay on the Principle of Population,* 5th ed. (London, 1817), 2:42–43.

deed demoralize and crush? When and why, on the other hand, does want remain for some individuals a spur to industry, ambition, and ultimate escape from want? This question, a confession of ignorance regarding all the possible effects of poverty—and one whose relevance has hardly diminished over time—was passed on to twentieth-century discourse by British classical economics and by subsequent American commentators such as the *Evangelist* operating in their own economic and political context, even as their uncertainty and ambivalence about poverty's effects could never truly compete with the moralistic attitudes that came more easily to them.

Little of such ambivalence toward poverty was expressed by members of a third antebellum configuration: skeptics and gainsayers of American economic exceptionalism who claimed that, in emulation of the Old World, generous extrinsic rewards for legally free labor were rapidly disappearing in the northern states and had all but been supplanted there by the competitive free market's preeminent negative incentive—the exploitative and hateful "lash" of poverty. This general configuration, consisting of many of the critics of northern "wage slavery" and "white slavery," included urban, often British-born artisan trade union activists of the 1820s and 1830s; northern, upper-middle-class utopian socialists of the 1840s; and conservative, proslavery intellectuals and politicians from the southern states. These last dominated the configuration in the 1850s as the northern criticisms were dissipated and mainstreamed into the antisouthern Republican Party crusade for "free soil, free labor, free men." Most of these diverse critics of American exceptionalist mythology tied the erosion and disappearance of positive labor incentives to the spread of the dependent wage labor condition itself—to the commodification of labor power in the North. While lacking Marx's theoretical model of surplus value, they shared Marx's view that a truly just recompense—as distinct from temporarily high wages—was necessarily precluded by the unequal, exploitative character of the employer–wage earner relationship.

These critics of northern wage slavery were, just like Whiggish American exceptionalists on the other side of the issue, typically playing off the Old World and making use of the conventional and harsh classical economic paradigm. They were articulating their own version of the maxim "like causes, like effects"—not George Arnold's version, which favorably invoked classical economy in warning of compulsory poor relief's universally destructive effects on the work habits of the poor, but rather a version that, to the contrary, *deplored* the penetration of classical economy's underlying principles and values into antebellum American culture. Thus the *Chronotype* refuted Calvin Colton's argument that classical economy was irrelevant to American conditions; indeed, it was proving all too relevant. As the *Chronotype* explained: "For the truth is that the system of things here is essentially the same as in Europe. It is not the accident of a surplus population on which Ricardo and Say reason, but the mere law of supply and demand which must regulate the price of labor every where, where it is a commodity in the market, where competition among laborers and between laborers and machinery is the prevailing fact."[23]

Republican and agrarian traditions and a related yearning for insulation from the pressures and vagaries of the capitalist market at times led members of this configuration, such as the printer and labor leader George Henry Evans, to valorize poverty when wedded to a condition of freehold independence.[24] But the same traditions stimulated their antipathy to poverty and even to the mere fear of want as components of the competitive labor market; the salutary impact of such work "incentives" was limited to the capitalist's profit sheet.

There were ironies in the tendency of many of the antebellum American critics of wage slavery and free market competitive processes to underscore the applicability of a European-derived political economic model that they despised.[25] Perhaps these ironies were particularly pronounced in the case of certain southern proslavery intellectuals—individuals who embraced Malthusian population theory to explicate American exceptionalism's ongoing displacement in the free states by a dog-eat-dog, immiserating competition for subsistence and yet who glossed over the extent to which the same harsh Malthusian pressures threatened their own peculiar institution by rendering free, white wage labor ever cheaper and more competitive.[26] During the 1850s, however, northern commentators who engaged in rhetorical battle with slavery's defenders also did their

[23] Review of *The Rights of Labor,* by Calvin Colton, *Chronotype* (Boston), October 28, 1846. This third configuration's overriding image of the North as a locale of superheated economic competition and insecurity, one that received pernicious doctrinal reinforcement from transatlantic political economic maxims, was also fed by cultural anxieties that both encompassed and transcended white racism. For discussion of some of the insights and limitations of recent raced-based cultural studies regarding notions of "wage slavery" and "white slavery," see Jonathan A. Glickstein, "Pressures from Below: Pauperism, Chattel Slavery, and the Ideological Construction of Free Market Labor Incentives in Antebellum America," *Radical History Review,* 69 (Fall 1997): 114–59.

[24] "To Gerrit Smith," from Evans, *Working Man's Advocate* (New York), August 17, 1844.

[25] I also note those other antebellum critics of northern wage slavery, particularly associated with "Jacksonian democracy," who identified the root evil not as an excess of economic competition but rather as an insufficiency of fair competition. Yet despite its own sanctification of free competition in the marketplace, British classical economics, post–Adam Smith, also failed for a variety of reasons to draw a generally enthusiastic response from this group of wage slavery's critics.

[26] Eugene D. Genovese and Elizabeth Fox-Genovese, "Slavery, Economic Development, and the Law: The Dilemma of the Southern Political Economists, 1800–1860," *Washington and Lee Law Review* 41 (Winter 1984): 23–30. There were also the different southern apprehensions regarding the continuing natural increase of the slaves themselves and their eventual "death struggle" with the white race (or some similar calamity) should the slaves be penned up in the existing slave states by an increasingly hostile northern majority. Such apprehensions over healthy, proliferating black bodies constituted an interesting variant on British Malthusian fears earlier in the century.

part to ignore the ironies and contradictions in proslavery Malthusianism. There always had been a substantial school of thought that had found unrelenting antislavery implications in Malthus's population principle. But precisely because members of this school had tended to predicate the dislodging of slave labor on the catastrophic, cheapening impact of "natural laws" on American free laborers—on the erosion of their positive incentives—this antislavery Malthusianism could be of little use to the late-antebellum celebrators of northern free labor. They were inspired only by the intensified proslavery Malthusianism of the period to further the long tradition of demonizing classical economics. Thus a contributor to Philadelphia's *North American and United States Gazette* opined in 1858 that Carlyle had been right to characterize as the "dismal science" what were still, unfortunately, the "prevalent theories" in political economy—Malthus's population doctrine and Ricardo's theory of rent. These theories were "malignant" not merely for the death sentences that they, by their intrinsic nature, erroneously passed on the laboring masses but also because they revealed their pernicious character by being "pressed into the service of every form of tyranny. . . . [P]ractical application is given to it [their "faith"] in the assertion that slavery is the natural condition of the laborer, and it is otherwise still more closely applied in the declaration that our northern freemen are merely in a state of wages-slavery, at some disadvantage, as compared with the chattel laborers of the south."[27]

Classical economics, above all its earlier and gloomiest prognostications regarding the wage levels and general condition of laboring populations, exerted influence that was both great and largely "negative" in antebellum America—influence that was commonly registered through the resistance and revulsion it generated within the extensive public domain of ideas. Merely by serving as a powerful weapon in the hands of both supporters and gainsayers of the mythology of American economic exceptionalism, the harsh Malthus-Ricardo scenario affected that mythology and with it the debates over antebellum labor's extrinsic inducements and rewards.

Yet beyond the popular interpretation of economic principles, these debates always encompassed a host of "extraeconomic" considerations that were themselves continuously shaping new formulations of the mythology of American exceptionalism. One consummate, late-antebellum example of such an ideological construction was an address by Henry Ward Beecher, which the famous minister delivered in October 1858 to help raise funds for a free library for New York City's seamstresses and other impoverished workingwomen.[28] Like others before him, Beecher

[27] Review of *Principles of Social Science*, by H. C. Carey, *North American and United States Gazette* (Philadelphia), March 27, 1858.

[28] There are at least two slightly different versions of Beecher's address. One, a paraphrase by the *New-York Tribune*, is in "A Free Library for Women," in the October 27, 1858,

recognized that the conditions that these wage-earning women had long experienced—the segmented and crowded labor markets, the fierceness of competition, the "hard conditions and oppressive tyrannies of overseers and employers," the subsistence wages and fifteen-hour work-days—were in considerable measure social constructions; they were at least in part the products of cultural norms and expectations that restricted women's acquisition of marketable skills.[29] Poor, uneducated females, above all single females who do not marry, should be given some chance to rise out of their "menial" employments and "the disadvantages of their earlier years." Otherwise, Beecher declared, northern free labor society must remain uneven and deficient in the encouragement it gave its praiseworthy principle—a principle altogether absent from the slave South—by which individuals were "taught to take care of themselves."[30]

Scholars have long recognized Beecher's special talent for assimilating, mixing, and packaging popular themes and images in an increasingly competitive antebellum marketplace of ideas. Consistent with this talent, Beecher's 1858 address is a hodgepodge of negotiations among themes reflective of widespread social and political tensions. Beecher concedes the economically destructive effects of metropolitan industrialization and other baleful "Europeanizing" tendencies for the city's workingwomen. Yet he insists that the beauty of the northern social order, and its superiority over the slave South, resides in its exaltation of manly economic self-help and independence. He defers to conventions stigmatizing single status for adult women as an undesirable, even unnatural condition. But he maintains that northern women who do remain single and are forced by economic pressures out of their proper "sphere" are entitled (within reason) to increased access to masculine avenues of striving and competition and to the greater extrinsic rewards which that access would bring. In lending his support to limited efforts to redress the seamstresses' lack of "starting gate" equality, Beecher is, in effect, negotiating on "the boundaries"—he would preserve the core of dominant free labor capitalist ideology and render it less vulnerable to attack by altering within some of its areas definitions of the just and the possible.[31] Or put another way,

---

issue. The other version is in *The Pulpit and Rostrum* (New York, 1859), 21–31. This pamphlet also contains the address given on the same occasion by the New York Democratic Party leader James T. Brady.

[29] Beecher, in *Pulpit*, 26. The structural characteristics of the wholesale clothing trade, particularly its system of subcontracting, did its part to depress seamstress wages. Beecher blunted his general criticisms of the "oppressive tyrannies of overseers and employers" with praise for "some of the largest employers" who were beginning to rise above short-term profit considerations "to make their establishments in some sort an artificial family" (*Pulpit*, 30.)

[30] Ibid., 30; Beecher, "Free Library."

[31] Marc W. Steinberg, "The Dialogue of Struggle: The Contest over Ideological Boundaries in the Case of London Silk Weavers in the Early Nineteenth Century," *Social Science History* 18 (Winter 1994): 505–41. Whereas Steinberg's focus is on the contesting done by an

Beecher is simultaneously embracing and retreating from a completely uncritical American exceptionalist mythology.

By the same token, Beecher's address is one illustration of the morass of intellectual currents and social attitudes that informed commentary on labor's extrinsic rewards in the antebellum North—commentary on both the existing level of wages and on the reform measures needed to elevate labor's extrinsic rewards to a level consistent with "economic justice." Beecher's address reflected the long-standing, fundamental debates over labor incentives, to which he referred when he spoke of the "stimulants and aids" that induced inhabitants of the free states to "govern themselves."[32] But the address was also a response to immediate issues and pressures in the late-antebellum period, and as such it illustrated how the period's representations of wages could reflect a complex amalgam of considerations. These included, but were hardly limited to, responses to escalating sectional conflict over slave labor, reactions to northern industrialization and technological change, and attitudes toward the gendering of work. Such extraeconomic considerations were pervasive in the culture, and they would ensure that not merely working-class ideological constructions but many middle-class ones as well would either contest or at least go beyond one of our principal stereotypes for this period: that of a one-dimensional political economic and entrepreneurial dogma that represented wages as the outcome of insuperable and impartial supply-and-demand market forces.

The early to mid–nineteenth century, in the United States as in England, is conventionally understood as the period in which the middle classes, and entrepreneurs and other capitalists most of all, began routinely to cite supply-and-demand conditions within the labor market as the preeminent determinant of an individual wage earner's recompense. Endorsement of supply-and-demand market rules and an attendant hostility to labor unions came all the more easily, if anything, to many of the American commentators who rejected the specific axioms of the Malthusian-Ricardian harsh scenario. Invoking the mythology of American exceptionalism, they could embrace those rules on the grounds that, whatever the "temporary" gluts in specific local labor markets, supply and demand in the United States overall would work for an indefinite period in behalf of the labor-

---

assertive subordinate group, mine is on Beecher's own negotiations with the internal threats and contradictions to American exceptionalism and free labor ideology that resided in such stubborn facts as northern metropolitan industrialization and segmented labor markets. Beecher's address is a treasure-house of middle-class assumptions and attitudes regarding working-class education, prostitution, and such "labor-saving" technology as the sewing machine. And in thinking of the library plan in terms of its benefits for single women, Beecher also exhibited the common tendency to screen out the no less onerous waged outwork and unpaid housework performed by working-class wives.

[32] Beecher, "Free Library."

ing population that enjoyed formal freedom. Market achievement here, at least, need not exact the social costs of a brutalizing and dangerous class competition and conflict. Such a characterization of this period as one in which supply-and-demand market dogma enjoyed ascendance, if not hegemony, is of some use in broadly differentiating this period both from earlier ones, in which traditional hierarchies and customs within trades enjoyed greater prevalence and strength as regulators of labor's rewards, and from a later era in which a bargained wage won increased recognition and legitimacy throughout society.

Yet the liberal-capitalist, supply-and-demand characterization of the wage arguments of the antebellum era remains inadequate, and not merely for the more obvious reason that it hardly pretends to encompass the assorted oppositional arguments used by labor activists and radicals which regarded market capitalist–determined rewards as incompatible with economic justice for individual wage earners. The inadequacy of the supply-and-demand characterization extends even to entrepreneurial and other middle-class elements that did invoke it because embedded in a "law" that addressed aggregate conditions in the labor market at any one time were assumptions and value judgments regarding the moral character, personal habits, and economic behavior of the market's individual participants.[33] This much itself has long been obvious since at least the time the Reverend Malthus offered a formulation of the supply-and-demand dictum that turned principally on the laboring poor's propensity for sexual gratification. And in the United States as well as in England, the invocation of ostensibly "blind" supply-and-demand laws to legitimate market rewards and inequality of outcomes was closely bound up in an emergent entrepreneurial and professional "success" ethos. That ethos broke down "just price" and other traditional arguments and also provided a new principle of social stratification in its insistence that capitalist profits as well as wage differentials reflected legitimate differences in talent, enterprise, and virtue. One of Friedrich A. Hayek's arguments against distributive justice— that it is a meaningless concept inside a market economy because of the gamelike character of the market—would have found little obvious ap-

---

[33] For example, the material suffering of the seamstresses was characterized by many middle-class commentators (if not Beecher) as largely self-imposed, attributable to the "false pride" and "stubbornness" of working-class females who turned down positions in domestic service and voluntarily "chose" to remain in a more overcrowded and poorly recompensed employment. See the criticisms cited in Glickstein, *Concepts of Free Labor*, 426 n. 170. The proposed solution of the *Evening Post* (New York) demonstrated its own fidelity to supply-and-demand principles: "As long as the larger proportion of women are incompetent or unwilling to earn anything except by plain sewing, . . . it would be better for all of them, in the long run, to reduce wages to the famine point, so as to force all who had sufficient strength into other employments. This at least would diminish competition, and give the remaining ones a better chance." Quoted in Carey, *Principles of Social Science*, 1:240.

peal among the free market defenders of an earlier era (or, for that matter, of our own era), who assumed the existence of an intimate link between material rewards and personal "merit."[34]

But even more to the point, the very middle-class perception that the behavior and misbehavior of individual wage earners were merely among the "thousand causes" that affected supply-and-demand did not always act to increase complacency regarding the distribution of market rewards.[35] There was also a recurrent sensitivity to the fact that the "law" of supply-and-demand, in determining aggregate wage levels, would prove unjust to individual laborers. In his reworking of the tenets of classical economics, John Stuart Mill most explicitly grappled with one dimension of the so-called free rider problem, whereby responsible laborers who practice "moral restraint" fail to reap the full material fruits of their good behavior because of the irresponsible behavior of others who continue to multiply and drag down overall wage levels.[36] But tension arising from the inability of individual workers, for any number of reasons, to enjoy their "just" deserts under the operation of "supply and demand" is evident in more inchoate form in a multitude of the most mainstream middle-class texts, including Beecher's address.

There is, finally, the most fundamental curiosity of all regarding supply and demand and the closely related dogma of "free competition." And here we are touching on an old and big issue that has grown only bigger in recent years. On the one hand, there is the market revolution—above all, perhaps, the pervasive rhetoric of the market revolution—in both Western Europe and the United States: "buy cheap and sell dear," and accompanying this aphorism the chronic complaints of early- to mid-nineteenth-century radical and plebeian movements that labor, especially wage labor, was indeed being commodified and cheapened through supply-and-demand market processes. On the other hand, there is the continuously mounting evidence that truly free and open competition—the unfettered operation of supply and demand—was, if not a chimera, nonetheless obstructed in this period in any number of ways and usually, it seems, to the disadvantage of wage earners and other small producers, as some of their spokesmen in fact recognized. This evidence as to the myth of a truly self-regulating market comes from a variety of sources and angles. There is, for example, Louis Hartz's old finding that the antebellum activities of the Pennsylvania state government were unequivocally regulatory and that there was, moreover, not even a fully-blown, laissez-

[34] Hayek himself suggested the limited appeal of his argument in Friedrich A. Hayek, *Law, Legislation, and Liberty* (Chicago, 1976), 2:71–74.

[35] "The Labor Question," *New-York Tribune*, April 2, 1851.

[36] Samuel Hollander, *The Economics of John Stuart Mill* (London, 1985), 2:950–54.

faire philosophy in evidence opposing these activities. Karl Polanyi's evidence shows that the liberal proponents of England's Poor Law Amendment, in their devotion to the principle of a self-regulating market in labor and wages, created new almshouses and other state institutions, holding much centralized authority, that grossly violated laissez-faire practices—"free competition," in other words, did not inevitably lead to governmental laissez-faire, because many of the lower classes had to be forcibly "trained" to compete. There are the newer Foucauldian embellishments of Polanyi's position, which invoke Jeremy Bentham's notorious Panopticon as well as the New Poor Law, to illustrate how liberal middle-class "biopower" was directed in the early nineteenth century as never before to establishing moral intervention in and surveillance over the lives of the laboring poor. There are the recent labor law studies indicating that in the realm of antebellum labor relations adjudication, either liberal competitive individualist tenets remained "abstractions" or hierarchical and restrictive master and servant common laws, rooted in the feudal order, privileged American employers over wage laborers in the new industrial settings, skewering the already "asymmetrical" relationships of power and exchange that existed between them in the marketplace. And there are, lastly, the recent feminist studies showing that a "woman's wage," above all, together with its determinants, is much more subjective and political than how economists commonly perceive the operation of individual choice in labor market analysis—that the lower wages paid women have often, historically, been justified by reference to their supposed lesser needs, rather than to the market value of their labor.[37]

Some historians—most of all, perhaps, Marxist historians—have had a ready explanation for many of these deviations, both ideological and actual, from the shibboleth of an open and meritocratic free competition: employers simply failed to observe it in situations where strict observance did not suit their perceived best interests.[38] Such an explanation, needless to say, is not terribly satisfying for those who crave intellectual consistency in the larger body of the period's commentary on labor's extrinsic rewards. But possibly only limited amounts of such consistency are to be expected. Mill noted that within contemporary societies, generally speaking, "the really exhausting and the really repulsive labours, instead of being better paid than others, are almost invariably paid the worst of all, because per-

[37] Louis Hartz, *Economic Policy and Democratic Thought* (Chicago, 1948); Karl Polanyi, *The Great Transformation* (Boston, 1944); Mitchell Dean, *The Constitution of Poverty* (London, 1991); Christopher L. Tomlins, *Law, Labor, and Ideology in the New Republic* (Cambridge, 1993); Karen Orren, *Belated Feudalism* (Cambridge, 1991); William M. Reddy, *Money and Liberty in Modern Europe* (Cambridge, 1987); Alice Kessler-Harris, *A Woman's Wage* (Lexington, 1989).

[38] E. J. Hobsbawm, *Labouring Men* (London, 1964), 352.

formed by those who have no choice."[39] This was a material reality that was as much a part of antebellum America as it was of any other country of the time (particularly when chattel slavery is included within that reality), even as it may have been no more true for nineteenth-century market capitalist societies in general than it was for earlier and different kinds of societies. In shibboleths such as "supply-and-demand" and "free competition" for capitalists and wage earners, middle-class Americans preeminently found devices appropriate enough to their early industrial capitalist development for addressing the age-old social paradox, whereby individuals engaged in society's most basic and indispensable labor—"dirty" and other kinds of manual labor occupations—received the poorest material and status rewards. Employer abandonment of the slogans when self-interest dictated could serve as its own form of testimony to the mere existence of this paradoxical situation. It was left to utopian socialist and other alternative ideological constructions, and less decisively to a more mainstream and intermittent middle-class angst, actually to perceive the paradox as a moral dilemma.

[39] John Stuart Mill, *Principles of Political Economy* (1871; 7th ed., New York, 1965), 388.

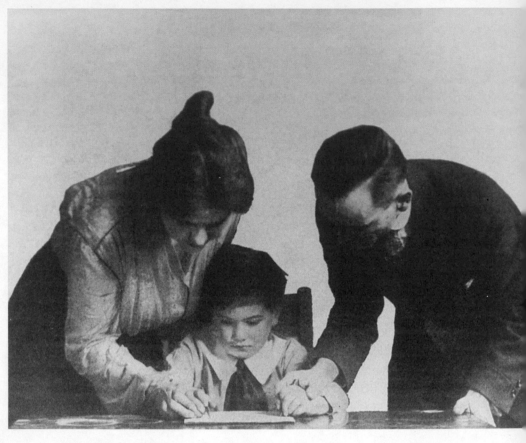

The plight of the left-handed in early-twentieth-century America: enforced right-handedness. From J. J. Terrell, "Let Left-Handedness Alone!" *Illustrated World* 27 (April 1917): 190.

Chapter Four

Deviance, Dominance, and the Construction of Handedness in Turn-of-the-Century Anglo-America

Tamara Plakins Thornton

Left-handed people have long had a rough time of it. Peasant superstition associated left-handedness with bad luck; long-standing tradition held that the devil was left-handed; and it was common school practice until well into the twentieth century to insist, by force if necessary, that all children write with their right hands. But it was only in the late nineteenth and early twentieth centuries that science, far from dispelling antique superstitions, was used to reinforce the notion that right-handers ruled the world by right and that left-handers were bad.

In updating the rationale for enforced right-handedness, turn-of-the-century scientists acted in typical fashion, assuming the cultural authority once granted to religion, fashioning biological arguments for the inferiority of some groups. To contemporaries, however, far more was at issue than the latest argument for hand binding and knuckle rapping. They invested the phenomenon of handedness with broad scientific and, ultimately, moral significance. For them, handedness was directly related to such categories as gender, race, and ethnicity and associated with a number of conditions—delinquency, criminality, "idiocy," "lunacy," epilepsy—that stigmatized individuals as somehow defective. They used the evolutionary victory of right-handed dominance to explain the dominance of whole peoples over others, while characterizing left-handedness as the marker of a host of genetic mistakes and a generalized mental and moral inferiority. Thus inferior and superior races would be distinguished by characteristic patterns of handedness, even as left-handers themselves would be constituted as a kind of composite race of genetic throwbacks and deviants.

How could a seemingly inconsequential behavior have been invested with such grand moral implications? One answer lies in its very insignificance. Preference for left over right in no way corresponds to the usual variables of prejudice—gender, race, ethnicity—but instead of rendering handedness void of moral import, that very irrelevance invested it with moral potential. Precisely because left-handedness and right-handedness exist independent of human categories of oppression and domination, they can function as abstract symbols of both deviance and mastery. Thinking about handedness, in other words, can act as a way to think about the nature and implications of human marginality, inferiority, and superiority.

Furthermore, that kind of thinking made particular sense in the turn-of-the-century period, because it was in these decades that scientific disciplines reconceptualized human beings into human organisms. Once moral philosophers had studied the mind and the will; their intellectual successors, the psychologists, studied the brain. For the latter, human superiority and inferiority were somatic not merely in expression but also in origin. It was logical, even logically necessary, then, that a seemingly isolated physiological trait such as handedness would be the sign and source of mental and moral qualities. That line of reasoning generated intellectually extravagant conclusions and morally insidious notions: a causal link between the dominance of the left hemisphere of the brain and the northern hemisphere of the globe, the eugenic elimination of left-handers, the creation of a master race of ambidexters. More important, it reminds us that moral issues have been conceptualized in what are now strange and unfamiliar ways, ways that for all their quaintness once held considerable moral power. We still live with the same moral problems—the dilemmas and conflicts posed by human difference—even as the terms in which these problems were once cast have lost their hold over the moral imagination.

Until well into the nineteenth century, there is almost nothing in the written record about left-handedness. In 1648, the English physician Thomas Browne published a treatise in which he argued that the perception of left-handers as somehow dangerous was a "vulgar error." In the next century, Benjamin Franklin pleaded the sinistral's case in his witty "Petition of the Left Hand."[1] But that was about it. Even penmanship man-

[1] Thomas Browne, *Pseudoxia Epidemica, or Enquiries into Very Many Received Tenets and Commonly Presum'd Truths, Which Examined Prove but Vulgar Errors* (London, 1648), quoted in Michael Barsley, *The Left-Handed Book: An Investigation into the Sinister History of Left-Handedness* (London, 1966), 193–97; Benjamin Franklin, "A Petition of the Left Hand to Those Who Have the Superintendency of Education," in *The Works of Benjamin Franklin*, comp. John Bigelow, 12 vols. (New York, 1904), 7:369–70.

uals, where we would expect mention of left-handedness if only to pro-hibit it, are silent on the subject.[2] Then from about 1860 and accelerating into the next century, there transpired a marked quickening of interest in the phenomenon, primarily among physicians and, to a lesser extent, among psychologists and experts in anatomy and physiology. When these scientists first took up the topic, however, it was less to investigate the pref-erence for left over right than the phenomenon of preference itself—handedness, in other words, not left-handedness.

Very little was known about handedness at the time of these early inves-tigations, and well into the twentieth century, very little remained firmly established.[3] Is handedness inherited, or is it an acquired characteristic? In the 1860s and 1870s, experts presented arguments for both sides. By the turn of the century, most medical and scientific authorities had come to the conclusion that handedness was a hereditary trait, but well into the twentieth century, most teachers and parents—and an occasional scien-tist—viewed manual preference as a matter of habit or custom.[4] Whatever the origin of handedness, it was difficult to explain exactly what it was and where in the body it existed separate from its behavioral manifestation. Some scientists claimed that it was a simple matter of anatomy. Dextrals have longer right forearms; sinistrals have longer left forearms.[5] Another school of thought pushed the question one step back; which hand domi-nates, they argued, is really a function of which eye dominates.[6] Increas-ingly, especially after experiments with those having aphasia led to an un-derstanding of the brain as a two-sided organ, handedness was located in the brain. But just how it was located there remained unclear; some scien-tists hypothesized that one side of the brain might receive a greater blood

[2] The very first reference to left-handedness that I have found in the dozens of British and American penmanship manuals I have examined is in Gideon Bixler, *Physical Training in Pen-manship* (Wooster, Ohio, 1892), 43.

[3] Useful overviews of the various theories of handedness can be found in Laura G. Smith, "A Brief Survey of Right- and Left-Handedness," *Pedagogical Seminary and Journal of Genetic Psychology* 24 (1917): 19–35, and Beaufort Sims Parson, *Lefthandedness: A New Interpretation* (New York, 1924), 1–19.

[4] Thomas Dwight, "Right and Left Handedness," *Journal of Psychological Medicine* 4 (1870): 535–42; William Ogle, "On Dextral Pre-eminence," *Lancet*, July 8, 1871, 49; H. E. Jordan, "The Inheritance of Left-Handedness," *American Breeders Magazine* 2 (1911): 19–29, 113–24; Andrew Buchanan, "Mechanical Theory of the Predominance of the Right Hand over the Left," *Proceedings of the Philosophical Society of Glasgow* 5 (1862): 142; Walter G. McMullin, "What Shall We Do with Our Left-Handed Pupils?" *Teacher* 18 (December 1914): 331–38; John B. Watson, "What the Nursery Has to Say about Instincts," *Pedagogical Seminary and Jour-nal of Genetic Psychology* 32 (1925): 319–22.

[5] W. Franklin Jones, "The Problem of Handedness in Education," in National Education Association, *Journal of Proceedings and Addresses of the Fifty-Third Annual Meeting . . . 1915* (Ann Arbor, Mich., 1915), 959–63; Jones, "What Shall Be Done with the Left-Handed Child?" *Chi-cago Sunday Herald Magazine*, February 18, 1917, 4.

[6] George M. Gould, *Righthandedness and Lefthandedness* (Philadelphia, 1908).

supply, whereas others argued that another structural factor distinguishes the two hemispheres.[7]

Even if one could determine the origin and nature of handedness, it was still difficult to explain why it was the right side, in particular, that had established itself as the dominant one. Almost all authorities agreed that at least as far back as the written record exists, human beings had always been predominantly dextral. They cited biblical and classical references as evidence. It was also a matter of general—though not, as we shall see, unanimous—agreement that all peoples are almost exclusively right-handed. Even "the barbarians who tattoo their faces, compress their skulls, distort their feet, and otherwise mutilate and disfigure the human frame," wrote the Scottish doctor Andrew Buchanan, "are, nevertheless, just as unanimous as civilized nations in the preference of the right hand over the left." Thomas Dwight, another physician and expert in the phenomenon, concurred. "Throughout literature, with scarcely an exception, the right is the fortunate and favored side," he wrote in 1891. "It is thus not only in the most ancient languages, but in the dialects of the American Indians, of Pacific Islanders, and even of such degraded races as the aborigines of Australia."[8]

Many explanations for the universality of right-hand predominance emerged. Some were anatomical, such as the argument that the greater weight of the organs on the right side of the body gave that side a mechanical advantage. Scientists who associated handedness with the brain searched for anatomical differences between the two sides of that organ, hoping to find that the right side is heavier, bigger, better supplied with blood, or more structurally complicated. Other authorities looked for clues in the early development of the human species. Perhaps the westward movement of the sun across the sky, in conjunction with primitive sun worship, held the key. Perhaps primitive man quickly came to recognize that he should wield his weapons with his right hand, the better to protect his most vital organ, his heart, with a shield. To many this second narrative was particularly preposterous. How could "ignorant and brutal savages" possibly act in so rational a manner? asked Thomas Dwight. And how can we account for the fact that not all left-handers were killed off? "Were they wicked and perverse people who refused to listen to the good prehistoric surgeon-general, when he told them to carry the shield on the left, and who, through some lapse of justice, escaped their deserts?"[9]

[7] Daniel Wilson, *The Right Hand: Left-Handedness* (London, 1891): D. J. Cunningham, "Right-Handedness and Left-Brainedness," *Journal of the Anthropological Institute of Great Britain and Ireland* 32 (1902): 288–94; Jordan, "Inheritance of Left-Handedness," 20–23.

[8] Buchanan, "Mechanical Theory," 142; Thomas Dwight, "What Is Right-Handedness?" *Scribner's* 9 (April 1891): 474.

[9] Dwight, "What Is Right-Handedness?" 475.

Despite critiques like these, the shield and weapon theory persisted for decades, surviving until well into the twentieth century.[10]

Just when right-handedness had caught on for good was also a matter of some disagreement. Consistent with their perception of non-Westerners as backward and inferior, some commentators insisted that it still had not taken universal hold. In 1886, a correspondent to the *Medical Record* reported that among the inhabitants of the Punjab "nearly seventy percent, use the left hand by preference" and "the Hottentots and Bushmen of South Africa are also said to be, for the greater part, left-handed." Others went in the opposite direction and cited evidence that even apes and monkeys are predominantly right-handed. By the end of the nineteenth century, however, the prevailing wisdom seemed to be that handedness emerged as the human species did and certainly went back no further. In his Huxley Lecture of 1902 delivered before the Anthropological Institute of Great Britain and Ireland, D. J. Cunningham summarized his observations on this topic. "For many years I have had an intimate experience of both the higher and the lower apes in the Gardens of the Royal Zoological Society of Ireland," he reported, "and I have never been able to satisfy myself that they show any decided preference for the use of one arm more than the other."[11]

Cunningham supported his argument by citing the work of Sir Daniel Wilson, Gabriel de Mortillet, and Daniel G. Brinton, all of whom had conducted investigations in the 1880s and 1890s into prehistoric art and artifacts and concluded that right-handedness was by no means as firmly fixed among our earliest ancestors as it was in their day. Wilson studied paleolithic cave paintings, assumed a correlation between the manual dominance of the artist and the side of the animal depicted in profile, and reasoned that a substantial proportion of those artists must have been left-handed. Mortillet drew a similar inference from a study of neolithic tools; indeed, he believed that *most* of his early toolmakers preferred left over right. In his study of stone implements, Brinton found that two-thirds were made for right-hand use, suggesting that, then as now, most people were right-handed. But it was the remaining third that captured Brinton's interest. They indicated to him "either that there were more left-handed persons" among prehistoric than modern humans, "or, as I prefer to believe, that there were more who were ambidextrous."[12]

---

[10] P. H. Pye-Smith, "On Left-Handedness," *Guy's Hospital Reports,* 3d ser., 16 (1871): 141; George M. Kellogg, "The Physiology of Right- and Left-Handedness," *Journal of the American Medical Association* 30 (1898): 356; Gould, *Righthandedness and Lefthandedness,* 45–60; Parson, *Lefthandedness,* 11–12, 64–65, 69.

[11] "Left-Handedness," *Medical Record,* November 20, 1886, 579; Cunningham, "Right-Handedness and Left-Brainedness," 285.

[12] Wilson, *Right Hand: Left-Handedness;* Gabriel de Mortillet, "Formation des Variétés,"

These narratives of prehistory were taken seriously because scientists in this age of Darwin could not understand handedness apart from an evolutionary framework. If almost every human being favored right over left, they insisted, it must be because that trait gave our progenitors an edge in the struggle for survival. What left-handers remained would be understood as hereditary degenerates, genetic sports, or evolutionary throwbacks. It required no great imagination, then, to correlate left-handedness with other forms of "defect." Among the first such suggestions came in 1880, when William Ireland conducted research among feeble-minded children. Ireland recorded with what one suspects is almost disappointment that left-handedness was as statistically frequent among normal children as among the mentally defective ones. He managed to salvage something from his research, however, when he added that "the imbeciles were much more decided in their left-handedness." Over the next several decades, physicians and psychologists continued to investigate the statistical links between left-handedness and various forms of defect. In 1912, P. B. Ballard followed Ireland's lead in comparing children in "special" schools with those in regular elementary schools, but unlike Ireland, he was successful in finding significantly higher rates of sinistrality among the feeble-minded. Hugh Gordon achieved similar results and expanded on them in a series of twin studies. He noted that in cases where one twin favored the right hand and the other the left, it was almost always the left-hander who exhibited some kind of abnormality—being mentally slow, physically stunted, "backward," "nervous"—while his or her sibling did not.[13] Subsequent researchers linked left-handedness with not only feeble-mindedness but also blindness, epilepsy, delinquency, immorality, criminal behavior, and what was loosely termed "the psychopathic constitution."[14]

Probably the most damning of these studies was conducted by Cesare Lombroso, the Italian criminologist. In 1903, Lombroso published his "Left-Handedness and Left-Sidedness" in the *North American Review,* asserting that a disproportionate number of criminals and lunatics favor left over right. For Lombroso, these "statistics" fit into a broader picture

Bulletin de la Société d'Anthropologie, pt. 3 (1890); Daniel G. Brinton, "Left-Handedness in North American Aboriginal Art," *American Anthropologist* 9 (May 1896): 179.

[13] William W. Ireland, *The Blot upon the Brain: Studies in History and Psychology* (New York, 1886), 290; P. B. Ballard, "Sinistrality and Speech," *Journal of Experimental Pedagogy* 1 (1912): 298–310; Hugh Gordon, "Left-Handedness and Mirror Writing, Especially among Defective Children," *Brain* 43 (January 1921): 313–66.

[14] Jordan, "Inheritance of Left-Handedness," 23–24; Smith, "Survey of Right- and Left-Handedness," 31–33; E. A. Doll, *Anthropometry as an Aid to Mental Diagnosis,* Research Publication no. 8, Training School, Vineland, N.J. (Baltimore, 1916), 58; Clarence Quinan, "A Study of Sinistrality and Muscle Coordination in Musicians, Iron Workers, and Others," *Archives of Neurology and Psychiatry* 7 (March 1922): 352–60.

of inferiority. Thus, he wrote, "persons who are more agile with the left hand . . . are ordinarily found among women, children, and savages, and they were more numerous in ages past than they are now." He was therefore able to explain why "the woman buttons her clothes from right to left, while the man does so from left to right" and why, "in early times, and still among people little civilized, such as Arabs, the writing was preferably from right to left, which is the habit of children until corrected."[15]

Scientists who correlated left-handedness with deviant behaviors and inferior abilities regarded left-handedness as a genetic defect, a form of hereditary degeneracy or atavism. Either way, they implied a genetic solution to left-handedness, the slow but certain purging of the defect from the population through controlled reproduction—in other words, eugenics. In 1911, Harvey E. Jordan's research on left-handedness appeared in the *American Breeders Magazine;* his other publications included "The Biological Status and Social Worth of the Mulatto," *Eugenics: The Rearing of the Human Thorough-bred,* and *War's Aftermath: A Preliminary Study of the Eugenics of War.*[16] The following year, Francis Ramaley characterized left-handedness as a "Mendelian recessive," not too ominous until one considers that he added the grim corollary that these "recessive mutants"—left-handers—"must tend to increase in number at the expense of the originally dominant right types."[17] A generation later, Alfred Gordon described sinistrality as an "abnormal condition" and a "physiological deviation," this in an article titled "Family Stock Betterment, with Response to Left-Handedness" that appeared in *Eugenical News.*[18]

It was the popular press, however, that most explicitly laid out the case for a eugenic remedy when in 1913 *McClure's,* in its finest muckraking tradition, published Edwin Tenney Brewster's exposé "The Ways of the Left Hand." Following the latest in scientific studies, the article noted "a disproportionate number of left-handed adults among criminals, insane persons, imbeciles, epileptics, vagrants, and social failures of various sorts." Echoing and extending Lombroso's equation of the deviant with the primitive, Brewster argued "that sinisterity is slightly more common, in the lower strata of society than in the higher, among negroes than among white persons, and among savages than among civilized persons." Again

[15] Cesare Lombroso, "Left-Handedness and Left-Sidedness," *North American Review* 177 (September 1903): 440, 442.

[16] Jordan, "Inheritance of Left-Handedness," 19–29, 113–19; H. E. Jordan, "The Biological Status and Social Worth of the Mulatto," *Popular Science Monthly,* June 1913, 573–82; *Eugenics: The Rearing of the Human Thorough-bred* (n.p., 1912); and *War's Aftermath: A Preliminary Study of the Eugenics of War* (Boston, 1914).

[17] Francis Ramaley, "Mendelian Proportions and the Increase of Recessives," *American Naturalist* 46 (1912): 334–51.

[18] Alfred Gordon, "Family Stock Betterment, with Response to Left-Handedness," *Eugenical News* 17 (May–June 1932): 87–88.

like Lombroso, Brewster admitted that a greater proportion of women than men are left-handed, but here he found it convenient to suspend his line of reasoning. "This fact," he simply declared, "has probably no significance." Females aside then, "all these unfortunate beings have something the matter with them"—the "brain is jerry-built"—"and that something is, in most cases, congenital and beyond all hope of avoidance or reform." Precisely what that "something" was Brewster soon made clear.

> The curious thing about the inheritance of left-handedness—which, as we have seen, depends on a peculiarity of the brain—is that it resembles closely the inheritance of two other peculiarities which are also dependent on brain structure—namely, mental ability and moral excellence. A sound and capable stock, like a right-handed one, breeds true generation after generation. Then something slips a cog, and there appears a left-handed child, a black sheep, or an imbecile. An imbecile or scapegrace parent married to a normal spouse may have half his children like himself. Two weak-minded, criminal, or degenerate parents always have all their children bad.

The eugenic implications were clear. If "the one overwhelming and significant difference among men is in the native quality of their brains" and "the one difference in human brains that is most easily made out and most conveniently studied, as it is transmitted from one generation to another, modified by training or affected by breeding," is handedness, then the eugenic solution presented itself irresistibly. Ensuring a "sound and capable stock" meant ensuring a right-handed one, in other words, breeding out the lefties.[19]

Brewster represented sinistrality not merely as a type of defect but also as a genetic marker for all others. Left-handedness was not just an isolated trait. Instead, it signified a total condition that defined a particular category of human being. Here one is reminded of Michel Foucault's description of the invention of the homosexual. Where once homosexuality had been understood as a wicked act, he argues, by the end of the nineteenth century and under the aegis of the new science of sexology, it had come to refer to a certain kind of person, whose entire being was suffused with and shaped by his sexuality. Inherent in this process of invention is the assertion of power not merely in the sense that, once identified, homosexuals could then be oppressed but also in the sense that the very process of creating the category of homosexual constituted a form of control.[20] Is this what happened with the left-handed? Certainly there is the same initial,

[19] Edwin Tenney Brewster, "The Ways of the Left Hand," *McClure's*, June 1913, 179, 180, 183.
[20] Michel Foucault, *The History of Sexuality*, trans. Robert Hurley (New York, 1978), vol. 1, *An Introduction*.

religious disapproval; then as the nineteenth century wanes, a sudden scientific recognition of the phenomenon; its definition in terms of degeneracy and atavism; and, finally, the scientific creation of a human type—the homosexual, the left-hander—whose "defect" is his or her essence and entirety. Is control part and parcel of this process? Certainly eugenics is the ultimate restraint. Even where lenience was prescribed, however, there remained an element of discipline. Let us take a brief look at the stance of a second group of scientists, the educational psychologists.

Unlike the physicians and physiologists whose ideas we have been examining so far, educational psychologists did not accept the construction of left-handedness as bad germ plasm. They regarded it as the expression of a relatively rare but nonetheless normal Mendelian trait, not unlike red hair or color blindness. Because sinistrality was perfectly normal, they argued, there was no justification for forcing left-handed children to write with their right hands. Because it was innate, such efforts would prove futile. Indeed, these attempts were liable to create neurological confusion and damage, manifested most conspicuously in stuttering.[21] On the surface, this was a far cry from both the biological eugenics hinted at by scientists and the pedagogical eugenics practiced in the classroom, but in fact educational psychologists turned left-handed children into subjects of observation quite as much as the white-coated researchers and knuckle-rapping teachers. They theorized that there is a continuum of handedness, encompassing hard-core lefties whose preference could not be altered as well as a much larger group less firmly committed in their sinistral tendencies who could indeed be trained in right-handedness. What was required, then, was a lengthy process of testing and diagnosis, consultation and record keeping, followed by individualized pedagogical guidance.[22] Here too was a regimen, if not one to eliminate or convert the left-hander, then at least to mark him or her as an individual in need of institutional attention and oversight.

Nevertheless, we should hesitate to apply Foucault's model too completely. As Ian Hacking has reminded us, there is "no reason to suppose that

[21] Jones, "The Problem of Handedness"; Lewis M. Terman, *The Hygiene of the School Child* (Boston, 1914), 345–46; J. J. Terrell, "Let Left-Handedness Alone!" *Illustrated World* 27 (April 1917): 190–92; Frank N. Freeman, "Present-Day Issues in the Teaching of Handwriting," *Elementary School Journal* 24 (September 1923): 40–41; Guy Montrose Whipple, "The Left-Handed Child," *Journal of Educational Psychology* 2 (1911): 574–75; M. M. Nice, "The Speech of a Left-Handed Child," *Psychological Clinic* 9 (1915): 115–17; M. G. Blanton and S. Blanton, "What Is the Problem of Stuttering?" *Journal of Abnormal Psychology* 13 (1919): 303–13; Ballard, "Sinistrality and Speech," 298–310.

[22] Freeman, "Teaching of Handwriting," 41; J. Merle Rife, "Types of Dextrality," *Psychological Review* 29 (November 1922): 474–80; June E. Downey, "Types of Dextrality and Their Implications," *American Journal of Psychology* 38 (July 1927): 317–67; Norma V. Scheidemann, "A Study of the Handedness of Some Left-Handed Writers," *Journal of Genetic Psychology* 37 (December 1930): 510–16.

we shall ever tell two identical stories of two different instances of making people up," and indeed there are critical differences between the making of the homosexual and the making of the left-hander.[23] The existence of left-handers had been recognized all along and in a totalizing fashion—they were deemed to be wicked people. Part of what changed was the framework in which that recognition proceeded. Once left-handedness had been the sign of the devil, a curse; now, in an age in which science had replaced religion as the dominant source of cultural authority, it was a genetic defect or rarity. But it was not only the way people thought about sinistrality that changed; it was also *why* they thought about it. Independent as it was from such variables as race and gender, left-handedness existed as an almost platonic type in nature, an ideal of deviance, that shed light on the nature and implications of human difference, marginality, and perversity of all sorts. If it had not been seized on before to fulfill this function, it was because the cultural climate did not allow for physiological deviance to be given such deep significance. By the end of the nineteenth century, however, the body was coming to replace the mind and the will as the prime mover of human behavior. Darwinism had something to do with that intellectual shift, of course, but so too did the requirements of the modern, industrial order. One need only think of the manual training movement, touted far more as a means of mental and moral than physical development, to recognize with what symbolic meaning—and disciplinary potential—the body, and even in particular the hand, could be invested.[24] In this context, exploring the nature and implications of left-handedness became a way to explore the nature and implications of any sort of "abnormality" or "inferiority"—physical, mental, social, cultural, and racial. Sinistrality, in other words, functioned as an intellectual proxy for deviance.

Furthermore, the cultural conversation surrounding sinistrality was especially compelling because it necessarily involved discussion of the broader phenomenon of manual preference. Not just left-handedness but also handedness, in other words, not just deviance but also dominance, were open for exploration. If the study of left-handedness offered a way to conceptualize social and cultural marginality, the study of handedness offered a way to think about the power exercised over the marginal. That

[23] Ian Hacking, "Making Up People," in Thomas C. Heller, Morton Sosna, and David E. Wellbery, eds., *Reconstructing Individualism: Autonomy, Individuality, and the Self in Western Thought* (Stanford, 1986), 236.

[24] On the reconfiguration of the relationship between body and mind, see Anson Rabinbach, *The Human Motor: Energy, Fatigue, and the Origins of Modernity* (New York, 1990); John M. O'Donnell, *The Origins of Behaviorism: American Psychology, 1870–1920* (New York, 1985); and John C. Burnham, "The Mind-Body Problem in the Early Twentieth Century," in *Paths into American Culture: Psychology, Medicine, and Morals* (Philadelphia, 1988), 26–37, 239–41.

issue was of particular interest to Anglo-Americans in the late nineteenth and early twentieth centuries. Both Great Britain and the United States were engaged in establishing empires and regarded dominion over other peoples as proof of a kind of national evolutionary fitness. For Americans, relations with inferior peoples was also very much a domestic issue; the majority of the foreigners emigrating to the United States in unprecedented numbers came from parts of the world, most notably southern and eastern Europe, regarded by the native-born as primitive and degenerate. Handedness provided a perfect opportunity to think about civilization and savagery.

In examining the phenomenon of manual preference, scientific experts explicitly linked the acquisition of a dominant hand with a move up the evolutionary ladder. "There is no doubt that this inclination to use one side more than the other is far greater in man than in the lower animals," wrote Thomas Dwight in 1870. "It may at first sight seem strange that asymmetry of function should be most marked in man, the highest of animals; but it may be shown that this is one of the elements of his superiority." The skilled use of tools, scientists further reasoned, could come only with the functional differentiation and specialization of hands. Our ancestors were ambidextrous, but as they grew more clever, they figured out a better way. "Ceasing to be a mere animalian machine without preference for right or lefthand usage," Beaufort Sims Parson wrote, early man "in his first attempts to fabricate his weapons and tools would of necessity rapidly develop unequal manual function." Now fully handed—again, whether right- or left-handed was irrelevant—he would be able to make more effective weapons, allowing him to win "his battles with the hairy rhinocerous along the banks of the Thames and the Somme." It "is by the superior skill of his right hand," concluded James Crichton-Browne triumphantly, "that man has won his tremendous victory for supremacy in the struggle for existence."[25]

Narrowly construed, what these grand evolutionary narratives were constructing was the basis for human ascendancy of the animal world. But it is impossible to ignore their broader commentary on human affairs, their imperialistic vision of the superiority of some people and their consequent dominion over others. That vision was implicit in the linking of the superiority of handedness with the values and attributes of modern Western civilization. One factor that made the preference for one hand over another a superior trait was that it allowed for specialization, in particular, the specialization of labor. Given Herbert Spencer's interpretation of evo-

[25] Dwight, "Handedness," 540; Parson, *Lefthandedness,* 58–59; James Crichton-Browne, quoted in "A Protest against the Ambidexterity Craze," *Current Literature* 44 (June 1908): 671.

lution as a process of differentiation, that understanding of the evolutionary advantage of handedness made sense. Paraphrasing the Spencerian
principle, one authority explained that the development of handedness
"illustrates the great biologic law that all progress consists in differentiation of function."[26] But the emphasis on specialization was also rooted in
a celebration of the advanced, industrial, bureaucratic economy and society of this era. After all, the same criterion that established handedness as
the more advanced state also stigmatized preindustrial people as primitive
and held up Western nations as advanced.

Another factor that seemed to point to the superiority of handedness
was the theory that the active speech center is located in just one half of
the brain and that it controls and determines manual preference. Some
scientists argued that each individual has only one such center, whereas
others countered that, although speech centers are located in both hemispheres, only one is actually used. Either way, the active mobilization of a
single center—left- or right-handedness, in other words, but not ambidexterity—was regarded as most desirable, again as an aspect of specialization. But a good deal more was at stake than just developing the power
of speech. Consistent with the larger cultural tendency to view the body as
prime mover of human behavior, most scientists located mental activity of
all sorts, not just speaking but thinking and writing as well, within this particular bit of gray matter. The development of humans as intelligent, articulate, and literate creatures, they argued, was therefore contingent on
the dominance of one lobe and the continual exercising of that dominance through preferential use of a single hand. What lay behind this correlation of handedness with evolutionary superiority was the notion that
what made a society civilized was not just its level of specialization but also
the degree to which it epitomized intellectual activity and written culture.
Not surprisingly, that standard could not be met by what one expert on
handedness described as "the grunting savage or peasant," the product of
a "simple," oral society.[27]

A prime example of the ways in which the hierarchy of values that privileged modern Western civilization shaped science is offered by the "dominant hemisphere" theory of handedness. According to this hypothesis, the
left hemisphere of a right-hander's brain is the dominant one and controls handedness; the opposite is true for a left-hander. Although we accept this explanation now, in earlier decades there was little empirical evidence for it, because laboratory scientists were hard pressed to detect
actual differences in the two halves of the brain. "The quest for the struc-

[26] Gould, *Righthandedness and Lefthandedness*, 32. See also Parson, *Lefthandedness*, 60–61.
[27] Gould, *Righthandedness and Lefthandedness*, 28.

tural conditions upon which the functional superiority of the left cerebral hemisphere depends," D. J. Cunningham conceded in 1902, "is surrounded with great difficulty." It has been hypothesized that the two halves
of the brain are unequally supplied with blood, he continued, that one
side is heavier and bulkier, and, most promising, that the dominant hemisphere is richer and more complex in its convolutions—in other words,
more specialized. None of these speculations could be demonstrated in
the laboratory, however. Still Cunningham saw no reason to abandon the
theory. "That I should have so far been baffled in the attempt to discover
some structural character to account for the functional superiority of the
left cerebrum," he concluded, "does not lessen my belief that such exists."[28]
Cunningham's conviction seems to have rested more on the cultural apt-
ness of the guiding metaphor than on the empirical evidence. For if handedness was a matter of specialization, and specialization was what made
Western civilization superior to savagery, then certainly handedness would
prove to be a matter of one "hemisphere" dominating the other by virtue
of its greater "complexity." It had to be that the brain, like the globe, could
be analyzed into its superior and inferior halves and that these, like human societies, would prove to be complex and simple, respectively.

Of course, if it really were handedness, and not right-handedness, that
spelled evolutionary superiority, then ambidexterity, not left-handedness,
would be the primary sign of atavism associated with inferior genetic stock.
That is precisely the line of reasoning followed by many scientists when
they interpreted the usual lineup of defectives. Thus Daniel Brinton would
"prefer" to interpret his prehistoric subjects as ambidextrous, rather than
left-handed. Now the primitive Murray Islanders would be seen as un-
commonly inclined to prefer neither hand, rather than the left one. The
same would be said of that other brand of primitive, the mentally defective. When Cunningham reported that ambidexterity—but not sinistrality—is found more often among individuals who are microcephalic than
among normal individuals, he explained that microcephalics "present in
the brain and the cranium certain remarkable atavistic characters, which
would seem to have been distinctive of an early stem-form of man." Similar conclusions were reached in America by Fred W. Smedley in his work
among the feeble-minded pupils of Chicago. And now the way was open
for "deviants" of every sort to join the ambidextral ranks. Savages, criminals, epileptics, delinquents, and blacks—all were observed as exhibiting
higher than statistically normal rates of ambidexterity.[29]

[28] Cunningham, "Right-Handedness and Left-Brainedness," 288–93.
[29] Ibid., 279 n, 286–87; Fred W. Smedley, "Child Study Report," no. 3, in *Report of the
United States Commissioner of Education* (Washington, D.C., 1902), 11–40; Jordan, "Inheritance

Oddly enough, the scientific discussion of handedness yielded another, precisely opposite interpretation of ambidexterity. If to some ambidexterity represented an atavistic state, others would see it as the liberation of the full complement of humankind's natural powers. In 1904, several dozen of these contrary-minded Britons established an organization for the promotion of "two-handed training" in the schools and the general goal of an ambidextrous population. The members of the so-called Ambidextral Culture Society were not marginal members of British society. Their names were followed by liberal sprinklings of initials and abbreviations indicating the acquisition of scholarly degrees, the honor of knighthood, and fellowship in handfuls of learned societies. Their president, E. Noble Smith, was a prominent Scottish surgeon and the author of respected treatises on gynecology and spinal deformities. Their vice presidents included Sir James Sawyer, a physician and professor of medicine in Birmingham; William H. Cummings, a musicologist; and Major General R. S. S. Baden-Powell, hero of the Boer War.[30]

The founder and guiding inspiration of the society was John Jackson, whose 1905 treatise, *Ambidexterity: or Two-Handedness and Two-Braineddness*, served as the bible of this unusual reform movement. Jackson contended that most human beings, like other animals, would use both hands if allowed to follow their instincts. He estimated that 3 percent of humans are strongly left-handed and 17 percent strongly right-handed by nature, but that a full 80 percent are "naturally either-handed" and with proper instruction would become perfectly ambidextrous. In the main, he continued, one-handedness is an artifact of civilization, and an unfortunate one at that. The right hand is made the dominant one only by means of "nothing less than a deliberate, regularly recognized, and systematic, cold-blooded crippling of the left member from the tenderest age up to the very end of school-life." To create a one-handed person, in other words, takes some effort and involves repressing the natural abilities of one hand, forbidding it "to assert its equality with the right, and to take its proper share in the daily duties of life."[31]

Jackson condemned the orthodox notions that "the greatest intellect and the greatest dextral pre-eminence are invariably associated together," that "the most civilized nations are the most strongly right-handed," that "it is only in idiots and criminals that there is any reversion to original type in the form of greater or lesser development of Ambidextral skill," that "in

---

of Left-Handedness," 23–24; Guy Montrose Whipple, "Simpler Processes," pt. 1 of *Manual of Mental and Physical Tests* (Baltimore, 1914), 107.

[30] On the Ambidextral Culture Society, see the appendix to John Jackson, *Ambidexterity: or Two-Handedness and Two-Braineddness* (London, 1905), 247–48.

[31] Ibid., 7–9.

brief, the history of *civilization* is merely the history of *right-handedness.*" Indeed, he argued quite the reverse, maintaining that it was one-handed education that leaves the child's mental powers undeveloped. "There can be no doubt that neglect of sinistral hand culture entails a corresponding and permanent Dextrocerebral Atrophy," he warned, "with an inseparable mental inferiority." The present state of affairs thus leaves us "living at some 30 per cent, below our maximum strength."[32]

Jackson proposed that parents and teachers train both hands much as they had been training only the right one. In practical terms, that meant ambidextrous training in penmanship, drawing, and all other manual activities. Not only could children be taught to shift the pen or paintbrush from hand to hand to relieve fatigue, they could also be taught to use their hands simultaneously—that is, to write two letters or draw two pictures at the same time.[33] As Jackson represented them, the advantages of ambidexterity were tremendous. Economic productivity would increase as the left hand was mobilized into service. The level of skill and efficiency achieved in athletics, handicrafts, domestic labors, and even the art of war would soar as men and women were released from the handicap of one-handedness. It was not just manual labors—throwing a ball, sawing wood, sewing a shirt, firing a gun—that would improve when both hands were used. Work involving the mind, not just the hands, would improve as well, because now both halves of the brain—in particular, both speech centers, the core of intellect—would be stimulated and strengthened to the height of their powers. "The entire mentality," argued Jackson, "would consequently be quickened, and the intellectual powers materially strengthened."[34]

But there was yet more. "I cannot help but thinking," continued Jackson, "that by the equal training of both hands . . . the moral sense will be perceptibly, if not proportionately, raised" and that the ambidexter will therefore "be stronger both to follow the right and to resist the wrong than he could be as a lopsided person with only one brain-lobe fully and perfectly organized." In his *Ambidexterity and Mental Culture* of 1914, Henry Macnaughton-Jones, one of Jackson's most devoted followers, stressed the moral benefits of two-handedness above all others. The distinguished Irish physician did not pretend that learning to write and draw with both hands was an easy task, but for him, the discipline, effort, and resolution required was precisely the point. It was mastering the difficult, but not physiologically impossible, skill of ambidexterity that built character, and

[32] Ibid., 16–17, 106.
[33] Ibid., 170–234.
[34] Ibid., 125–29, 134–38; Henry Macnaughton-Jones, *Ambidexterity and Mental Culture* (London, 1914), 31–33. An American edition of this latter work was also published in 1914.

for Macnaughton-Jones, character was ultimately what the ambidexterity reform was all about.[35]

The ambidexterity movement created quite some brouhaha. Opponents denounced the movement as a fad and a craze and branded its advocates the "ambidexterity sillies" and "ambidexterity mongers." Philadelphia physician George M. Gould commented wryly that the Ambidextral Culture Society "might better call itself the 'Society for nullifying the law of the differentiation of function necessary to all progress.'" In a speech titled "Dexterity and the Bend Sinister," James Crichton-Browne insisted that training all children to use both hands was "simply to fly in the face of evolution." The "practice of ambidexterity would be a social calamity," Sir James warned the audience at London's Royal Institution, "for it would compel the enlargement of our already overcrowded lunatic asylums." The brain, he explained, could not "withstand the cerebral strain of ambidexterity, which is essentially the character of the idiot."[36]

Despite their very real and heated opposition to each other, however, the ambidexterity advocates and dominance defenders were really not so terribly different in outlook and motivation. Both assumed the vital influence of the hand over the brain, arguing that the form taken by handedness shapes optimal mental and moral development. Both were captivated with the image of the West, and in particular the British Empire, asserting dominion over primitive peoples by virtue of its inherent superiority. Where Jackson and his followers differed was in their assessment of how the British Empire was faring. Britons, the ambidexterity advocates argued, were beginning to lose out in the race for global dominance. Those in the ascendancy, they invariably pointed out, use both hands. Military setbacks offered the most dramatic evidence of this decline. Japan's stunning defeat of Russia capped its "phenomenal national activity and development," certified it as "one of the most advanced and powerful of all civilized peoples," and, Jackson (erroneously) claimed, stemmed from its near universal practice of ambidexterity. Far more ominous, of course, was the recent course of events in the Boer War. "In these modern times," wrote Jackson darkly, "is there not convincing proof of the inferiority of one-handed or lopsided development in the prolonged war in South Africa, that so heavily taxed our resources and all but defied our most strenuous efforts to successfully terminate it? Do not the Boers use two hands where our soldiers can only use one?" It is well known, of course,

---

[35] Jackson, *Ambidexterity*, 129; Macnaughton-Jones, *Ambidexterity and Mental Culture*, 39–45, 47–57, 60–61.

[36] Gould, *Righthandedness and Lefthandedness*, 29; Gould quoted in "Ambidexterity: Its Possibility and Advisability," *Westminster Review* 162 (December 1904): 649–64; "Sir J. Crichton-Browne on Ambidexterity," *London Times*, May 6, 1907, 3; "Protest against the Ambidexterity Craze," 671.

that Major General Baden-Powell, similarly horrified by the performance of Her Majesty's army in the South African war, established the Boy Scouts as a means to strengthen British manhood; it is less well known that he supported the cause of ambidexterity for the same reason. In his introduction to Jackson's book, he argued that "to train the human body completely and symmetrically, that is, to cultivate all its organs and members to their utmost capacity, in order that its functions may also attain their maximum development, is an obligation that cannot be safely ignored." He signed his contribution twice, once with his right hand and once with his left.[37]

The ability to compete in the international race for survival went beyond military strength. Just as critical to world dominance was a nation's performance in the realms of economics and technology, which required not just strong bones and muscles but superior minds and wills as well. "We cannot afford in these days of such keen competition," warned Jackson, "to neglect, or even to undervalue, any aid to efficiency, any element of strength, or any essential factor in the product of our individual personality, or of our national constitution." It was bimanual training, of course, that would get Britons working at full capacity, physically, mentally, and morally. Without it, Jackson feared for the very future of Britannia. "Let any serious-minded man," he wrote, "sit down and estimate, if he can, the appalling loss in brain power, in inventive genius, in muscular energy, in effective fighting strength, in time and money, that our British Empire is suffering every day of its existence by neglecting to avail itself of this wonderful potency that is lying dormant in its very (left) hand."[38]

The ambidextral reformers never did succeed in transforming the educational system, but they had more success than one might imagine. On the Continent, bimanual training was instituted in parts of Germany, Denmark, and Belgium; in England, it enjoyed a vogue among the upper classes, most notably taking hold of Eton for a time.[39] In America, it had its share of practitioners as well. As early as 1899, James Liberty Tadd was reporting remarkable success with his system of bimanual training in Philadelphia. "The result of this work has only to be seen for one to become impressed with its value as a medium for the education of the individual," he wrote. "The most skeptical" are convinced that ambidextral training does indeed build "a better and more symmetrical men-

[37] Jackson, *Ambidexterity*, xi–xii, 105, 147.
[38] Ibid., 133, 141; see also Macnaughton-Jones, *Ambidexterity and Mental Culture*, 98–99.
[39] Varia Kipiani, "Ambidextrie," *Revue Psychologie* 5 (1912): 151–248; Varia Kipiani, "La réforme de la lecture et de l'écriture chez les voyants et les aveugles en rapport avec les lois de la symétrie," *Revue Psychologie* 3 (1910): 51–55, 399–403; "Against Ambidexterity Fad," *New York Times*, August 16, 1908, pt. 3, p. 3; Ford C. Wales, "Doubling Both Hand and Brain Power," *Technical World* 20 (1914): 680–81.

tal fabric," with dramatic implications for the powers of reason and imagination.[40] Even a full generation after Jackson published his call to arms (literally), American authorities recorded the continuing currency of his theories.[41]

Once it reached the United States, however, the bimanual training movement underwent a subtle transformation. Even if the Boer War did not administer quite the same shock to the American system as it had to the British, Jackson's jeremiad for Western civilization might well have resonated on this side of the Atlantic; after all, fin-de-siècle Americans had experienced their own anxieties about decline. But decay was not the theme Americans chose to pick up on. Instead, it was the vision of untapped energies that captured their interest. Ambidexterity, as it turns out, joined the long list of what T. J. Jackson Lears has termed "abundance therapies," available to Americans in search of experiential intensity and vitality.[42]

It was long thought, explained Ford C. Wales in a 1914 article titled "Doubling Both Hand and Brain Power," that each person has only one speech center, in the left brain in the case of right-handers and in the right brain in the case of left-handers. But now science had demonstrated that everyone has speech centers in both halves of the brain, one of which lies "unused, asleep, wasting," waiting to be awakened. "Most of us are using just one-half our brain power," estimated Wales. "One-half of our brain cells are asleep—'subconscious'—and need to be aroused into activity by some method, and thus brought into the field of 'consciousness' and usefulness." That method, of course, was ambidextral activity. The use of the heretofore neglected hand would set those "dormant faculties" into motion, releasing great quantities of mental potential. Wales told the story of a junior partner in a New York business concern, desperate to learn Spanish lest his firm lose its Argentine market, and he, his job. Try as he might, he could not pick up the language—his memory failed him—until he took some odd advice from a stranger. "Have you ever heard about a 'speech center'?" the stranger inquired.

> Well, you've got one all right, on the left side of your brain, and it's carrying about as much of a load as it can carry in remembering and using the English language. Fortunately, you have, or ought to have, a second "speech-center"

[40] James Liberty Tadd, *New Methods in Education: Art, Real Manual Training, Nature Study* (Springfield, Mass., 1899), 47, 48.

[41] Dora Keen Mohlman, "A Preliminary Study of the Problems in the Training of the Non-preferred Hand," *Journal of Educational Psychology* 14 (April 1923): 215–16; Downey, "Types of Dextrality," 350.

[42] T. J. Jackson Lears, "From Salvation to Self-Realization: Advertising and the Therapeutic Roots of the Consumer Culture, 1880–1930," in Richard W. Fox and T. J. Jackson Lears, eds., *The Culture of Consumption: Critical Essays in American History, 1880–1930* (Chicago, 1983), 3–38.

on the other half of your brain, but it's never been used; it's like a white sheet of paper that's never been written on. It ought to absorb the Spanish you want just like a sponge taking up water. It's asleep, dormant—you'll have to trick it into life and action. In your instance, the only way I can think of your doing so will be by writing down every Spanish word and phrase you study with your left hand.

Within a month, the junior partner sailed for Buenos Aires, master of the new language.[43]

In examining these investigations into handedness, it is apparent just how intimately scientific hypotheses are linked to the cultural climates in which they arise. The theory of cerebral dominance made sense to British and European investigators who divided the globe into an advanced northern hemisphere and a primitive southern hemisphere. The superiority of handedness was self-evident to those who equated specialization and literacy with civilization. The call for ambidextral culture appealed to British anxious for the fate of their empire and Americans in search of inner sources of efficiency and vitality. Nor were the "facts" of science any less plastic. Some swore monkeys prefer their right hands, and others, that they prefer neither. Primitive humans were variously described as almost always right-handed, preponderantly left-handed, and disproportionately ambidextrous. And what looked like preference for the left hand to one observer of feeble-minded children looked like preference for neither to another.

Just which facts would be pursued, just which theories sounded reasonable, was determined by the degree to which fact and theory fit in with an accepted hierarchy of cultural values. To contemporaries, of course, the "facts" of handedness seemed to prove the scientific validity of that hierarchy. Crafted into a grand evolutionary chronicle, they functioned to provide scientific legitimation of domination over "inferior" peoples, both abroad and at home, and to establish the superiority of the modern, industrial order. If the British rule the Hottentots and the Americans the Filipinos, if their economic systems reign supreme, was it not because specialized, literate societies are simply better? Surely that was proved by the master narratives of handedness: the hunter, weapon in dominant hand, conquers the animal world; the handed human, strengthening the power of speech, advances beyond the senseless clamor of the jungle. Ambidexterity advocates offered an alternate master narrative, of course—the fall from and return to primeval grace—but they too celebrated the potential of "advanced" societies.

---

[43] Wales, "Hand and Brain Power," 678–84.

The degree to which scientific theories and facts are shaped by prevailing ideologies is something historians have long explored, but something more was happening in the case of handedness. Certainly facts were perceived in such a way as to reinforce existing cultural assumptions and to bolster scientific theories that would support those assumptions. But even more critical, the entire area of inquiry was defined, indeed came into being, by virtue of its resonance with broader cultural concerns. Until the 1860s, the phenomenon of handedness was invisible to scientists. In a very real sense, handedness did not yet exist because it did not yet need to. By the second half of the nineteenth century, however, that necessity did exist. The issue of "inferior" peoples and individuals called for attention— How should we approach them? Why do we dominate them?—and to contemporaries, it seemed logical to turn to the phenomenon of handedness for insight into these questions. It was logical because left- and right-handedness, in their independence from the cultural variables of power and prejudice, functioned as pure types of deviance and dominance, surrogates for human categories of marginality and dominion. It was also logical because men and women of the turn of the century perceived the body as the key to the mind and the will. It made sense, then, that superiority and normalcy, on the one hand, and inferiority and deviance, on the other, would be somatic not only in expression but also in origin. The hand was an especially fruitful place to search because here, it was believed, lay the key to cerebral—that is, mental and moral—functioning. If left-handers never did get bred out of the gene pool to rid the world of degenerates and ambidextral education never did take hold to produce a master race, it was not for the lack of ability to imagine handedness in these terms.

RACE AND THE PROBLEM OF SLAVERY

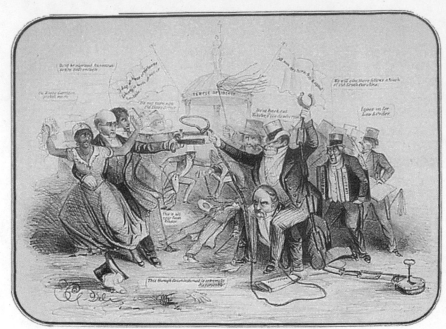

PRACTICAL ILLUSTRATION OF THE FUGITIVE SLAVE LAW.

Frederick Douglass and William Lloyd Garrison brandish weapons to protect a fugitive woman from enslavers, one of whom rides Daniel Webster. Edward W. Clay, cartoonist, "Practical Illustration of the Fugitive Slave Law," 1851, Museum of American Political Life, University of Hartford, West Hartford, Conn. Photograph by Stephen Laschever.

CHAPTER FIVE

Black Abolitionists and the Origins of Civil Disobedience

LEWIS PERRY

"Remember I am a slave," the clergyman Jermain Wesley Loguen proclaimed in 1856 to a white colleague who objected to his support for the underground railroad, "and hold my freedom only by setting the laws and ordinances which you respect in open defiance." Loguen had escaped from slavery in Davidson County, Tennessee, about twenty years before. He was, from the perspective of black abolitionists, "self-emancipated," but in the parlance of slave owners and catchers he remained a runaway who aided other fugitives; his remark epitomized one obvious justification for disobeying laws and resisting government.[1] But many black leaders, including Loguen, sought the privileges of citizenship and protection of the laws, and in justifying acts of noncompliance and resistance, they tested and explored key issues related to moral obligation in a republican government. While some acknowledged almost no limits to the right of armed self-defense and insurrection, others identified themselves, even while violating laws, with republican civility and Christian obedience. In explorations of borderlines separating—

Research for this essay was supported by a grant from the Harry Frank Guggenheim Foundation. Christopher L. Brown offered incisive comments on a draft of the essay.

[1] C. Peter Ripley et al., eds., *The Black Abolitionist Papers*, 5 vols. (Chapel Hill, N.C., 1985–1992), 4:350. Hereafter cited *BAP.* For blacks' use of the term "self-emancipated," see 2:69. Like many others, Loguen was self-named—his slave name had been Jarm Logue. His mother had been kidnapped as a child in Ohio, enslaved, and given a slave name. His father was one of her "demi-civilized" owners. *The Rev. J. W. Loguen, as a Slave and a Freeman* (1859; New York, 1968), 12–15.

and connecting—civil order and disobedient protest, they contributed to distinctive American traditions of civil disobedience at least as much as did some of their white contemporaries. In fact, it is impossible to understand the practice and justification of civil disobedience in the United States without paying attention to the words and deeds of those whose citizenship was curtailed.[2] It is one thing to listen to a white reformer defending his actions as expressions of his individual righteousness, but quite another to listen to a voice like Loguen's, in some ways accepting the values of American republicanism while recognizing his own freedom as won through defiance.

"Although the phenomenon of civil disobedience is today a world-wide phenomenon," Hannah Arendt noted in 1972, "it still is primarily American in origin and substance; . . . no other country, and no other language, has even a word for it."[3] When Arendt wrote, memories of the civil rights movement in cities like Montgomery and Greensboro were still vivid, and protests against the Vietnam War had made civil disobedience a topic of urgent concern to philosophers, the clergy, public officials, and jurists. Since that time, antiapartheid and antiabortion activists have referred back to a tradition which flows from the abolitionists and which surely includes such names as Susan B. Anthony, Alice Paul, A. J. Muste, and A. Philip Randolph.[4] Historians have generally ignored this tradition and said little about its origins, with the important exception of William G. McLoughlin, who illumined the New England Baptists' persistent disobedience of laws that required their support of the religious establishment. McLoughlin also noted that before Henry David Thoreau spent his famous night in jail during the Mexican War, he had conflicted with the state over support for the religious establishment. Thus McLoughlin was able to point out, as an "ironic epilogue" to the phases of New England intellectual and religious history that he studied so masterfully, "that the civil disobedience of pietistic Baptist martyrs was justified (and by America's civil

---

[2] The women's rights movement would demonstrate this point again after the Civil War, with women often drawing parallels between their tactics and the "wild, unaccountable things" done by abolitionists. See Elizabeth Cady Stanton's comments in *Revolution,* January 29, 1869, 48. For suffragists' criticism of Loguen for not including women in demands for suffrage, see October 22, 1868, 96.

[3] Hannah Arendt, *Crises of the Republic* (New York, 1972), 83. She usefully separated the tradition from Henry David Thoreau's focus on *individual* conscience (60) and contended that "civil disobedients are nothing but the latest form of voluntary association, and that they are thus quite in tune with the oldest traditions of the country" (96).

[4] See the excellent collection of writings in David R. Weber, ed., *Civil Disobedience in America: A Documentary History* (Ithaca, 1978). I have examined the tradition in "Civil Disobedience," in Jack P. Greene, ed., *The Encyclopedia of American Political History,* 3 vols. (New York, 1984), 1:210–17.

religion sanctified) by a pantheistic Transcendentalist."[5] We may add that some Garrisonian abolitionists, by no means all Transcendentalists, also dismissed government as an organization from which they might withdraw by certifying their choice to have no part in it.[6]

Although links clearly existed between church-state controversy and acts of protest such as Thoreau's, antebellum civil disobedience cannot be understood simply as a sign of unbroken continuity with the Protestant past. It was, at best, a complicated reassertion in an era when churches were easily conceived as separate from the state but the state could no longer be thought of as something separate from the people. In such an era, appeals to a superior law signified an endeavor to reserve a sphere for religious action in a republic that threatened to become overwhelmingly secular; the goal was to extend the influence of religion, not to shield religion from the sway of the public, or at least to demonstrate that some Americans placed their religious allegiances above any claims that the state might make of them. "Years before Henry David Thoreau," says the historian Robert Abzug, Angelina Grimké in 1836 "advocated civil disobedience: 'If a law commands me to *sin I will break it;* if it calls me to *suffer,* I will let it take its course *unresistingly.*'"[7] One motive for a stance of civil disobedience was to demonstrate religious allegiance; a second was to signify respect for law. Many antislavery people were concerned about the preservation of law and order in a republic, or at least they were too moderate and respectable to be comfortable in a movement charged with unruliness. During the Mexican War and again in response to the Fugitive Slave Act, some of them offered elaborate arguments to show that courteous acts of dissent could strengthen the state rather than weaken its authority. Law-breaking and law-respecting, they fashioned a version of civil disobedience that constituted a kind of oxymoron. They were civil, compliant, submissive, and orderly, yet determined to disobey unjust laws, especially the Fugitive Slave Law. A seventy-five-year-old clergyman, Nathaniel Hall, promised to submit quietly to enormous fines and sit in jail without a lock or keeper, "so important in my mind is the maintenance of civil order."[8]

---

[5] William G. McLoughlin, *New England Dissent, 1630–1833: The Baptists and the Separation of Church and State,* 2 vols. (Cambridge, Mass., 1971), 2:1261. Thoreau's "sanctification," or canonization, occurred in the twentieth century.

[6] Few abolitionists actually went to jail for their no-government convictions. One exception, who preceded and surely influenced Thoreau, was also a Transcendentalist: Bronson Alcott. See my *Radical Abolitionism: Anarchy and the Government of God in Antislavery Thought* (Knoxville, 1995), 85–86.

[7] Robert Abzug, *Cosmos Crumbling: American Reform and the Religious Imagination* (New York, 1994), 211, quoting from Grimké's *Appeal to the Christian Women of the South* (1836).

[8] I have emphasized the importance of Nathaniel Hall and other moderates in "Civil Disobedience," 1:214, and *Civility, Disobedience, and the Constitution* (Bloomington, Ind.,

Black abolitionists confronting oppressive laws sometimes relied on America's colonial religious past as well. It was to Quaker rather than Baptist history that a woman named Zillah turned, for example, while the Pennsylvania legislature considered a bill to prohibit black immigration, in particular to the story of a martyr who sang joyously while being whipped, was "strengthened by an invisible power, and afterwards declared if she had been whipped to death, she should not have been dismayed. Earnestly have I prayed . . . that a double portion of her humility and fortitude may be ours."[9] Blacks' expressions of fealty to divine law could be as uncompromising as Grimké's. In an 1842 Thanksgiving Day sermon, *Covenants Involving Moral Wrong Are Not Obligatory upon Man,* J. C. W. Pennington asserted: "If my Saviour were again to be on earth, I should as soon go to Jerusalem, and there in obedience to the mandate of Jewish prejudice, betray him for thirty pieces of silver, as to be an agent in delivering on demand a poor fugitive from bondage."[10] Sometimes black leaders, stating a concern for public order matching that of white moderates, recommended against mob action and insisted on peaceful responses to injustice.[11] But here the parallel breaks down. Despite similar expressions of allegiance to higher law and respect for civil order, northern blacks were not in a position like Grimké's or Hall's; their Christianity was always to some degree segregated, and their political rights were curtailed. When they counseled peaceful compliance with legal penalties, the reason was more likely to be tactical prudence than belief in the holiness or justice of submission.

Free blacks could not take citizenship for granted and thus had little reason to dismiss its importance with a morally superior gesture. As the example of Loguen illustrates, blacks found themselves poised at a boundary: sometimes their freedom came from defying the law, but in the longer run their protection depended on extending its reach. They stood at this boundary, moreover, at a moment when American republicanism offered very little room for law-breaking, unlike later eras when styles of agitation and dissidence were open to experiment and negotiation. For any ante-

---

1986), 10. I now regard that emphasis as a distortion without equivalent examination of the black abolitionists. The moderates' rhetorical civil disobedience was in part a reaction to black militancy.

[9] Zillah to "A Friend," *Liberator,* June 30, 1832, in *Black Abolitionist Papers 1830–1865,* 17 reels (New York, 1981–1983; Ann Arbor, 1984), microfilm, reel 1, 198A. Hereafter cited *BAP* (microfilm).

[10] J. C. W. Pennington, *Covenants Involving Moral Wrong Are Not Obligatory upon Man, BAP* (microfilm), reel 4, 485–90A. Pennington was reacting to the seizure of the fugitive George Latimer.

[11] See, for example, Samuel E. Cornish's editorials against assemblages of illiterate men who might, in the context of a trial of "Negro Catchers," lose "self-government and become mere subjects of passion." *Colored American,* April 15, 29, 1837, in *BAP* (microfilm), reel 2, 28B, 39B.

bellum abolitionist to advocate law-breaking required considerable courage and much effort of justification, for what they counseled was easily attacked as treason. No doubt one implication of the doctrines deployed in justification of the American Revolution had been to undercut unexamined obedience to the powers that be, but the reaction to those doctrines in subsequent decades had been Thermidorean.[12] As American governments came more and more to be thought of as based on the sovereignty of the people and representing the people's will, acceptable grounds for resistance to law were probably diminished rather than augmented. It became harder to think of government as sovereign in itself, somehow apart from and unaffected by the realm of the people—to be "rendered unto" but not participated in. In a representative government, citizens were said to have surrendered some of their autonomy, and disobedience to a law would be taken as disloyalty to the community or a violation of an agreement that the lawbreaker had helped to make.

A good illustration of this political logic was Andrew Jackson's proclamation to the citizens of South Carolina in 1831. Although Jackson believed more strongly in democratic government than did many other leaders, he voiced the Thermidorean consensus that turned the revolutionary origins of the United States into a theory of compulsory obedience. South Carolinians were misled in thinking they possessed "the revolutionary right of resisting all laws that were palpably unconstitutional and intolerably oppressive" and that nullification was "a peaceable remedy" based on that right. They were in no sense comparable to the revolutionary generation as an oppressed people. To the contrary, they were "free members of a flourishing and happy union." Better still, they lived under a constitutional government, uniting the states and "giving to *all* their inhabitants the proud title of *American citizen."* Jackson acknowledged that people suffering under oppression possessed "a natural right" to break their "obligations to the Government," but he restricted this right to "the last resort," unavailable until all other remedies are exhausted. Natural it might be, but it was "necessarily subjected to limitations in all free governments," which provided means for peaceful changing of the laws. To be faithful to the memory of the "fathers" and preserve the "rich inheritance" they bequeathed in the form of a government of laws based on popular representation, the nation must put down and punish open resistance to law.[13]

In hindsight, this use of the idea of citizenship to disallow the right of revolution was double-edged. By limiting protests against extreme griev-

[12] Many scholars have pointed to an American "Thermidor," including Daniel T. Rodgers in his highly relevant *Contested Truths: Keywords in American Politics since Independence* (New York, 1987), 63.

[13] James D. Richardson, comp., *A Compilation of the Messages and Papers of the Presidents* (New York, 1897), 3:1218 (emphasis added), 1184–88.

ances to the right of revolution, national political leaders equated resistance to law with treason and cautioned citizens to think gravely before entering on such a course. The implication was that citizens should operate within the political process and accept in good grace outcomes that displeased or injured them. But how did this logic apply to inhabitants of the nation who were not fully citizens? Would they be justified in taking up arms? This question arose sharply with regard to northern free blacks. Jackson, after all, had conceded that misrule, if "great and lasting," justified revolution, and sustained curtailment of the rights of citizenship might meet that standard.[14] For black Americans the right of revolution might have appeared the only option, if they had not been so badly outnumbered and if so many of them had not sought acceptance within the political system. They constituted a small but important group pressing American republicanism to modify the stark disjunction of obedience and revolution, to recognize a distinction between civil disobedience and treason, and to find ways of strengthening the law by extending citizenship.

It is hard to find a precise analogy to fit the condition of antebellum northern blacks. In some respects, they resembled a colonial people, except that they were a minority made to feel out of place in the land in which they found themselves. Perhaps they were more like out-workers in nations of the European Economic Community of recent years, defined by race, their rights seriously impaired. But they were also defined in relation to slaves; some were fugitives, and many others accepted responsibility for aiding fugitives. Enduring halfway between slavery and freedom, they were excluded by race from the suffrage in some states and subjected to discriminatory property qualifications in others. As the right to vote spread among white males, some states actually took it away from blacks.[15] In addition, laws and customs denied them civil rights to serve on juries or to give testimony in cases involving whites. Some states impeded black settlements or required surety bonds for black residents. In the notorious *Dred Scott* decision (1857), Chief Justice Roger Taney observed that blacks historically had been treated as a subject race with "no rights which white men are bound to accept"; he concluded that, "whether emancipated or not," they were simply not "included, under the word 'citizens' in the Constitution."[16]

---

[14] Ibid., 3:1187.

[15] "By 1840, some 93 per cent of the northern free Negro population lived in states which completely or practically excluded them from the right to vote." Leon Litwack, *North of Slavery: The Negro in the Free States, 1790–1860* (Chicago, 1961), 75.

[16] Paul Finkelman, ed., *Dred Scott v. Sandford: A Brief History with Documents* (Boston, 1997), 58, 61. While Taney's words are widely quoted and deplored, it is less often recognized that Taney was trying to clarify "what was, in *his* time, one of the most confused and unprecedented areas of American constitutional development: the problem of citizenship," in

To deprivations of political rights must be added segregation in schools, churches, theaters, and public conveyances. Few blacks benefited from the economic opportunity of the Jacksonian era. Even white antislavery organizations, as blacks complained repeatedly, were reluctant to employ blacks in positions of responsibility. Widespread poverty only deepened as Irish immigrants took many of the marginal jobs for which unskilled blacks might have been eligible. Those few who acquired some wealth and achieved some respectability were detested by urban mobs as much as casual laborers competing with whites for jobs. Those who spoke out against northern prejudice and southern slavery were especially likely to encounter violence in the riots that became commonplace in Jacksonian cities.

In view of the cruelties of life in a nation where even self-styled free states curtailed black citizenship, it is no surprise that some black leaders ridiculed patriotic depictions of America's mission to lead the world toward liberty. When the historian George Bancroft extolled America's world-historical role, the black educator William Watkins retorted that the world should not imitate a nation that tolerated the whipping of slaves and punished those who gave succor to fugitives.[17] In the 1820s and 1830s most black leaders opposed the program of the American Colonization Society to remove unenslaved blacks to Liberia; this was too clearly an instance of the racism that polluted American republicanism. But in time some thoughtful leaders came to regard emigration as the only possible response to slavery and racism. Watkins, for example, who in 1833 had led Baltimore blacks to declare the United States their "only *true and appropriate home*," recruited prospective settlers for the Haitian Emigration Bureau on the eve of the Civil War.[18] Others came to feel, especially in the 1850s, so discouraged by deprivations of citizenship that they debated and launched plans to resettle in Canada, the Caribbean, or West Africa. "Broad fertile Africa is the true home of the black man," was one response to complaints about segregation on northern railroads. "He can never conquer this land or the *prejudices* . . . of its inhabitants."[19]

In spite of threats and setbacks, however, many black leaders continued to insist that "we are American citizens. . . . 'Colored Americans' will do in the United States, but 'Africans' never."[20] Even in moments of severe discouragement, many expressed ardent patriotism. They praised black par-

---

particular, national citizenship. Harold M. Hyman and William M. Wiecek, *Equal Justice under Law: Constitutional Development, 1835–1875* (New York, 1982), 181.

[17] *BAP,* 4:256–57.

[18] *BAP,* 3:6, 4:155.

[19] *African Repository,* March 1853, in *BAP* (microfilm), reel 8, 147B.

[20] Uriah Boston to Frederick Douglass, April 1855, in *BAP,* 4:279.

ticipation in the American Revolution; they repeatedly noted that Andrew Jackson had honored free black volunteers at the Battle of New Orleans as brave "fellow citizens."[21] When South Carolina's legislature asked northern states in the 1830s to suppress antislavery societies, James Forten Jr. called all Americans to "the standard of patriotism which their fathers reared," one that protected freedom of speech. "I love America; it is my native land; . . . I love the stars and stripes, emblem of our National Flag— and long to see the day when not a slave shall be found resting under its shadow."[22] In protest against the Fugitive Slave Law in 1850, leaders referred back to the Massachusetts of the Puritans as "our father land" and to England, where traditions of liberty had been nurtured, as "our mother country." How dare the Congress strike down habeas corpus and trial by jury, "those great bulwarks of human freedom, baptized by the blood, and sustained by the patriotic exertion of our English ancestors."[23] There are numerous examples of northern black leaders claiming descent from the Puritans, the revolutionaries, the founding generations of Americans. Unmistakably, they claimed more than the right of consent to the American political order; they claimed inclusion in the American people.[24] If his children were nothing more than "*little Africans,*" one man asked whether "all white children in New England are any thing but a countless swarm of Englishmen, Scotchmen and Swiss."[25]

As the historians Jane and William Pease have shown, blacks gave crucial support to white antislavery endeavors, but they also developed their own separate movements, which paid much greater attention to northern discrimination and the absence of true liberty among nominally "free" blacks.[26] Programs to advance temperance, education, and self-improvement went hand in hand with protests against Jim Crow and the curtailment of civil rights. Emphasis on moral improvement may have

[21] *BAP,* 3:112, 115, 254–55, 4:153, 260, 5:335, 386. They did not mention Jackson's concerns about slave rebelliousness or invasions from Jamaica.

[22] *BAP,* 3:159–60.

[23] Quotations from Samuel Ringgold Ward and H. Ford Douglas in *BAP,* 4:49 and 74, respectively. According to Wilson Jeremiah Moses, *Alexander Crummel: A Study of Civilization and Its Discontent* (New York, 1989), despite scholarly emphasis on African and folk traditions, "it was from the English/American literary and intellectual traditions that the literate classes of black Americans derived their conceptions of what black culture ought, ideally, to become" (9).

[24] For examples, see *BAP* (microfilm), reel 5, 401B, 401AB, and reel 6, 731A, 818B; Samuel Ringgold Ward, *Autobiography of a Fugitive Negro* (London, 1855), 123. A probing investigation of links between lineage and rights is Werner Sollors, *Beyond Ethnicity: Consent and Descent in American Culture* (New York, 1988).

[25] Charles Caples to *Liberator,* September 6, 1834, in *BAP* (microfilm), reel 1, 523A.

[26] Jane H. Pease and William H. Pease, *They Who Would Be Free: Blacks' Search for Freedom, 1830–1861* (Urbana, Ill., 1990), 3–16.

been partly tactical, though some leaders went to the extreme of arguing that alcohol imposed a bondage equal to slavery.[27] There was some initial hope that respectable blacks would combat prejudice and win their rights by the example of their behavior. It soon became evident, however, that prejudice against their color, rather than judgment of their character, caused blacks' rights actually to shrink in the North while those of white males universally expanded. More than tactics were at stake in any case; to believe that self-improvement must accompany full citizenship was consistent with American republicanism, which once attempted to restrict the franchise to respectable men and by the Jacksonian era regarded education and moral uplift as essential to democracy's survival.[28]

In accepting such beliefs, while pressing for civil rights and the suffrage, blacks began to explore underlying tensions between political equality and civic respectability and ventured in the direction of what became the paradoxical American tradition of civil disobedience. On the one hand, they repeatedly encountered injustices in American laws, law enforcement, and social prejudice. The "hallmark of antebellum black radicalism," according to Vincent Harding, was "a careful, sober capacity to see the entire American government, and the institutions and population which it represented, as the basic foe of any serious black struggle." On the other, they frequently adhered to the conviction that civility and good character, even if inadequate to win fair treatment in the immediate future, were still essential to the transformation of the republic.[29]

Blacks amply demonstrated their acceptance of the legitimacy of disobedience. Of the many cases where blacks refused to be restricted to Jim Crow sections of streetcars and railways, the most notorious occurred when Elizabeth Jennings, a teacher on her way to church in lower Manhattan, defied a conductor's order to get off a streetcar. The conductor and driver dragged her off despite her insistence that she was "a respectable person" and it was wrong to "insult genteel persons." After suing the Third Avenue Railroad Company, she was awarded $225 and the right to ride.[30] When other blacks tried to translate this case into a victory against segregation

[27] See William Whipper in *BAP,* 3:120–22.

[28] On receptiveness to socialization as a sign of merit in Jacksonian political society, see the interpretation in David Brion Davis, ed., *Antebellum American Culture* (University Park, Pa., 1997).

[29] Vincent Harding, *There Is a River: The Black Struggle for Freedom in America* (New York, 1981), 200. This account of black culture stresses a "Great Tradition," including recurrent instances of "civil disobedience" throughout the antebellum era. For an important reminder that moral improvement was consistent with other goals and programs, even the most militant or separatist, see Peter P. Hinks, *To Awaken My Afflicted Brethren: David Walker and the Problem of Antebellum Slave Resistance* (University Park, Pa., 1997), 109–10.

[30] *BAP,* 4:230–32.

on all New York lines, they met disappointment. The clergyman James Pennington, for example, was ejected from a white car of the Sixth Avenue line in 1856. He did not go easily but instead held on to the railing and was dragged beside the car with a conductor stomping on his hands. He also lost his legal complaint, which threatened, in the court's view, both the company's profits and the system of segregation in all city institutions.[31] In protests of this kind, black leaders usually stressed the unfairness of categorical discrimination, regardless of individual character. "All hope of reward for right conduct is cut off" by Jim Crow, Charles Lenox Remond in 1842 told a Massachusetts legislative committee considering a bill (which was not passed) against segregation on public conveyances. "It is not true that we all behave alike. There is a marked difference, and we claim a recognition of this difference."[32]

Robert Purvis, a prosperous Pennsylvania landowner, was furious when local school officials in 1853 excluded his children from public schools. He refused to pay his school tax, second largest in the town, and ridiculed a pious Quaker who directed him to a miserable shanty in a nearby town that served as a school for blacks. "To submit by voluntary payment of the demand is too great an outrage upon nature, and with spirit, thank God, unshackled by this, or any other wanton and cowardly act, I shall resist this tax, which before the unjust exclusion had always afforded me the highest gratification in paying. With no other than the best feeling towards yourself," he wrote the tax collector, "I am forced to this unpleasant position, in vindication of my rights and personal dignity, against an encroachment upon them as contemptibly mean, as it is infamously despotic." Local officials backed down, surely in part because they needed his substantial payments.[33] Purvis blended courtesy and dignity with resistance in a manner showing how the civil disobedience tactic of tax refusal could go well beyond the church-state controversies of earlier times. Similar conclusions apply to boycotts that induced the Massachusetts legislature to mandate school integration in 1855.[34]

More ambiguous were the actions of the author-lecturer William Wells Brown when he returned from England in 1854. Having forgotten, or so he said, how segregation worked in northern cities, Brown walked into three New York restaurants and was turned away at each. At a fourth he simply sat down, stabbed at a pickle and ate it, managed to get served, and paid for his dinner at the bar. When the proprietor called him an impu-

[31] R. J. M. Blackett, *Beating against the Barriers: Biographical Essays in Nineteenth-Century Afro-American History* (Baton Rouge, 1986), 60–62.
[32] *BAP*, 3:369.
[33] Ibid., 4:187–88.
[34] Ibid., 3:48.

dent "nigger" whom he would have thrown out except for fear of disturbing other customers, Brown claïmed to have replied: "If you had, you would have taken the tablecloth, dishes and all with me. Now sir, look at me; whenever I come into your dining saloon, the best thing you can do is to let me have what I want to eat quietly."[35] Brown's audiences enjoyed his swagger, but the story exaggerated the ease with which Jim Crow could be overcome—and Brown made no claims to meeting discourtesy with courtesy or violence with nonviolence.

Threats of violence and resorts to violence raised issues that divided black abolitionists. In part, this was due to the influence of William Lloyd Garrison and other white radical pacifists who took leading roles in the American Anti-Slavery Society. Blacks gave vital support to Garrison's newspaper the *Liberator,* and they honored him as a courageous and eloquent white ally. Few blacks followed radical pacifists to the extreme of denying the authority of human government and all other coercive institutions, but some regarded "non-resistance" as the appropriate method of protesting the violence of slavery and responding to proslavery hecklers and mobs of ruffians. The merchant William Whipper reflected the Garrisonian logic in urging a reform society in 1837 to use methods of reason and persuasion rather than trying to beat down an enemy by superior force. "If I intimidate him I have made him a slave, while I reign a despot," he argued, and nothing is gained in the ensuing passion and resentment.[36] When Rev. Theodore Wright was insulted, kicked, and driven out of a meeting of a literary society at Princeton, he took pride in his own fidelity to "the comforting, but self-denying doctrine of non-resistance, so effective in curbing that vindictive spirit which naturally rises when suddenly assailed. Thankful am I that I was kept from lifting so much as a finger in self-defense, but continued my way out of the house."[37]

If nothing else, nonresistance helped to preserve self-control and personal dignity and thus signified the civility of its practitioners. In some versions it amounted to a personal form of passive aggression resembling the oxymoronic qualities of civil disobedience at the level of collective action. But was it effective in all instances, and could anyone really advise the slaves to be nonresistants? Only a few black Garrisonians embraced the dogma that violence was inherently evil and thus unjustifiable even in pursuit of good ends. Whipper praised the examples of peace martyrs throughout history and identified their modern successors as the northern abolitionists, who were "beaten and stoned, mobbed and persecuted from city to city, and never returned evil for evil, but submissively, as a sheep brought

[35] Ibid., 4:341–42.
[36] Ibid., 3:244.
[37] Ibid., 182.

before the shearer, have they endured scoffings and scourges for the cause's sake, while they prayed for their persecutors."[38] William Powell, who ran a boardinghouse for sailors in New Bedford, thought the nonresistance doctrine "heaven-born" and joined the Garrisonians' radical peace organization. But he removed his family to England during the 1850s and avoided the most searching debates over violent means.[39]

Blacks expressed many doubts about nonresistance. In 1838 Augustus Hanson wrote Garrison to insist that he had done nothing wrong in ignoring Garrison's advice and defending himself physically against an assailant, probably on a streetcar or railway.[40] In 1841, under the pseudonym "Sidney," a black leader, perhaps Henry Highland Garnet, dismissed appeals to nonresistance. Oppressors never retreat, he maintained, until their victims show that they know their rights and will fight for them.[41] Few black leaders disagreed with William Wells Brown, who declared in 1848 that he had no wish to see "scenes of blood and carnage," but "if a favorable opening should occur to the slave population of this country, he could hardly subdue himself to counsel non-resistance, or to act upon its principles himself." The year was significant: the European revolutions of 1848 emboldened blacks to speak more freely of their support of armed uprisings than they had during Nat Turner's rebellion in 1831 or in subsequent years.[42]

In a powerful 1843 address to the nation's slaves, Garnet ridiculed the "unreasonable and unnatural dogmas of non-resistance." It was sinful for slaves to submit voluntarily to captivity; it was their duty to use every means of resistance at their disposal. American revolutionary precedent, the divine law, the examples of slave rebels—all supported the motto "RESISTANCE! RESISTANCE! RESISTANCE!" He did not counsel armed revolution, solely because it was "INEXPEDIENT." Slaves were outnumbered and lacked allies. Instead, they should "go to your lordly enslavers, and tell them plainly, that YOU ARE DETERMINED TO BE FREE." After speaking to the masters of the injustice and sinfulness of slavery, they should "forever cease to toil for heartless tyrants. . . . You had far better all die—*die immediately*, than live slaves, and entail your wretchedness upon your posterity."[43]

Garnet's speech was an unusual utterance of a suppressed thought. It criticized slaves for being too patient, for tamely submitting to rape and

[38] Ibid., 248–49.
[39] Ibid., 238, 303.
[40] Ibid., 283–85.
[41] Ibid., 357.
[42] William Wells Brown quoted in Pease and Pease, *They Who Would Be Free*, 235–36.
[43] *BAP*, 3:403–10. Herbert Aptheker notes the similarity between Garnet's appeal to the slaves and Samuel Sharpe's alleged call for "massive passive resistance" in Jamaica in 1831. The connection has not been proved but is certainly plausible. See his *Abolitionism: A Revolutionary Movement* (Boston, 1989), 170–71.

exploitation. Its call to widespread insubordination, tempered by considerations of expediency, envisioned something more like mass civil disobedience than armed rebellion. Still, it was treated as so controversial that it was not published until 1848. The following year, Garnet's thought emerged again when Thomas Van Rensselaer took satirical note of Louisiana's official expression of support for European revolutionaries and urged slaves to rise up with confidence in the governor's sympathy. Turning more serious, he added: "We do not tell you to murder the slaveholders, but we do advise you to refuse longer to work without pay. Make up your minds to die, rather than bequeath a state of slavery to your posterity."[44]

Blacks' belief in a right of self-defense by any means, including violence, was most evident in discussions of aid to fugitives. After New York police officers in 1836 arrested a "respectable free colored man," whom the city recorder swiftly "pronounced to be a SLAVE," David Ruggles wrote this warning: "We have no protection in law. . . . [W]e must look to our own safety and protection from kidnappers! remembering that 'self-defence is the first law of nature.'"[45] Views like these were somewhat controversial, even among blacks, before 1848 (Ruggles was removed as secretary of the New York Vigilance Committee for speaking and acting too indiscreetly). But from 1835 onward, national Negro Conventions repeatedly sanctioned civil disobedience in aid of fugitives.[46] After the enactment of the new Fugitive Slave Law, no advantage derived from remaining cautious about asserting rights that whites took for granted. Thousands of northern blacks fled the United States. Among those who remained, Purvis declared his readiness "to kill every oppressor" chasing fugitives. Frederick Douglass thought "two or three dead slave holders" the best way to combat the law. The clergyman William P. Newman announced his "fixed and changeless purpose to kill any so-called man who attempts to enslave me or mine, . . . though it be Millard Fillmore himself. To do this, in defence of personal liberty . . . would be an act of the highest virtue, and white Americans must be real hypocrites if they say not to it—amen!"[47] Other events of the 1850s only deepened repudiation of nonviolence. Edward Scott, a Providence pastor who was self-emancipated, asked, "How can fugitives join the Peace Society, with Judge Taney at their back?"[48]

[44] Quoted in Harding, *There Is a River*, 151.
[45] *BAP*, 3:168–69.
[46] Harding, *There Is a River*, 121. The 1835 Philadelphia convention resolved: "That our duty to God, and to the principles of human rights, so far exceeds our allegiance to those [laws] that return the slave again to his master . . . that we recommend our people to peaceably bear the punishment those [laws] inflict, rather than aid in returning their brethren again to slavery" (121).
[47] *BAP*, 3:81, 4:64, 227.
[48] Ibid., 4:367.

Atrocities such as the Fugitive Slave Law, Samuel Ringgold Ward proclaimed at Faneuil Hall, left no recourse except "the right of Revolution, and if need be, that right we will, at whatever cost, most sacredly maintain."[49] It was, indeed, a short step from the right of self-defense to the right of revolution. William H. Newby, a daguerreotypist and editor, told a California audience: "I would hail the advent of a foreign army upon our shores, if that army provided liberty to me and my people in bondage. This may be thought ultra, but in saying it I am influenced by the same motives and spirit which influenced [Patrick] Henry, when he said to the burgesses of Virginia, 'give me liberty, or give me death!'"[50] Such reasoning was not at all abstract to the community of fugitives and free blacks who lived in Lancaster County, Pennsylvania, in a condition of constant jeopardy and conflict with gangs of local whites and slave catchers from nearby states. Their self-emancipated leader, William Parker, had "formed a resolution that I would assist in liberating every one within my reach at the risk of my life, and that I would devise some plan for their entire liberation." One night in September 1851, as a Maryland slave owner, together with his son, other friends and family, a federal marshal, and a Philadelphia policeman, approached in pursuit of fugitives whom Parker was sheltering, a Quaker neighbor came to Parker and urged him "not to resist the Fugitive Slave Law by force of arms, but to escape to Canada." According to a subsequent interview with Frederick Douglass, Parker "replied that if the laws protected colored men as they did white men, he too would be non-resistant and not fight, but would appeal to the laws. 'But,' said he, 'the laws for personal protection are not made for us, and we are not bound to obey them. If a fight occurs I want the whites [like his neighbor] to keep away. They have a country and may obey the laws. But we have no country.'" The next morning, in a brief battle sometimes called "the Christiana Tragedy," the slave owner was killed, his son wounded, and the posse routed, while Parker and the young men he aided escaped to Canada.[51] One historian compares the event to the Boston Tea Party; another calls it a story that "goes to the heart of American slavery."[52] It was certainly a story that revealed limits to the obedience to law that could be expected, in the modern world, of those who are not fully citizens.

Parker appeared to suggest that if the laws had protected him, he would not have turned to arms. Blacks who did not share his jeopardy usually

[49] Ibid., 51.

[50] Ibid., 357.

[51] Thomas P. Slaughter, *Bloody Dawn: The Christiana Riot and Racial Violence in the Antebellum North* (New York, 1991), 49, 57.

[52] Ibid., xi–xii; David Brion Davis, "Life and Death in Slavery," *New York Review of Books*, January 30, 1992, 9.

posed the alternatives less starkly. Even as they complained angrily about lack of support and sympathy from whites, black leaders frequently acknowledged the benefits of law and imagined a day when all would be citizens enjoying equal protection. This may be one implication of the case of Nelson Hackett, who had taken his master's gold watch, overcoat, horse, and saddle when he fled from Arkansas to Canada West. His indictment for grand larceny was used to justify extradition to Detroit and thence back to slavery. The case provoked an international outcry, but it is hard to believe that Hackett derived much comfort from knowing, as Detroit's Colored Vigilance Committee suggested, that his fame resounded in the House of Lords. Many abolitionists might have thought that his larceny was excused by his owner's previous expropriation of his labor and liberty, but the committee did not take that position. Since "all had been legally done" and "he was a felon," as their lawyer determined from examining the papers, they decided "it was better to let him go back to the prison house of slavery, than to bring a reproach upon the cause of emancipation by instituting a suit on his behalf." Perhaps they were simply sensitive to the way in which previous acts of violence had discredited antislavery activity and led to a curfew on Detroit's blacks. In any case, they repeatedly emphasized that they had "learned from experience, the superiority of moral and intellectual power, guided by calm, and deliberate reason, over that of ignorance and physical force, guided by heated and inflamed passion." They were determined to "secure justice for our own people" but also sought "to impress upon their minds the great necessity of observing the law and becoming good and peaceable citizens."[53] Certainly Garrisonian blacks, in responding to the violence of the 1850s, praised a future rule of law. The lecturer H. Ford Douglas, for example, praised John Brown's single-minded dedication to ending slavery, but he added, "I am not an advocate for insurrection; I believe the world must be educated into something better and higher than this before we can have perfect freedom, either for the black man or the white."[54]

Perhaps the point seems too obvious. What else could black leaders say except that the law should be changed so that it protected all Americans equally? Many were clear, especially after the government began to enforce the Fugitive Slave Law of 1850, that their self-respect depended on

[53] *BAP,* 3:397–401. Detroit's blacks, like those in other cities, formed secret organizations to assist fugitives, though much about them remains hard to determine. See David Katzman, *Before the Ghetto: Black Detroit in the Nineteenth Century* (Urbana, Ill.: 1973), 40–41. Blacks sometimes cautioned slaves about "misinterpretations of the rights of property. . . . [W]ere you better informed, you would not scruple to break your master's locks and take all their money." Philip S. Foner and George E. Walker, eds., *Proceedings of the Black State Conventions, 1840–1865,* 2 vols. (Philadelphia, 1979), 1:45.

[54] *BAP,* 5:89.

defying, not obeying, the law. Douglas went on: "What is the object of Government? . . . [I]t is to make men; and if it fails in this—as your government has done—it fails in everything and is no government." Blacks asked no special favors but only "the same rights, legally," as whites and the same opportunities to improve themselves.[55] And Purvis made the relationship of blacks to existing law very clear: "I never will stultify or disgrace myself by eulogizing a government that tramples me and all that are dear to me in the dust."[56]

Loguen's similar statement equating freedom with disobedience came in the course of bitter protest against a white minister who denied permission to collect funds for the underground railroad from his pulpit. Loguen's extensive comments exemplify ways in which blacks availed themselves of canonical heroes and texts to give specificity to the universal, but vague and unrealized, precepts of republican ideology and thus to justify disobedience to law. The white clergyman, antislavery by his own lights, viewed it as his "duty as a citizen and a Christian" to comply with the law of the land, and he quoted many lines of Scripture associating earthly rulers with the ordinations of God. Loguen's reply was angry and eloquent:

> What if Moses and Aaron, and Daniel and Elijah had adopted this wretched doctrine. . . ! Why, your argument strikes at all righteousness, and blots out the only feature of the Bible which makes it merciful, sublime and Godlike. When commanded to teach no more in Christ's name, the apostle said, "we ought to obey God rather than men." . . . It was through disobedience to the Kings of Egypt and Babylon, and other false rulers, that the government of Jehovah was preserved in the Jewish dispensation. It is owing to such disobedience in the Christian dispensation that it has been preserved ever since, and that light and knowledge, liberty and religion, progress and civilization exist on earth. . . . Will you make me believe that the villain who raised his gory lash from my bleeding body, and who now holds it over the backs of my poor mother, brothers and sisters—that the scoundrels who made and execute the fugitive slave law, who chase my famishing countrymen through the States, are the ministers of the most High God, and that we ought to submit quietly to be tortured, and robbed, and murdered, "for the Lord's sake," and if [we] resist them we must be damned? . . . Sir, you don't understand the Scriptures. The very fact that there are "higher powers ordained of God," implies that there are lower powers ordained of Hell—that the former only are to be recognized as "the Powers that be," and the latter to be recognized as no Powers at all.[57]

[55] Ibid., 93–94.
[56] Ibid., 4:364.
[57] Ibid., 348–50. Carol M. Hunter, *To Set the Captives Free: Reverend Jermain Wesley Loguen and the Struggle for Freedom in Central New York, 1835–1872* (New York, 1993), 218–23, sets this controversy in the context of revivalism.

The contradiction between these two readings of the sacred past, one obliging the faithful to comply with earthly authority, the other liberating the righteous to stand against evil, was part and parcel of what David Brion Davis has termed "the problem of slavery" in Western culture.[58] But it would be hard to find a stronger statement than Loguen's, in all the years of the slavery controversy in the United States, of the duty of disobedience.

If there is an American civil disobedience tradition, Loguen's remarks place his activities in aid of fugitives near its center. He was a precursor of what A. J. Muste later called "holy disobedience."[59] Yet he differed from his successors in two respects: as we observed at the outset, he expressed absolutely no respect for American law in general; and though he was originally a Garrisonian, by the 1850s he had little aversion to violent resistance. He was indicted for his part in the rescue of William "Jerry" McHenry in Syracuse in 1851, and he boasted of assisting nearly fifteen hundred fugitives in the 1850s. In these rescues, he considered armed violence justifiable but went to some lengths to cooperate with authorities afterward. He refused bail and thus escaped punishment because his incarceration would have created an uproar. He recruited fighters for John Brown's raid on Harpers Ferry in 1859.[60] The nation did not bar him from becoming a clergyman and a lecturer, but it kept him in a limbo of noncitizenship and jeopardized the liberty of his fellows. That in the end is what differentiated him from contemporaries and successors who professed to love the law while defying it.

Few other blacks spoke exactly in Loguen's terms of traditional religious justifications for disobedience, though many said generally that slavery violated the laws of God. For the most part, blacks appealed to the right of revolution, which even Andrew Jackson had conceded was the recourse for people convinced they had no protection from the regime in power. To this way of thinking, acts of disobedience were only one set of options available to people who might legitimately resort to any means that promised victory over their oppressors. They must not even appear to be submissive; that would only deepen whites' prejudice that blacks were unfit to win their liberty. The stance of submissive disobedience did not really exist for blacks who felt that they had suffered too many blows and that it was

---

[58] See esp. David Brion Davis, *The Problem of Slavery in the Age of Revolution, 1770–1823* (Ithaca, 1975), 523–56. Just before the Christiana battle, Parker and the slaveholder argued over what the Bible said about slavery. See W. U. Hensel, *The Christiana Riot and the Treason Trials of 1851* (Lancaster, Pa., 1911), 108.

[59] Nat Hentoff, ed., *The Essays of A. J. Muste* (Indianapolis, 1967), 355. Accounts of this tradition frequently mention only whites, especially Garrison and the Friends in the antebellum period. For examples, see Hentoff's introduction, xv, and Reinhold Niebuhr's review in *New York Times Book Review*, April 16, 1967.

[60] *BAP,* 4:87–88; *Rev. J. W. Loguen,* 435–37.

time to strike back. The sword, the physician John S. Rock told a Boston audience in 1860, was "no doubt the method by which the freedom of blacks will be brought about in this country. It is a severe method; but to severe ills it is necessary to apply severe remedies."[61] A few years later, Rock was recruiting for the famous Fifty-Fourth Massachusetts Regiment.

Definitions of civil disobedience frequently insist on a commitment to nonviolence. Some may be uneasy about placing at the source of a civil disobedience tradition episodes and movements that are not purely nonviolent. The words and actions of such Garrisonian nonresistants as Whipper and Wright raise no difficulties, but most black leaders, including Loguen, were less categorical in rejecting violence. Although the black abolitionists' calls for revolution may perhaps be criticized by absolute pacifists, one should recall Mohandas K. Gandhi's teaching, often cited by Martin Luther King, that "if cowardice is the only alternative to violence, it is better to fight."[62] Surely not everyone would agree with Gandhi's prescription that only those who *revere* the law are entitled to disobey the law (though antebellum black leaders had praised the rule of law even when deploring American injustice).[63] Those blacks who contemplated insurrection included artisans, clergy, physicians, educators, and authors; these men and women appreciated civil order—but they were not fully citizens, and they spoke and acted on behalf of slaves. It is hard to see how any white critics could have denied the claim that if their liberty were similarly curtailed, they would not be constrained by teachings of nonviolence.

The point to emphasize is that some antebellum blacks, in an era when governmental leaders offered no middle ground between revolution and submission and when some contemporaries saw their only hope in emigration, showed remarkable creativity in finding ways of protesting against law, even violating law, without forsaking the quest for citizenship. Instances of tax refusal, school boycotts, railway sit-ins, and aid to fugitives may appear familiar enough in retrospect, but at that time they carried the risk of being defined as treason.[64] These efforts by black militants, joined by some white allies, surely influenced the more polite and proper versions of civil disobedience originated by moderate white counterparts. There were links, moreover, between black abolitionism and protest movements of later

---

[61] *BAP,* 5:59.

[62] Gandhi quoted in Staughton Lynd, ed., *Nonviolence in America: A Documentary History* (Indianapolis, 1966), 391.

[63] Gandhi's view, as he sometimes explained it, resembled the Calvinist distinction between those who eschew sin because of its penalties and those with deeper motivations. See *Gandhi, an Autobiography: The Story of My Experiments with Truth* (Boston, 1957), 470.

[64] In the legal aftermath of the conflict at Christiana, those who sought to play a conciliatory role and refused to aid the posse were indicted for treason. Hensel, *Christiana Riot,* 57–58.

eras.[65] Religious conviction and the wish to fulfill ideas of citizenship continued to blend in powerful and intricate ways long after the language of nonresistance and the right of revolution began to fade into disuse. Black abolitionists stand as exemplars warning against dogmatic definitions of civil disobedience and reminding us of the importance of citizenship, and curtailments of citizenship, in shaping American reform traditions.

[65] The March on Washington Movement in 1948 pointed to the underground railroad as a forerunner proving that nonviolent civil disobedience was not alien to American society or black culture. See Committee against Jimcrow in Military Training and Service, "Questions on Civil Disobedience," Bulletin no. 2, June 17, 1948, 3, mimeographed copies in A. Philip Randolph Papers, Library of Congress, and Swarthmore Library Peace Collection.

"Flogging American Women" from George Bourne, *Picture of Slavery in the United States of America* (Middletown, CT: Edwin Hunt, 1834)

CHAPTER SIX

"The Right to Possess All the Faculties That God Has Given": Possessive Individualism, Slave Women, and Abolitionist Thought

AMY DRU STANLEY

The problem of possessive individualism haunts the study of slavery and emancipation. It lies at the heart of the ambiguities of antislavery reform, distilling the moral contradictions involved in the transition from chattel slavery to free market relations that was envisioned by abolitionists. It marks the limits of an ideal of freedom defined by the negation of property in the persons of others. It lies as well at the heart of the perplexities of liberalism as a theory of woman's emancipation, distilling the contradiction between affirmations of universal human rights and assumptions of sexual inequality based on immutable physical difference.[1]

This essay reconsiders antislavery ideas of possessive individualism in light of the circumstances of enslaved and freed women. In a 1992 essay the British historian Catherine Hall concludes that abolitionists in England always saw slave emancipation in "gendered terms." "Freedom for men," she states, "was going to be different from freedom for women."

In formulating my thoughts on the historical complexities of ideology, morality, and hegemony, I am indebted to the ideas of David Brion Davis as expressed throughout his published works as well as in his unpublished comments on my work. I am grateful for the support of the Humanities Institute of the University of Chicago and for the insights of Craig Becker, Lorraine Daston, and Dirk Hartog.

[1] On the ideological ambiguities of abolitionism, see David Brion Davis, *The Problem of Slavery in the Age of Revolution, 1770–1823* (Ithaca, 1975); Thomas Bender, ed., *The Antislavery Debate: Capitalism and Abolitionism as a Problem in Historical Interpretation* (Berkeley, 1992). On liberalism and female emancipation, see Carole Pateman, *The Sexual Contract* (Stanford, 1988).

The nub of that gender difference was proprietorship, predicated on the cardinal right of property in the self. In the British abolitionist view, only freedmen would be entitled to be self-owning individuals. As Hall writes, "only men . . . could claim to own . . . property in this way."[2] This strain of thought was no less pronounced in the worldview of American abolitionists.

My intent is to analyze divergent strains of American antislavery thought—to show that the intellectual and political relationship between theories of sex difference and theories of emancipation rooted in possessive individualism was hardly as clear-cut as Hall suggests. The interpretation centers on antislavery rhetoric of the body. It focuses particularly on the complex ideological consequences of abolitionists' use of the symbol of the suffering female slave to condemn the human chattel's self-dispossession. I argue that this symbolism—as it was handled by black, female antislavery thinkers—worked to disrupt, rather than to validate, the conventional categories of sex difference customarily associated with liberal belief. The essay also addresses the rights consciousness of freedwomen, in which, I argue, the right of self-proprietorship was of no small importance. The glaring ideological limits, evasions, and contradictions of possessive individualism as an antislavery theory have been well plumbed by historians.[3] But very little is known about how that theory figured in black women's aspirations to freedom. Exploring this body of thought casts new light not only on the moral implications of possessive individualism but also on the meaning of freedom in the age of slavery and emancipation.

In an 1850 sermon on "The Rights and Duties of Masters," the South Carolina minister James Henley Thornwell, who was one of slavery's most formidable defenders, decried the abolitionist theory that the slave owner held property in the slave's limbs, organs, and soul. Arguing from the standpoint of moral philosophy, Thornwell insisted that no human personality, not even the slave's, could be owned by another or transformed

---

[2] Catherine Hall, "In the Name of Which Father?" *International Labor and Working-Class History* 41 (Spring 1992): 25.

[3] See Davis, *Slavery in the Age of Revolution;* Eric Foner, *Politics and Ideology in the Age of the Civil War* (New York, 1980), 57–76; Thomas C. Holt, *The Problem of Freedom: Race, Labor, and Politics in Jamaica and Britain, 1832–1938* (Baltimore, 1992); and Julie Saville, *The Work of Reconstruction: From Slave to Wage Laborer in South Carolina, 1860–1870* (New York, 1994). See also C. B. Macpherson, *The Political Theory of Possessive Individualism: Hobbes to Locke* (Oxford, 1962). On writing "black women into history"—in this case the intellectual history of possessive individualism—see Evelyn Brooks Higginbotham, "Beyond the Sound of Silence: Afro-American Women in History," *Gender & History* 1 (Spring 1989): 50–67.

into "an article of barter or exchange." The master was entitled merely to labor (however forcibly it might be extracted), not to the slave's person, which was understood as distinct from labor. Like the free laborer, therefore, the slave remained essentially self-owning—in Thornwell's words, the slave's body was "not mine, but his."[4]

Arguments such as Thornwell's cut to the heart of abolitionist faith. In the eyes of virtually all antislavery advocates, self-ownership constituted the taproot of freedom. For them, the defining sin of slavery was its denial of property in the self. As Theodore Dwight Weld proclaimed in 1838, "SELF-RIGHT is the *foundation* right—*the post in the middle,* to which all other rights are fastened." The primacy of the conviction so unambivalently announced by Weld is well documented in recent historical scholarship on abolitionism. Less well known is how widely this conviction was espoused beyond the circle of the movement's most famous spokespersons, uniting a constituency cleft not only by disagreements over principles and tactics but by differences of sex and race, as well. In 1838, for example, the Second National Anti-Slavery Convention of American Women declared that women had the authority to assert the core right of self-ownership on the slave's behalf, to ask whether a man's "bones and sinews shall be his own, or another's." Black abolitionists, born both free and slave, also adopted the rhetoric of possessive individualism. Free blacks considered self-entitlement an indispensable aspect of liberty, though recognizing that it hardly toppled the barriers of racial prejudice or economic privilege. Of the "colored men and women" in Jamaica, Nancy Prince, a free black born in Massachusetts, wrote, they were "determined to possess themselves, and to possess property besides." Fugitive slaves advocated the right of self-sovereignty with particular fervor borne perhaps from knowing its denial. The former slave Samuel Ringgold Ward made the point succinctly in an 1850 speech: "This is the question, Whether a man has a right to himself." To most abolitionists the conflict between fundamental rights and self-dispossession was a guiding assumption.[5]

[4] James H. Thornwell, *The Rights and the Duties of Masters: A Sermon Preached at the Dedication of a Church, Erected in Charleston, S.C., for the Benefit and Instruction of the Coloured Population* (Charleston, 1850). See also Eugene D. Genovese, *The Slaveholders' Dilemma: Freedom and Progress in Southern Conservative Thought, 1820–1860* (Columbia, S.C., 1992).

[5] See Jonathan A. Glickstein, "'Poverty Is Not Slavery': American Abolitionists and the Competitive Labor Market," in Lewis Perry and Michael Fellman, eds., *AntiSlavery Reconsidered: New Perspectives on the Abolitionists* (Baton Rouge, 1979), 195–218; Eric Foner, "The Meaning of Freedom in the Age of Emancipation," *Journal of American History* 81 (September 1994): 435–60; Foner, *Politics and Ideology,* 57–76; Ronald G. Walters, "The Boundaries of Abolitionism," in Perry and Fellman, *AntiSlavery Reconsidered,* 3–23. Quotations are from Walters, "Boundaries of Abolitionism," 9; Elizabeth Cady Stanton, Susan B. Anthony, and

In exalting the inviolable right of self-ownership, antislavery advocates did not simply argue on the abstract plane of natural law; they turned to the body's palpable torments and reasoned in sensual, empirical ways. They compiled excruciating evidence of physical suffering, which was meant to incite a visceral response and played upon the cult of feeling dominant in Victorian America. Abolitionists were by no means alone in deploying images of suffering bodies; the literature of antebellum humanitarian reform was stocked with them. Conceivably, even the most empathetic of white abolitionists might not have been able to exclude all traces of voyeurism from their representations of the suffering slave. For black abolitionists, however, these images may have represented not only the singular horrors of slavery but also the vulnerability to violence and coercion shared by all members of their race. Again and again, Frederick Douglass summoned his audience to feel the slave's pain as his back was "torn all to pieces . . . flesh . . . cut with the rugged lash . . . warm brine . . . poured into . . . bleeding wounds." In Douglass's metaphorical description of the destruction of slave marriages, the "hearts of husband and wife" were rent by slave dealers, "bleeding ligaments . . . which before constituted the twain one flesh." And the crimes of the domestic slave trade came alive through an inventory of marketable body parts. "At these auction-stands," stated William Wells Brown, a leader of the black abolitionist movement, "bones, muscles, sinews, blood and nerves, of human beings, are sold."[6]

The bodily images reflect how seriously abolitionists took the corporeal dimension of the formal right of self-proprietorship, which they regarded as the only secure guarantee of personal autonomy. The obverse of the slave whose person was dismembered, through punishment and as a commodity, was the autonomous individual whose body was inviolate. Freedom, as Douglass curtly defined it, was "appropriating my own body to my use." Here abolitionism differed from other contemporary expressions of liberal thought, in which the attributes of individualism characteristically

Matilda Joslyn Gage, eds., *History of Woman Suffrage*, 6 vols. (Rochester, N.Y., 1887), 1:339; *A Narrative of the Life and Travels of Mrs. Nancy Prince. Written by Herself*, 2d ed. (Boston, 1853), 49–50, reprinted in Henry Louis Gates Jr., ed., *Collected Black Women's Narratives* (New York, 1988); C. Peter Ripley et al., eds., *The Black Abolitionist Papers*, 5 vols. (Chapel Hill, 1985–1992), 4:50.

[6] Frederick Douglass to William Lloyd Garrison, *Liberator*, November 18, 1842, in *The Life and Writings of Frederick Douglass*, vol. 1, *Early Years, 1817–1849*, ed. Philip S. Foner (New York, 1950), 108–9; William Wells Brown, "The American Slave-Trade," *Liberty Bell* (1848): 235–36. See Karen Halttunen, "Humanitarianism and the Pornography of Pain in Anglo-American Culture," *American Historical Review* 100 (April 1995): 303–34; Elizabeth B. Clark, "'The Sacred Rights of the Weak': Pain, Sympathy, and the Culture of Individual Rights in Antebellum America," *Journal of American History* 82 (September 1995): 463–93; Elizabeth Alexander, "'Can You Be BLACK and Look at This?' Reading the Rodney King Video(s)," *Public Culture* 7 (1994): 77–94.

implied a renunciation of bodily experience and the irrationality and carnality long associated with matters of the flesh. Rather than being unintelligible in the terms of Enlightenment political theory, the body's claims were formulated by abolitionists in the classical, legal language of rights. To be sure, antislavery rendered freedom abstract by enshrining ownership of self, at the expense of an older republican emphasis on ownership of productive property. But by conceiving free individuals (in contrast to slaves) as unmistakably embodied bearers of rights, abolitionists rendered self-ownership concrete while suggesting a new moral and ideological framework for thinking about the vicissitudes of human bodies. By their lights, soul and body were inseverable; spirit could not be emancipated where flesh was bound.[7]

Above all, abolitionists dwelled on the circumstances of the enslaved female body. In their eyes, the two sexes suffered differently under slavery. They constantly stressed that the bondswoman alone endured sexual violence, as well as bloody punishment and the terror of the auction block. As one writer observed, only in regard to women chattel did the master's lust swell his sadism and greed, mingling "the effervescence of lewdness with the wantonness of ferocity."[8]

The flesh of female slaves thus took center stage in abolitionist propaganda. Within the antislavery repertoire of bodily metaphors, the predominant one was the scourged body of the bondswoman, an image that symbolized the slave's utter debasement. Even abolitionists left to private fantasy the master's rape of his female slave, but they did not flinch from depicting other abuses that were disturbingly full of sexual meaning. In his autobiography Frederick Douglass dwelled on the wounds of slave women, giving a detailed account of the punishment delivered by a jealous master on a female slave for daring to meet illicitly with her lover: "Esther's wrists

[7] Douglass to Garrison, 109. See Clark, "'Sacred Rights of the Weak'"; Leonore Davidoff, "'Adam Spoke First and Named the Orders of the World': Masculine and Feminine Domains in History and Sociology," in Helen Corr and Lynn Jamieson, eds., *Politics of Everyday Life: Continuity and Change in Work and Family* (London, 1990), 229–55; Karen Sanchez-Eppler, *Touching Liberty: Abolition, Feminism, and the Politics of the Body* (Berkeley, 1993), 1–49. For recent scholarship stressing the opposition between liberal theory and circumstances of human embodiment—an opposition that abolitionist rhetoric challenges—see Michel Foucault, *The History of Sexuality*, vol. 1, *An Introduction*, trans. Robert Hurley (New York, 1978), esp. 145–59; Pateman, *Sexual Contract*, esp. 189–234; Lauren Berlant, "National Brands/National Body: *Imitation of Life*," in Bruce Robbins, ed., *The Phantom Public Sphere* (Minneapolis, 1993), 176–79.

[8] George Bourne, *Slavery Illustrated in Its Effects upon Woman and Domestic Society* (1837; Freeport, N.Y., 1972), 59. On female slaves, see Jacqueline Jones, *Labor of Love, Labor of Sorrow: Black Women, Work, and the Family from Slavery to the Present* (New York, 1985); Deborah Gray White, *Ar'n't I a Woman? Female Slaves in the Plantation South* (New York, 1985); Elizabeth Fox-Genovese, *Within the Plantation Household: Black and White Women of the Old South* (Chapel Hill, 1988).

were firmly tied. . . . Her back and shoulders were bare to the waist. Behind her stood old master, with cowskin in hand, preparing his barbarous work with all manner of harsh, coarse, and tantalizing epithets. The screams of his victim were most piercing. He was cruelly deliberate, and protracted the torture, as one who was delighted with the scene." Douglass recalled that he was first aroused to slavery's wickedness as a young boy, watching the whipping of his own cousin: "Her neck and shoulders were covered with scars . . . her face literally covered with blood."[9]

In accounts tinged with eroticism, abolitionists evoked a corporeal slave economy that was diametrically opposed to the sexual order of free society, in which female purity was valued as a priceless possession. Witness after witness divulged the slave masters' "'habit not only of stripping their female slaves of their clothing . . . but of subjecting their naked persons to the most minute and revolting inspection.'" Horror at such lewdly intimate practices of calculating profit drew together a diverse antislavery following—black and white, male and female, those born both slave and free. Abolitionists joined in describing scenes that were all but pornographic, lingering particularly over the unclothed body of the female slave. Routinely, they testified, she was put up for exhibition as a commodity, entirely naked. In "thrilling tones" the antislavery lecturer Sarah Parker Remond told of the display she had escaped as a Yankee-born, free black: "In the open market place women are exposed for sale—their persons are not always covered." The former slave Louisa Picquet spoke from more personal experience, recounting the procedure of her own sale at a public auction: "whoever want to buy come and examine, and ask you whole lot of questions. They began to take the clothes off of me." According to Thomas Wentworth Higginson, when a female slave was for sale, slave traders bid buyers to "*strip her naked and examine every inch of her.*"[10]

---

[9] Frederick Douglass, *My Bondage and My Freedom* (1855; New York, 1969), 87, 82. See also Jean Fagan Yellin, *Women and Sisters: The Antislavery Feminists in American Culture* (New Haven, 1989), 71–89; Margaret M. R. Kellow, "The Divided Mind of Antislavery Feminism: Lydia Maria Child and the Construction of African American Womanhood," in Patricia Morton, ed., *Discovering the Women in Slavery: Emancipating Perspectives on the American Past* (Athens, Ga., 1996), 107–26; Hazel V. Carby, *Reconstructing Womanhood: The Emergence of the Afro-American Woman Novelist* (New York, 1987), 35; Hortense J. Spillers, "Mama's Baby, Papa's Maybe: An American Grammar Book," *diacritics* 17 (Summer 1987): 65–81; Ronald G. Walters, "The Erotic South: Civilization and Sexuality in American Abolitionism," *American Quarterly* 25 (1973): 177–210; Ann duCille, "The Occult of True Black Womanhood: Critical Demeanor and Black Feminist Studies," *Signs* 19 (Spring 1994): 592. Not only female abolitionists dwelled on sexual matters, as has been suggested in recent scholarly assessments; see, for example, Sanchez-Eppler, *Touching Liberty*, 22–23.

[10] Theodore Dwight Weld, *American Slavery As It Is: Testimony of a Thousand Witnesses* (New York, 1839), 154; Remond cited in Vron Ware, *Beyond the Pale: White Women, Racism, and His-*

Such representations were no less potent in abolitionist polemics against slavery as an immoral labor system and an illegitimate exercise of power. Jehiel Beman, a free black, recounted journeying for the first time in the South and being stricken nearly speechless by the sight of "my sisters toiling, pitchfork and rake in hand, under the scorching rays of the sun . . . but little on the body . . . my feelings were such as I cannot describe. I tried to raise my cries to Heaven, but in this I was interrupted, for the flowing tear forced its way down my care-worn cheek." Matter-of-factly, the Yankee reformer Samuel Gridley Howe sought to touch a nerve in northern audiences by describing a public whipping at a New Orleans slave prison: "There lay a black girl, flat upon her face on a board . . . a strap passed over the small of her back. . . . Below the strap she was entirely naked."[11]

On the bodies of female slaves, therefore, abolitionists saw most spectacularly branded the crimes of slavery that accrued from treating human beings as property to be bought and sold. Notably, just when blackface minstrel performances were fetishizing black bodies in a new form of commercial entertainment, antislavery reformers were calling public attention to the commodified bodies of female slaves for insurrectionary purposes.[12] Dishonored, stripped bare, the bondswoman literally embodied the denial of property in the self, which for abolitionists counted as the ultimate wrong. In antislavery literature she served as the symbol of the dispossessed self, someone without any rights, the paradigmatic chattel. Through her image abolitionists sanctified, by negation, the liberal ideal of self-ownership as the essence of freedom.

This method of reasoning had no precedent in the classical liberal thought of the seventeenth and eighteenth centuries from which American abolitionists derived central lineaments of their critique of slavery. Although contrasting freedom and bondage, Enlightenment writers certainly did not take the subjugation of slave women as a platform for asserting the fundamental rights of free men; it is doubtful that they even considered women within the category of autonomous, self-owning indi-

---

tory (London, 1992), 78; H. Mattison, *Louisa Picquet, The Octaroon: A Tale of Southern Slave Life, Or Inside Views of Southern Domestic Life* (New York, 1861), in Gates, *Collected Black Women's Narratives*, 16; Higginson cited in Charles K. Whipple, *The Family Relation, as Affected by Slavery* (Cincinnati, 1858), 15. See also Halttunen, "Pornography of Pain"; Darlene C. Hine and Kate Wittenstein, "Female Slave Resistance: The Economics of Sex," in Filomina C. Steady, ed., *Black Women Cross-Culturally* (Cambridge, Mass., 1981), 290–96.

[11] Jehiel C. Beman to Joshua Leavitt, August 10, 1844, in Ripley et al., *Black Abolitionist Papers*, 3:451; Samuel Gridley Howe, "Scene in a Slave Prison," *Liberty Bell* (1843): 177.

[12] On the centrality of the black male body and sexuality in minstrelsy, see Eric Lott, *Love and Theft: Blackface Minstrelsy and the American Working Class* (New York, 1993), 111–22. For a differing interpretation, see David R. Roediger, *The Wages of Whiteness: Race and the Making of the American Working Class* (New York, 1991), 115–31, esp. 121–22.

viduals.[13] For abolitionists, however, there was obvious utility in attacking the slave system on behalf of the female sex; indeed, diverse battles had long been rhetorically waged in the name of violated womanhood.

But for antislavery thinkers to anchor visions of freedom in the negative symbolism of the bondswoman's body was something new, and the imagery was full of ambiguities. According to reigning cultural beliefs, the body of a black woman exemplified both degenerate female sexuality and the alleged natural inferiority of her race. Yet this abject icon became central to an antislavery politics of human emancipation. Since ancient times the idea of personal freedom had entailed the right to an inviolate body—but only for men. By defining freedom through the negative example of the female slave's physical subjection, abolitionists opened to question the right of women to own themselves. Thus the eroticized symbolism of antislavery held the potential to challenge the categories of sex difference embedded in classical liberalism and Victorian scientific theory as well as in older intellectual traditions.[14]

For most abolitionists that was hardly the intended outcome of their outcry against slavery. Virtually all of them foresaw emancipation as transforming chattels into self-proprietors: "righting the slave—restoring him to himself." But they differed over whether this form of deliverance would abolish distinctions based on sex as well as on race. At stake were opposing visions not only of possessive individualism but of the relationship between freedom and marriage.[15]

[13] See Amy Dru Stanley, *From Bondage to Contract: Wage Labor, Marriage, and the Market in the Age of Slave Emancipation* (New York, forthcoming), chap. 1; Pateman, *Sexual Contract*.

[14] Recent scholarship suggests that emphasis on the corporeal dimensions of individual sovereignty was newly fashioned in the nineteenth century by antislavery feminists; see Sanchez-Eppler, *Touching Liberty*, 1–21; Ellen Carol DuBois, "Outgrowing the Compact of the Fathers: Equal Rights, Woman Suffrage, and the United States Constitution, 1820–1878," *Journal of American History* 74 (December 1987): 856; Foner, "Meaning of Freedom," 450; and Elizabeth B. Clark, "Self-Ownership and the Political Theory of Elizabeth Cady Stanton," *Connecticut Law Review* 21 (1989): 905–41. In fact, this idea originated among male political thinkers in ancient Greece; see David M. Halperin, "The Democratic Body: Prostitution and Citizenship in Classical Athens," *differences* 2 (1990): 1–28. On age-old corporeal rationales for female subjection, see Lorraine Daston, "The Naturalized Female Intellect," *Science in Context* 2 (1992): 209–35. On conventional constructions of the black, female body, see Sander Gilman, "Black Bodies, White Bodies: Toward an Iconography of Female Sexuality in Late Nineteenth-Century Art, Medicine, and Literature," in Henry Louis Gates Jr., ed., *"Race," Writing, and Difference* (Chicago, 1986), 223–61; and Londa Schiebinger, *Nature's Body: Gender in the Making of Modern Science* (Boston, 1993), 115–83. On the ambiguity of abolitionist iconography of the chained female slave, see Yellin, *Women and Sisters*.

[15] *The Antislavery Argument*, ed. William H. Pease and Jane H. Pease (New York, 1965), 68. Recent studies, focusing on the late nineteenth and twentieth centuries, highlight the profound and complex ideological significance of marriage in the tradition of antislavery and African American women's writing; see Ann duCille, *The Coupling Convention: Sex, Text, and*

The dominant abolitionist position was that slave emancipation would convert freedmen alone into sovereign, self-owning individuals. Property in women would simply be conveyed from slaveholders to husbands. This conception recapitulated the gender rules of classical liberal theory, which defined men as masters of the household with proprietary rights to their dependent wives. Upon the abolition of the slave master's "prior right," the former bondsman would gain the birthright of all free men: title not only to himself but to his wife—to her person, labor, and sexuality. In an argument inconsistent with his commitment to women's rights and his opposition to restrictive gender distinctions, William Lloyd Garrison affirmed the sovereignty of husbands as a fundamental element of freedom. The freedman, he declared unequivocally, would be "master of his own person, of his wife." As masters at home, former bondsmen could lay claim to the chastity of black women violated under slavery.[16]

So entrenched, so authoritative, was this definition of freedom that even leading female abolitionists who condemned patriarchal institutions employed its terms. In her 1836 *Appeal to the Christian Women of the South*, Angelina Grimké asserted the right of free women to combat slavery but rather contradictorily set forth only the manhood rights annulled by slavery. Slavery, she argued, "is a violation of the natural order of things." It *"robs the slave of all his rights* as a *man"*: slaves were "robbed of wages, wives, children." By the order of nature, therefore, the freedman's property in his wife would be as irrevocable as in his wages, while the freedwoman would become entitled to her husband's protection—a reciprocity of marriage rights denied to slaves. For the freedwoman, emancipation would lie not in rights of individual ownership but rather in coverture—what one antislavery writer termed *"woman's grand shield,* MATRIMONY."[17] Thus would freedom represent slavery's antithesis, as interpreted by the binary laws of gender.

But this was not the only abolitionist construction of the freedom entailed in "righting the slave" through restoring ownership of the self. A di-

Tradition in Black Women's Fiction (Oxford, 1993); Claudia Tate, *Domestic Allegories of Political Desire: The Black Heroine's Text at the Turn of the Century* (New York, 1992); and Hazel Carby, "'On the Threshold of Woman's Era': Lynching, Empire, and Sexuality in Black Feminist Theory," in Gates, *"Race," Writing, and Difference,* 315.

[16] Bourne, *Slavery Illustrated,* 61, 121; *Liberator,* December 7, 1855. See also Stanley, *From Bondage to Contract,* chap. 1.

[17] Angelina E. Grimké, *Appeal to the Christian Women of the South* (New York, 1836), 24, 12; Bourne, *Slavery Illustrated,* 121. See also Kellow, "Divided Mind of Antislavery Feminism"; Pateman, *Sexual Contract;* Catherine Hall, *White, Male, and Middle Class: Explorations in Feminism and History* (New York, 1992), 205–54; Hall, "In the Name of Which Father?"; and Kristin Hoganson, "Garrisonian Abolitionists and the Rhetoric of Gender, 1850–1860," *American Quarterly* 45 (December 1993): 558–95.

vergent strain of antislavery thought made subversive use of the figure of the bondswoman and of appeals grounded in the body to voice women's claim to the rights of possessive individualism. Emancipation was prophesied in terms not of marriage bonds but of female self-ownership. Here, the symbolic power of the debased female body established the logic of personal sovereignty as a universal right, unqualified by sex difference. Even though this remained a recessive strain of abolitionism, it was not without highly articulate and influential exponents, particularly in the black antislavery community.

Foremost among them was Frances Ellen Watkins Harper, the most prominent black woman writer and orator of her generation. Contemporaries called her the "bronze muse" and recognized her as a "glorious speaker"—"one of the ablest advocates . . . of the slave." In an address to the annual meeting of the American Anti-Slavery Society in 1858, Harper set forth a heterodox vision of freedom. She invoked the accepted principle that the slave must be granted "the rights of a man." But she argued that the right of a man to himself must also belong to a woman.[18]

Eloquently fusing the rhetoric of possessive individualism with that of radical Christianity, Harper extended the scope of natural rights to guarantee women property in the self. She began by equating personal freedom with proprietary rights, as she pointed out that the "bondman . . . does not own the humblest joint that does the feeblest services . . . that the slave mother who clasps her child . . . does not own it by right of possession." She then veered off in more radical ways, as she spoke in the first person of her own individual rights. Although freeborn, she pictured herself as a fugitive slave brought to trial in the North. "To prove—what?" she demanded. "To prove whether I have a right to be a free woman or am rightfully the chattel of another; whether I have the right to possess all the faculties that God has given, or whether another has the right to buy and sell, exchange and barter that temple in which God enshrined my hu-

---

[18] Dorothy Sterling, ed., *We Are Your Sisters: Black Women in the Nineteenth Century* (New York, 1984), 160; William Still, *The Underground Rail Road: A Record of Facts, Authentic Narratives, Letters* (Philadelphia, 1872), 779, 158, and see also 758–61; Frances Smith Foster, ed., *A Brighter Coming Day: A Frances Ellen Watkins Harper Reader* (New York, 1990), 5; *National Anti-Slavery Standard*, May 22, 1858. See Carby, *Reconstructing Womanhood*, 62–94; Bert J. Loewenberg and Ruth Bogin, eds., *Black Women in Nineteenth-Century American Life: Their Words, Their Thoughts, Their Feelings* (University Park, Pa., 1976), 243–51; Shirley Yee, *Black Women Abolitionists: A Study in Activism, 1828–1860* (Knoxville, 1992), 112–35; Julie Winch, "'You Have Talents—Only Cultivate Them': Black Female Literary Societies and the Abolitionist Crusade," and Anne M. Boylan, "Benevolence and Antislavery Activity among African American Women in New York and Boston, 1820–1840," both in Jean Fagan Yellin and John C. Van Horne, eds., *The Abolitionist Sisterhood: Women's Political Culture in Antebellum America* (Ithaca, 1994), 101–18 and 119–37, respectively.

man soul."[19] Harper's vision of emancipation powerfully demonstrated the multivalence of the symbol of the female slave. For her, this symbol's antithesis was a freedwoman fully endowed with rights, whose body was as sacred as a holy shrine. Not only did her argument counterpose religious and market metaphors, it also joined soul and body, thereby controverting the racist association of black women with the body's most squalid habits and carnal passions. Simultaneously, it represented the freedwoman as a sovereign, self-owning individual, not as the object of her husband's property rights.

Harper herself did acquire a husband. But throughout her life she challenged the theory of marriage as a property relationship based on male dominion and female dependence. Her poems and fiction writing repeatedly portrayed women who, as wives, lost neither economic independence nor independence of spirit. In a short story published in 1859 she expressly criticized coverture in language echoing the attack on chattel slavery. Marriage should not "be a matter of bargain and sale," the heroine declares. But the villain regards it "as the title-deed that gave him possession of the woman."[20] For Harper, the husband's claim to property in his wife violated inalienable rights much as did the slave master's claim to his human chattels.

The pursuit of self-entitlement was also the central drama of Harriet Jacobs's slave narrative *Incidents in the Life of a Slave Girl, Written by Herself*, which was promoted by leaders of the abolition movement. Unlike Harper's work, however, Jacobs's story of her own passage from slavery to freedom directly confronted the problem of sexual property in women. For Jacobs, freedom entailed self-ownership of a clearly sexual character. As a slave she chose to take a white lover rather than submitting to her master's claims. Idealizing relations of voluntary exchange, insisting on bodily autonomy, she defended her desperate resort to illicit sexual relations as a matter of free contract. "It seems less degrading to give one's self, than to submit to compulsion," she wrote. "There is something akin to freedom in having a lover who has no control over you, except that which he gains by kindness

---

[19] *National Anti-Slavery Standard*, May 22, 1858.
[20] Frances Ellen Watkins [Harper], "The Two Offers," *Anglo-African Magazine*, September/October 1859, 288, 290. By Harper, see, for example, *Sketches of Southern Life* (Philadelphia, 1890), 12–15, 19, 21; "John and Jacob—a Dialogue on Woman's Rights," in Foster, *Brighter Coming Day*, 240–42; and *Iola Leroy; or, Shadows Uplifted* (1893, 2d ed.; Boston, 1987), 154–55, 172–73, 178, 205, 210, 242, 277. See also Carby, *Reconstructing Womanhood*, 79–80; Frances Smith Foster, *Written by Herself: Literary Production by African American Women, 1746–1892* (Bloomington, Ind., 1993), 88–93, 183–86; duCille, *Coupling Convention*, 3–12, 32–34, 44–47; Tate, *Domestic Allegories*, 147–49, 169–71; Barbara Christian, *Black Women Novelists: The Development of a Tradition, 1892–1976* (Westport, 1980), 3–29; and Still, *Underground Rail Road*, 755–80.

and attachment." Jacobs refused to recognize herself as property, even to the extent of having her freedom bought (though eventually it was) against her will. For she explained that the more she became used to the values of free society, the more intolerable she found even the most benevolent owner, implying that genuine freedom meant owning herself. "The more my mind had become enlightened, the more difficult it was for me to consider myself an article of property. . . . Being sold from one owner to another seemed too much like slavery." Jacobs did not directly protest the proprietary character of marriage. But, contrary to the prevailing view, she hardly assumed that the slaveholder's sexual rights should rightfully pass to a husband. Nor did she see marriage and freedom as one and the same. Rather, she counterposed them in a way suggesting their asymmetries, declaring at her narrative's close, "my story ends with freedom; not in the usual way, with marriage." Jacobs became a freedwoman, but not a wife.[21]

Marriage had no place either in the contrast between freedom and slavery that was formulated by Sarah Parker Remond, a popular abolitionist lecturer in both England and America. In her reworking of standard abolitionist themes, the description of the sexual abuse of female slaves culminated in an affirmation of women's rights as autonomous, propertied individuals. Addressing a London audience in 1859, she put the plight of slave women at the center of her appeal. As a British antislavery newspaper reported, she spoke as the representative of her own race but also "pleaded especially on behalf of her own sex." Like other abolitionists, she began by explaining that words failed to express the unique suffering of women on southern plantations: "the unspeakable horrors," the "depth of the infamy into which they were plunged by the cruelty and licentiousness of their brutal masters."[22]

But the argument Remond went on to develop broke with formulaic expressions. She favorably compared the situation of poor English needlewomen with the plight of American slaves. Evoking the misery of seamstresses made famous in Thomas Hood's poem "Song of the Shirt," she acknowledged "the trials and toils of the women of England—how, in the

[21] Harriet A. Jacobs, *Incidents in the Life of a Slave Girl, Written by Herself,* ed. Jean Fagan Yellin (Cambridge, Mass., 1987), 55, 199, 201. On the subversive quality of Jacobs's narrative, see Carby, *Reconstructing Womanhood,* 36–61; Foster, *Written by Herself,* 95–116; duCille, *Coupling Convention,* 4–5; Yellin, *Women and Sisters,* 87–96; Beth Maclay Doriani, "Black Womanhood in Nineteenth-Century America: Subversion and Self-Construction in Two Women's Autobiographies," *American Quarterly* 43 (June 1991): 199–222; and Sanchez-Eppler, *Touching Liberty,* 83–104. For an alternative interpretation, see Fox-Genovese, *Plantation Household,* 375–76.

[22] "Lectures on American Slavery," *Anti-Slavery Reporter,* July 1, 1859. See also Clare Midgley, *Women against Slavery: The British Campaigns, 1780–1870* (London, 1992), 143–45.

language of Hood, they were made to 'Stitch, stitch, stitch,' till weariness and exhaustion overtook them." This was a common ploy of Remond's fellow Garrisonians: granting the degradation of wage laborers, only to assert their absolute elevation above chattel slaves. Even the worst-off hireling, went the usual argument, was a free man with a right to his wages and to own himself. But in speaking on women's behalf, Remond altered the sex of the figures contrasted in this model of slavery and freedom—a change that radically transformed the antislavery tribute to possessive individualism. With regard to the needlewomen, she declared, "But there was this immeasurable difference between their condition and that of the slave-woman, that their persons were free and their progeny their own, while the slave-woman was the victim of the heartless lust of her master, and the children whom she bore were his property."[23] In Remond's exposition, the theory of self-ownership—freedom of one's person—did not only embrace women, it took on an explicitly sexual content. For her, the heart of the difference between slavery and freedom was not property in the laboring body but property in the sexual body. Children, not wages, were the fruits of the body's toil.

It is noteworthy that Remond contended that the progeny of free women were "their own." Her argument circumvented the claims of marriage, treating the rules of coverture as a dead letter, depicting free women's rights as greater than they actually were. She did not mention either the duties or rights of a husband or a father. Nor did she see female chastity as an emblem of male honor. Rather, the needlewomen owned in themselves—fee simple—the same property possessed by slave masters in their women chattel. As Remond proclaimed, "their persons were free and their progeny their own," in contrast to the female slave who was the "victim of the heartless lust of her master" and whose children were "his property."[24] For Remond, free women's title to their children arose from the still more basic right of bodily freedom that was understood to hinge on self-ownership. Thus her conception of personal autonomy was stamped with classical liberal doctrines of individual proprietorship. But in juxtaposing these doctrines to the antithetical symbol of the female slave, Remond constructed a theory of women's emancipation that subverted the very tradition of liberal individualism to which it was heir.

In recent historical scholarship the theory of female self-ownership has most commonly been identified with feminist reformers who were

---

[23] "Lectures on American Slavery." See Stanley, *From Bondage to Contract*, chap. 1; Foner, *Politics and Ideology*, 57–76; and Glickstein, "'Poverty Is Not Slavery.'"

[24] "Lectures on American Slavery."

allied with abolitionism but whose primary cause was the woman move-ment. It is well known that advocates of women's rights adopted antislav-ery rhetoric—pairing women with slaves, and marriage with bondage—and that they viewed self-entitlement as paramount. The "real question," as Lucy Stone wrote privately in 1856, was whether a wife had an "absolute right" to her "body, and its uses"—"Has woman a right to herself?" Stone confessed to being "not ready" to bring this momentous and sexually charged question before the public. But, in fact, it was already tacit in women's temperance reform and quite explicit in mounting feminist at-tacks on coverture, which as Elizabeth Cady Stanton said, designated the wife's "person . . . the property of another." And by the postbellum era, this question had come to dominate the politics of women's rights.[25]

But among the antislavery vanguard decades earlier, it was black women who most unequivocally asserted a woman's right to herself. Some of them had directly known the dominion of a slave master; most of them had never known dependence on a husband. Like other abolitionists, they as-sailed the subjection of female slaves and defended free women's liberty to speak on their behalf. Yet in their hands the symbol of the black woman came to represent not only the terrors of bondage but also the rights of freedom. Their black abolitionist brethren did not directly engage the question; nor did they expressly defend or disown the prevailing aboli-tionist theory of the freedman as his wife's master.[26] But in affirming the

[25] Lucy Stone to Susan B. Anthony, September 11, 1856, quoted in Blanche G. Hersh, *The Slavery of Sex: Feminist-Abolitionists in America* (Urbana, Ill., 1978), 66; Ellen Carol DuBois, ed., *Elizabeth Cady Stanton, Susan B. Anthony: Correspondence, Writings, Speeches* (New York, 1981), 48. See also Clark, "Self-Ownership and the Political Theory of Elizabeth Cady Stanton"; DuBois, "Outgrowing the Compact"; Ellen Carol DuBois, *Feminism and Suffrage: The Emergence of an Independent Women's Movement in America, 1848–1869* (Ithaca, 1978); Linda Gordon, *Woman's Body, Woman's Right: A Social History of Birth Control in America* (New York, 1976), esp. 95–115; and William Leach, *True Love and Perfect Union: The Feminist Reform of Sex and Society* (New York, 1980).

[26] On the individualist strains of black women's writing in the mid–nineteenth century, see Foster, *Written by Herself.* On black women's antislavery feminism, see Nell Irvin Painter, "Dif-ference, Slavery, and Memory: Sojourner Truth in Feminist Abolitionism," in Yellin and Van Horne, *Abolitionist Sisterhood,* 139–58; Nell Irvin Painter, *Sojourner Truth: A Life, a Symbol* (New York, 1996); Yee, *Black Women Abolitionists,* 136–54; Carby, *Reconstructing Womanhood;* and Yellin, *Women and Sisters,* 77–96. The position of black male abolitionists on the specific ques-tion of female self-sovereignty is hard to pin down. They identified the slave's lack of rights to his wife as one of slavery's chief wrongs, and scholars have documented the patriarchal views of free black men; see James O. Horton, "Freedom's Yoke: Gender Conventions among Antebellum Free Blacks," *Feminist Studies* 12 (Spring 1986): 51–76; bell hooks, *Ain't I a Woman: Black Women and Feminism* (Boston, 1981); Julie Winch, *Philadelphia's Black Elite: Ac-tivism, Accommodation, and the Struggle for Autonomy, 1787–1848* (Philadelphia, 1988), 86. But the sources do not show that black male abolitionists expressly proclaimed free men's pro-prietary rights to or dominion over their wives. Moreover, leading black male abolitionists, such as Frederick Douglass and Charles Lenox Remond, supported the women's rights move-ment; see Stanton, Anthony, and Gage, *History of Woman Suffrage,* 1:668, and Rosalyn Terborg-

right of the bondswoman to own herself—in disrupting any simple connection between marriage and freedom—black female thinkers recast the emancipatory potential of possessive individualism as a theory of slave liberation. It has recently been argued that the Western ideal of personal freedom emerged in ancient times from the longing of female slaves to negate their condition (since women first underwent mass enslavement) but that this ideal was rediscovered and appropriated by male thinkers. If so, then black female abolitionists could be said to have reclaimed their rightful intellectual legacy.[27]

To their way of thinking, the autonomous, self-owning freedwoman would not be fenced off from the interdependencies of social relationships. Instead, she would take her place as an equal member of a community of rights-bearing individuals. Her ties to her children were categorically affirmed, as a bond that was considered indispensable rather than contrary to personal autonomy, an extension of self-sovereignty claimed in the language of proprietorship. As the former slave Bethany Veney put it, in "my Northern home . . . I had the same right to myself that any other women had. No jailor could take me to prison, and sell me at auction to the highest bidder. My boy was my own, and no one could take him from me." However much feminists such as Stanton and Stone insisted that wife and husband must have equal legal rights to their children as well as to marital property, they were more inclined to imagine the essence of freedom in absolutely individual terms, as a solitary ideal. But a line of black female thinkers stretching from Remond to Anna Julia Cooper at the end of the nineteenth century did not conceptually sever property in the self from ownership of one's children. Like the rights consciousness of other subordinate groups, this creed of propertied individualism expressed a longing for both collective and personal emancipation, a release from the coercions of sex and race.[28]

Penn, "Black Male Perspectives on the Nineteenth-Century Woman," in Sharon Harley and Rosalyn Terborg-Penn, eds., *The Afro-American Woman: Struggles and Images* (Port Washington, N.Y., 1978), 28–42. Exceptional, even among the most radical of white male abolitionists, was the language used by Henry C. Wright, who stated that female slaves' bodies "belonged 'not to the women themselves, but to their masters,'" quoted in Hoganson, "Garrisonian Abolitionists," 571.

[27] See Orlando Patterson, *Freedom* (New York, 1991), esp. 1:xv, 50–63, 78, 106–132; Gerda Lerner, *The Creation of Patriarchy* (New York, 1986), 77–100.

[28] *The Narrative of Bethany Veney, a Slave Woman* (Worcester, 1889), in Gates, *Collected Black Women's Narratives*, 38. On Cooper, see Carby, *Reconstructing Womanhood*, 3. On Stanton and the solitary dimension of feminist possessive individualism, see "The Solitude of Self," in DuBois, *Elizabeth Cady Stanton, Susan B. Anthony*, 247–54; Clark, "Self-Ownership and the Political Theory of Elizabeth Cady Stanton"; Wai-chee Dimock, "Rightful Subjectivity," *Yale Journal of Criticism* 4 (1990): 25–51; Margit Stange, "Personal Property: Exchange Value and the Female Self in *The Awakening*," *Genders* 5 (Summer 1989): 106–19. For a critique of pos-

In no single figure was the merger of black abolitionism and feminism more famously embodied than in the fugitive slave and itinerant preacher Sojourner Truth. Indeed, so well known are her ideas about her rights, her body, and her womanhood that they would almost be clichés, were they not so historically important. Speaking to an Ohio women's rights convention in 1851, Truth announced that man was "in a tight place, the poor slave is on him, woman is coming on him." Flaunting the strength of her body to falsify assumptions about the natural incapacities of her sex and to justify "woman's rights," she said: "I have as much muscle as any man, and can do as much work as any man. I have plowed and reaped and chopped. . . . I can carry as much as any man, and can eat as much too." In the name of equal rights Truth reportedly exposed her body to public view, her arm in 1851 and then her breast in 1858. An ironic proof of her femininity, the display also parodied the slave auction.[29]

With respect to the intellectual tradition at issue here, Truth's importance lies not simply in the fact that she spoke about rights through her body or that she was taken by her contemporaries to personify black antislavery feminism. She embodied as well the process by which the antislavery ideas of free black women in the North were transmitted to former slaves in the postbellum South. Truth worked with former slaves as an agent of the National Freedmen's Relief Association, and she reported that she broadcast her beliefs to them. "I . . . go around among the Freedmens camps," she stated in 1864. "They are all *delighted* to hear me talk." Something she might have talked about was her apprehension that freedom

---

sessive individualism as isolating rights-holders from the larger political community, see Hendrik Hartog, "The Constitution of Aspiration and 'the Rights That Belong to Us All,'" *Journal of American History* 74 (December 1987): 1013–34. But see Eileen Boris, "Gender, Race, and Rights: Listening to Critical Race Theory," and Melinda Chateauvert, "Response," both in *Journal of Women's History* 6 (Summer 1994): 111–24 and 125–32, respectively; and Ellen Carol DuBois, "Taking the Law into Our Own Hands: *Bradwell, Minor,* and Suffrage Militance in the 1870s," in Nancy A. Hewitt and Suzanne Lebsock, eds., *Visible Women: New Essays in American Activism* (Urbana, Ill., 1993). It is beyond the scope of this essay to examine fully the differing feminist inflections of possessive individualism broached here, but I would caution that the distinction should not be pushed too far.

[29] Quotation from Nell Irvin Painter, "Representing Truth: Sojourner Truth's Knowing and Becoming Known," *Journal of American History* 81 (September 1994): 489. On the complexities of Truth's persona and body language and on conflicting accounts of her famed 1851 speech, see Painter, "Representing Truth"; Painter, "Difference, Slavery, and Memory," esp. 154–57; Carleton Mabee, *Sojourner Truth: Slave, Prophet, Legend* (New York, 1993); Painter, *Sojourner Truth,* 121–31, 164–78, 258–80. For another transcription of this speech, see Stanton, Anthony, and Gage, *History of Woman Suffrage,* 1:116. See also Erlene Stetson and Linda David, *Glorying in Tribulation: The Lifework of Sojourner Truth* (East Lansing, 1994); Paula Giddings, *Where and When I Enter: The Impact of Black Women on Race and Sex in America* (New York, 1984), 65–71; duCille, *Coupling Convention,* 34–35; and Yellin, *Women and Sisters,* 77–87, 96.

would remain unrealized: "colored men will be masters over the women, and it will be just as bad as it was before. . . . I want women to have their rights." Perhaps she reiterated the themes of her famous speech, themes she sounded again and again over the years. "If I have to answer for the deeds done in my body just as much as a man, I have a right to have just as much as a man. . . . You [men] . . . think, like a slave-holder, that you own us. . . . I have plead with all the force I had that the day might come that the colored people might own their soul and body. Well, the day has come, although it came through blood. . . . We are now trying for liberty that requires no blood—that women shall have their rights."[30] Precisely what Truth said in the freedmen's camps went unrecorded, but it is plausible that she spoke there, as elsewhere, on the bodily dimensions of individual rights.

In the wake of slave emancipation, scores of other black female abolitionists besides Truth acted as ambassadors of freedom, traveling south to work as teachers and missionaries among the former slaves. Along with Bibles, clothing, and spelling books, they undoubtedly dispensed their views on female emancipation.

Frances Ellen Watkins Harper crisscrossed the South between 1867 and 1871, giving public lectures to former slaves, staying in their cabins. "How busy I am," she wrote from South Carolina in May 1867. "Traveling, conversing, addressing day and Sunday-schools." In some ways her efforts resembled those of Elizabeth Cady Stanton, who traversed the country during the same years while campaigning for women's emancipation. Stanton met separately with small groups of white women to discuss marriage and sexual matters. Harper met alone with freedwomen, speaking out on the same issues. "Sometimes I speak twice a day," she wrote from rural Georgia. "Part of my lectures are given privately to women, and for them I never make any charge." These lectures expressed the complexities of her understanding of the link between freedom and marriage. On the one hand, Harper urged fidelity to marriage conventions as a mark of racial progress: "the colored man needs something more than a vote in his hand: he needs to know the value of home life; to rightly appreciate and value the marriage relation . . . to leave behind him the old shards and shells of slavery." But on the other hand, she taught that female subjection ran counter to a right valuing of marriage as a form of emancipation. "Part of the time I

[30] Sterling, *We Are Your Sisters,* 253; Stanton, Anthony, and Gage, *History of Woman Suffrage,* 2:193–94, 224–25. On the importance of body arguments in black women's thought, see also Elizabeth Alexander, "'We Must Be about Our Father's Business': Anna Julia Cooper and the In-Corporation of the Nineteenth-Century African-American Woman Intellectual," *Signs* 20 (Winter 1995): 336–56.

am preaching against men ill-treating their wives," she stated. "The condition of the women is not very enviable in some cases. They have had some of them a terribly hard time in Slavery, and their subjection has not ceased in freedom. . . . One man said of some women, that a man must leave them or whip them." By this time, Harper had attended women's rights conventions and doubtless aimed to promote freedwomen's sense of their personal autonomy. Hearing such talk, meeting apart from their menfolk, some freedwomen might well have reached a greater consciousness of their right to themselves, one antagonistic to the doctrine of male masterhood.[31]

More cryptic were the remarks of Charlotte Forten, a black abolitionist who went south to teach freedpeople on the South Carolina Sea Islands. On witnessing the marriage ceremonies of former slaves, she wrote in her diary she was "*truly* glad that the poor creatures are trying to live right and virtuous lives." But for herself, she confided in a later entry, "Think *I* sh'ld dread a funeral much less."[32] Was she thinking of the rule of coverture that rendered the wife dead in the eyes of the law? Perhaps her ambivalence (inadvertently) colored the perceptions of the former slaves she taught.

To suggest possible resonances between the ideas of reformers such as Forten, Harper, and Truth and the beliefs and activities of freedwomen is not to suppose that freedwomen were akin to blank tablets on which their Yankee sisters wrote their own worldview wholesale. Rather, the point is that in the shaping of freedwomen's complicated consciousness of their rights, one potent source may have been the encounter with female abolitionists, particularly of their own race, who were also apostles of feminism.[33]

That virtually no freedwomen possessed an education in classical liberal theory is obvious. Yet their views in some cases had much in common with liberal precepts. Based on evidence from the Freedmen's Bureau and other sources, it is plain that many freedwomen strove to control their own bodies, to possess their labor and its proceeds, and to enforce voluntary relations of exchange. Even as wives, within newfound bonds of marriage, many saw themselves, at some level, as autonomous individuals vested with rights of proprietorship. Mostly, as the legal documents attest, their renegade views were expressed by acts

[31] Still, *Underground Rail Road*, 767, 772, 770, 773, 777; Stanton, Anthony, and Gage, *History of Woman Suffrage*, 2:178, 182–83. See duCille, *Coupling Convention*, and Tate, *Domestic Allegories*.

[32] Ray Allen Billington, ed., *The Journal of Charlotte Forten: A Free Negro in the Slave Era* (London, 1953), 153, 207.

[33] See Patricia Hill Collins, "The Social Construction of Black Feminist Thought," *Signs* 14 (Summer 1989): 750.

rather than by words, and by negations of their husbands' claims rather than by explicit assertions of positive individual rights. In the early years of emancipation freedwomen participated actively in the mass politics of black communities, a form of public franchise that may have highlighted the private contradictions of wifely submission. Seeking to exercise the contract rights denied by coverture, some freedwomen opposed their husbands signing labor agreements for them and claimed title to their own wages. Others invoked their legal rights within the marriage relation, suing their husbands to oblige them to fulfill their half of the domestic bargain. Still others had their husbands arrested for whipping them. Although they closely embraced the kin ties forged in slavery, not all freedwomen willingly reckoned themselves tokens of their menfolk's emancipation. For them, no less than for black men, freedom heightened—or perhaps generated—a sense of their rights as both individuals and family members.[34]

Paradoxically, at the very moment many freedmen were collectively invalidating self-ownership as a sufficient material basis for freedom, some of their wives were claiming a right to own themselves. Thus a Georgia freedman in an 1876 divorce petition alleged that his wife had defiantly declared, "I am my own woman and will do as I please." Perhaps this freedwoman translated unarticulated notions of bodily integrity and personal autonomy into a full-fledged assertion of self-entitlement. Or perhaps this was a stock complaint, formulaically invoked by husbands against wives, for the same phrase appeared in another divorce suit filed the same year in the same county.[35] Even if a formula, the complaint suggests that freedwomen transgressed by staking a claim to property in the self.

Abolitionism's recessive strain thus lived on in the minds of some freedwomen, though the extent to which its antebellum exponents planted it

[34] See Eric Foner, *Reconstruction: America's Unfinished Revolution, 1863–1867* (New York, 1988), 88; Elsa Barkley Brown, "Negotiating and Transforming the Public Sphere: African American Political Life in the Transition from Slavery to Freedom," *Public Culture* 7 (1994): 107–46; Stanley, *From Bondage to Contract,* chap. 1; Sara Rapport, "The Freedmen's Bureau as a Legal Agent for Black Men and Women in Georgia: 1865–1868," *Georgia Historical Quarterly* 73 (Spring 1989): 39–41; Victoria Bynum, "Reshaping the Bonds of Womanhood: Divorce in Reconstruction North Carolina," in Catherine Clinton and Nina Silber, eds., *Divided Houses: Gender and the Civil War* (New York, 1992), 330–32.

[35] Quotation appears in Bynum, "Reshaping the Bonds of Womanhood," 330, and in Laura F. Edwards, "Sexual Violence, Gender, Reconstruction, and the Extension of Patriarchy in Granville County, North Carolina," *North Carolina Historical Review* 68 (July 1991): 255. For contending visions of the contours of freedom, see Saville, *Work of Reconstruction;* Foner, "Meaning of Freedom"; Foner, *Reconstruction;* Leon F. Litwack, *Been in the Storm So Long: The Aftermath of Slavery* (New York, 1979); and William S. McFeely, *Yankee Stepfather: General O. O. Howard and the Freedmen* (New Haven, 1968).

there is admittedly unclear. For those who espoused this logic, freedom could mean nothing less than purging sex difference from the ascendant abolitionist ideal of the emancipated slave: "He is free, and his own master, and can ask for no more."[36]

Recognizing these currents of thought runs against the grain of recent scholarship, for historians have made much of black women's familial image of freedom and the collective nature of their values, at the expense of insight into their desires as possessive individuals. Black women (freedwomen especially), it is said, did not subscribe to modern notions of personal autonomy. Their rights claims were not animated by the self-interested tenets of liberal political economy or by the radical individualism of evangelical Christianity. Yet the evidence suggests otherwise. However intensely black women in the nineteenth century valued kinship bonds and strove for collective emancipation, they were also keenly aware of their rights as individuals—rights premised on possession of the self.[37]

To acknowledge this intellectual tradition is scarcely to provide an uncritical celebration of the liberal theory of possessive individualism, which historically has obscured and legitimated the unfreedoms of market relations—an issue I have addressed elsewhere. Rather, I have undertaken to explore why, at a critical historical juncture, that theory provided a language for black women's aspirations to freedom. Its appeal derived not least from its negation of the domestic bonds that constituted chattel slavery and marriage as similar, though not identical, property relationships: its negation of the status of being dispossessed. As the legal theorist Patricia Williams, herself the descendant of slaves, has written of individualistic rights rhetoric: "Where . . . one's experience is rooted . . . in *being* illegitimate, in being raped, and in the fear of being murdered, then the black adherence to a scheme of negative rights—to the self, to the sanctity of one's personal boundaries—makes sense."[38] The intellectual history studied here constitutes a crucial moment in the forging of that adherence.

---

[36] Statement of William Jay, quoted in Foner, *Politics and Ideology,* 64.

[37] For the prevailing scholarly view that black women in nineteenth-century America did not conceptualize their freedom or rights in terms of individual autonomy, see, for example, Jones, *Labor of Love,* 58; Fox-Genovese, *Plantation Household,* 372–96; Brown, "Negotiating and Transforming the Public Sphere," esp. 124–25; Edwards, "Sexual Violence, Gender"; and Laura F. Edwards, *Gendered Strife and Confusion: The Political Culture of Reconstruction* (Urbana, Ill., 1997), 146, 182, 211. However, the ambition of self-proprietorship is intimately linked to what Hazel Carby has termed the desire at the turn of the century for "the uncolonized black female body"; see her "'On the Threshold,'" 315.

[38] Patricia Williams, "Alchemical Notes: Reconstructing Ideals from Deconstructed Rights," *Harvard Civil Rights-Civil Liberties Law Review* 22 (1987): 417. See Stanley, *From Bondage to Contract,* esp. chap. 2. On the debate among legal scholars over rights talk, see Hartog, "The Constitution of Aspiration"; Peter Gabel, "The Phenomenology of Rights-Consciousness and the Pact of the Withdrawn Selves," *Texas Law Review* 62 (May 1984): 1563–99; Mark Tushnet, "An Essay on Rights," *Texas Law Review* 62 (May 1984): 1363–1403; Frances

That the ethos of self-ownership is inextricably connected to a cast of mind that reduces all human experience to the calculus of buying and selling remains indisputable. Admittedly, difficulty lies in squaring the market's abstract values with the antislavery symbolism of bleeding, naked, black, female bodies. But to lose sight of the contradictory moral implications of the ideal of possessive individualism is to render its hegemony inexplicable. If the ideal of self-ownership had not carried such emancipatory power, it could not have disguised the existing coercions of free society.

Olsen, "Statutory Rape: A Feminist Critique of Rights," *Texas Law Review* 62 (May 1984): 387–432; Mark Tushnet, "Rights: An Essay in Informal Political Theory," *Politics and Society* 17 (1989): 403–451; and Martha Minow, *Making All the Difference: Inclusion, Exclusion, and American Law* (Ithaca, 1990).

Headstone, Staunton National Cemetery, Staunton, Va. Photographed by Bill Humm.

CHAPTER SEVEN

Worrying about the Civil War

EDWARD L. AYERS

In 1995 the United States Post Office issued a stamp set commemorating the end of the Civil War; the set's motto was "Once Divided. Now Perforated." The stamps balanced carefully—Lee and Grant, Davis and Lincoln, Clara Barton and Phoebe Pember, Sherman and Jackson, the *Monitor* and the *Virginia,* Harriet Tubman and Mary Chesnut, Chancellorsville and Gettysburg. The banners across the top also gave equal time, describing the conflict both as the "Civil War" and the "War Between the States." At the same time the federal government sold that artfully poised historical document, however, an episode of *The Simpsons,* a popular animated satire of American life, conveyed a different kind of message. Apu, an industrious South Asian immigrant in the Simpsons' hometown of Springfield, U.S.A., has studied hard for his citizenship test. The final question on the oral quiz is, predictably, "What was the cause of the Civil War?" "Actually, there were numerous causes," begins Apu. "Aside from the obvious schism between the abolitionists and the anti-abolitionists, there were economic factors, both domestic and inter——." The official, clearly bored with such superfluous erudition, intones flatly, "Just say slavery." Apu eagerly concedes the point—"Slavery it is, sir"—and wins his citizenship.[1]

The Civil War has never been more popular. Soldiers on both sides of

---

[1] An instructive overview of other current uses of the war is Jim Cullen, *The Civil War in Popular Culture: A Reusable Past* (Washington, D.C., 1995). On *The Simpsons,* see the transcript for the episode "Much Apu about Nothing," written by David S. Cohen and directed by Susie Dietter, production code 3F20, original airdate in North America: May 5, 1996, capsule revision C:June 10, 1996, in "The Simpsons Archive" on the World Wide Web, http://www.snpp.com/.

the war receive reverential treatment from magazines that lovingly examine every facet of the war, from cavalry to cooking, reporting on battles as if they are late-breaking news. Reenactors gather at battlefields, getting the feel of heavy wool clothing on a suffocating August day, of a heavy rifle, stiff boots, and hardtack. The "Confederacy" finds no shortage of those willing to play the role of the gallant losers. Civil War encyclopedias, atlases, biographies, sweeping surveys, and minutely detailed volumes devoted to single days of battle fill the history sections at bookstores across America. The business sections of those bookstores often carry Donald T. Phillips's *Lincoln on Leadership: Executive Strategies for Tough Times,* in which Phillips proclaims that Lincoln steered the country through the war "with a naturalness and intuitiveness in leading people that was at least a century ahead of his time." Lincoln's lessons to today's executives include "Get Out of the Office and Circulate among the Troops" and "Keep Searching Until You Find Your 'Grant.'" For the Southern point of view, the businessperson can consult *From Battlefield to Boardroom: The Leadership Lessons of Robert E. Lee,* by Bil Holton, Ph.D.[2]

There is no animosity in any of these historical or practical interpretations of the Civil War. It is clear that the North fought for purposes entirely good—for Union and the end of slavery—but Confederate soldiers also win respect for their bravery, their devotion, and their struggle against long odds. They seem to have been playing historical roles for which they are not to blame. The reenactors, the books in stores, and the battlefield tours generally avoid talking about the cause of the war, focusing instead on the common bravery and hardships of soldiers North and South. The war has become common property, with the treacherous parts helpfully roped off.

Michael Shaara's *The Killer Angels,* the most acclaimed fictional portrayal of the Civil War since *Gone with the Wind,* bears the major hallmarks of the current understanding of the war. Shaara's 1974 novel and the 1994 movie based on it, *Gettysburg,* view the conflict from the perspectives of men on both sides of the battle. We glimpse the anguish of Lee and Longstreet, the uncertainty and glory of Joshua Chamberlain, and the humanity of all involved. The moral centerpiece of both the book and the film is an Irish-American Union sergeant's soliloquy on freedom and dignity. The book, like other representations of the Civil War in recent decades, combines a respect for the warriors on both sides with an idealistic vision of the war's purpose.[3]

[2] Donald T. Phillips, *Lincoln on Leadership: Executive Strategies for Tough Times* (New York, 1992), 173. First published in 1992 and now in its eighth printing, the book bears rows of endorsements from prominent political figures, coaches, and corporate leaders. Bil Holton, *From Battlefield to Boardroom: The Leadership Lessons of Robert E. Lee* (Novato, Calif., 1995).

[3] Michael Shaara, *The Killer Angels* (1974; paperback ed., New York, 1975); *Gettysburg,* a film directed by Ronald F. Maxwell, 1994.

The paperback edition of *The Killer Angels* carries the imprimatur of the two leading interpreters of the war. James McPherson calls Shaara's book his "favorite historical novel," and Ken Burns tells readers that the book changed his life: "I had never visited Gettysburg, knew almost nothing about that battle before I read the book, but here it all came alive." A work on the Civil War could not have more influential endorsements. McPherson's *Battle Cry of Freedom* and Burns's television series *The Civil War* have shaped the ways millions of Americans understand the central event in their nation's history. In 1988, McPherson's history of the Civil War won the Pulitzer Prize and remained ensconced for months at the top of the bestseller list. In 1991, Burns's nine-part series attracted the largest audience ever to watch public television in the United States and became a nationwide media event. Both men have gained growing audiences over the years, their works becoming fixtures in the nation's libraries and classrooms. McPherson has produced a steady stream of books and essays since *Battle Cry of Freedom,* amplifying his basic tenets about the war's cause and conduct. Episodes of Burns's film are often the first sustained exposure young Americans have to the Civil War and a major influence on those who have already finished their schooling. Many people have purchased their own copies of the tapes so they can watch them whenever they wish.[4]

Different media create different emphases, of course. Burns assembled an impressive team of academic historians to guide him, including McPherson, yet Burns is most interested in uncovering and recovering the feelings of the past. He offers an impressionistic account of the war, full of quotation, image, and sound. He focuses on the battlefields but uses private expressions of love and grief to powerful effect. McPherson, by contrast, is a professional historian, attuned to the debates, standards, and innovations of the academy. Like Burns, McPherson is most interested in the battles, but he connects the military conflict to politics and the social structures of the North and the South more rigorously than his counterpart.

Despite their different purposes and means, however, the interpretations of Burns and McPherson share a common perspective. They both dramatize the ways that antislavery opinion, progress, war, and national identity intertwined at the time of the Civil War so that each element became inseparable from the others. Slavery stands as the antithesis of prog-

[4] James M. McPherson, *Battle Cry of Freedom: The Civil War Era* (New York, 1988); *The Civil War,* a nine-part documentary film directed by Ken Burns and shown by the Public Broadcasting System in 1990. McPherson has deepened and extended his interpretation in several books since *Battle Cry of Freedom,* including *Abraham Lincoln and the Second American Revolution* (New York, 1991), *What They Fought For, 1861–1865* (Baton Rouge, 1994), *Drawn with the Sword: Reflections on the American Civil War* (New York, 1996), and *For Cause and Comrades: Why Men Fought in the Civil War* (New York, 1997). McPherson's earlier overview of the era was called *Ordeal by Fire: The Civil War and Reconstruction* (New York, 1982).

ress, shattering nation and creating war; war is the means by which antislavery feeling spreads and deepens; the turn against slavery during the
war re-creates national identity; the new nation is freed for a more fully
shared kind of progress. This story has become common sense to Americans: emancipation, war, nation, and progress all seem part of one story,
the same story.

Both Burns and McPherson make sophisticated use of their preferred
medium. Burns explains the coming of the war in just a few minutes of his
long film, introducing the cotton gin and portraying the resulting conflicts
as the inevitable result of the growth of slavery. Familiar faces and events
flash past, from William Lloyd Garrison to Frederick Douglass to Harriet
Beecher Stowe to Abraham Lincoln, from Bleeding Kansas to Harpers
Ferry to Fort Sumter. McPherson, by contrast, spends hundreds of pages
explaining the origins of the war. Like Burns, McPherson uses quotation
extensively and effectively; he lets the words of his protagonists carry his
story. Persuasive Northern speakers come in at key points to make the liberal and nationalist statements attractive to McPherson.

White Northerners, white Southerners, and black Americans all grow
morally during the war that Burns and McPherson portray. The white North
comes truly to abhor slavery; white Southerners recognize the limits of
their power and the meaning of full nationhood; black Americans gain not
only freedom but also heightened dignity when they take up arms for their
freedom. Abraham Lincoln embodies this moral growth of his nation, as
the slaughter on the battlefield gradually persuades the cautious president
that the war must become a war against slavery. Lincoln's transformation
represents that of the North as a whole, and his assassination brings the
story to its end.[5]

Burns and McPherson hold up the story of the Civil War as an inspiration to Americans of today. As Burns puts it, "If there's one political theme
in this film, it's this: The Civil War is a chronicle of making permanent
that which was promised, but not delivered, in the Declaration of Independence and the Constitution." McPherson, long known as a historian of
abolitionism, stresses that the war was about freedom in its many manifestations. "Lincoln led the country through the worst of times to a triumph
that left America stronger, more free, and more democratic," he has written recently. "And that offers a lesson not only for Americans but also for
'the whole family of man.'" These historians celebrate the outcome of a

[5] As a recent survey observes, Lincoln "now enjoys extremely high approval-ratings"; older
"doubts and reservations seem to have evaporated." Michael Perman, "Lincoln, the Civil War,
and the New Approval Ratings," *American Studies* 36 (Spring 1995): 131–34. Penetrating
comments on McPherson's interpretation appear in Michael Johnson, "Battle Cry of Freedom?" *Reviews in American History* 17 (June 1989): 214–18, and in Jon L. Wakelyn's review
of *Battle Cry of Freedom* in *Civil War History* 34 (December 1988): 344–47.

war that put the country on the long path to the civil rights movement and greater equality. Their powerful histories tell a story of freedom emerging through the trial of war, of a great nation becoming greater through suffering.[6]

Despite the harrowing picture of war in Burns's film, where severed limbs and bleaching bones appear frequently and memorably, his North and South are engaged in a collaborative effort. "Between 1861 and 1865, Americans made war on each other and killed each other in great numbers," Burns's narrator David McCullough tells viewers early in the film, "if only to become the kind of country that could no longer conceive of how that was possible." The beginning and the end of the war fuse into one; the soldiers kill each other for the common purpose of discovering the depth and the nature of their nationalism. The final scene in Burns's epic shows footage from 1913, when aging veterans of Gettysburg return to the scenes of carnage to stroll peacefully together through fields now regrown green and alive. McPherson has less of a reconciliationist bent than Burns, but he uses the first page of his book to emphasize that versions of the song "The Battle Cry of Freedom" were popular in both the North and the South. His title is nonpartisan.[7]

Burns and McPherson work hard to protect the memory of the war. They defend its integrity from the evasions of those who insist that the South fought for something other than slavery; they guard it from those who emphasize the North's narrow self-interest; they protect it from the many historians who hold military history in disdain; they shield it from cynics on both the right and the left. For Burns and McPherson, the war's sacrifices must not be wasted; the people of the United States must not become unaware and unappreciative of what was at stake and what was won. McPherson continually reminds Americans, as his recent book titles put it, "what they fought for," that "we cannot escape history," that Lincoln led "the second American Revolution," and that soldiers fought "for cause and comrades." He has spearheaded efforts to protect battlefields, "sacred soil," from development.

McPherson is so vigilant because he recognizes that this interpretation has become established only after long struggle. The elegance and directness with which he and Burns tell their stories can lead us to forget what a complicated event the Civil War was. It was, after all, simultaneously a

---

[6] Burns's press kit for *The Civil War*, quoted in Cullen, *Civil War in Popular Culture*, 11; James M. McPherson, ed., *"We Cannot Escape History": Lincoln and the Last Best Hope of Earth* (Urbana, Ill., 1995), 12.

[7] Geoffrey C. Ward, with Ric Burns and Ken Burns, *The Civil War: An Illustrated History* (New York, 1990), xix. For stimulating and divergent discussions of the issues raised by Burns's series, see Robert Brent Toplin, ed., *Ken Burns's "The Civil War": Historians Respond* (New York, 1996).

war among citizens and among states, a war fought by disciplined soldier-citizens and a war that continually threatened to spin out of anyone's control, a war whose opponents were driven by hatred and yet who quickly reconciled when it became convenient, a war in which slavery died at the hands of soldiers who often fought against slavery reluctantly and even then because slavery's destruction seemed the only practical way to win. The current interpretations contain these tensions in an overarching story of emergent freedom and reconciliation. While acknowledging the complicated decisions people faced, Burns and McPherson resolve them through narrative. White Northerners, including Lincoln, announce early on that the war is not about slavery, but the words do not disturb us because we know these people change their minds later on. White Southerners claim plausible support from the Constitution, but their arguments have little weight because they lost the war and thus their arguments. Black Americans denounce the war at first as irrelevant or worse, but we know they were, fortunately, mistaken.

So self-evident does the dominant interpretation seem that many Americans of today never suspect how hotly historians have contested these issues throughout much of the twentieth century. Although vestiges of older interpretations still crop up in people's vague recollections, no one has stepped forward in a very long time to offer a popularly accepted counterargument to the explanation codified in Burns and McPherson. Major American thinkers last offered strong dissent three decades ago, when Robert Penn Warren and Edmund Wilson expressed visions of the Civil War that now seem startling in their vehemence and skepticism. Wilson made audacious comparisons in his influential book *Patriotic Gore,* a survey of wartime writing. "All animals must prey on some form of life that they can capture, and all will eat as much as they can," Wilson dryly observed as he compared the North and the South to sea slugs he had seen in a Walt Disney documentary. Man is different only because he "has succeeded in cultivating enough of what he calls 'morality' and 'reason' to justify what he is doing in terms of what he calls 'virtue' and 'civilization.'" Abraham Lincoln, Wilson thought, should be grouped with other leaders who sought to build nations through force and appeal to transcendent meaning: Bismarck and Lenin.[8]

Robert Penn Warren offered a more generous, yet still critical, meditation in his book *The Legacy of the Civil War.* The war, Warren cautioned, had produced two dangerous habits of mind in Americans. For the South, it offered "the Great Alibi," the great excuse for everything that was wrong or lacking in the region. For the North, the war offered "the Treasury of Vir-

[8] Edmund Wilson, *Patriotic Gore: Studies in the Literature of the American Civil War* (New York, 1962), xv–xix.

tue," in which the war appeared as "a consciously undertaken crusade so full of righteousness that there is enough overplus stored in Heaven, like the deeds of the saints, to take care of all the small failings and oversights of the descendants of the crusaders, certainly unto the present generation." Warren, like Wilson, did not shun dramatic effect: it was tempting, he argued, for Americans to regard the war as "part of our divinely instituted success story, and to think, in some shadowy corner of the mind, of the dead at Gettysburg as a small price to pay for the development of a really satisfactory and cheap compact car with decent pick-up and road-holding capability."[9]

Wilson and Warren wrote during the one-hundredth anniversary of the war—"this absurd centennial," Wilson called it—when histories, plays, reenactments, products, and commemorations of all sorts proliferated. Wilson and Warren wrote to dampen the self-righteousness and materialism to which Americans inclined in those stressful years of the cold war. The two authors considered themselves voices in the wilderness, delivering jeremiads, for a once-powerful tradition of skepticism about the Civil War had crumbled and a new tradition of acceptance and celebration was rising in its place.[10]

The skeptical viewpoint had peaked decades earlier, in the 1920s and 1930s, when "revisionism" flourished. The "revisionists" challenged the comforting bargain put forward in the years before World War I by Southern journalists such as Henry Grady and scholars such as Woodrow Wilson. Without sacrificing any respect for the Lost Cause, the reconciliationist bargain admitted that secession had been a mistake and that the nation should never have been divided. It argued that emancipation had been a fortunate occurrence for the white South, for whom slavery had been a burden. Southerners who made such concessions won in return the admission by white Northerners that Reconstruction and its elevation of black Southerners had been a mistake. This understanding of the Civil War, in other words, was simultaneously antislavery and racist, emphasizing the triumph of white reconciliation and progress at the expense of black rights. All white people emerged from the conflict looking high minded and principled.[11]

Charles and Mary Beard's immensely popular *Rise of American Civilization,* first published in 1927 and reflecting the disillusionment that fol-

[9] Robert Penn Warren, *The Legacy of the Civil War: Meditations on the Centennial* (New York, 1961), 64, 49–50.

[10] Wilson, *Patriotic Gore,* xxxi. A blistering assessment of the Civil War from the perspective of the centennial also appears in Oscar Handlin, "The Civil War as Symbol and Actuality," *Massachusetts Review* 3 (Autumn 1961): 133–43.

[11] Willie Lee Rose discusses the turn-of-the-century sectional compromise in *Race and Region in American Historical Fiction: Four Episodes in Popular Culture* (Oxford, 1979), 21–24.

lowed World War I, scoffed at this interpretation. They argued that neither side had been high minded, that the Civil War had been fought over neither slavery nor states' rights. Rather, economic issues stood paramount. "If the southern planters had been content to grant tariffs, bounties, subsidies, and preferences to northern commerce and industry," the Beards declared, "it is not probable that they would have been molested in their most imperious proclamations of sovereignty." The skeptical view broadened and deepened throughout the 1930s. In *The Repressible Conflict* of 1939, Avery Craven argued that the Civil War should be judged by its consequences and that those consequences looked bleak indeed at the end of the 1930s: the black American had escaped "little of the hard fate destined for his race in 1850. Industrial capitalism, with the banners of righteousness, patriotism, and progress over its head and with all critics hushed in disgrace and defeat, went on to its fullness and perhaps its ruin." Something precious had been lost in the Civil War, Craven lamented: "a Constitution which might have protected rights, an agrarian way of life which might have fostered a rich American culture and a sane economic order, a decentralized government wherein individuals and localities might have realized a more satisfactory democracy." Craven believed, along with many Americans, that those dreams had died with the Civil War.[12]

In 1940 James G. Randall delivered his presidential address to the leading organization of historians of the United States. In the address, titled "The Blundering Generation," he concluded that "the Civil War mind seems a sorry *melange* of party bile, crisis melodrama, inflated eloquence, unreason, religious fury, self-righteousness, unctuous self-deception, and hate." The war could, and should, have been avoided, Randall argued, for it was not fought over irreconcilable differences between the North and the South. Randall, like his fellow revisionists, thought he was moving discussion of the war to more realistic grounds, puncturing Northern arrogance and Southern apology. The Civil War was not to be glorified. It stood as an example of how democratic politics could run out of control, of the way moral absolutism could blind people to their own faults and to the consequences of their actions.[13]

---

[12] Charles Beard and Mary Beard, *The Rise of American Civilization* (New York, 1927), 51–54; Avery O. Craven, *The Repressible Conflict, 1830–1861* (Baton Rouge, 1939), 62–63. For useful overviews see Thomas J. Pressly, *Americans Interpret Their Civil War* (1954; 2d ed., New York, 1962); David Donald, "American Historians and the Causes of the Civil War," *South Atlantic Quarterly* 59 (Summer 1960): 351–55; David M. Potter, "The Literature on the Background of the Civil War," in *The South and the Sectional Conflict* (Baton Rouge, 1968), 87–150; Peter Novick, *That Noble Dream: The "Objectivity Question" and the American Historical Profession* (Cambridge, 1988), 72–80, 234–38, 354–59; Michael Perman, *The Coming of the American Civil War*, 3d ed. (Lexington, Mass., 1993).

[13] James G. Randall, "The Blundering Generation," *Mississippi Valley Historical Review* 27 (June 1940): 18.

Such claims did not go completely uncontested, for black historians warned that such views distorted all American history. Throughout the Gilded Age, abolitionists such as Frederick Douglass, trying to create a usable past, argued in vain that the war had been fought over slavery. In 1935, during the peak of revisionism, W. E. B. Du Bois argued that the Beards' work created the "comfortable feeling that nothing right or wrong is involved. Manufacturing and industry develop in the North; agrarian feudalism develops in the South. They clash, as winds and waters strive, and the stronger forces develop the tremendous industrial machine that governs us so magnificently and selfishly today." Du Bois wondered how "anyone who reads the *Congressional Globe* from 1850 to 1860, the lives of contemporary statesmen and public characters, North and South, the discourses in the newspapers and accounts of meetings and speeches, [could] doubt that Negro slavery was the cause of the Civil War?" Du Bois granted that the "North went to war without the slightest idea of freeing the slave" but showed how the abolitionists and the slaves themselves forced Lincoln into making the war a war against slavery. These arguments won little attention or respect from white historians. This was the heyday of revisionism: "everyone" knew the war had been a mistake.[14]

Yet revisionism, so powerful in the first half of the twentieth century, faded away with remarkable speed in the second half. No sooner had World War II ended than commentators called for a rethinking of the dominant skeptical interpretation of the Civil War. Arthur Schlesinger Jr. argued in 1949 that the revisionists, despite their claims to the contrary, had been "sentimentalists," insensitive to the evil of slavery and excessively squeamish about using violence to end it. "The unhappy fact is that man occasionally works himself into a log-jam; and that log-jam must be burst by violence," Schlesinger lectured. "We know that well enough from the experience of the last decade." In 1953, the year that James Randall died, the black historian Benjamin Quarles published his *Negro in the Civil War,* arguing that black people had played central roles in transforming the Civil War into a war to end slavery. Avery Craven began toning down his earlier views, and no one picked up the revisionist banner. David Donald, a student of Randall's who, more than any other leading scholar, seemed sympathetic to the revisionists, explained in 1960 why the perspective no longer won converts: "To those who reached maturity during the years when irresistible and complex forces brought the United States, and the whole civilized

---

[14] David W. Blight, "'For Something beyond the Battlefield': Frederick Douglass and the Struggle for the Memory of the Civil War," *Journal of American History* 75 (March 1989): 1156–78; W. E. Burghardt Du Bois, *Black Reconstruction: An Essay toward a History of the Part Which Black Folk Played in the Attempt to Reconstruct Democracy in America, 1860–1880* (New York, 1935), 714–16.

world, into a disastrous world war, it no longer seems so simple to unravel the causes of the conflict and to pass out praise and blame like honors at a college commencement exercise."[15]

The decline of revisionism was part of a larger rethinking of the American past. Historians in the 1960s, 1970s, and 1980s changed the way Americans understood nineteenth-century America, reflecting the influence of the civil rights movement, the War on Poverty, and the counterculture. Many of the country's most visible historians valued rapid reform, through nonelectoral means if necessary, far more than they did the political stability, gradual change, and regional compromise championed by the revisionists. A self-consciously reformist, often radical, social history swept the profession, displaying and analyzing evidence of injustice and dominion. Southern slaves emerged as fully human, anguished by their bondage and determined to be free in whatever ways they could. Abolitionists no longer appeared as deluded zealots but rather as men and women willing to risk their lives for the highest religious and political ideals. The Republicans came to be seen primarily as advocates of free labor and economic progress, hating the South for its political arrogance and its violation of American virtues. Politicians in general no longer appeared to be blundering but responding, and rather timorously at that, to the very real dilemmas of their society.[16]

Despite penetrating essays and books by historians attentive to the complexities of the party system, no aggressive Civil War revisionism swept over America in the 1960s. This absence of antiwar thinking is surprising. After all, if the disappointments following World War I helped create the first revisionism, why did the far greater disillusionment with the war in Vietnam not create another surge of revisionism? Although disgust with the military and with warfare, with claims of national virtue and innocence, permeated the academy in the late 1960s and early 1970s, only one young scholar, a graduate student, issued a call for "a new revisionism." In 1969, he argued that "the limited improvement in the status of the Negro in this country was not worth the expenditure in lives required to make that improvement possible."[17]

[15] Arthur Schlesinger Jr., "The Causes of the Civil War: A Note on Historical Sentimentalism," *Partisan Review* 16 (October 1949): 980, 981; Benjamin Quarles, *The Negro in the Civil War* (Boston, 1953); Donald, "American Historians," 354. We can trace Craven's self-revisions in his *An Historian and the Civil War* (Chicago, 1964).

[16] Perhaps the most important book in this regard was Eric Foner's *Free Soil, Free Labor, Free Men: The Ideology of the Republican Party before the Civil War* (New York, 1970).

[17] John S. Rosenberg, "Toward a New Civil War Revisionism," *American Scholar* 38 (Spring 1969): 261; for the debate that ensued, see the response to Rosenberg in Phillip S. Paludan, "The American Civil War: Triumph through Tragedy," *Civil War History* 20 (September 1974): 239–50, and John S. Rosenberg, "The American Civil War and the Problem of 'Presentism': A Reply to Phillip S. Paludan," *Civil War History* 21 (September 1975): 242–53.

David M. Potter, while not an aggressive revisionist, wrote several brilliant essays in which

Merely to quote the argument today is to show why it did not succeed: the antiwar spirit directly conflicted with the other great ideal of the sixties, black freedom. Revisionists in the 1920s and 1930s had argued that the end of slavery was not worth six hundred thousand lives because those historians did not consider slavery intrinsically immoral and certainly not much worse than what followed. By the late 1960s, however, slavery seemed so uniquely and undeniably wrong that the calculus of sacrifice had changed. The moral passion that earlier generations had invested in explaining why there should have been no Civil War now focused on explaining why the war and Reconstruction had not been more thorough, why Reconstruction had not been more aggressively supported by confiscation and military power. Scholars' compassion now focused more on the former slaves than on the soldiers in the war. The war itself became something of a scholarly backwater, neglected by the leading historians of nineteenth-century America. The distaste for the war in Vietnam manifested itself in an aversion to any kind of military history, while the fascination with social history made generals and their maneuvers seem irrelevant and boring at best.

Scholars, if not interested in the events on the battlefields, did remain intrigued by the causes of the Civil War. To scholars mindful of either mainstream social science or Marxist thought, the North increasingly appeared as a modern and modernizing society locked in an unavoidable struggle with an antimodern, archaic, and stagnant slave South. The economic conflict between the two societies no longer seemed one merely of tariffs and taxes, issues that could have been worked out, but rather a fundamental clash of free labor and slavery, of the future and the past. The two societies, historians of widely differing perspectives came to agree, could not, should not, have coexisted within the same nation-state. Slavery had to be destroyed as soon as possible, and given the white South's intransigence, only violence was likely to accomplish that purpose.[18]

By the 1970s and 1980s, in sum, the Civil War no longer appeared as a moral problem to the people who wrote the major books about the struggle. Such authors wasted little ink on what had been lost in the war other than precious lives; they worried little about how the war might have

---

he asked hard questions about comforting interpretations of the Civil War. They are collected in *The South and the Sectional Conflict*. While his posthumous and magisterial *The Impending Crisis, 1848–1861* (New York, 1976) cannot be clearly labeled, Potter's revisionist leanings are clear in the textbook *Divisions and the Stresses of Union, 1845–1876* (Glenview, Ill., 1973).

[18] For an influential statement of this argument, see Eric Foner, "The Causes of the American Civil War: Recent Interpretations and New Directions," *Civil War History* 20 (September 1974): 197–214.

been avoided. Slavery displaced other questions that had long agitated Americans, questions about state power, centralization, democracy, war itself. The Civil War came to seem like bitter medicine the country had to swallow for its own good.

Today's stories pivot around moments of wartime cohesion, purposefulness, and decision, especially the growing recognition among white Northerners that the war had to be a war to end slavery and not merely one to save the Union. The war appears as a crucible that burned away the impurities in the Union purpose: this is what Americans were willing to die for, the story says, this is how America atoned for the sin of slavery. The Civil War stands as the origins of our better selves, of the time when we threw off the slavery of our inheritance and became truly American. To Ken Burns, the war marked the equivalent of a "traumatic event in our childhood." To James McPherson, a generous reckoning of the war's purposes and consequences can help Americans overcome "the climate of disillusionment produced by the Vietnam War and the aftermath of the civil rights movement."[19]

So what is wrong with a generous interpretation? After all, it puts the ideals of democracy and nationhood at the center of the story, offering a counterweight to those who have appealed to less expansive interpretations of the nation's ideals. It holds up heroes worth emulating. It reconciles the North and South to each other, giving respect where it has not always been found. It places the struggle for black freedom and equality at the heart of American history. It connects Americans with their past. All these worthy purposes have been won only after great effort, and a person of goodwill might think twice before questioning them. And yet if we do not question them, we close ourselves off from other kinds of understanding and other perspectives on the American nation.

The current interpretation reassures Americans by reconciling the great anomaly of slavery with an overarching story of a people devoted to liberty. These stories reassure Americans by reconciling the horrors of fratricidal war with a vision of a peace-loving republic devoted to democracy and prosperity. They tell the story of a devastating war so that it seems not merely unavoidable but transformative and ultimately healing. The stories help restock Robert Penn Warren's "Treasury of Virtue" in the wake of the war in Vietnam. White Southerners have been permitted limited access to parts of the treasury, handed the keys to the rooms that contain honor, bravery, and even idealism—though not justice. Black Americans have finally been acknowledged as agents in their own freedom. But it is white Northern

---

[19] According to Burns, "If you see history like the life of a human being, this [the Civil War] was the traumatic event of our childhood." *Newsweek,* October 8, 1990, 59; McPherson, *Lincoln and the Second American Revolution,* 13.

men who come off best in these stories, martyrs for the Union and the liberty of others.[20]

The new interpretation contains little of the cynicism and irony of the revisionists of the 1920s and 1930s. Today's stories tend to be earnest accounts, clear and linear, with motives and emotions close to the surface. Indeed, it is in part the very appeal of these stories as stories which makes them so resistant to revision and which makes them seem so self-evident. The accounts of the war have a familiar narrative shape; they present an apparently unresolvable problem and then, after great trials, show its resolution, echoing other basic stories of Western and American culture.

We understand the plot lines of war, dramatized every day on sports fields and in action films: good causes and bad, cowardice and bravery, sacrifice and glory, winners and losers, sudden victories and unexpected reverses. Fundamental ideas of history, religion, and science, as Hannah Arendt has argued, incline twentieth-century people to see wars as major engines of beneficial social change, even as we loathe and fear the conflict itself. Not only does the Judeo-Christian religious tradition accustom us to think of violence and blood as necessary accompaniments of progress, but evolutionism also leads us to conceive of violence as a part of nature, a way for bad ideas and institutions to be culled. These assumptions, combined with a widespread belief in the divine favor enjoyed by the United States, have made it easy for Americans to believe that the Civil War was not merely necessary but actually good for the country in the long run.[21]

Our current understanding of the war makes us impatient with those in the North—the great majority, at the beginning—who argued that they were fighting only for the Union, not for the end of bondage. We are befuddled by black Northerners who argued that a war fought to protect the Union—"this unholy, ill-begotten, would-be Republican government, that summons all its skill, energy, and might, of money, men, and false philosophy that a corrupt nation can bring to bear, to support, extend, and perpetuate that vilest of all vile systems, American slavery"—was not a war worth fighting. We are disappointed with those many white men who died

[20] For an example of black agency and white leadership, see *Glory*, a film directed by Edward Zwick, 1989. Ironically, Warren served on Burns's team of advisers and is quoted in the introduction to the book based on the series (Ward, *Civil War*, xix). Burns focuses on Warren's statement that the war was so central and complex an event that it tends to create a personal connection between it and Americans. In many ways, though, Burns's *Civil War* seems an example of the sentimental nationalism that Warren warned against thirty years earlier.

[21] McPherson, *Battle Cry of Freedom*, 858; Thomas Cripps, "Historical Truth: An Interview with Ken Burns," *American Historical Review* 100 (June 1995): 741–64; Hannah Arendt, *On Violence* (New York, 1970), paraphrased in Jean Bethke Elshtain, "Reflections on War and Political Discourse: Realism, Just War, and Feminism in a Nuclear Age," in *Just War Theory* (Oxford, 1992), 270.

for the Union who would not willingly have risked their lives for the end of slavery. As the *Chicago Times,* commenting on Lincoln's Gettysburg Address, put it, "They were men possessing too much self-respect to declare that negroes were their equals, or were entitled to equal privileges."[22]

Garry Wills, in *Lincoln at Gettysburg* (1992), used such quotations to explain the great transformation of the North. In this best-selling and prize-winning interpretation of the war, Wills argued that Lincoln, in the mere 272 words of the address, cleared "the infected atmosphere of American history itself, tainted with official sins and inherited guilt." Rather than burning the Constitution because it countenanced slavery, as William Lloyd Garrison had proposed, Lincoln instead "altered the document from within, by appeal from its letter to the spirit, subtly changing the recalcitrant stuff of that legal compromise, bringing it to its own indictment." Lincoln's redefinition of the Constitution to embrace black equality, Wills admiringly noted, was "one of the most daring acts of open-air sleight-of-hand ever witnessed by the unsuspecting. Everyone in that vast throng of thousands was having his or her intellectual pocket picked. The crowd departed with a new thing in its ideological luggage, that new constitution Lincoln had substituted for the one they brought with them."[23] Lincoln tricked Americans into being better than they really were, into fighting for a higher cause. Wills's Lincoln transmogrified a war for the Union into a war for freedom.

There are, of course, scholarly dissenters from this standard interpretation. Historians such as David Potter, J. Mills Thornton, Michael Holt, William Gienapp, and William Freehling have questioned the political narrative that makes the conflict over slavery seem relatively straightforward, in either the North or the South. Their regions are marked by strong countercurrents, compromises, and possibilities for alignments other than those that brought on the war.[24] Other historians have argued that African Americans did more to free themselves than Abraham Lin-

[22] First quotation from James M. McPherson, *The Negro's Civil War: How American Negroes Felt and Acted during the War for the Union* (New York, 1965), 34. The quotation from the *Chicago Times,* November 23, 1863, is in Garry Wills, *Lincoln at Gettysburg: The Words that Remade America* (New York, 1992), 38–39.

[23] Wills, *Lincoln at Gettysburg,* 37–39, 183–85. David Brion Davis has explored, with characteristic subtlety, the conflation of Lincoln with the images associated with individual emancipation. See his "The Emancipation Moment," in Gabor S. Boritt, ed., *Lincoln, the War President* (New York, 1992), 63–88.

[24] Potter, *Impending Crisis;* J. Mills Thornton III, *Politics and Power in a Slave Society: Alabama, 1800–1860* (Baton Rouge, 1978); Michael F. Holt, *The Political Crisis of the 1850s* (New York: Wiley, 1978), and Holt, *Political Parties and American Political Development from the Age of Jackson to the Age of Lincoln* (Baton Rouge, 1992); William E. Gienapp, *The Origins of the Republican Party, 1852–1856* (New York, 1986); William W. Freehling, *The Road to Disunion: The Secessionists at Bay* (New York, 1990), and Freehling, *The Reintegration of American History: Slavery and the Civil War* (New York, 1994).

coln ever did. In the eyes of Leon Litwack, Ira Berlin, Barbara Fields, and Armstead Robinson, the focus on white Northern soldiers and civilians gives undue credit to reluctant friends of freedom. Without the desperate efforts by slaves to free themselves, they argue, the Union cause would have remained a cause for union alone. It was anonymous African Americans who forced Union generals to take a stand on slavery—to recognize that only by ending slavery could the North win the war. Assuming an implicit and intrinsic push toward freedom on the part of the North, these historians warn, gives that society far too much moral credit.[25]

Other historians have argued that the conflict was considerably more vindictive, hateful, and destructive than the new orthodoxy emphasizes. Michael Perman, Charles Royster, Michael Fellman, and Steven Ash stress the chaotic violence that swirled around the regimented violence of the war, tormented the border regions from Missouri to occupied South Carolina, ravaged the postwar period throughout the South, and nullified much that the war claimed to have won. Noncombatants as well as leading generals, these historians show, were often less eager to rejoin the foe as part of the Union than to see them dead. As Royster puts it, Northerners and Southerners fell into "visions of purgation and redemption, into anticipation and intuition and spiritual apotheosis, into bloodshed that was not only intentional pursuit of interests of state but was also sacramental, erotic, mystical, and strangely gratifying." Such imagery has little place in the way most Americans prefer today to remember the war, in which violence was inflicted almost reluctantly, brother against brother.[26]

The dominant story of the war can absorb a great deal of such amendment, however, without changing its fundamental outlines. The standard interpretation, after all, never makes the war seem painless; in fact, the suffering, struggle, conflict, and uncertainty constitute crucial parts of the "ordeal by fire" that tried the nation and its ideals. Arguments about the complexities of the antebellum period can complicate without undermining a belief that the war, as Lincoln put it, was "somehow" about slavery.

[25] On blacks' efforts to strike their freedom, see Leon F. Litwack, *Been in the Storm So Long: The Aftermath of Slavery* (New York, 1979); Ira Berlin, Barbara J. Fields, Thavolia Glymph, Joseph P. Reidy, and Leslie Rowland, eds., *Freedom: A Documentary History of Emancipation, 1861–1867,* 1st ser., vol. 1 (New York, 1985); and Armstead Robinson, "Day of Jubilo: Civil War and the Demise of Slavery in the Mississippi Valley, 1861–1865" (Ph.D. diss., University of Rochester, 1976). For strong criticism of Burns on this issue, see Litwack, "Telling the Story: The Historian, the Filmmaker, and the Civil War," in Toplin, *Ken Burns's "The Civil War",* 119–40.

[26] Michael Perman, *The Road to Redemption: Southern Politics, 1869–1879* (Chapel Hill, 1984); Michael Fellman, *Inside War: The Guerrilla Conflict in Missouri during the American Civil War* (New York, 1989); Charles Royster, *The Destructive War: William Tecumseh Sherman, Stonewall Jackson, and the Americans* (New York, 1991); Michael Fellman, *Citizen Sherman: A Life of William Tecumseh Sherman* (New York, 1995); and Stephen V. Ash, *When the Yankees Came: Conflict and Chaos in the Occupied South, 1861–1865* (Chapel Hill, 1995).

Arguments that Southern slaves helped free themselves can fit into and even enrich a story of the war that emphasizes the growth of liberty. Though arguments about the irrationality, brutality, and bloodthirstiness of the war may signal a new, darker school of interpretation, defenders of the standard interpretation have argued that the American Civil War actually saw less inhumanity than most other wars, that the American war was distinguished by the rigor with which soldiers and leaders played by agreed-upon rules. Even historians find it hard, in other words, to convey an overall interpretation of the war that fundamentally challenges the one that has become so deeply entrenched in American culture.[27]

This lack of far-reaching debate over the Civil War—so unlike that which has surrounded other major historical events such as the French Revolution, the Holocaust, or the cold war—may not be a cause for self-congratulation. It is not merely that all the evidence is in and accounted for and historians have finally found the one true interpretation. It may be, rather, that we like the current story too much to challenge it very deeply and that we foreclose questions by repeating familiar formulas. The risk of our apparent consensus is that we paper over the complicated moral issues raised by a war that left hundreds of thousands of people dead. The risk is that we no longer worry about the Civil War.

The American Civil War presents great narrative opportunities. No one could ask for a richer subject, a better plotline of conflict and resolution, struggle and triumph, good and evil. But with those opportunities also come temptations. All the struggle, conflict, and uncertainty can appear as so many plot complications in a story that drives to its natural conclusion. Because the secession conflict led to the Civil War, war now seems to be the intention of those who sought to leave the Union. Because the war became a bloodbath of incalculable scale, that scale now seems inevitable. Because the war ended with the survival of the Union, that survival now seems the natural outcome of the war. Because slavery came to an end in 1865, that victory has suffused the purposes of the North throughout the war and before. The story has been settled upon, assuming the shape of an elaborate play. Every American schoolchild learns the set pieces, the way that generals and presidents personified various traits: Grant's cool purposefulness, Lee's selfless dedication to homeland, Sherman's prescient destructiveness, Lincoln's forgiveness and suffering.

Yet things may not have been so settled. The contingencies of the war, we might recognize, could easily have changed not only the outcome of the conflict but its apparent moral meaning as well. If the North had

---

[27] A counterargument that has received McPherson's endorsement is Mark Grimsley, *The Hard Hand of War: Union Military Policy toward Southern Civilians, 1861–1865* (Cambridge, 1995).

overwhelmed the South in 1862, the victory would have brought the restoration of the Union without the immediate end of slavery. If that had happened, the war's causes as well as its outcome would be understood differently today. Similarly, if Lincoln had escaped assassination and had overseen the conciliatory form of Reconstruction he seemed to have had in mind, he likely would not appear to be the transcendental visionary he is considered now. Not only events were contingent, in other words—so were apparently fixed ideologies, values, personalities, and memories. With one key victory, after all, George McClellan might well be pictured on classroom walls throughout a very different kind of United States.[28]

We might rethink, too, the role of modernity in causing and deciding the war. Modernity is perhaps the single most deeply embedded part of the standard story; Americans of all regions and generations, for different reasons, accept the idea that the North was a modern society that could not long coexist with a South that had rejected modernity. McPherson, for example, divides the country into two halves with different orientations toward "modernization." He characterizes that process as one marked by "an evolution from the traditional, rural, village-oriented system of personal and kinship ties, in which status is 'ascriptive' (inherited), toward a fluid, cosmopolitan, impersonal, and pluralistic society, in which status is achieved by merit." A 1996 book that offers "everything you need to know about America's greatest conflict but never learned" boils things down this way: "The America of the Union states was racing toward the twentieth century, with banks, booming factories, railroads, canals, and steamship lines. . . . The southern states of the Confederacy were, in many respects, standing still in time." The prominent historian George Fredrickson has argued that a modern society such as the North, in conflict with a nonmodern or less modern society such as the South, will benefit from modernity in wartime because "its greater social mobility and emphasis on achievement will bring to the fore more effective leaders, and its more highly differentiated structure of social and occupational roles will make possible a more efficient allocation of tasks."[29]

Such views may give modernity more credit than it deserves as the driving force behind freedom and military victory. Modern economies, after all, have often found ways to make their peace with nondemocratic gov-

---

[28] Battlefield contingency is the major analytic argument in McPherson's *Battle Cry of Freedom,* where he posits four points at which the North could have lost the war; see pp. 857–58.

[29] McPherson makes this point explicitly in *Ordeal by Fire,* 13, and implicitly in *Battle Cry of Freedom;* Kenneth C. Davis, *Don't Know Much about the Civil War: Everything You Need to Know about America's Greatest Conflict but Never Learned* (New York, 1996), 151–52; George Fredrickson, "Blue over Gray: Sources of Success and Failure in the Civil War," in *A Nation Divided: Problems and Issues of the Civil War and Reconstruction* (Minneapolis, 1975), 78.

ernment, coercive labor, and constrained liberties. And while the events of the twentieth century show that a technologically sophisticated, "highly differentiated" society can become a terrifyingly effective war machine, Americans have learned that more advanced societies do not always triumph over less developed enemies. If the South had won the Civil War, in fact, historians could plausibly argue that a defensive, highly mobilized, self-sacrificing, organic South would naturally defeat the commercial, aggressive, polyglot, individualistic North, with its draft riots, paid substitutes, and indecisive president. They would look to the American Revolution as foreshadowing the inevitable success of the Confederacy—just as the Confederates themselves did.

Even this counterfactual perspective does not go far enough, for it neglects how "modern" the slave South itself had become by the late antebellum period. This topic has been hotly debated by historians for decades, revealing that modernity is among the most slippery of concepts, especially as it related to slavery. It seems fair to say that from the perspective of most other societies in the world in 1860, the slave South was an advanced society, rich in the machinery and trappings of modernity. Railroads, telegraphs, cities, newspapers, active political parties, factories, and reform societies emerged in the 1840s and 1850s. Slavery grew no weaker as a result, however, showing itself dismayingly adaptable. Where the incentives existed, as in Virginia, slaves were put to work in the machinery of the new age, laboring in industries such as iron foundries. White Southerners considered themselves a progressive people, taking the best of the new while maintaining social stability and responsibility for their workers. They prided themselves on their white democracy, their widespread church membership, and their strict adherence to the Constitution. They saw themselves on a different, smoother, more humane path to progress.[30]

Modernity, slavery, and nation appeared in strange combinations in the secession crisis and war. Some of the largest planters and richest slave areas in the Deep South tended to be Unionist, whereas cities, where modern ways had made the greatest inroads in the slave South, often voted for secession. The machinery of print and telegraph, rather than moderating the opinions of city dwellers and inclining them toward freedom, could inflame them against the North. The most heavily Unionist districts, for their part, were those least connected to the South and the rest of the nation;

[30] Richard Graham, "Economics or Culture? The Development of the U.S. South and Brazil in the Days of Slavery," in Kees Gispen, ed., *What Made the South Different?* (Oxford, Miss., 1990). For insightful portrayals of "modern" influences in the South, see Thornton, *Politics and Power;* Eugene D. Genovese, *The Slaveholders' Dilemma: Freedom and Progress in Southern Conservative Thought, 1820–1860* (Columbia, S.C.; 1992); and Kenneth W. Noe, *Southwest Virginia's Railroad: Modernization and the Sectional Crisis* (Urbana, Ill., 1994).

up-country people seemed bound to older ideas of nation, not newer ones. Once the war began, the Confederacy innovated quickly on the battle-field, on the oceans, and behind the lines, even as it held stubbornly to slavery.

There is no doubt that the North was more economically developed than the South and that slavery rendered the South economically back-ward by comparison. But seeing the war as a conflict between the future and the past tempts us to think that modernity naturally, if often violently, creates freedom. It tempts us to bifurcate and simplify the causes of the war into easy-to-understand formulas that flatter Americans, including white Southerners, into thinking that things unfolded pretty much as they were destined to unfold. It conflates slavery with the agrarian past and ig-nores the viruslike ability of slavery to insinuate itself into diverse kinds of societies. An interpretation based on modernization ignores how inter-twined North and South, black and white, and slavery and freedom were in antebellum America.

Slavery and freedom remain the keys to understanding the war—but they are the place to begin our questions, not end them. The interpreta-tion of the Civil War that appeals to so many Americans today weaves antislavery sentiments, war, economic progress, and nationalism into an inseparable whole. Freedom, it seems, was driven by the machinery of modern life, achieved through cathartic violence, and embodied in a government that valued freedom above all else. The triumph, moreover, seems to have operated retroactively. A nation that tolerated slavery at its founding can seem, in retrospect, fundamentally opposed to slavery. A national economy that for generations depended on slavery as its main-spring can seem intrinsically antagonistic to slavery. A war that began as a fight to maintain the Union with strong protections for slavery can be seen as inherently antislavery from the beginning. Given these assumptions, a conflagration on the scale of the Civil War appears inevitable.

Those who resist this argument, its assumptions, and its implications are often conservatives of various kinds. Some are white Southerners unwill-ing, as they see it, to abandon their ancestors and their heritage. Other critics resent the power of the national government and are jealous for the power of states and localities.[31] Others are racists, denying to black Ameri-

[31] Jeffrey Rogers Hummel offers iconoclastic and penetrating commentary on the war in his *Emancipating Slaves, Enslaving Free Men: A History of the American Civil War* (Chicago, 1996). Hummel, from the viewpoint of one who finds the market and its values more just and efficient than the state and its values, challenges some of the orthodoxies of the liberal in-terpretation. He argues that a war to maintain the Union alone was not the worthy crusade it often appears: "As an excuse for civil war, maintaining the State's territorial integrity is

cans the freedoms and aspirations available to other Americans. As a result, liberals have stood staunchly behind the standard interpretation, hoping it can help strengthen the activism and authority of the national government, the claims of African Americans for full citizenship, and the tradition of white reform.

Perhaps, however, the standard interpretation is no longer serving liberal ends as it once did. The story of the Civil War has become a story of things being settled, of scores being righted. Movies and books that tell of Americans killing more than six hundred thousand other Americans somehow convey a sense of the greatness of everyone concerned and of the nation for which they died. Such faith in the transformative effects of warfare can make it easier for Americans to find other wars natural and inevitable. Celebrating the martyrdom of whites for black freedom can reduce white guilt. Celebrating the bravery of Confederate soldiers and the brilliance of Confederate generals can trivialize the stakes of the war. Celebrating sectional reconciliation can mask the struggles over justice, power, and arrogance that have marked relations between the North and the South for generations.

A new Civil War revisionism may help us avoid some of these temptations. That revisionism, unlike its predecessors, might focus on the way we relate the Civil War rather than on matters of interpretation alone. It might resist the very notion of the war as a single story, with a beginning, middle, and end, with turning points and near misses. The war did not have a single chronology, a rising and falling, an obvious pivot, but rather competing and intertwining chronologies in different theaters, on different home fronts, in politics and in economy. The sequence of sectional crisis, war, and aftermath did not follow a cumulative and linear development. To some, war seemed less impending in 1859 than in 1854, less threatening in February of 1861 than in November of 1860. The war seemed more pointedly about slavery in late 1863 than it did six months later when the presidential election in the North threatened to capsize the Lincoln administration. Black freedom promised more liberation in 1865 than it had delivered by 1876.

---

bankrupt and reprehensible" (352). Hummel believes that the war was not the only, or even the best, way of ending slavery, pointing out that the amount of money the North alone spent on the war "was enough to buy all slaves and set up each family with forty acres and a mule" (354). The source of his dissent, reflected in his title, is that "in contrast to the whittling away of government that had preceded Fort Sumter, the United States had commenced its halting but inexorable march toward the welfare-warfare State of today" (359). Hummel's notes on the historical literature are often biting, but his narrative of the war's coming, fighting, and aftermath does not differ markedly from more conventional accounts. His political perspective has revealed to him the evasions and conventions of the current orthodoxy and suggested promising areas for further reflection and research, but he has not yet offered a coherent counternarrative of the conflict.

A new revisionism might also set aside the Olympian perspective and voice of our dominant books and films to provide a different sense of the war's depth and scale. It might give up older reassurances to provide new kinds of clarity. It might convey what Stephen Crane's *Red Badge of Courage* conveyed—the swirl of action and reflection, the partial knowledge of those swept up in war. A new revisionism might inspire battle histories that leave some of the fog of battle on the page.

A new revisionism would place more distance between nineteenth-century Americans and ourselves, the very distance that lets us see ourselves more clearly. If Americans resist the temptation to count every cost of the Civil War as a "sacrifice," we might be more grateful for our simple good fortune and perhaps less self-satisfied with the people we have become. If we acknowledge that we inherit all the past and not merely those parts we like to call our "heritage," we would better respect the past's complexity, weight, and importance. If we recognize that the Civil War did not represent the apotheosis of American ideals, we might look for that culmination in the future rather than in the past. All we need is the faith to approach these threatening years without a comforting story already in hand.

CHAPTER EIGHT

Caste, Class, and Equal Citizenship

WILLIAM E. FORBATH

The interplay of moral insight and moral blindness has long occupied David Brion Davis; so has the intricate and vexed relationship between race- and class-based bondage and freedom. At the intersection of these two interests stands *The Problem of Slavery in the Age of Revolution,* a work and a pair of interests that place Davis in a tradition with W. E. B. Du Bois.[1] In 1992 Davis wrote an essay offering a distinctly Du Boisian view of the "American dilemma."[2]

On the eve of *Brown v. Board of Education,* Gunnar Myrdal, in his famous *American Dilemma,* maintained that "in principle, the Negro Problem was solved long ago."[3] The solution to racial subordination in the United States lay in extending our creed of equal rights and equal citizenship to black America. It remained only to put the solution into practice. The task was daunting but clear. Written almost thirty years after *Brown,* Davis's essay implies that the liberal common sense of Myrdal—and *Brown*—was mistaken. Instead of a solution, Davis points to another problem.

America, Davis suggests, will never overcome its "pathology of race" until the nation confronts its class divisions and the "destructive myth of a classless society."[4] Nor can the United States effectively attack class in-

[1] David Brion Davis, *The Problem of Slavery in the Age of Revolution, 1770–1823* (Ithaca, 1975).
[2] David Brion Davis, "The American Dilemma," *New York Review of Books,* July 16, 1992, 13–18.
[3] Gunnar Myrdal, *An American Dilemma: The Negro Problem and Modern Democracy* (New York, 1944), 24.
[4] Davis, "American Dilemma," 17.

equalities without confronting its racial cleavages. Call this idea the historical knot of race and class. Beginning with Du Bois's *Black Reconstruction,* historians and political analysts have understood much of our past in these terms, from the Revolution of 1776 to the revolt of the Reagan Democrats.[5] Black slavery, in this view, not only financed the American Revolution but, by keeping the propertyless laboring class in chains, also enabled the colonial gentry to forge a revolutionary "equal rights" outlook and republican political culture among all ranks of white colonists, freed from the threat of social revolution.[6] Thereafter, black subordination remained a potent element of American national identity, binding white Americans together as "equals" across the unacknowledged breaches of class.

To be sure, the Reconstruction amendments extended equal rights to blacks. This prompted Myrdal's view that "the Negro problem" had been "solved" in principle. But if black subordination were more than an aberration from the equal rights creed, if it were also part of the creed's cultural and socioeconomic groundwork, then attaining equal citizenship for black America would require changing the meaning of that moral and political principle for all Americans. That is Davis's point. The equal rights creed can go but so far in undoing the subordination of black Americans, unless it addresses the ways that class inequalities mock equal citizenship for all. Many analysts have pointed to this knot of race and class to explain

[5] In the early 1930s Du Bois rendered his famous verdict on Reconstruction: the federal government betrayed the freedmen by failing to protect their rights. This betrayal allowed the former slaveholders to prevail in the South, spelling the end of democracy there. But it also enabled elites to gain an enduring advantage everywhere, injuring the whole nation's political development. "Property and privilege" North and South concluded a bargain, and the "black laboring class" was robbed of the right to vote "with the aid of white southern labor and the silent acquiescence" of white workers in the North. W. E. B. Du Bois, *Black Reconstruction in America, 1860–1880* (New York, 1935; reprinted, 1963), 630–31.

The advantages of whiteness often showed up on payday. But even when white workers "received a low wage" and had little sway in the polity, they were "compensated in part by a . . . public and psychological wage." A measure of status and privilege, the very rights and standing of citizenship, hinged on whiteness and compensated for exploitative class relationships in both sections of the reunited nation. Half a century later, the "wages of whiteness" continued to buy the white workingman half a loaf, and still, the "unending tragedy of Reconstruction," Du Bois said, remained the "utter inability of the American mind to grasp its real significance, its national implications" for both black and white (700, 708). An important rekindling of Du Bois's perspective on the American working class is David R. Roediger, *The Wages of Whiteness: Race and the Making of the American Working Class* (New York, 1991).

Historians also have taken up Du Bois's broader challenge, exploring the relationship of race and class during Reconstruction and other formative moments in the nation's political development. See, for example, Eric Foner, *Free Soil, Free Labor, Free Men: The Ideology of the Republican Party before the Civil War* (New York, 1970); Eric Foner, *Politics and Ideology in the Age of the Civil War* (New York, 1980); Eric Foner, *Reconstruction: America's Unfinished Revolution, 1863–1877* (1988), Edmund S. Morgan, *American Slavery, American Freedom: The Ordeal of Colonial Virginia* (New York, 1975); C. Vann Woodward, *Origins of the New South, 1877–1913* (xxxxxxxx, xxxx); and Barbara J. Fields, "Ideology and Race in American History," in J. Morgan Kousser and James M. McPherson, eds., *Region, Race, and Reconstruction: Essays in Honor of C. Vann Woodward* (New York, 1982).

[6] See Morgan, *American Slavery, American Freedom.*

the political and moral vulnerability of "civil rights liberalism" in today's America. They highlight the fact that contemporary liberal "rights talk" addresses the injuries of caste for black and other non-white Americans but not the overlapping injuries of class many share with whites.[7] That is certainly true in the context of constitutional law, politics, and punditry. But, colleagues in the liberal and left precincts of constitutional law may object: class inequalities lie outside our jurisdiction. We may lament the fact, and our conservative counterparts may applaud it. But while the meaning of our constitutional tradition is forever debated, everyone seems to agree that redressing class inequalities has not been part of the debate.

Here, our colleagues are mistaken. They overlook a rich history of constitutional concern about economic dependence and powerlessness. A broad, positive conception of equal citizenship—encompassing adequate social provision, livelihoods, and work, and a measure of economic democracy—has had a distinguished career in the constitutional history they claim to describe. Borrowing a phrase from its Progressive Era proponents, I will call this conception of constitutional equality, and the arguments and understandings that supported it, the "social citizenship tradition."[8]

The egalitarian constitutional tradition we know well is court-centered and countermajoritarian. Springing from *Brown v. Board of Education*, it defends the rights of "discrete and insular minorities." The social citizenship tradition, by contrast, was a majoritarian one and addressed its arguments to lawmakers and citizens, not courts. From Reconstruction through the New Deal, it insisted that the political economy was shot through with constitutional infirmities that the nation was obliged to mend. Aimed against harsh class inequalities, it found classic expression in Franklin Delano Roosevelt's "second Bill of Rights" and provided New Dealers with not only a rights rhetoric but also arguments and modes of interpretation that supported their constitutional revolution.

My thesis is that the seemingly separate fates and flaws of these two egalitarian visions have long been joined. The moral insights of each speak to the other's blindness. By retrieving their buried historical links, I hope to

---

[7] See, for example, Thomas Edsall and Mary Edsall, *Chain Reaction: The Impact of Race, Rights, and Taxes on American Politics* (New York, 1991); Kevin P. Phillips, *Boiling Point: Republicans, Democrats, and the Decline of Middle-Class Prosperity* (New York, 1993), and Phillips, *The Politics of Rich and Poor: Wealth and the American Electorate in the Reagan Aftermath* (New York, 1990); Jim Sleeper, *The Closest of Strangers: Liberalism and the Politics of Race in New York* (New York, 1990).

[8] See, for example, Florence Kelley, *Some Ethical Gains through Legislation* (New York, 1905). Today, we associate the term "social citizenship" most readily with the English sociologist T. H. Marshall and his classic lectures on the rise of the welfare state as a new "stage" in the development of citizenship. See T. H. Marshall, *Citizenship and Social Class* (Cambridge, 1949). For a thoughtful assessment of Marshall from a U.S. perspective, see Nancy Fraser and Linda Gordon, "Contract versus Charity: Why Is There No Social Citizenship in America?" *Socialist Review* 22 (1992): 45–67. This essay approaches Fraser and Gordon's question quite differently from theirs.

suggest the outlines of a new constitutional narrative, one that reflects Davis's and Du Bois's insights and shows how Du Bois's "unending tragedy of Reconstruction" conditioned the constitutional dramas of the twentieth century. The abandonment of Reconstruction by the federal government and white America, I'll argue, did more than deprive black Americans of civil and political rights for almost a century. By allowing the emergence and consolidation of the Solid South, this same constitutional bad faith also operated in the New Deal era to prevent all Americans from securing the boon of social citizenship.

In constitutional history, as in Faulkner's novels, the past is never past. The tangled knot of race and class lies unexamined at the heart of this history. Ignoring it has prevented liberal and progressive theorists from fully understanding the embattled constitutional legacies of the New Deal and civil rights eras. Retrieving this history will not reveal a truer New Deal "moment" for courts to preserve but instead a recurrent constitutional conflict which was concluded by racism and fraud and deserves to be reopened.

I.

The language of equal citizenship did not loom large in the Constitution prior to the adoption of the Civil War and Reconstruction amendments.[9] Since then, however, subordinated groups have laid claim to the status of citizens and rights bearers in language rooted in those amendments. As Hendrik Hartog observes, "the long contest over slavery did more than any other cause to stimulate the development of an alternate, rights-conscious interpretation of the federal constitution." The varying meanings that have been drawn from the phrase "equal protection of the laws" are "rooted in contending visions of what it was that was overthrown by the end of slavery."[10] From Reconstruction onward through the New Deal, industrial workers, farmers, middle-class and elite reformers, African Americans, and women's rights advocates mounted repeated efforts to realize the distributive and enabling economic dimensions of the Reconstruction amendments' promise of equal citizenship.

Abraham Lincoln and the new Republican Party laid a fresh foundation for the old idea that constitutional interpretation was a popular project, not limited to a professional elite; they coupled it to the vision of an evolving antislavery constitution whose egalitarian meanings must unfold in time. The framers, in Lincoln's famous phrase, had made the egalitarian

[9] See Stanley Katz, "The Strange Birth and Unlikely History of Constitutional Equality," *Journal of American History* 75 (1988): 747.

[10] Hendrik Hartog, "The Constitution of Aspiration and the 'Rights that Belong to Us All,'" *Journal of American History* 74 (1988): 1017.

principles of the Declaration of Independence the "apple of gold" around which the Constitution was merely a "silver frame."[11] Lincoln called on fellow citizen-interpreters to spurn the proslavery Constitution of the Court and instead complete the founders' "unfinished" work of "Liberty for All."[12] The hermeneutics of an evolving antislavery Constitution, renewed and realized over time by citizens and opposed by the courts, would find many later practitioners who called on succeeding generations to complete the "unfinished work" not of the founders but of Lincoln and the Antislavery amendments.

By dint of these amendments, "We, the People" had become in 1867 "all persons born or naturalized in the United States," irrespective of "race, color, or previous condition of servitude." The nation broke this promise of equality, but not before those who led the battles for the Thirteenth, Fourteenth, and Fifteenth Amendments outlined an understanding of equal citizenship that spoke to the social and economic circumstances not only of former slaves but also of white free laborers. Even the most conservative Republicans agreed on the core rights of contract, property, and personal liberty. Above all, what had distinguished the lowliest hireling in the North from the southern slave were the rights to contract and "earn the fruits of his own labor" and to marry and be protected in his home and family." Now these rights were "universal."[13] But to the Radical Republicans, they were hardly sufficient to underpin the freedmen's new status as citizens. Citizenship demanded suffrage, and the independence of the freedmen's ballots required material foundations, which entailed not only equal rights to contract and own property but also public education and training. Some agreed with Thaddeus Stevens that equal citizenship for the freedmen also demanded land redistribution—"forty acres and a mule," in the famous phrase.[14] The idea was not limited to former slaves. Stevens and other Republicans pressed for generous homestead laws and land grant colleges for white hirelings in the North. They thought, in traditional republican terms, that property was "so essential for both individual and collective self-governance" that "every citizen should have some."[15]

---

[11] Paul W. Kahn, *Legitimacy and History: Self-Government in American Constitutional Theory* (New Haven, 1992), 32–35; Don Fehrenbacher, *Lincoln in Text and Context* (Stanford, Calif., 1987), 126; Gyora Binder and Robert Weisberg, *Literary Criticisms of Law* (Princeton, forthcoming).

[12] Harry Jaffa, *Crisis of the House Divided* (Seattle, 1982), 316; Abraham Lincoln, "Speech at Chicago, July 10, 1858," in *The Life and Writings of Abraham Lincoln,* ed. Peter Stern (New York, 1940), 442–43.

[13] Amy Dru Stanley, "Conjugal Bonds and Wage Labor: Rights of Contract in the Age of Emancipation," *Journal of American History* 75 (1988): 492.

[14] See Foner, *Reconstruction,* 235–36.

[15] See Akhil Reed Amar, "Forty Acres and a Mule," *Harvard Journal of Law and Public Policy* 13 (1990): 37.

As the "Labor Question" eclipsed the "Slavery Question" in the politics of the rapidly industrializing postbellum North, it too had a constitutional cast. Elite reformers who styled themselves "New Liberals" assailed union-sponsored labor laws as trampling workers' constitutional liberties. Labor leaders, by contrast, said the Constitution demanded these measures to combat wage slavery and corporate tyranny.[16] Invoking constitutional provisions aimed at protecting the rights of black former slaves in the South to support rights for white workers in the North was not far-fetched. As Eric Foner has shown, defending white free labor always had loomed large in the Republicans' antislavery outlook,[17] and the party's leadership repeatedly declared that the Antislavery amendments embodied a promise of universal freedom, limited to "neither black nor white."[18] Thus during debates on the Fourteenth Amendment, the Radicals in the Thirty-ninth Congress led by Stevens and Charles Sumner proposed a joint resolution declaring that in the reconstructed nation "there shall be no denial of rights . . . on account of color or race"—and also "no Oligarchy, Aristocracy, Caste or Monopoly invested with peculiar privileges and powers."[19] Slavery represented the extremity of caste subjugation based on race. The Black Codes, passed by the southern states in 1865–66, reinstated a race-based caste system, keeping blacks as an inferior and dependent class by disabling them from owning, renting, or transferring property, pursuing skilled callings, or seeking access to courts. At a minimum, all Republicans meant to outlaw those disabilities, but resolutions such as this one suggest that many thought the promise of equal citizenship went further. Beyond the unique harshness of this form of racial subjugation, the law could be used to hem resourceless white working people into a dependent and degraded—castelike—condition. It could invest groups or classes of the propertied with "peculiar privileges and powers" and enshrine, in Stevens's words, "the recognized degradation of the poor, and the superior caste of the rich."[20] This, too, the new amendments should forbid. Republicans celebrated the Thirteenth Amendment as a

---

[16] William E. Forbath, "The Ambiguities of Free Labor: Labor and the Law in the Gilded Age," *Wisconsin Law Review* (1985): 756; Christopher Tomlins, *Law, Labor, and Ideology in the Early American Republic* (Cambridge, 1993); Karen Orren, *Belated Feudalism: Labor, the Law, and Liberal Development* (Cambridge, 1991).

[17] See Foner, *Free Soil, Free Labor, Free Men*.

[18] Remarks of Sen. Wilson, *Congressional Globe*, 39th Cong., 1st sess., 1866, 343, quoted in Lea VanderVelde, "The Labor Vision of the Thirteenth Amendment," *University of Pennsylvania Law Review* 138 (1989): 446. See also Herman Belz, *Emancipation and Equal Rights* (New York, 1978), 108–40, and Charles Fairman, *Reconstruction and Reunion* (New York, 1971), 1117–49.

[19] Proposed by Sen. Sumner, *Congressional Globe*, 39th Cong., 1st sess., 1866, 674, quoted in Andrew Kull, *The Color-Blind Constitution* (Cambridge, Mass., 1992), 252 n. 27.

[20] Remarks of Rep. Stevens, *Congressional Globe*, 39th Cong., 1st sess., 1867, 3148, quoted in Foner, *Reconstruction*, 254.

charter of free labor, aimed at ending the degradation of labor, "both black and white,"[21] "subdu[ing] that spirit" which "makes the laborer the mere tool of the capitalist."[22]

Concern for the laborer's freedom found expression in the Supreme Court's first important encounter with the Reconstruction amendments. The plaintiff butchers in the *Slaughter-House Cases*[23] were exemplars of Lincoln's "free labor system."[24] They were shop-owning artisans, and in the new monopoly created by the Louisiana legislature, these "Free Laborers" saw a serious threat that they would be reduced to the condition of mere hirelings, with their "labor" and the "fruits of [their] toil" "subjected to the control of the new corporation."[25] Yet, as Justices Field and Bradley declared in their famous *Slaughter-House* dissents, the Reconstruction amendments had promised to secure "everyone's" right freely to "pursue a calling" and enjoy the "fruits of his own labor."[26] Indeed, this "equality of right" in the pursuits of life was "the fundamental idea upon which our institutions rest, and unless adhered to in the legislatures of the country, our government will be a republic only in name."[27] The Louisiana monopoly, so Field and Bradley reasoned, violated this "equality of right" and with it "the right of free labor."[28] This pristine free labor reading of the Fourteenth Amendment unfolded in strikingly different directions: toward *Lochner v. New York* and liberty of contract in the nation's courts, and toward an egalitarian and anticorporate radicalism in the hands of the labor movement.

Industrialization had changed the social meaning of constitutional equality, labor reformers argued. For Lincoln, the hireling's lot was almost as unfree as the slave's, but it was a brief way station on the road to owning productive property and laboring for oneself. That was the status of "Free Labor," but Lincoln's "free labor system" was no more. Today's hireling was no longer tomorrow's proprietor. Destined to remain propertyless, the lifelong industrial hireling's status was akin to bondage. Judges and treatise writers freely conceded that the common law of employment mingled free contract with the centuries-old law of "master and servant." Employment law bore the "marks of social caste," recognizing the employer/master's property in his worker/servant's labor and his rights "to direct and control the servant" and to unleash state violence against his servants' or-

[21] VanderVelde, "Labor Vision," 453.
[22] Remarks of Rep. Shannon, *Congressional Globe*, 38th Cong., 1st sess., 1864, 2948, quoted in ibid., 471.
[23] 83 US 36 (1873).
[24] See Forbath, "Ambiguities of Free Labor."
[25] Trial transcript quoted in ibid., 772–73.
[26] 83 US 36, 90 (1873) (Field, J., dissenting).
[27] Ibid., 93.
[28] Ibid.

ganizing efforts. Yet, labor advocates pointed out, the Constitution's guarantee of equal rights was meant to vouchsafe the material independence and dignity of free labor. This constitutional promise now demanded that lawmakers undo the common-law rules that were the legal underpinnings of "wage slavery" and supplant them with statutes that repealed the harsh common-law restraints on collective action, set legal limits to the industrial workday, underwrote industrial cooperatives, and generally restored a measure of working men's and women's dignity and independence. The work of Antislavery remained "unfinished," labor reformers declared, in an echo of Lincoln on the founders; uprooting "this subtler form of [wage] slavery" demanded "reconstructing the whole Social System, North and South." Restoring Lincoln's apple of gold—a republic of free labor and equal citizens—once more demanded reinterpreting and recasting the silver frame and spurning an oppressive, counterfeit Constitution being forged by the courts.[29]

Along with the rights of contract and free labor, the right to marry and have a family was the other fundamental freedom every Republican agreed was enshrined by the Civil Rights Act of 1866 and the Fourteenth Amendment. This account of core citizenship rights was all of a piece for the freedman, but not the freedwoman or women generally. Married women lacked not only the right to vote but also the right to contract; their labor and its fruits belonged to their husbands.[30]

Far from "universal," the "new birth of freedom," as Congress conceived it, was deeply gendered. But women's advocates, famously, seized on the mainstream constitutional language of freedom as self-ownership and equal rights. In addition to woman's suffrage, the organizations that led women's struggles for equal citizenship held that ending women's status as a "dependent and despised class" demanded that women "enjoy the fruits of their own labor." Equal rights meant legal autonomy in market and property relations and economic independence within the marriage relation. Yet the common law denied all these rights in favor of the husband. Law and social usage "oppressed [her] with such limitation and degradation of labor as mark the condition of a disabled caste." So, women's rights organizations campaigned for statutes that would overturn the husband's common-law rights to his wife's labor, both within the household and outside it.[31] Passage of married women's property and earnings statutes ac-

[29] See Forbath, "Ambiguities of Free Labor," 779–86; Eric Foner, *Politics and Ideology in the Age of Civil War* (New York, 1980), 61–72. On the English side, see Davis, *Problem of Slavery in the Age of Revolution*, 346–501.

[30] Stanley, "Conjugal Bonds and Wage Labor," 492.

[31] *Proceedings of the Woman's Rights Convention, held at Worcester, October 23 and 24, 1850* (Boston, 1851), 4–5, quoted in Reva Siegel, "Home as Work: The First Woman's Rights Claims

complished part of this project. The property statutes, however, generally covered only such property as wives brought with them to, or received as gifts during, the marriage relation, which, in most marriages, was none. The hard-fought earnings statutes entitled married women to keep their own wages; "Now," one law writer declared, the married woman "has the right to her labor."[32] But the new statutes left untouched the web of custom, union rules, and legal proscriptions that kept women out of most industrial jobs, skilled trades, and professions. Moreover, the earning statutes covered only wages or income earned outside the home, and so for the majority of workingwomen, who toiled inside the household, the earnings statutes left the old doctrine of marital service intact.

Here nineteenth-century feminists did not challenge the gender division of labor so much as the gendered definition of labor.[33] The "economy of the household," a woman's rights convention resolved, "is generally as much the source of family wealth as the labor and enterprise of man"; yet the law effaced women's contribution, categorically defining them as "dependents" and embedding their contribution to the family economy in property to which men held title. No less economically productive than men, the convention went on, women were entitled to participate equally in managing assets both helped to accumulate. In this manner, as Reva Siegel has shown, woman's rights advocates cannily employed the mainstream constitutional language of self-ownership and labor rights to dismantle and reconstruct the legal and cultural discourse that cast women as unproductive dependents.[34]

Most freedmen and freedwomen apparently agreed with Thaddeus Stevens on the necessity of confiscating the largest plantations of the South and redistributing them to former slaves in order to secure the African Americans' liberty. Like the industrial workers in the North, they insisted on hewing to the older republican definition of liberty and to Lincoln's understanding of free labor—not mere self-ownership but the independence that accompanies ownership and control of productive property. Only land, said former Mississippi slave Merrimon Howard, would enable "the poor class to enjoy the sweet boon of freedom."[35] When Congress refused to redistribute Southern property, the key sites of argument and

Concerning Wives' Household Labor, 1850–1880," *Yale Law Journal* 103 (March 1994): 1100; see also Norma Basch, *In the Eyes of the Law* (Ithaca, 1982), 162–99.

[32] Stanley, "Conjugal Bonds and Wage Labor," 492.

[33] I borrow this phrase from Jeanne Boydston, *Home and Work: Housework, Wages, and the Ideology of Labor in the Early Republic* (New York, 1990), xi–xv.

[34] See Siegel, "Home as Work," 1112–18.

[35] Quoted in Eric Foner, "The Meaning of Freedom in the Age of Emancipation," presidential address to Annual Conference of Organization of American Historians, April 14, 1994, in *Journal of American History* 81 (September 1994): 435.

struggle shifted to the hustings, legislatures, local courthouses, churches, and fields of the South. State and local black Republican leaders formed coalitions with representatives of white yeomen and tenant farmers to build up a southern base for the "party of Free Labor."[36] Meanwhile Republican judges and justices of the peace adjudicated contract disputes between freedmen and former masters in a fashion that confirmed the planters' worst fears about "Negro rule" and confirmed as well the mutability and redistributive potential of contract doctrine. "Equal rights under law" was anything but self defining; as is often the case in contract and property relations, the devil was in the details and who controlled them.[37] As these judges granted more power to sharecroppers, the planter class and Democratic Party turned to massive violence and economic coercion to quell black voting and political associations. The Democrats and the Ku Klux Klan also meted out violence against black property holders and skilled crafts workers, aiming, in one freedman's words, to "keep us hewers of wood and drawers of water to as mean a class of white men . . . as live in any one of these reconstructed states."[38] By 1874, northern weariness with Reconstruction and its readiness to "leave the South alone" enabled the Democrats to regain control of Congress. Over the next two decades all three branches helped dismantle the federal government's protections for the freedmen's recently enacted constitutional rights.

After Reconstruction, racial backlash in the South and intensifying class strife and agrarian unrest in the North and Midwest drove Republican leaders to remake the party into a bastion of business and laissez-faire. Their equal rights rhetoric gradually hardened into an antidemocratic and antiredistributive liberal orthodoxy, which became the liberal-legal orthodoxy expressed in cases such as *Lochner*. Yet the architects of this orthodoxy—such treatise writers as Christopher Tiedman and Thomas Cooley and elite lawyers and legal reformers such as David Dudley Field— anguished over the fate of the distributive ideal in an industrialized America.[39] To a surprising degree, these pioneers of laissez-faire jurisprudence

[36] See Foner, *Reconstruction*, 281–411.

[37] See Donald Nieman, "Black Political Power and Local Justice: Washington County, Texas, 1868–1885" (unpublished paper in author's possession); Nieman, *To Set the Law in Motion: The Freedmen's Bureau and the Legal Rights of Blacks* (Millwood, N.Y., 1979); Thomas Holt, *Black over White: Negro Political Leadership in South Carolina during Reconstruction* (Urbana, Ill., 1977); Edward Magdol, *A Right to the Land: Essays on the Freedmen's Community* (Urbana, Ill., 1977).

[38] Quoted in Peter J. Rachleff, *Black Labor in the South: Richmond, Virginia, 1865–1890* (Philadelphia, 1984), 145.

[39] See, for example, Thomas M. Cooley, *A Treatise on the Constitutional Limitations which Rest upon the Legislative Powers of the States of the American Union*, 7th ed. (Boston, 1903), esp. 512–14, urging that morally "the [employer's] business is as much that of those who bring to it their labor . . . [and not] exclusively their employers'" and so the latter should share "control" and "profits" with employees. See also David Dudley Field, "Industrial Co-operation,"

shared the conviction of Gilded Age radicals that the emerging corporate order offended the republican Constitution. And, like many in the agrarian and labor protest movements, these laissez-faire thinkers embraced the idea of cooperative ownership of the tools of industry as a way of rebuilding the material foundations of workingmen's equal citizenship—the modern equivalent of broadly distributed yeoman property.[40] Of course, as "new liberals," the elite reformers could not abide the use of state power to help bring about such measures. Instead, they exhorted captains of industry to address the widening gulf between labor and capital.[41] Not surprisingly, these pleadings produced more expiation than reform, and it fell to Gilded Age protest movements to write the first serious chapter on the significance for an industrialized America of the distributive and enabling dimensions of constitutional discourse about labor and property.

Populism marked an effort to rebuild a "poor man's party" akin to the southern Republicans on new foundations. Not since the abolitionists had reformers plunged so deeply into constitutional discourse. As the Populists' 1892 presidential candidate, James Weaver, put it, the power of "organized wealth" had arrayed itself against the "rights of the plain people as vouchsafed by the Constitution."[42] Like their labor-reform counterparts, Populists rejected the "dogma" that the "doctrine of equality laid down in our Constitution" was "limited to mere equality before the law." The "real theory" underlying "equal rights," the editor of the Populist *National Economist* explained, is that the "doctrine of political equality carries with it the idea that the republic and popular government can only be maintained by sustaining the practical equality of all the people." "Imbedded in our Constitution" is the "principle of securing the widest distribution of wealth and education by maintaining equality in the opportunities to gain them." This was "the great basic idea of our laws, the very cornerstone of the republican structure," and that structure was at risk.[43] Corporations "brought into existence by legislation" had arrogated to themselves the tools of industry, transportation, communication, and finance. Creating "egregious concentrations of wealth for the few and proportionate

---

North American Review 140 (1885): 411, decrying the dependency of wage earners on capital as incompatible with the status of citizenship and urging capitalists to transform corporations into labor-capital "cooperatives." Christopher Tiedman authored a constitutional treatise vilified by Progressives for spreading the doctrines of laissez-faire constitutionalism, but Tiedman's treatise was at one with the constitutional outlook of Gilded Age radicals in suggesting that the statutes and common-law decisions which provided the legal framework for the giant new corporations trenched on the Equal Protection Clause. See Tiedman, *A Treatise on the Limitations of Police Power in the United States* (St. Louis, 1886), 324–69.

[40] See Forbath, "Ambiguities of Free Labor," 787–92.

[41] See, for example, Cooley, *Treatise*, 511–15; Field, "Industrial Co-operation," 412–20.

[42] James B. Weaver, *A Call to Action* (Des Moines, Iowa, 1892), 34.

[43] Henry Tracy, "Corporations: Their Uses and Abuses, and Their Effect upon Republican Institutions and Productive Industries," *National Economist*, 187, 188.

poverty, dependency and powerlessness for the many," they wielded their power to destroy the "democratic social fabric"—all in "utter violation of the basic principles of our Constitution and common law."[44]

In Populists' view, the courts were eroding the common-law constraints on corporate expansion and endowing corporations with constitutional personhood and property rights that stymied regulation.[45] With the rise of the "trusts," Populists held, key functions of government—regulating interstate commerce, issuing and controlling currency—had been given over to private corporations and "leased to associated speculators." These were constitutional usurpations. Not only did the Constitution authorize Congress to perform these functions, but when Congress's powers were exercised by private actors in a fashion that violated the common good, dispossessing farmers and reducing wage earners to industrial slavery, the Constitution also *demanded* that Congress act.[46]

Gilded Age labor reformers concurred. Securing citizenship rights and republican government in an industrialized America meant "engrafting republican principles on property and industry." This "engrafting" meant, first of all, amending the Constitution to "free [it] from the courts." Appropriately enough, these agrarian and labor antimonopolists decried the judiciary's "asserted Monopoly on interpreting the Constitution," for which "no warrant can be found in the Constitution itself." By amending the Constitution to "tame" the courts, they sought to reclaim the "Power of the Co-Ordinate Branches and of the Sovereign People to render their own Interpretations."[47] Substantively, renewing farmers' and workers' citizenship rights meant freeing the "colored tenant and the white" one from the "iron grip of the money power." It meant ensuring for industrial workers the "right to a remunerative job" through public works and countercyclical spending and, through an end to the harsh common-law restraints on workers' collective action and the savagery of "government by injunction," encouraging robust unions and industrial cooperation. And finally,

[44] Ibid. For similar arguments, see also John Potter, "The Duty of a Reformer," in Nelson Dunning, ed., *The Farmers' Alliance History and Agricultural Digest* (Washington, D.C., 1891), 331–32; "Political Economy," *National Economist*, May 11, 1889, 115; "President Jone's Message," *National Economist*, September 7, 1890, 386; "Speech of Governor Pennoyer," *Non-Conformist*, April 4, 1892, 1.

[45] See, for example, James Davis, *A Political Revelation* (Dallas, 1894), 134–38; Henry Jelley, *The Voice of Labor* (Chicago, 1893), 45–51.

[46] Davis, *A Political Revelation*, 37.

[47] See "Speech of Governor Pennoyer," 1. For extended discussions of the right and duty of coordinate branches to make and enforce their own interpretations of the Constitution, see Davis, *A Political Revelation*, 13–73, and Jelley, *Voice of Labor*, 23–67. The constitutional amendments that the Populists championed to "tame" the judiciary and restore popular sovereignty ranged from election of federal and state judges to abolition of judicial review of various classes of reform statutes, direct election of senators, and initiative, referendum, and recall in state constitutions. For discussion, see William Ross, *A Muted Fury* (Princeton, 1994).

through these agencies, it meant enabling workers to exercise the rights and responsibilities of control over productive property.

Southern blacks continued to vote and form political associations for virtually two decades after Reconstruction. The rights talk of Gilded Age black labor and agrarian reformers "wove together the rhetoric of 'equal rights' and 'race pride.'"[48] They continued to rage against Klan violence and forcible exclusion from skilled callings, but they also struck more expansive chords, drawing out the links between the labor-Populist reform program and their Reconstruction-bred understanding of equal citizenship: a decent living and, with it, dignity, autonomy and equal standing in civil society and polity, secured by something beyond formal equality— enabling rights and resources, accessible land and credit, and new forms of civic association linking market and polity.[49]

Blacks joined the Populists in significant numbers in some southern states, but the threat of a biracial Populist alliance bred another concerted wave of terror, violence, and massive disenfranchisement, unopposed by federal authority. Waving the banner of white solidarity, southern "redeemers" sought to defuse the remnants of Populism by disenfranchising lower-class whites as well as blacks. They succeeded; the all-white primary and racial intimidation took precedence in blocking black voter participation, but in many southern states more whites than blacks—a majority of white voters—were barred from the ballot box by the new poll tax. This codification of white supremacy and widespread disenfranchisement secured a closed, one-party system dominated by the landholding elites of the Black Belt and by New South entrepreneurs.[50]

The United States Supreme Court played an important part in this process, almost strangling the Equal Protection Clause "in its infancy."[51] The Court lent its sanction to the reconstituted caste system of the New South,[52] and the Court's bad faith, shared by all branches of the federal government, led to a fatal anomaly in the constitutional revolution we are about to examine, producing a reactionary core, the Solid South, at the heart of the New Deal liberal coalition.

[48] Rachleff, *Black Labor in the South*, 145.

[49] Ibid.; Foner, *Reconstruction;* Philip S. Foner and Ronald L. Lewis, eds., *The Black Worker during the Era of the Knights of Labor* (Philadelphia, 1978).

[50] J. Morgan Kousser, *The Shaping of Southern Politics: Suffrage Restrictions and the Establishment of the One-Party South* (New Haven, 1976); Arthur Raper and Ira Reid, *Sharecroppers All* (Chapel Hill, 1941), 4.

[51] *Regents of the Univ. of Cal. v Bakke*, 438 US 265, 291 (1978).

[52] See, for example, *U.S. v Cruikshank*, 92 US 542 (1875); *U.S. v Harris*, 106 US 629 (1883); Civil Rights Cases, 109 US 3 (1883); *Plessy v Ferguson*, 163 US 527 (1896); and *Williams v Mississippi*, 170 US 213 (1898). A classic account of the Court's role is found in C. Vann Woodward, *The Strange Career of Jim Crow*, 2d ed. (New York, 1966), esp. 59–72.

What most separated Progressives from Gilded Age reformers was the death of racial liberalism among whites. Throughout the nation the vast majority of white Progressives concurred with or at least acquiesced without protest in the soured Tom Watson's conclusion: social reform for white southerners depended on black disenfranchisement and segregation. It was the inverted image of Du Bois's insight and the foundation of southern Progressivism. From the perspective of southern Progressive history, "the great race settlement of 1890–1910 . . . was itself the seminal 'progressive' reform of the era."[53] The plausibility of this outlook on the national scene hinged on a revaluation of Reconstruction, a new narrative, which the new social science and historical professions helped to frame. Reconstruction became a wildly misguided and self-regarding experiment on the part of northern reform. A backward people, blacks had "suffered much but benefited more" under the civilizing "tutelage" of slavery. Reconstruction interrupted the civilizing process, duping the "race" with delusions of political grandeur beyond its reach. Former slaveholders had been obliged to "redeem" the South from governmental corruption and the madness of interracial equality. Disenfranchisement of a "backward people" was a grim but "necessary reform." Now the gradual uplift of the "Negro in special and separate institutions" would lead him toward "industrial efficiency" without injuring the betterment of white farmers and workers.[54]

To this tidily evolutionary tale, the Progressive historians added their "economic interpretation" of the Radical Republican project—not a grand constitutional redefinition of "We, the People" but a shrewd capitalist scheme to clinch national policymaking for northern capital and open the South to northern industrial development and exploitation.[55] Thus debunked, Reconstruction could be set aside. Professor of political science at turn-of-the-century Princeton, Woodrow Wilson wrote in his American history textbook that the compromise of 1877 meant that the "supremacy of the white people was henceforth assured in the administration of the southern States" and the "Union restored . . . to normal conditions of government." With the "abandonment of federal interference with elections, the 'southern question' fortunately lost its prominence" in national politics, to be replaced by the great Progressive issues of the

[53] Jack Kirby, *Darkness at the Dawning: Race and Reform in the Progressive South* (Philadelphia, 1972), 4; C. Vann Woodward, *Tom Watson: Agrarian Rebel* (New York, 1938).

[54] That was Woodrow Wilson's resigned conclusion, distilling the wisdom of a series of articles on "the reconstruction of the Southern states" by leading academics in the *Atlantic Monthly*. See Woodrow Wilson, "The Reconstruction of the Southern States," *Atlantic Monthly*, January 1901, 87, 1–3.

[55] See Kirby, *Darkness at the Dawning*, 89–108; Richard Hofstadter, *The Progressive Historians: Turner, Beard, Parrington* (New York, 1968); Charles Beard and Mary Beard, *The Rise of American Civilization* (New York, 1933).

day: "the reform of the civil service, the control of corporations, conflicts between capital and labor . . . and the purification of the ballot." Wilson would address these Progressive concerns in the White House, where, as the first southern occupant since the Civil War, his administration brought Jim Crow to the capital and the federal bureaucracy.[56]

Standard accounts paint a different gulf between Progressive Era reformers and their Gilded Age predecessors. They emphasize the Progressives' accommodation to corporate dominance, their fondness for managerial and administrative solutions to social problems, and their role in recasting American "freedom" to mean abundance and security in the sphere of consumption, not dignity and independence in the sphere of production. The Progressives' vision of reform, the story goes, substituted a new consumerist welfare state for the old producerist commonwealth.[57]

There is much to this tale, but it paints over important continuities. The Progressives added state-based social provision to the rights contended for by the social citizenship tradition. Their administrative state-building ambitions were foreign to most Gilded Age reformers. But even the most modernizing Progressives such as Herbert Croly were engaged with the "political economy of citizenship."[58] "How," Croly repeatedly asked, "can the wage-earners obtain an amount of economic independence analogous to that upon which the pioneer democrat could count?" Social insurance and social legislation were necessary, but no substitute for transforming "the wage system itself in the interest of an industrial self-governing democracy . . . a new system, based upon the dignity, the responsibility and the moral value of human work." This was essential, in Croly's account, to "converting civil and political liberty" under the "old Constitution" into their "social consummation."[59]

[56] Woodrow Wilson, *Division and Reunion, 1829–1889* (New York, 1898), 287, 290.

[57] See, for example, Christopher Lasch, *The New Radicalism in America, 1889–1963: The Intellectual as Social Type* (New York, 1967); Lasch, *The True and Only Heaven: Progress and Its Critics* (New York, 1991); Alan Dawley, *Struggles for Justice: Social Responsibility and the Liberal State* (Cambridge, Mass., 1991); Lawrence Goodwyn, *Democratic Promise: The Populist Moment in America* (New York, 1976); David Montgomery, *The Fall of the House of Labor: The Workplace, the State, and American Labor Activism, 1865–1925* (Cambridge, 1987).

[58] The phrase "political economy of citizenship" is borrowed from Michael Sandel's important book *Democracy's Discontent* (Cambridge, Mass., 1996), 121–249, which makes fruitful use of the historical work on this tradition of discourse linking political economy and citizenship.

[59] Herbert Croly, *Progressive Democracy* (New York, 1914), 380, 384, 215. On Progressive efforts at creating state-based social insurance, see Arthur Link and Richard McCormick, *Progressivism* (Arlington Heights, Ill., 1983); David Thelen, *The New Citizenship: The Origins of Progressivism in Wisconsin, 1885–1900* (Columbia, 1972); Theda Skocpol, *Protecting Soldiers and Mothers: The Political Origins of Social Policy in the United States* (Cambridge, Mass., 1992); and Udo Sautter, *Three Cheers for the Unemployed: Government and Unemployment before the New Deal* (Cambridge, Mass., 1991). On the Progressives as state builders and would-be state builders, see William E. Forbath, "Labor Politics in England and America," in Christopher Tomlins, ed., *Labor Law in America: Historical Essays* (Baltimore, 1992), and Stephen Skow-

Like John Dewey, Croly's critique of the "old Constitution" extended to constitutionalism *tout court*. One can search in vain for any rights talk on the part of these thinkers; to them rights seem destined to ossify into impediments to practical change. Constitutionalism, they thought, was just what the *Lochner* Court insisted: a limit on the democracy's capacity to reconstruct its social environment by redistributive means. Yet, even such a thoroughgoing anticonstitutionalist as Croly framed the case for reform with a constitutional narrative and interpretation of the founding. "The American democracy," Croly argued, could accept "in the beginning an inaccessible body of [judge-made] Law" and the judiciary's "uncontrollable" sway over the political economy because "the Law promised property to all." This was the Constitution's "original promise": economic opportunity and a republic of freeholders secured by limited government and equal rights to own and hold property. This constitutional promise formed a "working compromise" between the "pioneer democrat" and "the monarchy of the law and aristocracy of the robe." In industrial America, however, the ideals of liberty and equality that were "wrought into our constitutions" no longer "consist[ed] in the specific formulation of legal and economic individualism" defended by the courts. Interpreting and safeguarding these constitutional ideals now properly belonged to the "active law-making and law-administering branches" watched over by an "active citizenry." Croly urged changing the amending process to create the conditions for the citizenry's playing a more frequent and active role in constitutional politics. Doing so, he hoped, would enable them, in turn, to alter the constitutional text and structure to accommodate the "active, democratic" branches' role in instituting the new meaning of the old liberties.[60]

Louis Brandeis's links to Gilded Age reform ideals are better known. Brandeis had no use for Croly's centralizing impulses or for his anticonstitutionalism. Like the latter, Brandeis was a stern critic of the laissez-faire Constitution and classical legal orthodoxy, but his critique demanded an enlightened rather than marginalized constitutional judiciary, one that still enforced tempered norms of federalism and separation of powers. Unlike Croly or Dewey, Brandeis—with Florence Kelly and most other law-trained Progressives—strove to reconstruct rather than relinquish the language of rights.[61] Thus Brandeis declared in a widely published 1915 address at Boston's Faneuil Hall, "The Constitutional protections of life and liberty are now being interpreted according to demands of social jus-

---

ronek, *Building a New American State: The Expansion of National Administrative Capacities, 1877–1920* (Cambridge, 1982).

[60] Croly, *Progressive Democracy*, 209–11.

[61] On Kelly's efforts to reconstruct rights, see Joan Zimmerman, "The Jurisprudence of Equality: The Women's Minimum Wage, the First ERA, and *Adkins v. Children's Hospital*," *Journal of American History* 78 (1991): 188–225.

tice and of democracy." All Americans "must have a reasonable income" and "regular employment"; "they must have health and leisure," "decent working conditions," and "some system of social insurance." However, the "essentials of American citizenship are not satisfied by supplying merely workers' material needs." There could be no more "political democracy" in contemporary America, Brandeis told the U.S. Commission on Industrial Relations that same year, without "industrial democracy," without workers' "participating in the [business] decisions" of their firms—with "not only a voice but a vote."[62] Only by bringing constitutional democracy into industry could the United States produce not only goods but citizens as well. No more than his grittier counterparts in the labor movement did Brandeis expect the courts to enact this vision, but that took nothing away from its constitutional moorings. Today, we remember the restraint the Progressives demanded of the judiciary. We tend to forget, however, the affirmative obligations their vision laid on the other branches of government. They sought not the divorce of constitutional discourse from political economy but the replacement of the judiciary by "democratic" state actors as the nation's "authoritative constitutional political economists."[63]

II.

By now we can see why it was more than happenstance that so many of the key cases marking off the New Deal's constitutional revolution— *Schechter Poultry, Morehead v. New York ex rel Tipaldo, West Coast Hotel v. Parrish, Jones and Laughlin Steel Co. v. NLRB*—were labor cases.[64] They were labor cases for the same reason that *Lochner*—the case that gave its name to the Constitution's ancien régime—was a labor case: the common-law ordering of labor-capital relations, invested by the judiciary with the permanence of fundamental law, was the social institution at the center of that regime.

Beginning with the Court's attack on key New Deal reforms in 1935 and climaxing with FDR's Court-packing plan and the Court's famous 1937 "switch in time that saved nine," by the early 1940s the ancien régime in Constitutional law had been overthrown. With the appointments of New Deal justices like Hugo Black, Felix Frankfurter, William Douglas, Harlan Stone, and Robert Jackson—all leaders of the intellectual and political

---

[62] Louis D. Brandeis, "Statement to United States Commission on Industrial Relations" (January 23, 1915, reprinted in Brandeis, *The Curse of Bigness: Miscellaneous Papers*, ed. Osmond Kessler (Port Washington, N.Y., 1935), 73–74, 78–79.

[63] John R. Commons, *Legal Foundations of Capitalism* (Clifton, N.J., 1924).

[64] *Schechter Poultry Corp. v U.S.*, 295 US 495 (1935); *Morehead v New York ex rel Tipaldo*, 298 US 587 (1936); *West Coast Hotel v Parrish*, 300 US 379 (1937); *National Labor Relations Bd. v Jones & Laughlin Steel Corp.*, 301 US 1 (1937).

battles against the old constitutional order—the New Deal Constitution seemingly supplanted the *Lochner* Constitution. Entire doctrinal structures were swept away. Democracy now could reach labor-capital relations, Congress had no limits on its power to regulate the nation's economy, and a fourth branch of government, the administrative agency, ran roughshod over the constitutional separation of powers.

But how did this new constitutional order legitimate itself? In theory, big changes in the Constitution come about by amendment. Yet no amendments accompanied this sea change. Until recently the issue hardly mattered; no one questioned the wisdom of interring the *Lochner* regime. Now, however, a great many law professors say *Lochner*ism should have won. They believe the New Deal changes were unjustified; they required but received no validating Constitutional amendment.[65] These conservatives go on to argue for undoing the New Deal changes and resurrecting the laissez-faire Constitution.[66] And some federal judges as well as several of the Republican Party's present congressional leaders seem to agree.

Faced with this new crisis of legitimacy, the New Deal Constitution has found its defenders. One theory argues that the New Dealers had merely returned to the faith of the fathers. It was the jurisprudence of *Lochner* that had departed from precedent and tradition. But this restorationist perspective won't wash. As far as fidelity to the framers is concerned, recent scholarship leans heavily in favor of the ancien régime.[67]

There is a second, more sophisticated defense, which Cass Sunstein and Laurence Lessig describe as "translation."[68] It also fails. By Sunstein's own account, the New Deal "refashioned the three basic cornerstones" of the

[65] For example, Gary Lawson has written, "The post-New Deal administrative state is unconstitutional, and its validation by the legal system amounts to nothing less than a bloodless Constitutional revolution." See Lawson, "The Rise and Rise of the Administrative State," *Harvard Law Review* 107 (1994): 1231.

[66] See, for example, Lawson, "Rise of the Administrative State"; Bernard Siegan, *Economic Liberties and the Constitution* (Chicago, 1980); Richard Epstein, *Takings: Private Property and the Power of Eminent Domain* (Cambridge, Mass., 1985); Richard Epstein, "A Common Law for Labor Relations: A Critique of the New Deal Labor Legislation," *Yale Law Journal* 92 (1983): 1357; and Richard Epstein, "The Proper Scope of the Commerce Power," *Virginia Law Review* 73 (1987): 1387.

[67] See G. Edward White, *The Marshall Court and Cultural Change, 1815–1835* (New York, 1991); Morton Horwitz, "The Constitution of Change: Legal Fundamentality without Fundamentalism," *Harvard Law Review* 107 (1993): 32, 57; and Stephen Siegel, "Lochner Era Jurisprudence and the American Constitutional Tradition," *North Carolina Law Review* 70 (1991): 1–111.

[68] See Cass Sunstein, "Constitutionalism after the New Deal," *Harvard Law Review* 101 (1987): 421–97; Cass Sunstein, "New Deals," *New Republic,* January 20, 1992, 32 (review of *We the People,* by Bruce Ackerman); Cass Sunstein, "Congress, Constitutional Moments, and the Cost-Benefit State," *Stanford Law Review* 48 (1996): 247, 253–57; and Lawrence Lessig, "Understanding Changed Readings: Fidelity and Theory," *Stanford Law Review* 47 (1995): 395–472.

"original Constitutional structure": federalism, by expanding the powers of the national government to "something close to general police powers"; checks and balances, by delegating "enormous policymaking power to the President and creat[ing] . . . powerful, autonomous executive and independent agencies" that combined "traditionally separated powers of adjudication, execution, and legislation"; and individual rights, by authorizing a "wide range of redistributive policies."[69] Sunstein rightly sees these changes as embodying a "revolutionary redefinition of constitutional commitments," a "New Deal Constitution."[70] Yet, at the same time, Sunstein sides with those who insist that the New Deal era saw no rupture with the constitutional past, only a "translation" of tradition in light of changed circumstances. He cannot have it both ways. True, the process of uprooting old institutional arrangements and creating and legitimating new ones necessitates new readings or "translations" of normative traditions, but it also entails collective choices and committed action.

Thus, Sunstein and Lessig are talking about politics, constitutive politics, and not simply "translation." Their account of New Deal constitutional change assumes constitutional actors besides the courts, but their theory puts all the burden of justification on judicial interpreters. Nonjudicial actors have no interpretive authority of their own; their constitutive choices and actions and their extrajudicial "translations" of constitutional tradition play no part in Lessig's and Sunstein's hermeneutics. And because courts may not enact such changes as Sunstein describes, their theory ends up papering over the New Deal's genuine rupture with the constitutional past and leeching politics, choice, and agency out of the story.

Putting "constitutional" or "higher lawmaking politics" at the center of his argument lends Bruce Ackerman's defense of the New Deal Constitution its originality and importance. Ackerman agrees with today's conservatives that the New Deal transformations were significant enough to require Constitutional amendment. But he interprets the political processes that attended those transformations as sufficient to amend the Constitution. For Ackerman the New Deal marked a "constitutional moment," a sustained, self-conscious political act by the citizenry that overthrows one constitutional regime and ushers in a new one.[71] Ackerman finds his warrant for this unconventional theory in the history of Reconstruction. That great constitutional revolution was also technically illegal. Despite the Union victory, it was all too easy to see how the former Confederate states

---

[69] See Sunstein, "Constitutionalism after the New Deal," 423–25.

[70] See Sunstein, "Congress, Constitutional Moments, and the Cost-Benefit State," 253–54.

[71] See Bruce Ackerman, *We the People: Foundations* (Cambridge, Mass., 1991); Ackerman, "Higher Lawmaking," in Sanford Levinson, ed., *Responding to Imperfection: Theory and Practice of Constitutional Amendment* (Princeton, 1995).

could block the Republicans' constitutional initiatives. Lincoln and then Johnson put extraordinary pressures on the South to ratify the Thirteenth Amendment, but with the Fourteenth Amendment, Johnson stopped in his tracks. This prompted the Republicans on Capitol Hill to transform the regular election of 1866 into "one of the great higher lawmaking events of American history," going to the people with the Fourteenth Amendment as their platform and winning a mandate for constitutional reform. Johnson, however, denied the mandate and led ten southern state governments to excrcise the veto seemingly offered by Article 5. The Republican Congress responded in turn, destroying those governments and demanding ratification as a condition for recognition of reconstructed governments in the South. Then Johnson sought to stymie this plan, and Congress impeached him. When Johnson backed down, he accepted the Republicans' claim to speak for the "people" in their newfound constitutional vision and thereby set the precedent for that later "switch in time" on the part of the Supreme Court in 1937. Generalizing the pattern, Ackerman sums up the process "in terms of a simple schema: "Constitutional Impasse . . . Electoral 'Mandate' . . . Challenge to Dissenting Institutions . . . the 'Switch in Time.'"[72]

It is not hard to see how the schema applies to New Deal history, and Ackerman is right about the self-consciously constitutional character of New Deal politics and that New Dealers claimed a constitutional mandate arising from their crushing victories in the election of 1936—or the sequence of elections in 1932, 1934, and 1936. But he is wrong in stating that the New Deal's "constitutional mandate" amounted simply to an authorization for expanded federal power and an activist national government.[73] Ackerman dodges the question of whether the New Dealers, like the Reconstruction Republicans, sought a mandate to redefine national citizenship. As we shall see, they did.

In May 1935 the Court decided *Schechter*, striking down the National Recovery Act and ruling that the federal government had no power to regulate wages and hours in the nation's industries, save where the workplace was directly part of interstate commerce. In May 1936, *Carter Coal Co.* reaffirmed that "Congress is powerless to regulate anything which is not commerce." Two weeks later, *Morehead* invalidated the New York minimum wage law for women and children, echoing the 1923 *Adkins* decision: "The State is without power by any form of legislation to prohibit, change or nullify contracts between employers and adult women workers as to the

---

[72] Ackerman, "Higher Lawmaking," 76–79.
[73] See Ackerman, *We the People,* 103.

amount of wages to be paid." The Court's "stone wall" across the path of New Deal reform seemed complete.[74]

Conservative Republicans and business organizations such as the Liberty League hailed the Court, and as the 1936 campaign got under way, they repeatedly accused FDR and the New Deal of "tearing down the Constitution." Roosevelt, the Republican platform declared, was "insist[ing] on the passage of laws that are contrary to the Constitution," "violat[ing] the rights and liberties of citizens," and "constantly seeking to usurp" the rights "reserved to the people and the States."[75] Roosevelt responded in kind. Throughout the summer and fall of 1936, FDR characterized the campaign as a moment of extraordinary popular deliberation and a time for basic, constitutive choices about the powers and duties of government and citizens' legitimate claims on the state.[76]

Looking back in early 1937, FDR and New Dealers in Congress depicted their crushing victory as a "great Revolution," a "repudiation of the Constitutional philosophy of the prevailing five-judge majority" and an embrace of the "philosophy of the New Deal."[77] By an "unprecedented majority," the people "upheld the legislation" the courts had struck down. In these terms Senator (soon to be Justice) Hugo Black put the case for the administration's controversial Court-packing plan. Congress, Black declared, had "not only the right but the imperative duty under the Constitution" to "protect the People from the miserable and degrading effects" of joblessness and poverty. This was the "Constitutional philosophy of progressive democracy" that "went before the People last fall." The people adopted it, but the "courts have not understood this revolution."[78]

In his second term's "first radio report to the people," Roosevelt put forward the constitutive-politics case for his controversial "Plan for Reorganization of the Judiciary." "I hope that you have re-read the Constitution of the United States in these past few weeks," he told his millions of listen-

[74] See *Schechter Poultry Corp. v U.S.*, 295 US 495 (1935); *Carter v Carter Coal Co.*, 298 US 238 (1936); *Morehead v New York ex rel Tipaldo*, 298 US 587 (1936). "Stone wall" is attributed to Franklin Delano Roosevelt's attorney general, Homer Cummings. See Irving Bernstein, *A Caring Society: The New Deal, the Worker, and the Great Depression* (Boston, 1995), 128.

[75] See Leroy Blanton, ed., *Platforms of the Two Great Parties, 1932–1940* (Washington, 1940), 373.

[76] See, for example, "Acceptance of the Renomination for the Presidency," Philadephia, Pennsylvania, June 27, 1936, in *The Public Papers and Addresses of Franklin D. Roosevelt*, ed. Samuel Rosenman, 13 vols. (New York, 1969), 5:234 ("Never since the early days of the New England town meeting have the purposes and affairs of government been so widely discussed").

[77] See speech of Sen. Hugo Black, 76th Cong., 1st sess., *Congressional Record* (March 25, 1937), 81, pt. 6:A636–38; see also speech of Sen. Logan, 75th Cong., 1st sess, *Congressional Record* (July 8, 1937), 81, pt. 6:6902–3.

[78] See "Radio Address by Hon. Hugo L. Black of Alabama, February 23, 1937," 75th Cong., 1st Sess., *Congressional Record*, 81, pt. 6:A306–8.

ers. Like the Protestant Bible, the Constitution was a "layman's document." No priesthood or legal elite enjoyed a monopoly of interpretive authority. To the contrary, at critical moments in the past, the "lay rank and file," "the American people," and their reform-minded leaders had set their own constitutional vision against the doctrines of the judiciary and legal elite and "ultimately prevailed." They "overruled" the Court. So it was today.[79]

In the end, FDR and the New Dealers had to depend on neither the amendment process nor the Court-packing plan to "save the Constitution from the Court."[80] While Congress was debating the latter, the Court made its famous "switch in time." Soon the appointments to the Court of Black, Jackson and other New Dealers would turn acquiescence into assent toward the New Deal "mandate." But what was the mandate's substance? The constitutional choices FDR and the New Dealers laid out during the 1936 campaign were not only about lawmakers' authority to regulate the economy but also involved the recognition of new rights and new rights bearers. Prior to the assertion of enlarged governmental powers was a redefinition of national citizenship, which entailed those expanded powers.

During the first New Deal, FDR had already promised to redefine the duties of national government. "Every man has a right to life," Roosevelt declared, and a "right to make a comfortable living." The "government," he went on, owes to everyone an avenue to possess himself of a portion of the nation's wealth sufficient for his needs, through his own work." Roosevelt and his allies in Congress also seized on the time-honored reformers' reliance on the language of the Preamble to undergird a positive vision of national responsibilities: "If our Federal Government was established among other things, 'to promote the general welfare,' it is our plain duty to provide for that security upon which welfare depends. . . . [T]he security of the home, the security of livelihood, and the security of social insurance . . . constitute a right which belongs to every individual and every family willing to work."[81] Thus did FDR introduce what he called the "general welfare Constitution." In Congress, too, New Dealers repeated earlier twentieth-century reformers' demands that the constitutional protections of life, liberty, and property be interpreted, in Brandeis's words, "according to the demands of social justice and of democracy." Their social and economic rights rhetoric echoed a protest language millions of

[79] See Franklin Delano Roosevelt, "A 'Fireside Chat' Discussing the Plan for Reorganization of the Judiciary," March 9, 1937, Washington, D.C., in *Public Papers*, 6:124; see also Roosevelt, "The Constitution of the United States was a Layman's Document, Not a Lawyer's Contract," address on Constitution Day, September 17, 1937, Washington, D.C., in *Public Papers*, 6:363–65.

[80] See Roosevelt "'Fireside Chat,'" 6:126.

[81] Franklin Delano Roosevelt, "Objectives of the Administration," June 8, 1934, in *Public Papers*, 3:291–92.

industrial workers encountered in the groundswell of organizing by the Congress of Industrial Organizations (CIO), and workers made this social rights talk part of mass consciousness. As Lizabeth Cohen has shown, during the 1920s the nation's millions of unorganized, largely new-immigrant factory workers looked on the national government and national elections with mistrust and indifference. Their welfare needs were met, if at all, by paternalistic employers or ethnic organizations. Now, they were ardent—and overwhelmingly Democratic—voters; they had turned away from employers and ethnic associations and looked instead to the national government for such basic goods as welfare, security, and employment. Experience with early New Deal programs and rhetoric engendered among these millions of working-class families a remarkable "new sense of entitlement." They made no apologies, Cohen shows, for taking relief, social security, insurance, mortgages, and jobs from the state. As contributing members of society, they had rights to such things, and they rallied behind those politicians, labor leaders, and other reformers who championed expanding the programs that backed up these rights.[82]

For his part, FDR continued to make the labor movement's social and economic rights rhetoric his own, both responding to and encouraging workers' new sense of entitlement. Famously "pragmatic" and often tentative in reform strategies, FDR proved constant in employing social citizenship as a language of ends. This public rhetoric—of which FDR and his speechwriters were more creatures than creators—shapes the texts to which Ackerman would have us look for the "Electoral Mandate" of 1936. Roosevelt's speech at the 1936 Democratic Convention rang in the oppositionist Constitution. He set out "the people's mandate" for new understandings of "liberty" and "equality" and of the citizen's legitimate claims on the state. Here was the oppositionist narrative of social change and constitutional usurpation. Like Brandeis in the second decade of the twentieth century and Weaver in the 1890s, FDR told of the dangers of a new kind of tyranny, not political but economic: a "new industrial dictatorship" that had "concentrated into their own hands an almost complete control over other people's property, other people's money, other people's labor—other people's lives."[83] Roosevelt's constitutional narrative reached the same crisis and turning point as had Weaver's and Brandeis's. Struggling against "such tyranny as this," Roosevelt proclaimed, has given "us as a people a new understanding of our Government and of ourselves." Our

[82] Lizabeth Cohen, *Making a New Deal: Industrial Workers in Chicago, 1919–1939* (Cambridge, 1990), 252–81. See also Bernstein, *A Caring Society;* and Bernstein, *Turbulent Years: A History of the American Worker, 1933–1941* (Boston, 1969).

[83] Franklin Delano Roosevelt, "Acceptance of the Renomination for the Presidency," 232–34.

inherited understandings had brought us to the brink of "economic slavery." Now we know, "freedom is no half-and-half affair." Government has an "inescapable obligation" to "protect the citizen in his right to work and his right to live" no less than "in his right to vote."[84]

Speechwriter and editor of Roosevelt's *Public Papers,* Samuel Rosenman, has described FDR's meetings with the National Resource Planning Board as they formulated the Declaration of Principles for their important 1942 report *Security, Work, and Relief Policies.* Roosevelt himself set about "simplifying and dramatizing" the declaration for his speeches.[85] In his 1943 and 1944 State of the Union addresses, FDR would advocate a "second, economic Bill of Rights" and, to undergird it, a reorganized federal budgeting process and an unequivocal federal commitment to full employment, as well as expanded social insurance and public investment. In addition to "adequate food and clothing and recreation," medical care, and "a decent home," Roosevelt's "Bill of Rights" included "the right to a useful and remunerative job . . . [and] the right to earn enough."[86]

By 1945, when Congress took up the administration's Full Employment Bill, the "all-important right to work" seemed secure, not only in labor reform rhetoric but in the mandarin legal culture of the day. That year the American Law Institute (ALI) appointed a committee of legal luminaries to draft a "Statement of Essential Human Rights." The staff of the Senate committee holding hearings on the Full Employment Bill asked the members of this ALI group to prepare "an analysis of the legal and philosophical considerations that led to the inclusion of the right to work" in the ALI Statement.[87]

Several of the liberal legal notables in the ALI group had helped inscribe FDR's "four freedoms" and "second Bill of Rights" into the founding documents and machinery—the Atlantic Charter, the UN Charter, Bretton Woods—of the postwar international order. As they surveyed those new institutions, as well as the "the forty nations whose current or recent constitutions contain provisions granting various social and economic rights," and put these alongside the "fundamental legislative measures passed in the United States in the last dozen years to secure such rights to its citizens," the drafters concluded that "the place of social and

[84] Ibid., 234.

[85] See Editor's Note to Roosevelt, "Letter to the Congress" accompanying National Resources Planning Board, *Security, Work, and Relief Policies,* in *Public Papers,* 7:52.

[86] See Franklin Delano Roosevelt, "Message to Congress on the State of the Union," January 11, 1944, in *Public Papers,* 13:32. See also Roosevelt, "Message to the Congress on the State of the Union," January 13, 1943, in *Public Papers,* 12:49.

[87] John Ellingston, William Draper Lewis, and C. Wilfred Jenks, Chair and members, Drafting Committee, American Law Institute, *Statement of Essential Human Rights,* "On the Right to Work," in *Full Employment Act of 1945: Hearings before a Subcommittee on Banking and Currency on S. 380,* 79th Cong., 1st sess., 1945, 1249–59.

economic rights in any modern declaration of the rights of man has already been decided."[88] To the reproach that the right to work did not lend itself to judicial enforcement, they responded, first, that "legal imagination could develop new procedures" and, second, that in any case judicial administrability was not the correct test of a right: "A Bill of Rights is more than a consolidation of the fractions of freedom already gained. . . . It is a directive to the whole society and a guide to legislatures and executives in the framing of laws and regulations that will gradually make the rights effective."[89]

III.

Some contemporary constitutional liberals such as Sunstein rely on FDR's "second Bill of Rights" to clinch the argument that the New Deal Constitution enacted a constitutional right to minimum welfare entitlements.[90] By contrast, Ackerman, despite his characterization of constitutional moments as occasions for considered popular judgments on "the rights of citizens and the permanent interests of the community," remains silent and seemingly unsure about how, if at all, the New Deal Constitution redefined citizenship rights.[91] And his uncertainty is justified. A real gulf separates the robust, encompassing rights talk of FDR's 1936 campaign and his "second Bill of Rights" from the partial patchwork of entitlements that was the New Deal's actual institutional legacy. There is a gap between the "mandate" and the outcome of the New Deal "moment" for which Ackerman's constitutional narrative provides no explanation. But an explanation is at hand, if one takes a more sober look at our constitutional moments and the reversals and contradictions bound up with them.

The explanation returns us to Davis's and Du Bois's insights about race and class. It lies in what V. O. Key called the "southern veto": the hammerlock on Congress that the southern Democrats enjoyed by dint of their numbers, their seniority, and their control over important committees. Key described how the Dixiecrats exercised this power to veto civil rights legislation—hence, the New Dealers' notorious failure to enact a federal antilynching law.[92] But the Dixiecrats used their veto power more broadly. By allying with northern Republicans, or by threatening to do so, they stripped all the main pieces of New Deal legislation of any design or pro-

---

[88] Ibid., 1253.
[89] Ibid., 1258.
[90] See Cass Sunstein, *The Partial Constitution* (Cambridge, Mass., 1993): 137–38.
[91] Ackerman, *We the People*, 240, 272–74.
[92] See V. O. Key, *Southern Politics in State and Nation* (Knoxville, 1949).

vision that threatened the separate southern labor market and its distinctive melding of class and caste relations, its racial segmentation, and its low wages. The Agricultural Adjustment Act, the National Industrial Recovery Act, and the Social Security, Wagner, and Fair Labor Standards Acts: all were tailored in this fashion. More encompassing and inclusive bills— ones with national, rather than local, standards and administration—enjoyed solid support from the northern Democrats (and broad but bootless support from disenfranchised southern blacks and poor whites); but the Southern Junkers and their "racial civilization" exacted a price, and FDR, willingly at first, paid up.[93]

As the new industrial unions of the CIO and the black voters of the North loomed large in FDR's 1936 reelection bid, however, and his social and economic rights talk grew more and more robust and universal, the southern attacks began. Governor Talmadge of Georgia convened a "Grass Roots Convention" to "Uphold the Constitution" against "Negroes, the New Deal and Karl Marx," while Senator Carter Glass of Virginia worried if the white South "will have spirit and courage enough to face the new Reconstruction era that Northern so-called Democrats are menacing us with."[94] By the late 1930s roughly half the southerners in the Senate voted consistently against FDR. Even more Dixiecrats "backed Roosevelt on a final vote but fought his program in their respective committees . . . supporting crippling amendments, and block[ing] consideration of many measures."[95]

Then, with the coming of war, southern members of Congress openly joined ranks with the minority-party Republicans to defeat those 1940s programs that looked toward "completing the New Deal" by enacting and implementing FDR's "second Bill of Rights."[96] The Dixiecrats allied with northern Republicans to scuttle FDR's executive reorganization plan; they took the lead in gutting the administration's 1945 Full Employment Bill

[93] See Ira Katznelson, Kim Geiger, and Daniel Kryder, "Limiting Liberalism: The Southern Veto in Congress, 1933–1950," *Political Science Quarterly* 108 (Summer 1993): 283; Harvard Sitkoff, *A New Deal for Blacks* (New York, 1978), 45–57; Francis Perkins, *The Roosevelt I Knew* (New York, 1952), 291; Arthur Altmeyer, *The Formative Years of Social Security* (Madison, 1968), 14–15; Edwin Witte, *The Development of the Social Security Act* (Madison, 1962); and James T. Patterson, *Congressional Conservatism and the New Deal: The Growth of the Conservative Coalition in Congress* (Lexington, 1967).

[94] Sitkoff, *New Deal for Blacks*, 142–44; Nancy Weiss, *Farewell to the Party of Lincoln: Black Politics in the Age of FDR* (Princeton, 1983), 186.

[95] Sitkoff, *New Deal for Blacks*, 123–24. See also Katznelson, Geiger, and Kryder, "Limiting Liberalism," which analyzes southern Democrats' voting patterns in eighty-nine Senate and sixty-one House roll call votes on critical New Deal (1930s and 1940s) bills and amendments; Jill Quadagno, *The Color of Welfare* (New York, 1994), 1–23.

[96] See Richard Bensel, *Sectionalism and American Political Development, 1880–1980* (Madison, 1984), 152–68; Barry Karl, *Executive Reorganization and Reform in the New Deal* (Cambridge, Mass., 1963); Marion Clawson, *New Deal Planning: and The National Resources Planning Board* (Baltimore, 1981), 283–332; and Katznelson, Geiger, and Kryder, "Limiting Liberalism."

and in abolishing the National Resources Planning Board.[97] Together, these would have laid an institutional foundation for active national labor market and full employment policies. These defeated and dismantled laws, agencies, and innovations were ones that would have sustained the public rhetoric and generated the new institutional capacities and commitments embodied in the "all-important right to work," in "the right to earn a decent livelihood," "to opportunity and advancement," and "to train and retrain."[98] As a consequence, we have forgotten that New Dealers uniformly insisted that the "right to a decent, remunerative job" was "the very hub of social security," that "employment assurance" was "paramount" over income transfers in the original architecture of the New Deal welfare state in all the major reports and proposals by New Deal cabinet commissions and congressional policymakers from 1934 onward through 1946.[99]

Between the popular "ratification" of social citizenship and its enactment into law fell the shadow of Jim Crow. By 1938 the Solid South had stopped the New Deal's legislative engine in its tracks. In the summer of that year, Roosevelt intervened in several primary elections in the South, hoping to defeat some of the most prominent reactionary Democrats. But this effort was doomed because the white primary, the poll tax, and other restrictions kept most blacks and a majority of low-income whites, the New Deal's constituency, from voting.[100]

By 1944 many New Dealers agreed with Vice President Henry Wallace that the future of New Deal reform depended on confronting Jim Crow. That year the Supreme Court decided *Smith v. Allright,* declaring the all-white primary unconstitutional;[101] this combined with an outpouring of money and organizers by the CIO to produce an extraordinary voter registration drive in the South. In a few southern states such as Alabama and Georgia, the number of black and poor white voters increased several-

[97] See Clawson, *New Deal Planning;* and Stephen Bailey, *Congress Makes a Law: The Story behind the Employment Act of 1946* (New York, 1946).

[98] *Full Employment Act of 1945,* 2, 4, 10, 59. See Ira Katznelson and Bruce Pietrykowski, "Rebuilding the American State: Evidence from the 1940s," *Studies in American Political Development* 5 (1991): 301; Katznelson, Geiger, and Kryder, "Limiting Liberalism"; Clawson, *New Deal Planning;* and Phillip Harvey, *Securing the Right to Employment: Social Welfare Policy and the Unemployed in the U.S.* (Princeton, 1988).

[99] "Preliminary Report of the Staff of the Committee on Economic Security," September 1934, 30, *Final Report of the Committee on Economic Security,* January 15, 1935, 1 reprinted in *Unemployment, Old Age, and Social Insurance: Hearings before the Committee on Labor on H.R. 2827, H.R. 2859, H.R. 185, H.R. 10,* 74th Cong., 1st sess. (1935); "Address to the Congress on the State of the Union, January 7, 1943," in Roosevelt, *Public Papers,* 12:21–34; U.S. National Resources Planning Board, *Report of the Committee on Long-Range Work and Relief Policies* (Washington, 1942): 1–3. See, generally, Harvey, *Securing the Right to Employment,* 1–23.

[100] Roosevelt, *Public Papers,* 7:399. The account of voting rights efforts in the following paragraphs is indebted to Patricia Sullivan, *Days of Hope: Race and Democracy in the New Deal Era* (Chapel Hill, 1996).

[101] 321 US 649 (1944).

fold. At a rally in Birmingham, one black leader recalled "those first bright days of Reconstruction [when] the legislatures controlled by the newly freed slaves and the emancipated poor whites gave to our region its first democratic governments." It was time, he said, for "history to repeat itself."[102] But that was not to be, not in time to complete the New Deal's unfinished reforms or enact the "second Bill of Rights." The constitutional bad faith that for half a century had led both parties and all three branches of the federal government to support Jim Crow and disenfranchisement produced the anomaly of a reactionary core at the heart of FDR's New Deal liberal coalition. This excluded most blacks from the benefits of many New Deal programs.

This same constitutional bad faith at black America's expense also deprived all Americans of the institutional foundations and ideological legacy of social citizenship. Broad social and economic rights talk fell into disuse after the decisive defeats that the New Deal agenda suffered in the 1940s. Blocked by the Dixiecrats at every legislative turn, social citizenship's only powerful, organized constituency, the industrial unions of the CIO, gradually abandoned their efforts to "complete the New Deal." By the mid-1950s they had begun instead to fashion with employers a private system of social provision and job security through collective bargaining in core sectors of the economy.[103] During the same moment, the rigid consensus politics of the cold war eclipsed the confident liberalism of the New Deal America.

The civil rights movement opened the door to reform for the first time since the 1930s, and many civil rights leaders and Great Society policymakers consciously set out to complete the New Deal moment, convinced that without social citizenship for all Americans, many black Americans would remain part of a subordinate caste.[104] As Bayard Rustin, chief organizer of the 1963 March on Washington, warned the Democratic National Convention in 1964, the "solution to our full citizenship" demanded more than "the Civil Rights Bill."[105] "What will [the Negro] gain by being per-

[102] Osceola McKaine, "For Victory at the Ballot Box," *Monthly Bulletin*, Southern Negro Youth Congress, August 1944, quoted in Sullivan, *Days of Hope*, 191. See also Thomas Krueger, *And Promises to Keep: The Southern Conference for Human Welfare, 1938–1948* (Nashville, 1967): 234–67, and Robert Sieger, *The CIO* (Chapel Hill, 1994).

[103] See Nelson Lichtenstein, "From Corporatism to Collective Bargaining: Organized Labor and the Eclipse of Social Democracy in the Postwar Era," in Steve Fraser and Gary Gerstle, eds., *The Rise and Fall of the New Deal Order, 1930–1980* (1989), 122, and Lichtenstein, *The Most Dangerous Man in Detroit: Walter Reuther and the Fate of American Labor* (New York, 1995). See also Kevin Boyle, *The UAW and the Heyday of American Liberalism, 1945–1968* (Ithaca, 1995).

[104] On the links between New Deal and Great Society liberalism, I am indebted to Lichtenstein, *The Most Dangerous Man in Detroit*.

[105] Bayard Rustin, "Address to Democratic National Convention, Atlantic City, N.J., August 1964," 27, The Bayard Rustin Papers, reel 3.

mitted to move to an integrated neighborhood if he cannot afford to do so because he is unemployed?" It was essential but insufficient "to outlaw discrimination in employment when there are not enough [jobs] to go around." Civil rights, Rustin told Congress, "are built on the right to a decent livelihood," or they rest on sand. Indeed, "it would be dangerous and misleading to call for [enforcement of antidiscrimination norms] without at the same time calling attention to the declining number of employment opportunities in many fields."[106] And Rustin detailed the "displacement of unskilled workers" in the nation's "relatively high-wage heavy industries into which Negroes have moved since World War I" and the vast numbers of black workers cast aside each year by the "diminishing number of [decently paid unskilled and semiskilled] jobs." "We cannot have fair employment," he warned, "until we have full employment."[107] This same insight drove Martin Luther King to launch the Poor People's Campaign. The "full emancipation and equality of Negroes and the poor," he repeatedly told rallies and demonstrations, legislative hearings, and White House conferences, demanded a "contemporary social and economic Bill of Rights." King's "bill," like FDR's, emphasized decent incomes, education, housing, and full employment.[108] The initiative that fleshed out King's "bill" was Bayard Rustin and A. Philip Randolph's Freedom Budget for All Americans. As an alternative to the administration's antipoverty programs, King and Randolph proposed a "multi-billion dollar social investment to destroy the racial ghettoes of America, decently house both the black and white poor, and to create full and fair employment in the process."[109] Randolph compared the idea to the "social investments of the New Deal," noting that the New Deal's labor legislation and public investments did more than provide jobs and foster collective bargaining; they "evoked a new psychology of citizenship" and A sense of dignity" among white workers, as would the Freedom Budget "among millions of Negroes." It would be "their New Deal thirty years late."[110]

The same genre of full employment and economic planning policies found bold champions among the New Dealers in the Johnson administration, above all in Secretary of Labor Willard Wirtz. Wirtz waged a sustained battle against the "partial and piecemeal" social services/work counseling approach adopted by the War on Poverty. Eloquent in his carefully documented accounts of the "human slag heap" emerging in

---

[106] Ibid.; Bayard Rustin, "Draft for Testimony on FEPC," n.d. [Fall 1963], The Bayard Rustin Papers, reel 4.

[107] *Id.* at 7.

[108] Martin Luther King Jr., *Where Do We Go From Here: Chaos or Community?* (New York, 1967), 163, 193.

[109] Bayard Rustin, "Freedom Budget," MS, n.d. [probably December 1965], 1, The Bayard Rustin Papers, reel 13.

[110] Ibid., 8–9.

the nation's industrial regions, including its central cities, where black unemployment had already begun to "explode," Wirtz, like the drafters of the Freedom Budget, urged regional and sectoral public investment, other incentives for job creation, and coordinated employment services and training.[111] But the Wirtz/Freedom Budget approach got nowhere. Most contemporaries explained its failure in terms of the escalating costs of waging the Vietnam War and President Johnson's desire for a cheap, quick fix for ghetto unrest. The impediments, however, were deeper. If civil rights laws were an inadequate response to the social and economic plight of black America, they were a forthright response to the standard liberal account of race discrimination. Committing the Democrats to the kind of social democratic political economy King now demanded would have required mobilization and coalition building on a much more vast scale. It required a palpable threat of mass protest on the part of the poor and working class, black and white—a felt crisis of governability— sufficient to give LBJ and the Democrats the kind of leverage that Roosevelt enjoyed in the 1930s.

But that too was not to be. Walter Reuther and other progressive labor leaders supported King's vision, but not the AFL-CIO leadership under George Meany's wing and not Reuther's own constituents. The latter, as Meany pointedly observed, cared about the pensions, health plans, and job security measures in their union contracts, not about raising hell until government provided these things for everyone. Ironically, as Nelson Lichtenstein has shown, Reuther's own accomplishments had helped ensure that organized labor's grievances now came in more administrable packages.[112] The defeats that social citizenship suffered in the 1940s, when the whole CIO demanded it, and the "private welfare state" its unions created in the 1950s and 1960s meant that the language of social and economic rights no longer resonated for organized workers.

So, black America never got its "New Deal thirty years late." Nor did white working-class America get the New Deal Constitution it was promised thirty years earlier. The reasons are many, but the central ones trace back to Du Bois's "unending tragedy of Reconstruction" and the tangled knot of race and class. From the perspective of this history, the New Deal constitutional legacy that is under unprecedented attack today is a marred one. We have enshrined the vast expansion of national governmental power but not what it was expanded for. This suggests why Ackerman's the-

---

[111] Memorandum from Willard Wirtz to Walter Heller, November 19, 1963, in *Administrative History of the Department of Labor,* vol. 3, Documentary Supplement, sec. 3-B, box 5, Lyndon Baines Johnson Library. See, generally, Margaret Weir, *Jobs and Politics* (Princeton, 1994).

[112] Lichtenstein, *The Most Dangerous Man in Detroit,* 346–69.

ory might explain how constitutional politics authorized the New Deal justices to hand down their transformative opinions, but it cannot readily show how the "rights of citizens" were transformed by the New Deal moment. Matters would be different if the only fault line were the exclusion of blacks from a newly enacted national commitment to social citizenship. But, as we have seen, the betrayal of Reconstruction had more pervasive consequences. It subverted white working-class America's capacity to enact even a racially exclusionary form of social citizenship. Accordingly, there is no "synthesis" of racial equality and social rights to be drawn here; the fault lines are too many.

Ackerman points to the Full Employment Act of 1946 as a "framework statute" that was "part of the New Deal Constitution" forged by "We, the People."[113] But, "we" hollowed the constitutional substance out of that statute. Ackerman gets the law's actual title wrong; it was the Employment Act of 1946, reflecting the removal of the new federal right to employment and the institutional and policy innovations proposed in the Full Employment Bill of 1945. What possible precommitment could one draw from the 1946 act to constrain the "ordinary politics" of today? In general, the commitments "we" made to ourselves in the New Deal moment were too deeply compromised by our past inconstancy to undergird the kind of "preservative" theory Ackerman desires.

My constitutional narrative offers the colder comfort of a deeper understanding of the most embattled dimensions of liberal constitutional theory. The historical knot of race and class has tied liberal constitutional theory today to a conception of the affirmative dimensions of constitutional equality that does not fit the moral and historical arguments meant to support it. Those arguments call for a broader conception, as did the New Dealers and the civil rights leaders we canvassed. The twice-told defeat of social citizenship prevented this. Synthesizing the majoritarian and countermajoritarian ideals of equal citizenship remains a task for future movements and a future moment; no theorist can reclaim such a synthesis from our flawed past.

But perhaps this history also yields a constitutional imperative. If so, it is a much weaker one that only binds us in the arena of public discourse and debate. If the narrative outlined here proves persuasive and we can agree that the question of social citizenship was concluded by the shadow of Jim Crow on the nation's polity, then perhaps we can agree it was concluded illegitimately and must be reopened.

If we do reopen the question, we may find that a conception of social citizenship centered on a decent livelihood is not only better grounded in our history but also more appealing as a normative matter. A right to wel-

[113] Ackerman, *We the People*, 107.

fare is insufficient to underpin the equal respect on which equal citizenship rests. Equality of worth, not in dollars but in the sense of having an opportunity to earn one's livelihood, is essential. Yet, it is no longer seriously disputed that the United States is witnessing a dramatic decline of decent jobs with decent pay. Estimates vary, but in one reasonable reckoning, as many as one-third of the American workforce are looking for more work than they now have, while the poverty rate for full-time workers has been increasing—a 50 percent increase since 1980. And both trends seem very likely to mount.[114]

As during the Gilded Age and the Progressive Era, the 1930s and the 1960s, our basic social policies are once more in issue. Broadening the base of citizenship by broadening the base of work is no simple task, and the capacity of government to do so is constrained in many ways. But this history suggests there are constitutional stakes in the present crisis of work—and in its consequences in second-class citizenship, where caste and class intersect for millions of Americans.

[114] See Joel Handler and Yehsekel Hasenfel, *Reform Work, Reform Welfare* (New Haven, 1997), 18.

RELIGION AND MORAL COMMUNITY

שַׁחֲרִית שֶׁל שַׁבָּת · צ

הַנּוֹתֵן תְּשׁוּעָה לַמְּלָכִים וּמֶמְשָׁלָה לַנְּסִיכִים ·
וּמַלְכוּתוֹ מַלְכוּת כָּל עוֹלָמִים: הַפּוֹצֶה אֶת
דָּוִד עַבְדּוֹ · מֵחֶרֶב רָעָה: הַנּוֹתֵן בַּיָּם דֶּרֶךְ · וּכְמַיִם
עַזִּים נְתִיבָה: הוּא יְבָרֵךְ · וְיִשְׁמוֹר · וְיִנְצוֹר · וְיַעֲזוֹר ·
וִירוֹמֵם · וִיגַדֵּל · וְיִנַּשֵּׂא לְמַעְלָה לְמַעְלָה · לַאֲדוֹנֵנוּ
הַמֶּלֶךְ: מֶלֶךְ מַלְכֵי הַמְּלָכִים בְּרַחֲמָיו יִשְׁמְרֵהוּ וִיחַיֵּיהוּ
וּמִכָּל צָרָה וְנֶזֶק יַצִּילֵהוּ: מֶלֶךְ מַלְכֵי הַמְּלָכִים בְּרַחֲמָיו
צָרוֹתָיו וְגַדֵּה כּוֹכַב מַעַרְכוֹתוֹ · וְיַאֲרִיךְ יָמִים עַל מַמְלַכְתּוֹ:
מֶלֶךְ מַלְכֵי הַמְּלָכִים בְּרַחֲמָיו · יִתֵּן כִּלְבוֹ וּבְלֵב כָּל
יוֹעֲצָיו וְשָׂרָיו · רַחֲמָנוּת לַעֲשׂוֹת טוֹבָה עִמָּנוּ · וְעִם כָּל
יִשְׂרָאֵל אַחֵינוּ · בְּיָמָיו וּבְיָמֵינוּ תִּוָּשַׁע יְהוּדָה · וְיִשְׂרָאֵל
יִשְׁכּוֹן לָבֶטַח · וּבָא לְצִיּוֹן גּוֹאֵל · וְכֵן יְהִי רָצוֹן ·
וְנֹאמַר אָמֵן:

הַנּוֹתֵן תְּשׁוּעָה לַמְּלָכִים וּמֶמְשָׁלָה לַנְּסִיכִים וּמַלְכוּתוֹ
מַלְכוּת כָּל עוֹלָמִים: הַפּוֹצֶה אֶת דָּוִד עַבְדּוֹ
מֵחֶרֶב רָעָה: הַנּוֹתֵן בַּיָּם דֶּרֶךְ וּבְמַיִם עַזִּים נְתִיבָה: הוּא
יְבָרֵךְ · וְיִשְׁמוֹר · וְיִנְצוֹר · וְיַעֲזוֹר · וִירוֹמֵם · וִיגַדֵּל ·
וְיִנַּשֵּׂא לְמַעְלָה לְמַעְלָה ·

A os grandes Epoderozos Señores , estados d
Hollanda, & West-Frieslant ,e aos altos Epoderozos Señores Estados gerais das Provincias Vni-
das (com todos feus aliados) E aos muy nobles
E dignissimos Señores Burgamestres , E Mage-
ftrado defta Cidade de Amsterdam.

כלך   יב ב א

During the recess of Congress

The President and Vice President
of the United States of America
The Governor the Lieutent Governor
and the People of this State
represented in Senate & Assembly
and the Magistrates of this City

During the setting of Congress

The President and Vice President of
the Union, The Senate and House
of Representatives of the United States
of America in Congress assembled
The Governor and the Lieutenant
Governor and the People of this
State represented in Senate and
assembly and the Magistrates
of this City

Handwritten changes introduced into the traditional Jewish prayer for the government in the wake of the American Revolution. From an eighteenth-century Amsterdam Hebrew prayer book in the possession of Rev. Gershom M. Seixas, Seixas Family Papers, American Jewish Historical Society, Waltham, Mass., and New York, N.Y. Reprinted with permission.

CHAPTER NINE

Jewish Prayers for the U.S. Government:
A Study in the Liturgy of Politics
and the Politics of Liturgy

JONATHAN D. SARNA

In an Orthodox synagogue in Cambridge in 1979, a student whose un-
happiness with the Carter administration was well known led the traditional Sabbath morning liturgy. Piously, he intoned the Jewish prayer for
the government, which he recited in Hebrew. "May the President, the Vice
President and all the constituted officers of the government be blessed,
guarded, protected, helped, exalted, magnified and raised ... *upward,*" he
shouted, his arms pointing heavenward. The congregation exploded in
laughter.[1] The student's mischievous supplication highlights an issue of
enduring moral significance in the relationship of religion and state: the
tension between patriotic loyalty and prophetic judgment. How people
pray for their government reveals much about what they think of their government. Changes over time in these prayers shed light on religion and
politics alike.

Prayer, while unquestionably a part of the American experience, is not
a phenomenon that most American historians study.[2] Yet, liturgical texts—

I am grateful to Jonathon Ament, Dr. Grace Cohen Grossman, Felicia Herman, Professor
Ruth Langer, Professor Nahum M. Sarna, Professor Moshe Sherman, Rabbi David Starr,
Ellen Smith, and Professor Saul Wachs for their assistance with various aspects of this paper.
    [1] I was present at this service, and the translation is mine. On substituting for the tradi-
tional blessing of the government a malediction that it be "speedily uprooted and crushed,"
see Ya'akov Navon, "Tefilah Le-Shlom Ha-Medinah Be-Metsiut Yamenu ... ," *Iture Kohanim,*
no. 124 (1995): 6–15 (Hebrew); cf. *Jerusalem Report,* August 10, 1995, 16.
    [2] James F. White, "Liturgy and Worship," in Charles H. Lippy and Peter W. Williams, eds.,
Encyclopedia of the American Religious Experience (New York, 1988), 1269–83, surveys the "little
scholarly research" that exists (1269).

as well as other aspects of prayer—may be subjected to historical analysis. In what follows, I focus on Jewish prayers for the government: fascinating texts, richly inlaid with multiple meanings, that necessarily underwent significant transformation as they accompanied American Jews through centuries of political, social, and religious change.[3] Close examination of these prayers, as we shall see, sheds light on the Americanization of Judaism and on the changing relationship between American Jews and the state. The prayers also make significant political and religious pronouncements, revealing attitudes not otherwise accessible to the historian. There is, finally, some connection between this project and the work of David Brion Davis. For he too has taught us that religion, politics, and moral judgment walk hand in hand, and he too has sought, in multitudinous ways, to read America between the lines.

Throughout their long history in the diaspora, Jews have recited special prayers "for the welfare of the government."[4] The biblical prophet Jeremiah, writing from Jerusalem to the Jewish community exiled in Babylonia, explained one rationale behind this practice: "Seek the welfare of the city to which I have exiled you and pray to the Lord in its behalf; for in its prosperity you shall prosper."[5] Jewish political philosophy as articulated later by the rabbis in the Ethics of the Fathers and then throughout rabbinic literature assumed that a government, even an oppressive government, is superior to anarchy.[6]

The practice of praying for the welfare of the sovereign was common not only in antiquity but also in medieval Christendom and Islam. Jewish

[3] Barry L. Schwartz, "The Jewish Prayer for the Government" (ordination thesis, Hebrew Union College-Jewish Institute of Religion, 1985), is the only full-length study; published articles by Schwartz are cited below. See also Macy Nulman, *Concepts of Jewish Music and Prayer* (New York, 1985), 100–106; Macy Nulman, *The Encyclopedia of Jewish Prayer* (Northvale, N.J., 1993), 155; Israel Abrahams, *A Companion to the Authorised Daily Prayerbook* (1922; New York, 1966), 160–61; J. D. Eisenstein, *Ozar Dinim u-Minhagim* (1917; Tel Aviv, 1975), 62 (Hebrew); Jacob Kabakoff, "Hebrew Prayers in Behalf of the Government and Its Leaders," in *Seekers and Stalwarts: Essays and Studies on American Hebrew Literature and Culture* (Jerusalem, 1978), 263–68 (Hebrew); and sources cited note 9.

[4] Stefan C. Reif, *Judaism and Hebrew Prayer: New Perspectives on Jewish Liturgical History* (Cambridge, 1993), 218, observes that the evidence for regular, formal prayers for the government dates back no earlier than the Middle Ages. Occasional prayers and regular sacrifices for the welfare of the ruler, however, are attested to much earlier; see, for example, The Letter of Aristeas, verse 185, in James H. Charlesworth, *The Old Testament Pseudepigrapha* (New York, 1985), 25; Josephus, *The Jewish War*, trans. G. A. Williamson (Baltimore, 1959), 129; and Philo, *Legatio ad Gaium*, ed. E. M. Smallwood (London, 1961), 142.

[5] Jer. 29:7; cf. Gen. 47:7 and Ezra 6:10.

[6] Ethics of the Fathers 3:2; Babylonian Talmud, Tractate Avoda Zara 4a; Joseph H. Hertz, *The Authorized Daily Prayer Book* (New York, 1948), 502–7; Martin Sicker, "A Political Metaphor in Biblical and Rabbinic Literature," *Judaism* 40, no. 2 (Spring 1991): 208–14.

prayers nevertheless stand out as expressions of minority group insecurity. In one case, for example, Jews added to their prayers a special plea for "all of the Muslims who live in our country." Another Jewish prayer book contains a special blessing for the welfare of the pope.[7] The uniquely plaintive quality of many of these prayers, beseeching God to incline the heart of the sovereign to treat Jews benevolently, bespeaks the distinctive political realities of diaspora Jewish life. "Throughout medieval Christian Europe," Yosef Hayim Yerushalmi observes, "the Jews inevitably, yet willingly, allied themselves to the Crown as the best, and, ultimately, the only guarantor of stability and security." From the thirteenth century onward, Jews in many of these countries also held the status of *servi camerae* (serfs of the chamber); the monarch was their direct legal protector. The result, in Yerushalmi's words, was a "royal alliance," born of necessity and confirmed by history, that "flowered beyond its obvious mundane realities into a guiding myth."[8] This myth, characteristic of Jews throughout the medieval world, inspired Jews not only to cast their lot with the sovereign authority but also to pray fervently for its welfare.

By the mid–seventeenth century, a cleverly written prayer known in Hebrew as Hanoten Teshua and beginning with the phrase (as traditionally translated) "He who giveth salvation unto kings and dominion unto princes" had become a fixed part of the liturgy in most of the Jewish world. Now believed to have been composed in the late fifteenth or early sixteenth century, the prayer likely emerged in the Sephardic diaspora, among Jews expelled from Spain and Portugal, and it then traveled "along the extensive network of Sephardic trade routes" and was adopted, with minor modifications, by Ashkenazic Jews, who carried it through Central and Eastern Europe. In 1655, the Dutch scholar and rabbi Menasseh ben Israel published a translation of the prayer into English as part of his apologetic effort to prove Jewish loyalty in order to secure the readmission of the Jews into England. He described the prayer (quite anachronistically) as part of "the continuall and never broken custome of the Jews, wheresoever they are, on the Sabbath Day, or other solemn Feast" to have the "Minister

---

[7] Yosef Yanun (Fenton), "Tefila Be'ad Hareshut Ureshut Be'ad Hatefila," *East and Maghreb* 4 (1983): 7–21 (Hebrew); Avraham Ya'ari, "Tefilot Misheberah," *Kirjath Sepher* 33 (1957–58): 247 (Hebrew); S. D. Goitein, "Prayers from the Geniza for Fatimid Caliphs, the Head of the Jerusalem Yeshiva, the Jewish Community, and the Local Congregation," *Studies in Judaica, Karaitica, and Islamica, Presented to Leon Nemoy on His Eightieth Birthday* (Ramat Gan, 1982), 47–57; S. D. Goitein, *A Mediterranean Society* (Berkeley, 1971), 2:164; Armand Lunel, "Prière des Juifs de Carpentras pour le pape," *Evidences* 1 (1949): 4–5.

[8] Yosef Hayim Yerushalmi, *The Lisbon Massacre of 1506 and the Royal Image in the "Shebet Yehudah,"* Hebrew Union College Annual Supplements no. 1 (Cincinnati, 1976), 35–66, esp. 37, 39.

of the Synagogue" bless "the Prince of the country under whom they live, that all the Jews may hear it, and say, Amen."[9]

The manifest language of Hanoten Teshua bespeaks Jewish loyalty and faithful allegiance. It calls on God to "bless, guard, protect, help, exalt, magnify and highly aggrandize" (literally, "raise upward") the king and the royal family, to grant them a long and prosperous rule, and to inspire them with benevolence "toward us and all Israel our brethren." At the same time, the prayer's esoteric meaning, presumably recognized only by an elite corps of well-educated worshipers, reveals much about the mentalité of diaspora Jews subjected to countless acts of discrimination under the dominion of foreign kings. The biblical verses quoted in the prayer conceal hints of spiritual resistance, a cultural strategy well known among those determined to maintain their self-respect in the face of religious persecution. Thus, for example, the prayer begins with a verse modified from Psalm 144:10: "You who give victory to kings, who rescue[s] His servant David from the deadly sword." The next line of that psalm, not included in the prayer but revealing in terms of its hidden meaning, reads, "Rescue me, save me from the hands of foreigners, whose mouths speak lies, and whose oaths are false." Barry Schwartz points out several more esoteric readings in the prayer, including Isaiah 43:16, which forms part of a chapter predicting the fall of Babylon; Jeremiah 23:6, cited in the prayer's conclusion, which preaches the ingathering of the exiles and the restoration of the Davidic dynasty; and Isaiah 59:20 ("He shall come as redeemer to Zion"), which is preceded two verses earlier by a call for vengeance, a sentiment not found in our prayer but likely on the minds of some Jews who recited it.[10] Simultaneously, then, Jews prayed aloud for the welfare of the sovereign on whom their security depended, and read between the lines a more subversive message, a call for rescue, redemption, and revenge.[11] Based on past diaspora experience, both messages were fully appropriate.

The Hanoten Teshua prayer accompanied Jews to the American colonies. Indeed, it is found in the very earliest published American Jewish liturgical composition, a "Form of Prayer" from Congregation Shearith

[9] Barry Schwartz, "*Hanoten Teshua*`: The Origin of the Traditional Jewish Prayer for the Government," *Hebrew Union College Annual* 57 (1986): 113–20; Aaron Ahrend, *Israel's Independence Day—Research Studies* (Ramat Gan, 1998), 176–200 (Hebrew); Lewis N. Dembitz, *Jewish Services in Synagogue and Home* (Philadelphia, 1898), 217–18; Simeon Singer, "The Earliest Jewish Prayers for the English Sovereign," *Transactions of the Jewish Historical Society of England* 4 (1903): 102–9, reprinted in I. Abrahams, ed., *The Literary Remains of the Rev. Simeon Singer: Lectures and Addresses* (London, 1908), 76–87.

[10] Schwartz, "*Hanoten Teshua*`," 119.

[11] In the Ashkenazic tradition, the prayer is shortly followed by the prayer Av Ha-Rahamim, usually dated to the time of the Crusades, which calls on God for "retribution for the blood of thy servants which hath been shed." See J. H. Hertz, *Authorized Daily Prayer Book*, 510–15.

Israel in New York, obviously geared for external consumption, marking the day (October 23, 1760) "Appointed by Proclamation for a General Thanksgiving to Almighty God, for the Reducing of Canada to His Majesty's Dominions." The published liturgy contains a complete translation of this prayer, mentioning by name not only "our Sovereign Lord King GEORGE the Second, His Royal Highness, George Prince of *Wales,* the Princess Dowager of *Wales,* the Duke, the Princesses, and all the Royal Family" but also "the Honourable President, and the Council of this Province; likewise the Magistrates of *New York,* and the Province." [12] Many of these same worthies are named in the translations of the prayer published in the only two Jewish prayer books from the colonial period, both English renderings of the traditional Hebrew text according to the Spanish and Portuguese rite. [13] These translations were not read aloud at New York's Congregation Shearith Israel. Instead, Hanoten Teshua continued to be recited, as per tradition, in Hebrew. Following the custom in Amsterdam and London, the section of the prayer containing the names of the "high and mighty" officials being blessed was read out in Portuguese—a language that few members of the congregation actually understood. [14]

Within a few years, however, this longtime practice had become a problem for American Jews. It was not just that their loyalties had changed—that, after all, was common to many Americans of the day and had in any case been a feature of Jewish life for centuries (causing no end of problems when prayer books extolling a previous sovereign in the text of Hanoten Teshua had to be hastily withdrawn). [15] The more vexing problem Jews faced in the wake of the American Revolution was whether the prayer familiar to them from regular use and fixed in their liturgy was appropriate at all in a country where leaders were elected and sovereignty rested with the people.

---

[12] *The Form of Prayer Which was performed at the Jews Synagogue in the City of New-York on Thursday October 23, 1760 . . . Composed by D. R. Joseph Yesurun Pinto . . .* (New York, 1760), 5–7, reprinted in *Studia Rosenthaliana* 13 (January 1979): following page 24.

[13] *Evening Service of Roshashanah, and Kippur . . .* (New York; 1761), 21; and with minor differences, *Prayers for Shabbath, Rosh-Hashanah, and Kippur . . . According to the Order of the Spanish and Portuguese Jews. Translated by Isaac Pinto* (New York, 1765–66), 20–21. Recitation of the prayer for the government as part of the evening (Kol Nidre) service on Yom Kippur conforms to Sephardic custom and may have been an attempt to allay fears that the Kol Nidre prayer was unpatriotic.

[14] *Publications of the American Jewish Historical Society* [hereafter *PAJHS*] 27 (1920): 392–93; H. P. Salomon, "Joseph Jesurun Pinto (1729–1782): A Dutch Hazan in Colonial New York," *Studia Rosenthaliana* 13 (January 1979): 26 n. 38. Samuel Pepys records in his diary (October 13, 1663) that this was similarly the practice in England; see Singer, "Earliest Jewish Prayers for the English Sovereign," 81.

[15] Eisenstein, *Ozar Dinim u-Minhagim,* 62.

The need for at least some change was apparent within a week of independence when, on July 11, 1776, the New York Convention to the Continental Congress circulated a letter suggesting that prayers for the royal family be eliminated in all American congregations. No minutes from this period in the history of New York's only Jewish synagogue survive, since most Jews (along with their minister, Gershom Seixas) fled the city in the summer of 1776 in advance of British troops.[16] Nor do records seem to be extant from America's other four Jewish congregations. Three changes, however, took place during the Revolutionary era that demonstrate that Jews were duly sensitive to the problem. First, when next we encounter Hanoten Teshua, in a prayer recited at the dedication of Congregation Mikveh Israel in Philadelphia (1782), the royal family has been replaced in the traditional blessing by "His Excellency the President, and Hon'ble Delegates of the United States of America in Congress Assembled, His Excellency George Washington, Captain General and Commander in Chief of the Federal Army of these States," the General Assembly of Pennsylvania, and "all kings and potentates in alliance with North America." Except for the mention of Washington, the prayer was noticeably depersonalized; forever after, in America, Jews would usually bless officeholders ("the President") rather than named individuals, in marked contrast to the personality cult that previously surrounded the king.[17] Second, Congregation Shearith Israel, once its membership returned, abandoned the practice of reading the names of government officials in Portuguese; henceforth, the names were read out in English.[18] Finally, and most remarkable, the congregants of Shearith Israel ceased to rise for Hanoten Teshua. According to an oral tradition preserved by H. P. Salomon, "The custom of sitting during this prayer was introduced to symbolize the American Revolution's abolition of subservience."[19]

Yet the prayer Hanoten Teshua itself, notwithstanding the obvious inappropriateness of some of its sentiments (including such lines as "may the Supreme King of kings exalt and highly aggrandize them, and grant them long and prosperously to rule") and notwithstanding the prayer's inevitable association in the public's mind with the prayer for the English monarch, underwent no other changes of any kind. A prayer book pre-

[16] *PAJHS* 27 (1920): 392; *PAJHS* 21 (1913): 140; Jacob R. Marcus, *The Colonial American Jew* (Detroit, 1970), 1272–73.

[17] Sabato Morais, "Mickve Israel Congregation in Philadelphia," *PAJHS* 1 (1892): 17; Edwin Wolf 2nd and Maxwell Whiteman, *The History of the Jews of Philadelphia from Colonial Times to the Age of Jackson* (1956; Philadelphia, 1975), 121; cf. *PAJHS* 27 (1920): 126.

[18] *PAJHS* 27 (1920): 392; David de Sola Pool and Tamar de Sola Pool, *An Old Faith in the New World* (New York, 1955), 87; Salomon, "Joseph Jesurun Pinto," 26 n. 38.

[19] Salomon, "Joseph Jesurun Pinto," 26 n. 38.

served in the papers of Gershom Seixas makes clear that into the nineteenth century, Shearith Israel's minister recited the identical Hebrew
text that he had used before and the same one that was read in the
Sephardic congregation of Amsterdam. The only textual difference, written out in longhand on a piece of paper pasted into the prayer book, was
the list of American notables (in English). When Congress was in session,
that list included "the President and Vice President of the Union, the Senate and House of Representatives of the United States of America in Congress assembled; The Governor and the Lieutenant Governor and the
People of this state represented in Senate and assembly and the Magistrates of this City." When Congress was in recess, as if to underscore that
its members were fellow citizens rather than noble aristocrats, the Senate
and House of Representatives were summarily dropped from the list of
those to be exalted.[20]

Shearith Israel's ardent attachment to its traditional prayer for the government stands in marked contrast to the rushing currents of Americanization and democratization that swept across the landscape of American
religion during the post-Revolution era. The Episcopal Church, to take an
obvious example, published a totally new prayer "for the President of the
United States and all in Civil Authority" appropriate to a democratic state,
and it modified other elements of its *Book of Common Prayer* as well. Jews in
France, following their emancipation, likewise altered their traditional
patriotic liturgy.[21] Why were American Jews, in their prayers, so reluctant
to follow suit? Certainly it was not due to any lack of patriotism on their
part. The bulk of Shearith Israel's members and particularly its minister
had been conspicuous supporters of the Revolution, and all major synagogues in the United States had Americanized their constitutions and de-
mocratized their procedures.[22] Nor is there any evidence that the prayer's
esoteric meaning attracted notice; that had long since been forgotten.
Most likely, the tenacious hold of Hanoten Teshua was due to the fact that
the prayer had become a fixed piece of the ritual at Shearith Israel, part of

[20] Seixas's Amsterdam prayer book, with the slip of paper pasted between page 69 and
page 70, is preserved in the Seixas Family Papers, American Jewish Historical Society,
Waltham, Mass.

[21] Nathan O. Hatch, *The Democratization of American Christianity* (New Haven, 1989);
Marion J. Hatchett, *Commentary on the American Prayer Book* (New York, 1980), 158–59,
338–39, 554; *The Book of Common Prayer According to the Use of the Protestant Episcopal Church in
the United States* (Philadelphia, 1822), 22, 27; V. Staley, "State Prayers," in *The Prayer Book
Dictionary* (1925), 9:760–70; Abrahams, *Companion to the Authorised Daily Prayerbook*, 161;
Ronald B. Schechter, "Becoming French: Patriotic Liturgy and the Transformation of Jewish
Identity in France, 1706–1815" (Ph.D. diss., Harvard University, 1993).

[22] Jonathan D. Sarna, "The Impact of the American Revolution on American Jews," *Modern Judaism* 1 (1981): 149–60.

the established Sephardic rite (*minhag*) that the congregation faithfully perpetuated and preserved.[23] Moreover, it was written in Hebrew, the "holy tongue" that American Jews respected even if they understood it no better than they did Portuguese. Rather than tamper with such sacred elements, the congregation prudently focused on the prayer's more profane vernacular section and on the rituals that accompanied the prayer's recitation. These, as we have seen, were suitably Americanized even as the rest of the prayer was left untouched. The result was a liturgical compromise that effectively reinforced three central messages that American synagogues of the day sought to inculcate: that Jews should maintain ancestral custom, distinguish between sacred and profane, and exercise extraordinary discernment in all matters connected with the outside world.

Prayers recited on special occasions and thus not part of the fixed liturgy offered America's foremost Jewish congregation far greater latitude for originality in prayer. At such services, particularly when the prayers were delivered in English and written with the knowledge that non-Jews would hear them, leaders of Shearith Israel often dispensed with the traditional prayer for the government and substituted revealing new compositions appropriate to the concerns of the day. A prayer composed in 1784 (in this case in Hebrew) by the otherwise unknown Rabbi (Cantor?) Hendla Jochanan van Oettingen, for example, thanked God who "in His goodness prospered our warfare." Mentioning by name both Governor De Witt Clinton and General George Washington, the rabbi prayed for peace and offered a restorationist Jewish twist on the popular idea of America as "redeemer nation": "As Thou hast granted to these thirteen states of America everlasting freedom," he declared, "so mayst Thou bring us forth once again from bondage into freedom and mayst Thou sound the great horn for our freedom."[24] Later, a 1799 day of thanksgiving proclaimed by the clergy of New York allowed Gershom Seixas the chance to pray for the government in staunchly republican terms: "Impart thy divine wisdom to the Rulers & Administrators of Government . . . and graciously extend thy protection & direction, to the good people of this State, and to the United States of America in general, with their representatives in the Legislature." Seixas also used the occasion to pray for an end to political infighting and

[23] Pool, *Old Faith in the New World*, 81–101.

[24] *PAJHS* 27 (1920): 34–37. Raphael Mahler, "The Historical Background of Pre-Zionism in America and Its Continuity," in B. W. Korn, ed., *A Bicentennial Festschrift for Jacob Rader Marcus* (New York, 1976), 347–48, and Jacob R. Marcus, *United States Jewry, 1776–1985* (Detroit, 1995), 1:288, offer contrasting interpretations of this prayer; for Christian parallels, see Ernest Lee Tuveson, *Redeemer Nation: The Idea of America's Millennial Role* (Chicago, 1968), 26–51, and Ruth Bloch, *Visionary Republic: Millennial Themes in American Thought, 1756–1800* (New York, 1985), esp. 94–115.

unseemliness among the politicians of his day: "Let peace and harmony reside perpetually among them," he declaimed, "that they may act in such manner as to command the approbation of their Constituents."[25]

A particularly remarkable prayer, delivered by Gershom Seixas at a special Jewish service on yet another day of "public Thanksgiving and Prayer," December 20, 1805, demonstrates that he had by then worked out a political theology appropriate to a democratic state and, as Barry Schwartz observes, felt "secure in his role as a participant in a system of representational democracy."[26] Instead of asking God to "exalt and highly aggrandize" the nation's leaders, as he did regularly every Sabbath and holiday, he now pleaded for these leaders to be granted "an emanation of thy divine wisdom," an expression far more consonant with the democratic ethos. Moreover, akin to his Christian counterparts, he used his prayer for the government to shed light, from a religious perspective, on contemporary events, as seen from his own Jeffersonian perspective:

> Let no party schisms in state affairs prevail, so as to destroy the principles of the Constitution, which is for the security of person & property, & sworn to be observed by the administrators of Government.
>
> May the Congress assembled, act in unison with each other to promote the welfare of all—and may they be able to deliberate and decide on all laws proposed for the advantage of their Constituents. May agriculture flourish & Commerce be prosperous, may the seminaries of education be continued under the direction of able Teachers & Professors—that the succeeding generations may gain the knowledge of freedom without licentiousness, & the usefulness of power without tyranny.
>
> May the people be convinced of the fidelity of their representatives, and may no cause of jealousy subsist among the different States of the Union—may the blessing of Peace attend their Councils.[27]

The Shearith Israel compromise—retaining the original Hebrew of Hanoten Teshua on a regular basis, Americanizing its vernacular section, and permitting new prayers for the government on special occasions—was reflected in the first new Jewish prayer book to be published in the United States, Solomon Henry Jackson's *The Form of Daily Prayers, According to the Custom of the Spanish and Portuguese Jews* (1826). In a prefatory note, Jackson wrote revealingly that "it was thought best to adapt the prayer Hanoten Teshua to our republican institutions." In fact, however, not one

---

[25] *PAJHS* 27 (1920): 134.
[26] Barry Schwartz, "The Jewish Prayer for the Government in America," *American Jewish History* 76, no. 3 (March 1987): 335.
[27] *PAJHS* 27 (1920): 137–39.

word of the original Hebrew was changed; Jackson merely printed the new vernacular section that Shearith Israel had introduced, complete with its different forms "during the Sitting of Congress" and "during the Recess." More interesting is the addition at the end of the prayer book of a long new "Prayer for Peace," which according to Jackson was "said during the war" (presumably the War of 1812). This new composition included a revised prayer for the government that borrowed language from Hanoten Teshua, but with the undemocratic hope for leaders "long and prosperously to rule" and the cowering plea for "benevolence towards us, and all Israel" conspicuously missing. The new prayer never caught on and is not found in later prayer books. It nevertheless adumbrates what would shortly become a widespread effort not just to adapt Hanoten Teshua, but also to replace it altogether.[28]

The first American prayer book to make this more radical change, replacing Hanoten Teshua with a completely new prayer, was *The Sabbath Service and Miscellaneous Prayers Adopted by the Reformed Society of Israelites*, the published 1830 prayer book of the Charleston Reform Movement. The young leaders of this incipient movement for Jewish religious reform in the United States advocated a radically abbreviated liturgy appropriate to the times and appreciative of "this happy land" that they called home.[29] Their prayer for the government, written by David Nunes Carvalho, a London-born merchant (whose brother had served as the ministering cantor of the city's Sephardic congregation), gave expression— and sacralized—their central reformist values.[30] The prayer also reflected their sense of security, for like their Christian neighbors they now depicted a God who influenced America for good, a far cry from the God of the traditional Jewish prayer who exalted monarchs and inclined their hearts to treat Jews mercifully. Written entirely in English, the new prayer had none of the regal language of its traditional counterpart. Rather than "exalting" the president and other federal and state officials, for example, it simply asked God to "bless," "preserve," and (a reflection of their highest ideal) "enlighten" them. Then, in an expression of patriotic piety not previously encountered in an American Jewish prayer book, it thanked God for having "numbered us with the inhabitants of this thy much favoured land . . .

[28] Solomon Henry Jackson, *The Form of Daily Prayers, According to the Custom of the Spanish and Portuguese Jews* . . . (New York, 1826), ii, 133, 232–34. On Jackson, see Marcus, *United States Jewry*, 1:193–94.

[29] Michael A. Meyer, *Response to Modernity: A History of the Reform Movement in Judaism* (New York, 1988), 228–35; James William Hagy, *This Happy Land: The Jews of Colonial and Antebellum Charleston* (Tuscaloosa, 1993), 128–60; and Gary Phillip Zola, *Isaac Harby of Charleston, 1788–1828: Jewish Reformer and Intellectual* (Tuscaloosa, 1994), 112–49.

[30] Zola, *Isaac Harby*, app. D; Charles Reznikoff and Uriah Z. Engelman, *The Jews of Charleston* (Philadelphia, 1950), 109.

where the noble and virtuous mind is the only crown of distinction, and equality of rights the only fountain of power," for having removed from the republic "the intolerance of bigotry," and for freeing its people "from the yoke of political and religious bondage." Finally, it sought divine blessings on "the people of these United States," called for charity, friendship and unity among them, and prayed that "the lights of science and civilization . . . defend them on every side from the subtle hypocrite and open adversary." The hope for Jewish redemption that closed the traditional prayer for the government went unmentioned.[31]

Here, more than in any previous text we have encountered, we see Jews reshaping their prayer for the government in response to changing conditions and shifting ideological currents. Concerned for the "future welfare and respectability" of the Jewish people, Charleston's reformers abandoned what they saw as an outmoded text and replaced it with one that invoked God's blessing on the national ideals that these young, enlightened Jews valued most highly.[32] Unlike Hanoten Teshua, which could be recited everywhere in the diaspora simply by substituting one set of "high and mighties" for another, the new prayer glorified America alone, implying that it might serve as a model for "all the nations of the earth." It also promoted universalism by including all "the people of these United States" and "all mankind" (but not "all Israel our brethren") among those whom it called on God to bless. In much of this, the prayer echoed central themes of Enlightenment era American Protestantism and anticipated what would later become known as American civil religion, both of which sacralized the land and nation of the United States in parallel terms.[33]

Charleston's Reform Jews notwithstanding, Hanoten Teshua was by no means forgotten. It continued to be recited at Shearith Israel, and although documentation is lacking, it almost certainly formed part of the liturgy in most other American synagogues in the first decades of the nineteenth century as well. Moreover, Isaac Leeser, the German-born minister of Congregation Mikveh Israel in Philadelphia and the foremost traditionalist American Jewish religious leader of his day, published Hanoten

---

[31] *The Sabbath Service and Miscellaneous Prayers Adopted by the Reformed Society of Israelites, Founded in Charleston, South Carolina, November 21, 1825* ([Charleston, 1830]; reprinted, with an introduction by Barnett A. Elzas, New York, 1916), 25–26; *The Isaac Harby Prayerbook* (Charleston, 1974), 22–23.

[32] Joseph H. Blau and Salo W. Baron, *The Jews of the United States, 1790–1840: A Documentary History* (New York, 1963), 554.

[33] Catherine Albanese, *Sons of the Fathers: The Civil Religion of the American Revolution* (Philadelphia, 1976), esp. 15; Lou H. Silberman, "American Impact: Judaism in the United States in the Early Nineteenth Century," in A. Leland Jamison, ed., *Tradition and Change in Jewish Experience* (Syracuse, 1977), 89–105; Barry L. Schwartz, "Expressions of Civil Religion in Jewish Prayer for the Government," *Journal of Reform Judaism* 37 (Spring 1990): 5–11.

Teshua in his pathbreaking, six-volume Sephardic Hebrew-English prayer book (1837), the most ambitious and impressive Jewish liturgical publication to that time in the United States.[34] Leeser actually printed two versions of the prayer for each service, one designated A Prayer for a Royal Government (he hoped to market his prayer book throughout the English-speaking world) and the other A Prayer for a Republican Government. The former was the traditional text of the prayer, complete with the hope that God would "bless, preserve, guard, assist, exalt, and raise unto a high eminence, our lord the king." The latter deleted this phrase, asking only that God "bless, preserve, guard and assist the constituted officers of the government"—not even the president was separately mentioned. This shift from the long list of officials found in earlier American prayers to the formulaic "constituted officers" anticipated a later trend and underscored a critical difference between autocratic monarchies and democratic republics.[35] Even more important, however, was the symbolic importance of offering two alternative prayers in the liturgy. By distinguishing monarchies and republics as he did, Leeser (perhaps unconsciously) divided the diaspora into two kinds of polities, implying that they stood differently before God. Everywhere that Leeser's prayer book reached (or its successor, edited by Abraham de Sola, that followed essentially the same practice), this dramatic distinction was underscored, reminding Jews who still lived under kings and queens that an alternative form of government existed.[36]

In 1848, in response to "the many communities of the German denomination lately sprung up in this country," Leeser published a prayer book "according to the custom of the German and Polish Jews," hoping that it would capture the growing market for prayer books opened up by the burgeoning Jewish immigration from Central Europe. For the most part, he relied on the Ashkenazic Hebrew text prepared in Germany by Rabbi Wolf Heidenheim. When it came to the prayer for the government, however, he published a revision of his own Prayer for a Republican Govern-

[34] See Lance J. Sussman, *Isaac Leeser and the Making of American Judaism* (Detroit, 1995), 93–94.

[35] Practical considerations may also have been involved, because political titles differed from state to state and officeholders changed frequently. I have found only two presidents, both highly popular among Jews, whose names were actually printed in the text of a regular prayer for the government: Theodore Roosevelt and Franklin D. Roosevelt. See *Magil's Complete Linear Prayer Book* (Philadelphia, 1905), 153 (later editions drop the Roosevelt name), and the frontispiece to *A Naye Shas Tehinah* (Brooklyn, [1943?]).

[36] Isaac Leeser, ed., *The Form of Prayers According to the Custom of the Spanish and Portuguese Jews* (Philadelphia, 1837), 1:114–15. In the revised edition by Abraham de Sola (Philadelphia, 1878; Philadelphia, 1925), A Prayer for a Royal Government was retitled Prayer for the Queen and Royal Family, and the appropriate members were listed by name, probably an attempt to increase sales within the British Empire.

ment. The Heidenheim text included the line, not found in Sephardic versions of the prayer,[37] "may he [the sovereign] subdue nations under his feet, and make his enemies fall before him, and in whatsoever he under-taketh may he prosper." Apparently finding these militant sentiments un-palatable in an American setting, Leeser quietly dropped them.[38]

Other texts prepared for German Jews, however, went much further in their changes. In 1846, just a few months after he arrived from Germany, the young Rabbi Max Lilienthal, serving as chief rabbi of a union of New York's three leading German-Jewish Orthodox congregations, abolished Hanoten Teshua altogether and replaced it with a new Hebrew prayer of his own composition beginning with the words "Master of the Universe" (*Ribon Kol Ha-Olamim*).[39] The surviving minutes of this short-lived syna-gogue union do not preserve Lilienthal's reasons—although given his neg-ative experiences with the governments of Germany and Russia and his ardent political liberalism they are not hard to fathom—nor do they pre-serve more than the first three words of the new prayer's text. But a New York prayer book published for German Jews in 1848 includes a prayer for the government beginning with these same words, and it seems safe to conclude that the new prayer—reprinted in Orthodox prayer books into the twentieth century—is, in fact, Lilienthal's formulation.[40] This is no small irony, because within a decade Lilienthal had cast his lot with Re-form Judaism and moved to Cincinnati.

Lilienthal's flowery Hebrew prayer is an extraordinary liturgical evoca-tion of the theme of Zion in America. Abandoning both the groveling tone and the sense of dependency reflected in Hanoten Teshua, it radiates op-timism and self-confidence. Where Hanoten Teshua drew its metaphors from the experience of the exile, the new prayer looks hopefully toward redemption, appropriating idyllic biblical depictions of the land of Israel

[37] Dembitz, *Jewish Services in Synagogue and Home*, 218, claims otherwise, but without substantiation.

[38] Isaac Leeser, ed., *The Book of Daily Prayers for Every Day in the Year According to the Custom of the German and Polish Jews* (Philadelphia, 1848), preface and 108–9. Near the end of his life, Leeser published a revised translation of a French meditation to be recited during the prayer for the government. His translation radically toned down the fawningly patriotic French original, Americanized the blessing for the ruler, and added a line calling for resto-ration to Zion. Compare *Prières d'un coeur Israélite-Imre Lev* (1848; reprint Montreal, 1945), 98–99, with *Imre Lev: Meditations and Prayers for Every Situation and Occasion in Life* (Philadel-phia, 1866), 29–30.

[39] Hyman B. Grinstein, "The Minute Book of Lilienthal's Union of German Synagogues in New York," *Hebrew Union College Annual* 18 (1944): 324, 338, 341. On Lilienthal, see Jonathan D. Sarna, "Max Lilienthal," in *American National Biography* (forthcoming).

[40] *Tefilot Yisra'el. Prayers of Israel, with an English Translation*, 5th ed. (New York, 1856), 198–99. See also Jonathan D. Sarna, "A Forgotten Nineteenth-Century Prayer for the United States Government: Its Meaning, Significance, and Surprising Author," in *Essays in Honor of Ernest Frerichs* (forthcoming).

and applying them to the United States: "Look down from Your holy dwelling and bless this land, the United States of America, whereon we dwell. Let not violence be heard in their land, wasting and destruction within their boundaries [Isa. 60:18]. . . . May you grant them rains in due season, may the earth yield her produce and the tree of the field yield its fruit [Lev. 26:4]." The prayer goes on to seek God's blessing on the president and the vice president, as well as on state and local officials, and prays for them to be divinely guided. It makes no mention, however, of their being exalted or preserved in office. It also includes a special blessing for New York City and its inhabitants—an appropriate blessing for Lilienthal to have written for his local congregants but very strange in a prayer book distributed across the country. Inevitably, if not intentionally, the prayer reinforced the mistaken belief that New York was a microcosm of American Jewry as a whole. Finally, the prayer evoked God's blessing on the whole House of Israel, praying for safety, material wealth, and growing strength, "until a redeemer shall come forth to Zion." [41]

Lilienthal's prayer reflected some of the fondest hopes of Central European Jews who immigrated to America's shores. Its publication in place of Hanoten Teshua in a widely circulated Orthodox prayer book did much to signify to them that America was different—if not actually Zion, then the closest thing to it. The prayer also heralded a period of intense Jewish liturgical creativity in the United States as the size of the community grew, its religious life became more variegated and diverse, and the hegemony of traditionalist Sephardic congregations was broken. Over the next 150 years, hundreds of new American Jewish prayers and prayer books appeared, covering a wide spectrum from Orthodoxy to Radical Reform. [42] Most contained a prayer for the government: sometimes the traditional Hanoten Teshua; sometimes a variant of that prayer; sometimes a totally new prayer in Hebrew, English, or both; and sometimes just an indication that following the reading of the Torah such a prayer was commonly said. Prayers for the government were likewise published in Jewish newspapers and in handbooks for rabbis; countless more were probably never recorded. [43] While several prayers won wide circulation, no single one ever

[41] *Tefilot Yisra'el*, 198; my translation. For parallel applications of the Zion theme to America, see Conrad Cherry, ed., *God's New Israel: Religious Interpretations of American Destiny* (Englewood Cliffs, N.J., 1971).

[42] Sharona R. Wachs, *American Jewish Liturgies: A Bibliography of American Jewish Liturgy from the Establishment of the Press in the Colonies through 1925* (Cincinnati, 1997); Eric L. Friedland, "The Historical and Theological Development of the Non-Orthodox Prayerbooks in the United States" (Ph.D. diss., Brandeis University, 1967).

[43] Surprisingly, the prayer book prepared by Isaac Mayer Wise, *Minhag Amerika* (Cincinnati, 1857), contains no prayer for the government. His congregation had commissioned a new prayer in 1850 (see note 44), and it likely remained in use.

again predominated, as Hanoten Teshua had done since the seventeenth century. Instead, a wide variety of liturgies for the government would henceforth coexist, a reflection, on the one hand, of the fragmentation of American Judaism and, on the other, of that same spirit of freedom and democracy that the prayers themselves so enthusiastically celebrated.

Three features found in a great many of the new Jewish prayers for the government, and already anticipated by the Charleston reformers and by Lilienthal, immediately set these prayers apart from Hanoten Teshua. First, they were identifiably *American* prayers, exhibiting a conscious effort to distinguish Judaism in America from its counterpart in Europe. Second, the prayers now included (and often began with) blessings for the country, as if to underscore that America, rather than any particular president, guaranteed Jewish liberty. Third, the exaggerated deference to leaders, characteristic of Hanoten Teshua (even as its subtext hinted that the "King of Kings" was greater) was replaced by an emphatic statement of the leaders' own subservience to God. Where Hanoten Teshua played to the vanity of the sovereign and underscored Jewish powerlessness, the new prayers, much more akin to parallel Protestant prayers, emphasized the vulnerability of political leaders and their consequent need for divine guidance.

The 1850 prayer for the government composed by Rev. Henry A. Henry for Cincinnati's Bene Yeshurun congregation effectively illustrates all three points. Composed at the request of the congregation's board of trustees, it was specifically written to be "a prayer for the welfare of the Government and people of the United States" and a replacement for Hanoten Teshua "formerly used . . . in accordance with the custom and practice of the European congregations." The prayer's first three paragraphs invoked God's blessing, first, on our "happy country, the Land of Freedom"; second, on the states "that Virtue, Truth, Charity and Mercy may flourish"; and third, on "the inhabitants of this Land . . . that they may all live as brethren." Only in the last two paragraphs did the prayer turn its attention to federal, state, and local officials, and then it called on God to "banish all errors from their minds," "teach them," and "instruct them"—a far cry indeed from the obsequious message of Hanoten Teshua.[44]

The Union Prayer Book, first published in 1895 and rapidly accepted by the vast majority of Reform Jewish congregations in the United States, followed this same pattern. "Fervently we invoke Thy benediction for this our

[44] *Asmonean* (New York), June 21, 1850, 70; Jay Henry Moses, "Henry A. Henry: The Life and Work of an American Rabbi, 1849–1869" (ordination thesis, Hebrew Union College-Jewish Institute of Religion, 1997), 32–33. In 1850, Henry's son, the folk-artist Moses Henry, still incorporated the traditional prayer for the government in a piece of liturgical art; see Alice M. Greenwald, "The Masonic Mizrah and Lamp: Jewish Ritual Art as a Reflection of Cultural Assimilation," *Journal of Jewish Art* 10 (1984): 100.

country and our nation," its untitled "Prayer" began, the cumulative emphasis on "our" underscoring native Jews' quest to belong and seem loyal.[45] America's leaders entered the prayer only in the middle, as subjects of its call on God to "enlighten and sustain with Thy power those whom the people have set in authority." In accordance with Reform Judaism's ethos, the prayer concluded on a universalistic note, calling for "peace and good will" among "all the citizens of our land" and for "religion to exalt our nation in righteousness." This is among the most widely known of all Jewish prayers for the government in the United States. With only slight changes in wording it remained in the Reform Jewish prayer book for eighty years. It was also reprinted in the prayer book prepared for Jewish soldiers in World War I. Astonishingly, it was even reprinted at the back of one Orthodox prayer book—but without attribution![46]

In calling for "peace and good will" among Americans, the *Union Prayer Book* echoed what was already a recurrent theme among the new Jewish prayers for the government. While Gershom Seixas in the decades following the Revolution was principally concerned with infighting among politicians, Jews arriving in America later on viewed with far more concern tensions among people of different regions, races, ethnicities, and creeds. Their own security, many Jews believed, was inextricably bound up with domestic tranquillity. Rabbi David Einhorn, who arrived in America in 1855 and became a fierce opponent of slavery, already wrote into his brief prayer for the government (1858) a specific line calling for "love" between America's "various tribes and denominations." Rabbi Morris J. Raphall, who disagreed with Einhorn concerning slavery, likewise prayed for unity. In his 1860 prayer delivered before Congress (the first Jewish prayer ever delivered before that body), he called on lawmakers to adopt "the way of moderation and equity . . . so that, from the North and from the South, from the East and from the West, one feeling of satisfaction may attend their labors; while the whole people of the land joyfully repeat the words

[45] In keeping with the precedent set in David Einhorn's prayer book *Olat Tamid: Gebetbuch für israelitische Reform-Gemeinden* (New York, 1858), 22, this prayer was embedded within a broader one for the congregation printed under the simple heading "Prayer." The *Union Prayer Book* prayer, however, was an entirely different (and later) composition. For the relationship between the two prayer books, see Lou H. Silberman, "The *Union Prayer Book:* A Study in Liturgical Development," in Bertram W. Korn, *Retrospect and Prospect* (New York, 1964), 46–80.

[46] *The Union Prayer-Book for Jewish Worship* (Cincinnati, 1895), 1 : 99; stylistically revised in *The Union Prayerbook for Jewish Worship* (Cincinnati, 1947), 1 : 148. See also *Abridged Prayer Book for Jews in the Army and Navy of the United States* (Philadelphia, 1917), 81, and the Orthodox *Form of Prayers for the Feast of New-Year* (New York, n.d.), 478; cf. page 192. Preliminary versions of the *Union Prayer Book*, prepared by I. S. Moses, lack this prayer. It may have been written by Gustav Gottheil, rabbi of Temple Emanu-El of New York; see Richard Gottheil, *The Life of Gustav Gottheil: Memoir of a Priest in Israel* (Williamsport, Pa., 1936), 163.

of thy Psalmist: 'How good and how pleasant it is when brethren dwell together in unity.'"[47]

East European Jews, immigrating a generation after the Civil War, stressed this same theme in their new prayers for the government. The twentieth-century Conservative rabbi Elias L. Solomon, for example, called on God to cause all Americans "to dwell in harmony and in peace with one another, and to seek one another's wellbeing, and the good of their common land."[48] The great rabbinic scholar Louis Ginzberg, in a prayer first published both in Hebrew and in English translation in the *Festival Prayer Book* of the Conservative movement (1927), and subsequently reprinted in standard Conservative Jewish prayer books and in the prayer books of the Reconstructionist movement as well, made this theme central to his message. "Plant among the peoples of different nationalities and faiths who dwell here, love and brotherhood, peace and friendship," he wrote in his original Hebrew. "Uproot from their hearts all hatred and enmity, all jealousy and vying for supremacy." While the English paraphrase toned these sentiments down (the recent prayer book of the Reconstructionist movement, *Kol Haneshamah,* has restored them), the core of the message was preserved: "May citizens of all races and creeds forge a common bond in true harmony to banish all hatred and bigotry." Ginzberg's prayer, which also contained all the other elements that had by now become standard for prayers of this kind, including a universalistic peroration, became one of the most frequently invoked twentieth-century Jewish substitutes for Hanoten Teshua. Long after other prayers for the government were forgotten, his remained timely.[49]

Even those prayers that proved evanescent, however, disclose much about the concerns of American Jews at particular moments. Like other occasional prayers that we have seen, they aimed to bring God into central questions of the day—often in tacit support of a particular point of view. During the Civil War, for example, Sabato Morais, the minister

[47] Einhorn, *Olat Tamid,* 22; Bertram W. Korn, *Eventful Years and Experiences* (Cincinnati, 1954), 100; Bertram W. Korn, *American Jewry and the Civil War,* 2d ed. (New York, 1970), 15–31; David Brion Davis, *Slavery and Human Progress* (New York, 1984), 82–84.

[48] Jacob Bosniak, ed., *Pulpit and Public Prayers* (New York, 1927), 81.

[49] *Festival Prayer Book* (New York, 1927), 201; *Sabbath and Festival Prayer Book* (New York, 1946), 130; Jules Harlow, ed., *Siddur Sim Shalom* (New York, 1985), 415; David Golinkin, ed., *The Responsa of Professor Louis Ginzberg* (New York, 1996), 54–55. All major Conservative Jewish prayer books contain essentially the same text of Ginzberg's prayer in Hebrew, along with English paraphrases that differ somewhat more. See also *Sabbath Prayer Book* (New York, 1946), 164–67. Rabbi Jacob Kohn took credit for the first sentences of the English paraphrase; see Bosniak, *Pulpit and Public Prayers,* 76. The new Reconstructionist prayer book, *Kol Haneshamah* (Wyncote, Pa., 1994), 418–19, revises Ginzberg's original Hebrew but translates it literally. For an alternate text used in some Conservative congregations, see the revision of Hanoten Teshua in Max D. Klein, *Seder Avodah* (Philadelphia, 1951), 278–79.

(*Hazan*) of Congregation Mikveh Israel was requested by his patriotic lay board (*adjunta*) to include in the prayer for the government the words "may our Union be preserved and its defenders be shielded from danger."[50] Later, during the long debate over immigration restriction, several rabbis included in their prayers the hope that America would remain, as Rabbi Aaron Wise put it in his 1891 prayer book, "the haven of rest and of refuge to the persecuted of all nations."[51] Rabbi Joseph Krauskopf of Philadelphia, long concerned about issues of social justice and urban reform, used his prayer in 1892 to remind congregants that "despite abundance, want lodges in our midst; and, despite peace, the voice of discontent is not yet hushed in our land." He called on God to "enable the people's representatives, wherever assembled, to wrestle with this harassing foe, and to conquer him."[52] Rabbis writing in the twentieth century went further, using prayers for the government to invoke God on behalf of such causes as pacifism, anti-imperialism, freedom of conscience, and equal opportunity. One rabbi prayed that America be prevented "from losing its own soul."[53] The contrast between these prayers and the traditional Hanoten Teshua could not be more glaring and underscores the aforementioned tension between patriotic loyalty and prophetic judgment. While the traditional prayer assumed Jewish dependency and curried favor from the ruling authorities, these new prayers exude self-confidence and offer direction to the ruling authorities on how to do their jobs better.

Some Orthodox Jews resisted this trend toward writing new prayers for the government. Committed to maintaining Jewish tradition in the face of social pressure to acculturate, they refused to tamper with any part of the prayer book, Hanoten Teshua included. Liturgical custom, they believed, was not something to be violated with impunity. Besides, America as they understood it was not much different from any other diaspora land; it was still exile and its Jews still depended on the benevolence of a non-Jewish government. For these "resisters," maintaining Hanoten Teshua, even if

[50] Congregation Mikveh Israel Minute Book, September 20, 1862, as cited in Ruth Alpers, "Traditionalism, Americanization, and Assimilation: The Struggles of Sabato Morais, 1851–1897" (ordination thesis, Hebrew Union College-Jewish Institute of Religion, 1994), 46.

[51] *Shalhevet Yah: The Temple Service Arranged for the Congregation Rodeph Sholom of New York by Dr. Aaron Wise* (New York, 1891), 19. Aaron Wise was the father of the famous Reform rabbi Stephen S. Wise.

[52] Joseph Krauskopf, *The Service Manual* (Philadelphia, 1892), 32.

[53] Julius Silberfeld, *The Sabbath Service* (New York, 1923), 187; Bosniak, *Pulpit and Public Prayers,* 76–82 (quote is from page 80); Morris Silverman, *The Junior Prayer Book* (New York, 1933), 38; Morris Silverman, *Sabbath and Festival Services* (Hartford, Conn.: 1936), 214. See also the supplementary prayer That America Fulfil the Promise of Its Founding, in the Reconstructionist *Sabbath Prayer Book,* 546–47.

only by reflex, made a powerful statement. It was another symbol of their proud stance against assimilation and all that it threatened.[54]

By contrast, Orthodox Jews who took a more positive view of America, believing that tradition and Americanization could be reconciled, did modify Hanoten Teshua. Some, as we have seen, even went further, rejecting the prayer altogether in favor of the Lilienthal prayer or some other new version. More frequently, however, especially in the twentieth century, the modifications they introduced were small—a few words added here or subtracted there—leaving the bulk of the prayer intact. One early text, for example, sought to universalize Hanoten Teshua by seeking the government's mercy not only on Israel but also on all America's ethnic groups. Another replaced the call for mercy with one for "wisdom and understanding." Still another, the very popular Orthodox prayer book edited by Philip Birnbaum, deleted both the plea for mercy and the call, that Isaac Leeser had earlier found offensive, to "subdue nations." But it kept the rest of Hanoten Teshua intact.[55] No less than the strategy of resistance, these various accommodationist strategies likewise made a powerful statement of cultural ideology. Both strategies demonstrated that the question of how to pray for the government raised issues that reached far beyond government, extending to Judaism's relationship toward American culture as a whole.

The establishment of the State of Israel in 1948 compounded the problem of how to pray for the government. As Jews across the spectrum of American Jewish life gradually added prayers for the State of Israel to their liturgy, they were forced to consider the appropriate relationship between prayers for the new Jewish homeland and prayers for the land that American Jews still called home. One of the first to deal with this problem was the Orthodox Jewish liturgist Birnbaum. In his prayer books published soon after the establishment of the Jewish state, he appended a Prayer for the Welfare of the State of Israel, by the Chief Rabbinate of Israel, to follow the traditional prayer for the government.[56] This pattern, praying for

[54] Jeffrey S. Gurock, "Resisters and Accommodators: Varieties of Orthodox Rabbis in America, 1886–1983," *American Jewish Archives* 35 (November 1983): 100–187. Prayer books that print the traditional text of Hanoten Teshua, sometimes with minor modifications, include *Form of Prayers and Blessing of Israel* (New York, 1901), 254; *Sephath Emeth* (New York, 1919), 196; M. Stern, ed., *Daily Prayers* (New York, 1928), 199; S. Singer, ed., *The Standard Prayer Book* (New York, 1947), 219.

[55] *Mahzor Kol Bo . . . Yom Kippur* (New York, [1912?]), 189 (the first American edition of this prayerbook [1909?], found in the American Jewish Historical Society, accidentally retained the prayer for the czar); *Magil's Complete Linear Prayer Book*, 153–54; Philip Birnbaum, *Daily Prayer Book* (New York, 1949), 379. *Sabbath Prayers: A Complete Ritual* (New York, 1925), 113, published the traditional Hebrew text and an unrelated Americanized prayer in English.

[56] Birnbaum, *Daily Prayer Book*, 379, 789; Philip Birnbaum, *High Holyday Prayer Book* (New York, 195[?]), 421–23.

America ("our country") first and for the welfare of the State of Israel second, quickly became standard, establishing as it were a hierarchy of priorities. Thereafter, some prayer books, notably most Orthodox ones and the Reconstructionist *Kol Haneshamah,* sought to establish a careful symmetry, printing prayers of approximately equal length for America and for Israel, with one immediately following the other.[57] Other prayer books, particularly those composed in the 1970s and 1980s by the Conservative and Reform movements, devoted more than twice as much space to the prayer for "our country" than to the prayer for the State of Israel, an accurate if not necessarily conscious reflection of both movements' central focus.[58] As so often before, so too here, liturgy sheds light on an issue of central importance to American Judaism: the immensely sensitive political and moral question of how to balance national loyalty with devotion to Zion.

The general practice of praying aloud for the welfare of the country declined during the Vietnam and post-Vietnam years. With many American Jews openly critical of their nation's foreign and domestic policies, chauvinistic prayers left over from an earlier era rang hollow. Declining patriotism and widespread public disillusionment with government—by no means unique to American Jews—spawned liturgical change. The new Reform Jewish prayer book, *Gates of Prayer* (1975), for example, abandoned the fervent supplication that was for so long a staple of Reform Jewish worship, replacing it with an occasional prayer, divorced from the regular liturgy, that covered the nation, its inhabitants, and its leaders in four short lines. A popular new Orthodox prayer book known as the ArtScroll Siddur (1984) included no prayer for the government whatsoever, only a note that "in many congregations, a prayer for the welfare of the State is recited."[59] Impressionistic evidence suggests that even where prayer books did include a regular prayer for the government, congregations recited it less frequently during these years. And where the prayer was recited, as in that Orthodox synagogue in Cambridge with which we began, vigorous expressions of dissent could not be ruled out.

The prayer for the government thus serves as a revealing historical barometer of the relationship between American Jews and the state. The changes we have seen in these prayers—the growing minority-group con-

---

[57] David de Sola Pool, *The Traditional Prayer Book for Sabbath and Festivals* (New York, 1960), 259; *Kol Haneshamah,* 418–21.

[58] Jules Harlow, ed., *Mahzor for Rosh Hashanah and Yom Kippur* (New York, 1972), 506; Harlow, *Siddur Sim Shalom,* 414–17; *Gates of Prayer: The New Union Prayerbook* (New York, 1975), 452; *Gates of Repentance: The New Union Prayerbook for the Days of Awe* (New York, 1978), 354–55.

[59] *Gates of Prayer,* 452; Nosson Scherman, ed., *The Complete ArtScroll Siddur* (New York, 1984), 450. *Service of the Heart* (London, 1967), upon which *Gates of Prayer* was based, is full of prayers for the (English) government; see 137, 156, 174, 194, 211. The special Rabbinical Council of America edition of *The Complete ArtScroll Siddur* restored both the traditional prayer for the government and the prayer for the State of Israel.

fidence that they display, the critical issues to which they point, and the complex moral tensions that they engender—speak to themes central to the American Jewish experience as a whole. They shed light not only on the faith of American Jews but on their politics, acculturation, and community conscience as well.

Oct. 26, '97.

Julia Collier on the day of her wedding to Julian Harris, October 26, 1897. Courtesy of Special Collections Department, Robert W. Woodruff Library, Emory University, Atlanta, Ga.

CHAPTER TEN

Interfaith Families in Victorian America

ANNE C. ROSE

In June 1897, Julia Collier, the daughter of the mayor of Atlanta, became engaged to Julian Harris, son of the popular creator of "Uncle Re-
mus," Joel Chandler Harris. The two were deeply in love. Following the
death of her mother in March, Julia had written to Julian that "the fact that
you are alive and love me is the very greatest possible comfort."[1] She worried, however, about the difference in their religions. Julia was a Protestant
and Julian was a Catholic, raised in the faith by a devotedly Catholic
mother with the consent of his nominally Protestant father. "Of course the
next subject touched upon was your religion," Julia explained to Julian in
her account of a private talk with a friend who had become a Catholic in
order to marry a Catholic man. She did not trust a letter to convey the
thoughts they shared: "I will wait until I see you to tell you about that part
of the conversation."[2] Julia did not record what she later said to Julian, but
the way they dealt with the question of religion in their family is clear. In
October, they were married in Julia's home by a Methodist minister. Family
members on both sides, Protestants and Catholics, attended the wedding,
and neither the bride nor the groom converted to the other's religion.[3]

I am grateful for fellowships from the American Jewish Archives, Hebrew Union College-
Jewish Institute of Religion; the College of the Liberal Arts, Pennsylvania State University;
and the Cushwa Center for the Study of American Catholicism, University of Notre Dame.
[1] Julia Collier [Harris] to Julian Harris, [March 23, 1897], box 24, folder 2, Julian LaRose
Harris Papers, Special Collections, Robert W. Woodruff Library, Emory University, Atlanta,
Georgia.
[2] Ibid., [June 5, 1897], box 24, folder 3, Julian Harris Papers.
[3] An account of the wedding appeared in the *Atlanta Constitution*, October 27, 1897; see
also Joel Chandler Harris to Julia Collier [Harris], June 21, [1897], box 34, folder 1, and [il-
legible] to Julia Harris, [October] 27, [1897], box 34, folder 8, Julian Harris Papers.

During the sixty-five years of the Harrises' marriage before Julian's death in 1963, they continued to be involved with religion, although never in an exclusive or dogmatic frame of mind. They blended Protestant and Catholic observances at home when their sons were young and in 1925 shared the Pulitzer Prize for journalism for contesting the religious and racial prejudices of the Ku Klux Klan in their role as joint editors of the *Columbus (Georgia) Enquirer-Sun*.

The Harrises' family history casts light on the moral challenges facing interfaith couples who married in America during the Victorian era. Because Julia and Julian did not allow traditional religious rules—and specifically the injunction to marry within one's faith—to dictate their choice in marriage, they transformed religion in their family from a set of moral imperatives into a series of moral problems. Only twenty-one and twenty-three years old, respectively, when they married, Julia and Julian did not set out to contest scriptural laws, ecclesiastical policies, or clerical authority. Nonetheless, their simple decision to intermarry enhanced the role of their independent judgments in their subsequent religious affairs. Julia's premarital discussions of religion with Julian and her friend represented more than a woman's reflections. In Victorian interfaith households, the family was the center of moral decision making, dialogue was the means, and change in response to new private circumstances was the rule. This is not to say that interfaith families commonly turned away from Judeo-Christian principles or avoided connections with churches or synagogues. Yet family members tried hard to embrace doctrines and rituals only to an extent consistent with an unspoken family ethic of forbearance, tolerance, and mutual respect. Not surprisingly, they did not always live up to the high standard of extending their love to husbands, wives, or children with whom they disagreed. Religious conflicts were capable of eroding a family's common emotional ground and leaving feelings of betrayal and alienation. All the Victorians who chose interfaith marriages, however, were risk takers from a moral perspective. Trusting, like Julia Collier, their capacity for communication and love, they accepted the ethical challenge of living in families divided by religion.

In this essay I examine the way American Victorian interfaith families dealt with the "moral problem" of coping with religious diversity among kin. The analysis is based on seventeen families begun by marriages involving members of America's three major religious groups—Protestants, Catholics, and Jews—that were contracted between 1819 and 1905.[4] These

---

[4] A table providing information on the couples studied appears in the appendix. Although I have tried to balance the sample by religion, place of residence, and date of marriage, my choices have been influenced by the availability of family papers. I use "Victorian" to denote a culture, and especially a religious culture, committed to tradition and innovation at once, as well as piety and civility. Understood in this sense, Victorianism persisted from about 1820 to the early twentieth century and flourished particularly among the educated middle classes. I

families were poised between tradition and self-determination, institutional policies and lay initiatives, formal doctrines and instinctive solutions. Their assumption that they were free to make moral choices was a sign of their modernity, but they also knew that ideas about interfaith marriage had deep roots in the Judeo-Christian past. The Hebrew Bible recorded policies enacted by Ezra and Nehemiah to restrict marriages between the Israelites and members of neighboring tribes. In the Christian Bible, Paul's first letter to the Corinthians cautiously approved intermarriage in the hope that the family might be an instrument of persuasion for the unbelieving husband or wife. His second letter, however, warned sharply against ties with the faithless. No Western religious community favored interfaith marriages.[5]

In America, republican principles invited more open relations among religious groups, including ties woven by romance and marriage. The separation of civil and ecclesiastical power, the legal equality of religions, and the sharp decline in the number of laws restricting religious minorites permitted men and women of dissimilar backgrounds to meet in a shared social space. Jews, for example, as one Jewish layman noted in 1845, suffered "no legal disabilities" for the first time in their history and could "mingle and associate with persons of different religious beliefs in society and friendly intercourse and business pursuits."[6] The growing freedom of women to move widely in society and, within marriage, to hold their own opinions favored interfaith households as well. Certainly religious prejudices continued to exercise a constant and occasionally virulent presence during the Victorian era and worked as a counterforce to friendly communication. Yet, on the whole, American circumstances were hospitable to the creation of interfaith families.

This essay chronicles the emergence of an informal family ethic of religious accommodation in interfaith homes. It is a story connected with two

---

focus on interfaith marriages within the religious triple melting pot because the nineteenth century was the key era of immigration from Europe that produced this threefold pattern. In none of these families did one partner formally convert to the other's religion at the time of marriage. In part, this was because American clergy of all groups did not develop consistent policies linking conversion and marriage until near the turn of the twentieth century.

[5] Key biblical passages include Ezra 10:2–19, Neh. 13:23–30, Ruth, 1 Cor. 7:12–16, and 2 Cor. 6:14–18. Teachings on interfaith marriage in both the Jewish and Christian Bibles contain subtleties and ambiguities, as the secondary literature suggests, esp. Louis M. Epstein, *Marriage Laws in the Bible and the Talmud* (Cambridge, Mass., 1942), and James A. Brundage, "Intermarriage between Christians and Jews in Medieval Canon Law," *Jewish History* 3 (1988): 25–40.

[6] Simeon Abrahams, "Intermarrying with Gentiles," *The Occident and American Jewish Advocate* 2 (March 1845): 586. Although the legal liberation of religious minorities during the nineteenth century occurred most fully in America, rates of intermarriage rose simultaneously in Europe. See Deborah Hertz, *Jewish High Society in Old Regime Berlin* (New Haven, 1988), esp. chap. 7, and Todd M. Endelman, *Radical Assimilation in English Jewish History, 1656–1945* (Bloomington, Ind., 1990).

trends in the relationship of interfaith couples to public religious communities: the families often questioned traditional authority, yet they still wished to participate in congregations or at least to advocate moral causes. I look first at the personal religious changes that led to interfaith marriages and then at moral issues in families, seen in relation to their public affiliations, over time. In all these settings, laypeople struggled to respond charitably to loved ones who held beliefs unlike their own.

The sociology of nineteenth-century American interfaith marriages is not difficult to grasp. Before the 1840s, small Catholic and Jewish populations made marriage to a Protestant almost a demographic necessity. When a priest visited Lancaster, Ohio, in 1810, nine-year-old Maria Boyle had to ask her aunt if they were Catholic. "Why yes child, we were in Brownsville [Pennsylvania]," Susan Beecher replied. The marriages of Susan and later Maria to Protestants made sense in light of their isolation as Catholics.[7] By 1900 there were substantial pools of marriageable men and women of all faiths, but now assimilation turned the romantic sights of many Catholics and Jews outward. There was a tacit logic to a cluster of articles in the periodical the *Israelite* in 1908 and 1909: "Jewish Girls in Private Schools," "Jewish Students in American Universities," and a jeremiad on intermarriage, "'The Melting Pot': Will the Jews Become Merged in It and Disappear?"[8] The social conditions of interfaith marriage reveal little, however, about the religious values of individuals who married outside the faith. These men and women commonly felt distanced from the traditions of their childhoods before they chose a spouse. As crucial, because they were both unconventional and thoughtful, they found creative ways

[7] Eleanor S. Ewing, "Maria Boyle Ewing," unpaginated typescript, Ellen Boyle Ewing Sherman Papers, Henry E. Huntington Library, San Marino, California.

[8] "Jewish Girls in Private Schools," *Israelite*, November 12, 1908, 4; Samuel J. Horvitz, "Jewish Students in American Universities," *Israelite*, September 3, 1908, 5; Emanuel A. Hirsch, "'The Melting Pot': Will the Jews Become Merged in It and Disappear?" *Israelite*, May 4, 1909, 1. Rates of interfaith marriage varied significantly in different locations even at a single point in time as a result of such factors as size of the ethnic community, degree of assimilation, and influence of the clergy. A rough overall estimate for intermarriage during the nineteenth century is between 5 and 10 percent of Protestants, Catholics, and Jews. Studies helpful in estimating the frequency of mixed marriage include Leslie Tentler, *Seasons of Grace: A History of the Catholic Archdiocese of Detroit* (Detroit, 1990), 100, and Jacob Rader Marcus, *United States Jewry, 1776–1985*, 4 vols. (Detroit, 1989–93), 1:606–8, 3:399–400. More impressionistically, periodicals, advice literature, and fiction, especially Catholic and Jewish sources, discussed interfaith marriage extensively. On Catholic attitudes, see, for example, Mary Anne Sadlier, *The Blakes and Flanagans: A Tale, Illustrative of Irish Life* (1855; reprint, New York, 1863); Alban Stolz, *Mixed Marriage: The Forbidden Fruit for Catholics*, trans. H. Cluever, 4th ed. (New York, 1883); and Lelia Hardin Bugg, *The Correct Thing for Catholics*, 12th ed. (New York, 1891), 39–40. On Jewish views, see articles in the Reform periodical the *Israelite*, including Isaac Mayer Wise, "Why They Should Not Intermarry," March 14, 1879, 4, and [David Philipson?], "Rabbis Officiating at Intermarriages," September 30, 1909, 4.

to build intimacy without religious consensus. Tolerance, energized by feeling, shaped their religious decisions.

The importance of freethinking as a prelude to interfaith marriage appeared as early as 1821. In that year Isaac Lea (1792–1886), a Quaker, married Frances Anne Carey (1799–1873), daughter of the Irish-born writer and publisher Mathew Carey, at St. Augustine's Catholic Church in Philadelphia. Lea possessed an impressive Quaker lineage dating back to a Friend who immigrated to Philadelphia in 1699. He himself quarreled, however, with the Society of Friends. In 1814, Lea forfeited his birthright as a Quaker when he volunteered for a musket company, and perhaps even before his provocative act, he was cool toward Quaker piety. As an adult, Lea's true love was science. During his lifetime, he published nearly three hundred works in the fields of conchology, mineralogy, and geology.[9]

It was on the common intellectual ground of the Enlightenment that Lea met Frances Carey. Her father was a loyal supporter of both the Irish and Catholicism as a founder of the Hibernian Society in Philadelphia in the early 1790s and the Society for the Defense of the Catholic Religion from Calumny and Abuse in 1826. Even so, he informed the Catholic hierarchy during the recurring controversies of the period between lay trustees and the clergy that American Catholicism must be made compatible with republicanism: "A different order of things prevails in this country."[10] This tempered attitude toward religion characterized his *Philosophy of Common Sense: Practical Rules for the Promotion of Domestic Happiness* (1838). A husband should "treat your wife as your equal," and a wife should "receive your husband with smiles," Carey advised, but he said nothing about religious doctrine.[11] An ethic of decency and respect was more important to families than was church affiliation.

How much Frances agreed with her father about the rule of goodwill in domesticity may be inferred from her actions. Fondly loved by Isaac, she accommodated her tastes to his. On a carriage journey in 1849 through the Pennsylvania countryside, Frances and Isaac stopped at the house of his uncle and aunt. "My good wife," Isaac wrote, "to whom this was all new

---

[9] "Isaac Lea (1792–1886)" and "Elizabeth Gibson (1762–1833)," manuscripts, in folder titled "Notes of Isaac Lea," Isaac Lea Papers, American Philosophical Society, Philadelphia, Pennsylvania; Edward Sculley Bradley, *Henry Charles Lea: A Biography* (Philadelphia, 1931), chap. 1; Arnold W. Green, *Henry Charles Carey: Nineteenth-Century Sociologist* (Philadelphia, 1951), 3–4. The sources disagree about whether the Leas were married in St. Augustine's or St. Joseph's Church; both churches, however, were Catholic.

[10] *Address to the Right Rev. the Bishop of Pennsylvania and the Members of St. Mary's Congregation* (1820), quoted in Patrick W. Carey, *People, Priests, and Prelates: Ecclesiastical Democracy and the Tensions of Trusteeism* (Notre Dame, 1987), 156.

[11] Mathew Carey, *Philosophy of Common Sense: Practical Rules for the Promotion of Domestic Happiness* (Philadelphia, 1838), 3, 6.

was interested for our sake as well as in this quaint old building."[12] Perhaps with the same amiability, Frances declined to continue an active practice of Catholicism after her wedding. This did not mean that her two sons grew up without an acquaintance with religion. Bible stories and moral teachings were among the lessons they did at home with a tutor during the 1830s and 1840s. The boys spent far more time, however, on languages, mathematics, and science.[13] Trusting human intelligence to discern what was right, the Carey and Lea families apparently agreed that basic kindness was the core of religion. Someone must have insisted that Fanny's marriage would not be legitimate without vows administered by a priest. But, for the most part, the families worked out their religious differences on their own.

Nearly a century later, Rachel Berenson (1880–1933) and Ralph Barton Perry (1876–1957) were similarly in agreement with each other about the primary role of generosity—as opposed to tradition or doctrine—in a family's moral relationships. For that reason they were surprised and troubled by the distress of Ralph's father in 1905 over his son's plan to marry a Jew. "You know I can't quite believe it—I mean—it doesn't seem quite real to me, his prejudice," Rachel wrote to Ralph. "My mind tells me it ought not to be pampered & sympathized with but my heart tells me all sorts of other things—that you are the dearest hope of his life & anything that touches that must be the ideal he has painted in his mind."[14] She did not burden Ralph with the pain she must have felt at George Perry's rejection. In fact, however, Rachel identified so marginally with Judaism that she must have reacted privately with a sense of his judgment's injustice.

Both Rachel and Ralph had complicated relations with their religious traditions by the beginning of their courtship in 1902. Rachel grew up in a family that constructed a hybrid form of Judaism. Her father was influenced by the Haskalah—the Jewish Enlightenment—before the family emigrated from Lithuania to Boston in 1875. Once in America, the Berensons indulged their eclectic tastes. Bessie, Rachel's sister, recalled in 1953 that her mother "read the new testament & even read Mary Baker Eddy." Her father "read lots of Voltaire to Rachel & us when we were tots."[15]

[12] "A Pencilled Memorandum in the Hand of and Signed by Isaac Lea (1792–1886)," manuscript, July 12, 1849, 3, folder "Notes of Isaac Lea," Isaac Lea Papers.

[13] "Isaac Lea," Isaac Lea Papers, notes simply that Frances became a Protestant. The "Juvenile Notebooks" of Henry Charles Lea (1825–1909) are catalogued in four boxes, Henry Charles Lea Papers, Special Collections and Rare Books, Van Pelt-Dietrich Library, University of Pennsylvania, Philadelphia. His lessons about Bible stories are in a notebook dated February 21, 1838, box 1.

[14] Rachel Berenson [Perry] to Ralph Barton Perry, May 12, 1905, HUG 4683.70, box 3, Ralph Barton Perry Papers, Harvard University Archives, Nathan Marsh Pusey Library, Harvard University, Cambridge, Massachusetts. Permission to quote from this collection is granted by courtesy of the Harvard University Archives and Ralph Barton Perry III.

[15] Elizabeth (Bessie) Berenson to Ralph Barton Perry, August 14, [1953], HUG 4683.8, box 1, Perry Papers. Departures from common capitalization in this and subsequent quotations appear in the original texts.

Rachel's older brother, Bernard, became an Episcopalian before he graduated from Harvard in 1887 and was baptized a Roman Catholic in 1891. Rachel, too, received a genteel education at Smith and then Radcliffe, where she received a master of arts degree in classics in 1904. There is no evidence that she or the other Berensons formally became Christians. Bessie's courtship by a rabbinical student in 1905 reveals the family's continuing ties with the Jewish community, and Judith, their mother, resumed synagogue attendance after her husband's death. Still, the Berensons felt comfortable enough in a predominantly Christian environment to invite their future son-in-law for Easter dinner in 1905 while Rachel was away studying in Europe.[16] It was more important to spend the day with Ralph than to adhere strictly to Jewish tradition.

Many native-born Protestants were rethinking their beliefs at the same time that immigrants were forming bonds with American culture. For Ralph Barton Perry, a doctoral student of William James who received his Ph.D. degree from Harvard in 1899, becoming a religious liberal was a gradual spiritual and intellectual process. He planned to train for the Presbyterian ministry after he graduated from Princeton in 1895 but instead entered Harvard the following year to study philosophy. A month after he arrived in Cambridge, Perry wrote in his diary that he wished to "harmonize orthodoxy and liberality, strong convictions and intellectual freedom, salvation and culture."[17] This ideal of an open-ended Christianity was easier to state in theory than enact in practice. When Perry taught at Williams and Smith Colleges between 1899 and 1902, he was still committed to traditional Christian service: he taught a Sunday school class, served on a missions committee, and lectured to the YMCA. By the spring of 1902, however, about the time he met Rachel, he was also pursuing bolder religious interests, including preaching to a Unitarian congregation and visiting Felix Adler, founder of the Ethical Culture movement and the son of a leading rabbi.[18]

Looking back in 1946 in an after-dinner speech to his Harvard colleagues, Perry summarized his ethical philosophy as the "idea of doing good" and observed that he had learned over the years to be "less dogmatic and pugnacious, more disposed to look to the minds of others for

---

[16] Ralph Barton Perry to Rachel Berenson [Perry], April 23, 1905, HUG 4683.70, box 3, Perry Papers. Bessie told Ralph about her courtship in a letter (June 28, 1905) located in the same box. On the Berensons' religion, see Ernest Samuels, *Bernard Berenson: The Making of a Connoisseur* (Cambridge, Mass., 1979), pp. 3, 15–16, 38–40, 136–37.

[17] Ralph Barton Perry, October 13, 1896, Diary, 1896, HUG 4683.71, box 1, Perry Papers.

[18] Ralph Barton Perry, January 28 and November 18, 1900 (Sunday school), Diary, 1900; January 17 and March 14, 1902 (missions), Diary, 1902; January 28, 1900 (YMCA), Diary, 1900; January 5, 1902 (Unitarians), Diary, 1902; April 1 and August 17, 1902 (Adler), Diary, 1902, HUG 4683.71, box 3, Perry Papers. On Perry's intellectual development, see Bruce Kuklick, *The Rise of American Philosophy: Cambridge, Massachusetts, 1860–1930* (New Haven, 1977), 254–55.

their kernel of truth than for their shell of error."[19] This was the outlook that enabled Ralph to marry Rachel Berenson in August 1905. So, too, did instinctive kindness and family feeling induce George Perry to put his opinions aside and reach out to his daughter-in-law in a letter in September. He was sad, he began, to lose his son "who has been to me, not half of my life, but quite all of it": "My joy, however, is real, & will become deeper & deeper, as I trust, for it is the thought of gaining a daughter such as you, whose fine qualities of mind & heart must make you a delightful personality."[20] To varying degrees, Rachel, Ralph, and, finally, George Perry were able to balance their attachment to inherited religion with a practical, family-centered humanism.

Not all the personal religious changes that led to mixed marriages were liberal in nature. One small but significant group of interfaith families came into being not through romance and compromise but as a result of the conversions of Protestant wives to Roman Catholicism.[21]

The decision of Wilhelmine Easby-Smith (1835–1918) of Alabama to become a Catholic in 1862 was a conservative step theologically but a risky choice for a married woman with children. Her conversion might have been predicted by her religious history: she was raised an Episcopalian in Washington, D.C., attended a Catholic convent school, and belonged to a High Church Episcopal congregation in Tuscaloosa after her marriage in 1854. Far different, her husband William (1815–96), a politician, had been allied with the nativist Know-Nothing Party in the mid-1850s, and Wilhelmine hid her religious intentions from him as long as possible. When she finally spoke on the evening before she was received into the church, he paled and "went out," she recalled, "shutting the door with enough force to make me understand how deeply he was offended."[22] She must have spent the night fearful that she would have to carry out her resolve to return to Washington with her children, if necessary, to live with her mother.

Despite the fact that Wilhelmine and William held strong and diverging religious views, they were able to construct a family peace nearly identical in temper to the household arrangements of couples who entered interfaith marriages with open eyes. William loved Wilhelmine with an unashamed sentimentality that carried him through the crisis of her conver-

---

[19] "Department Dinner," typescript, May 3, 1946, 3, HUG 4683.7, box 1, Perry Papers.

[20] George A. Perry to Rachel Berenson Perry, September 13, 1905, HUG 4683.70, box 1, Perry Papers.

[21] Among this group of families, the converts were Sophia Dana Ripley, Anna Barker Ward, and Wilhelmine Easby-Smith. It was generally the conversion of wives that produced interfaith marriages; male converts exercised sufficient power over their kin to bring their families into the Catholic Church. See my "Some Private Roads to Rome: The Role of Families in American Victorian Conversions to Catholicism," *Catholic Historical Review* (forthcoming).

[22] Undated letter to a daughter (probably the book's author), quoted in Anne Easby-Smith, *William Russell Smith of Alabama: His Life and Works* (Philadelphia, 1931), 139.

sion. Ardent feeling convinced him to put religious discord aside. The annual sonnets he composed on her birthday continued. "Forty today!" he wrote playfully in 1875. "Be not dismayed, sweet dame."[23] At the same time that affection softened the edges of disagreement, the Smiths confined religion to mutually acceptable channels. William consented to Wilhelmine's wish to raise their children as Catholics, but forbade religious discussions at home. Wilhelmine and the children, for their part, prayed for William's conversion without his resistance.[24] In sum, religious liberality in the family was within the emotional reach of a couple in which the wife took her beliefs so seriously that she jeopardized her marriage and the husband stood his ground as a Protestant for many years.

The experimental moral temper of interfaith households did not mean that their members acted without guidance or communal ties. In fact, critical thinking and compromise tended to become values passed down between generations, and extended families lent stability to ongoing religious discussions. More dramatically, interfaith marriage itself sometimes became a family tradition.

When Iphigene Bettman of Cincinnati completed a family questionnaire in 1964 for the American Jewish Archives, she reconstructed a four-generation saga in which interfaith marriage was the rule. The centerpiece occurred in 1878 when Bettman's mother, Helen Wise, daughter of the preeminent Reform rabbi Isaac Mayer Wise, eloped with James Molony, a Presbyterian. Although the *Cincinnati Enquirer* elevated the incident to a lighthearted scandal ("a runaway match" was the result when "cupid conquers"), the bride's father was deeply hurt and publicly embarrassed.[25] Set in a broad family context, however, Wise's distress was exceptional and its legacy muted. The father of James Molony was an Irish-born Catholic who married a Presbyterian in America and took his wife's religion. During Iphigene Bettman's own life, her "three children are married to Protestant, Jew, & Catholic."[26] As a child, she had accompanied her mother nearly every Saturday to services at her grandfather's Plum Street Temple. After her marriage to Gilbert Bettman in 1915, "we always regarded ourselves as Jews."[27] Nonetheless, it was the heritage of intermarriage itself, as much as Judaism, that bound her extended family together. The low-key tone of Bettman's report on her complex family perhaps grew from a habit of taking account of religious background as only

---

[23] Ibid., 187.

[24] Ibid., 139, 238.

[25] "Cupid Conquers," *Cincinnati Enquirer,* May 30, 1878, Small Collections 13082, American Jewish Archives (AJA), Hebrew Union College-Jewish Institute of Religion, Cincinnati, Ohio. See also Clifford M. Kulwin, "Helen Wise Molony and James Molony: A Look Back at a Nineteenth Century Intermarriage," typescript, no date, Small Collections 6508, AJA.

[26] Iphigene Molony Bettman, questionnaire, question no. 20, May 9, 1964, AJA.

[27] Ibid., question no. 30.

one component of an individual's character. Her tolerance, most likely nurtured in her parents' home, must have smoothed the way for her children's marriages.

Family liberalism did not guarantee individual freedom, however, or domestic peace. Private strategies for resolving religious issues could become as rigid as public proscriptions against interfaith romance. If expectations were violated, compromises carefully constructed over many years might explode. This occurred when Tom Sherman, the oldest son of William Tecumseh Sherman (1820–91) and his wife, Ellen (1824–88), decided to become a Catholic priest in 1878. For three generations in the family, Protestant husbands of limited fervor had wed Catholic wives: Philemon Beecher and Susan Gillespie (married in 1803), Thomas Ewing and Maria Boyle (1820), and William T. Sherman and Ellen Ewing (1850). Intimacy among the women as Catholics made it easier to cope with their religious distance from their husbands. In 1854, for example, Ellen conferred with Maria about her daughter Minnie's exposure to her Sherman kin during Minnie's stay with her grandmother in Ohio: "I wish her Aunts and cousins all to know as soon and as emphatically as possible that she is to be raised with no tinge towards protestantism."[28]

At the same time that intergenerational bonds lent the family support, they laid the groundwork for the crisis over Tom. Tom broke with male precedents because he was Catholic and deeply religious. William Tecumseh Sherman summed up his own beliefs so succinctly that there was no chance they would intrude on his worldly business. "God governs this world" through "invariable laws," he explained to a friend in 1878, and "good works," he told Ellen in 1842, are the duty of humankind.[29] Tom, "whom I had trained to assist me in the care of a large and expanding family," betrayed his father's idea of what Sherman men did when he chose instead to be "shut up in a Cloister."[30] Ellen tried to reason with her husband, just as "we would freely offer our son's life in battle for his country,"

---

[28] Ellen Sherman to Maria Ewing, February 19, 1854, Ellen Sherman Papers. Susan Gillespie Beecher was the aunt of Maria Boyle, but Maria grew up in the Beechers' interfaith household after her mother's death. Especially helpful on the complicated genealogy of the family are Eleanor Ewing, "Maria Boyle Ewing" (typescript), "Neal Gillespie Chart and Note" (manuscript), and "Hugh Boyle" (typescript), all undated, Ellen Sherman Papers; Ellie Ewing Brown, "Notes on Boyhood of Philemon Beecher Ewing and William Tecumseh Sherman" (typescript, ca. 1932), William Tecumseh Sherman Family Papers (CSHR), Archives of the University of Notre Dame, University of Notre Dame, Notre Dame, Indiana (UNDA). See also Michael Fellman, *Citizen Sherman: A Life of William Tecumseh Sherman* (New York, 1995), and Katherine Burton, *Three Generations: Maria Boyle Ewing (1801–1864), Ellen Ewing Sherman (1824–1888), Minnie Sherman Fitch (1851–1913)* (New York, 1947).

[29] William T. Sherman to Henry Turner, July 7, 1878, quoted in Joseph T. Durkin, *General Sherman's Son* (New York, 1959), 53; Sherman to Ellen Ewing [Sherman], April 7, 1842, box 1, Sherman Family Papers.

[30] William T. Sherman to Minnie Sherman Fitch, June 16, 1878, and Sherman to Henry Turner, July 7, 1878, quoted in Durkin, *Sherman's Son,* 52, 53.

we must accept his sacrifice "for the country which has no bounds."[31] Yet Sherman confessed to Minnie that he was "embittered" toward the Catholic Church, and he remained cool toward his wife and Tom.[32] His family history better prepared him for a son's interfaith marriage than for Tom's religious vocation.

The deep roots of interfaith marriage in the families of Iphigene Bettman and the Shermans drive home the point that the Victorians did not cross religious boundaries precipitously but in response to experiences of long gestation. Intermarried couples were touched by the movements of modernity that shook people loose from tradition and offered them new values favorable to mutual respect without consensus: critical religious reflection and reorientation, Enlightenment and later forms of liberalism, and, quietly but powerfully behind these intellectual influences, a tenacious attachment to the family and domestic life. Indeed, it was romance that commonly impelled individuals who were prepared by their backgrounds to take an unconventional step actually to do so, and love of family that fueled intellectual compromise.

No doubt love has struggled with religious doctrines on marriage throughout Judeo-Christian history, but in Victorian America romance gained unprecedented legitimacy as a mode of self-validation. Interfaith couples, no more or less than others in a sentimental culture, delighted in playful intimacy. "My sweetheart," my "blessed love," Zebulon Vance of North Carolina wrote to Florence Martin on various occasions before their wedding in 1880, signing "your own boy" and "your big boy."[33] Vance's pleasure in communicating his affection was not diminished by the fact that he was a fifty-year-old widower and a Presbyterian courting a Catholic widow with a child. Pet names, in fact, convey the importance of love in persuading interfaith couples that their decisions to marry were right and in holding marriages together. Julia Collier addressed Julian Harris mysteriously as "Richard" during their courtship (1896–97) and called herself the "Marchioness." Ralph Barton Perry and Rachel Berenson corresponded as "Nunky" and "Niecy," diminutive versions of uncle and niece, before their wedding in 1905. After nearly fifteen years of marriage Julia Harris still wrote to Julian as "Dear Boy" and signed "M," and Rachel Perry

[31] Ellen Sherman to William T. Sherman, May 25, [1878], box 2, Sherman Family Papers.

[32] William T. Sherman to Minnie Fitch, June 16, 1878, quoted in Durkin, *Sherman's Son*, 52. Although there had often been tensions in the Shermans' marriage, their letters during the last decade of Ellen's life seem impersonal (box 2, Sherman Family Papers).

[33] Zebulon Vance to Florence Martin [Vance], March 11, 1880, April 4, [1880], March 22, [1880], Zebulon Baird Vance Papers, Division of Archives and History, Department of Cultural Resources, State of North Carolina, Raleigh, North Carolina. On Vance's marriages, see my *Victorian America and the Civil War* (Cambridge, 1992), 29, 150. On romantic love, see esp. Karen Lystra, *Searching the Heart: Women, Men, and Romantic Love in Nineteenth-Century America* (New York, 1989).

addressed "Darling Nunk" in 1933, the year of her death.[34] In the Victorian setting, being in love became an argument, despite religious difficulties, in favor of marriage.

The values and emotions that pushed men and women forward toward interfaith marriage also prepared them, to a great extent, to behave with fairness in families where questions of belief and commitment were bound to recur. Religiously unconventional, interfaith couples brought moral creativity to the down-to-earth problem of making room for diverging convictions. Wedding days did not bring resolutions but marked the beginning of continuing religious change. Responding to the dissimilar beliefs of family members in new situations gave domestic life in these homes the flavor of moral adventure.

The conversion of Thomas Wren Ward (1844–1940) to Catholicism is a compelling example of how questions about personal identity and family relations persisted in interfaith households. Ward was fourteen years old when his mother, Anna, decided to become a Catholic and ninety-six when he entered the Catholic Church himself. For most of his life, he was a Protestant bystander in a Catholic family. He grew up to marry a Catholic and help raise Catholic children. In this, he followed the precedent of his father, Samuel, who remained a Unitarian after his wife's conversion but respected Anna's beliefs enough to build her a chapel at their home in Lenox, Massachusetts. Unlike his father, however, Thomas died a Catholic after he resolved a lifelong struggle between his "search for contact with God" and his "old prejudice" against Catholicism.[35] Ward wrestled with the moral problem of satisfying conscience while also honoring his family's convictions. His story unfolded against the background of two generations of Catholic practice by his mother and his wife, as well as widespread anti-Catholic bias, which he shared. Private issues and public influences typically interacted in American Victorian interfaith families. Their day-to-day ethic of tolerance did not work in isolation but in relation to Judeo-Christian culture.

Interfaith couples who married before the early twentieth century did not dismiss public observance, despite their freethinking habits. All family members gravitated toward one religious community. Whether churches

[34] Julia Harris to Julian Harris, [August 2, 1912], box 24, folder 7, Julian Harris Papers; Rachel Perry to Ralph Barton Perry, January 12, 193[3], HUG 4683.70, box 5, Perry Papers. Samples of earlier letters are Julia to Julian, April 21, [1896], and [December 25, 1896], box 24, folder 1, Julian Harris Papers; and Ralph to Rachel, January 4, [1903], and Rachel to Ralph, [April 3, 1903], HUG 4683.70, box 3, Perry Papers.

[35] The quotation comes from an unidentified 1935 source and appears in Margaret Snyder, "The Other Side of the River," *New England Quarterly* 14 (1941): 434. On the Ward family, see also David Baldwin, *Puritan Aristocrat in the Age of Emerson: A Study of Samuel Gray Ward* (Ph.D. diss., University of Pennsylvania, 1961; Ann Arbor: University Microfilms, 1973), esp. 289–90.

and synagogues dealt with them patiently or inflexibly affected not only their choice of affiliation but the temper of their private discussions as well. Families composed of Catholic wives and Protestant husbands settled most comfortably into an institutional home: the Catholic Church. Although Catholic advice literature, periodicals, and fiction consistently pronounced the evils of mixed marriage; priests and nuns welcomed Catholic wives and urged them to pray for their husbands.[36] These intermarried women were not limited to marginal roles in Catholic communities. Esther LaRose Harris, the Canadian-born wife of Joel Chandler Harris, described herself around 1900 in a letter to the bishop of Savannah as one of the "original promoters" of a Catholic parish in Atlanta's West End. Her marriage to a Protestant did not diminish the self-confidence of her request for money to construct a building that would be "an honor to God, a credit to Catholics, and an ornament to this part of our city."[37] Wives of Protestants were judged by the Catholic Church on their own merit and perhaps even held in special esteem because of their family evangelism.

Their husbands leaned toward their wives' Catholicism. Respect for their Catholic wives and love for their frequently Catholic children created a kind of community of religious interest that did not extend, however, as far as doctrinal agreement. George Ripley (1802–80) walked this line between Catholic sympathies and personal independence after the conversion of his wife Sophia (1803–61) in 1847 or 1848. A leading Unitarian minister and later transcendentalist in Boston during the 1830s and 1840s, Ripley occasionally attended Mass and visited convents with Sophia in the 1850s when they lived in Brooklyn. On one occasion, Sophia reported to her cousin Charlotte, he defended a lecture by Orestes Brownson, a convert and friend, "when it was attacked at the breakfast table" of the Ripleys' boardinghouse.[38] Through the years, Sophia prayed for her husband's conversion. "Sister M[ary]. C[atherine]. & I are uniting in the Thirty Day's Prayer for him," she wrote characteristically to Charlotte in 1848.[39] She watched for signs of his change of heart. In 1857, he asked Sophia to see an "agnus dei" when he prepared an entry on these wax prayer disks, imprinted with a picture of a lamb, for *Appleton's Cyclopedia*. He "put it on with perfectly childish delight, & would not lay it aside on any ac-

[36] See sources cited in note 8.

[37] Esther Harris to Rt.-Rev. B. J. Kelly, n.d., box 7, folder 4, Joel Chandler Harris Papers, Special Collections, Robert W. Woodruff Library, Emory University, Atlanta, Georgia. On the marriage of Esther and Joel Chandler Harris, see Julia Collier Harris, *The Life and Letters of Joel Chandler Harris* (Boston, 1918), and Hugh T. Keenan, introduction to his *Dearest Chums and Partners: Joel Chandler Harris's Letters to His Children, a Domestic Biography* (Athens, Ga., 1993), xvii–xxxii.

[38] Sophia Ripley to [Charlotte Dana], [1855?], box 14, Dana Family Papers, Massachusetts Historical Society, Boston. On the Ripleys, see Charles Crowe, *George Ripley: Transcendentalist and Utopian Socialist* (Athens, Ga., 1967).

[39] Sophia Ripley to Charlotte Dana, September 15, 1848, box 10, Dana Papers.

count," she observed hopefully. "The church has a place for everything, & everything in its place," George told Sophia. "It is a great institution."[40]

The cordiality of the church to George Ripley lent support to the peace made by the couple at home. Yet his affinity for Catholicism grew from his bond with his wife and did not survive her. On the first anniversary of her death in 1862, George thanked Charlotte for arranging a memorial Mass: "You know that it has always been my wish that such a faithful Catholic heart should enjoy, to its fullest extent, every rite & promise which the good motherly Church affords to those who look to her for blessings."[41] Ripley himself, however, became active in the radical Unitarian congregation of Octavius Brooks Frothingham. When he married again in 1865, he wrote to his sister that his new wife, Louisa, was "entirely in opinion & feeling with the liberal Unitarians of the school of Mr. Frothingham—& myself."[42] Ripley's circuit from radical Protestantism through interfaith marriage and back to Protestant loyalty reveals the powerful influence of conjugal love as a force of religious persuasion. No less important was the openness, based in evangelical hopes, of the Catholic Church.[43]

Beyond institutions, prejudice inescapably complicated the commitments of interfaith families. The sympathy of a Protestant husband for his wife's Catholicism turned easily from a private preference to a source of public rebuke. "I beg you will not allow yourself to be beguiled" into running for president, Ellen Sherman urged her husband in 1876, because "you could not be elected by reason of your family being Catholic."[44] Being charged as crypto-Catholics was not a new experience for Ellen's Protestant kin. In 1854, a political opponent of Thomas Ewing stooped to "wording and arranging his sentences so as to make it appear that Father is a Catholic," Ellen complained to her mother, "as if he thought it so disgraceful that he dare not venture upon the open libel."[45] Two years later, Ellen wrote home from San Francisco that her husband's "defense of the Sisters of Mercy (whom some of the papers have been abusing) and his condemnation of the common schools" raised the "ire" of the newspaper press. One critic wrote that "Mrs. T[ecumseh]. S[herman]. is a Catholic

[40] Ibid., December 6, 1857, box 15.

[41] George Ripley to Charlotte Dana, February 8, 1862, box 16, Dana Papers.

[42] George Ripley to Marianne Ripley, April 9, 1865, George Ripley Letters, microfilm (1824, 1852–82), Division of Archives and Manuscripts, State Historical Society of Wisconsin, Madison. See also his letter to Marianne of March 26 on his relationship to Unitarianism.

[43] Although Ripley's circular history clearly illustrates the religious influence of marital love, it was perhaps more common for Protestant husbands finally to become Catholics. Among the couples studied, this occurred in the cases of William Russell Smith, Joel Chandler Harris, and Thomas Ewing. The key difference between these men and Ripley is that the converts either predeceased their wives or had Catholic children or both.

[44] Ellen Sherman to William T. Sherman, May 8, 1876, box 2, Sherman Family Papers.

[45] Ellen Sherman to Maria Ewing, October 29, 1854, Ellen Sherman Papers.

and that accounts for the 'milk in the cocoanut [*sic*].'"[46] Sherman's impulse as a husband to stand up for Ellen's religion opened the way for these mean-spirited words. Cutting innuendo not only imposed a burden of hate on the family but, casting Sherman in a role of Catholic fellow traveler, also violated his sense of himself as a moral rationalist.

Anti-Semitism similarly imposed the constraints of public opinion on families uniting Christians and Jews. Prejudice followed Jews even after years of intermarriage. Although Judah Benjamin married into a prominent Creole family in New Orleans in 1833 and discontinued any visible practice of Judaism, he was later hounded by prejudice as a member of the Confederate cabinet. The "mob only calls him 'Mr. Davis's pet Jew,'" Mary Chesnut noted in her journal in 1862, "a King Street Jew, cheap, very cheap, &c&c."[47] The Protestant majority could imagine that a Protestant husband, like Sherman, might be swayed in the bedroom to embrace Catholic errors, but a Jew was inexorably a Jew.

Like most prejudices, this judgment contained much falsehood and a kernel of truth, although even then the truth was construed in a damaging way. In fact, most couples composed of Jews and Christians inclined toward Christianity as their family religion. Yet the Jewish spouse rarely crossed easily into the Christian world. These families were pushed away from the Jewish community at the same time as they were pulled toward Christianity by the advantages of belonging to the religious majority. Isaac Leeser, the leading Jewish clergyman in America before midcentury, declared in his periodical the *Occident* in 1845 that the conversion of Gentile spouses to Judaism was inadvisable and that intermarried couples should be shunned. Parents may "love their children," Leeser instructed, "but they must love God more."[48] In light of Jewish opposition to mixed marriage, it is not surprising that when David Levy Yulee (1810–86) of Florida married Nannie Wickliffe in 1846, he reached out to her by voicing Christian beliefs, though phrased in a way that did not flagrantly offend his Jewish heritage. "We must love all our fellow beings and sympathise with all of

[46] Ibid., October 3, 1856.

[47] Mary Chesnut, February 13, 1862, in *Mary Chesnut's Civil War*, ed. C. Vann Woodward (New Haven, 1981), 288–89. On the Benjamins' marriage and his experience of anti-Semitism, see Eli N. Evans, *Judah P. Benjamin: The Jewish Confederate* (New York, 1988), 23–26, 33–34, 103–7, 201–7, 385, 395–99.

[48] [Isaac Leeser], "The Dangers of Our Position," *Occident and Jewish Advocate* 2 (January 1845): 463. Leeser acknowledged his authorship in his commentary on Abrahams, "Intermarrying with Gentiles," 588. Virtually no Reform rabbis after midcentury openly approved of interfaith marriage, but debate about how to respond to mixed couples gave interfaith families a tiny measure of legitimacy. See, for example, writings on the circumcision of adult converts and the status of children of Jewish fathers: Henry Berkowitz, "An Important Inquiry to Learned Rabbis," *Israelite*, July 31, 1890, 4; [Isaac M. Wise?], "Some Remarks on Milah," *Israelite*, October 2, 1890, 4; [Isaac M. Wise?], untitled article, *Israelite*, August 1, 1879, 4.

them," he wrote philosophically to his wife in 1848, "and especially those who are good."[49] Yulee also reasoned his way toward Christianity because he was a man on the way up. In 1845, he was elected to the U.S. Senate and in November purchased twenty-four slaves for more than seven thousand dollars at an auction in St. Augustine. His success now positioned him socially to propose to a Gentile about whom he seemed sincerely to care. At the same time, Nannie's father, recently a member of the cabinet of President Tyler, could be expected to help Yulee's political career.[50] The question of whether to live as Jews or Christians did not even arise for David and Nannie Yulee.

Their public image as churchgoing Protestants nonetheless obscured David's troubled relations with his father, Moses Elias Levy (ca. 1781–1854). The amicable religious compromises of the Yulees' marriage did little to still David's private war with his heritage, embodied in this complex man. Born in Morocco, Moses Levy was a peripatetic Jewish philosopher who dabbled in Kabbalah, Swedenborg, mesmerism, phrenology, and Christianity. He believed that the Jews would bring on the millennium— "Christians (*spiritual* Israel) will ask Israel to establish a theocracy"—if they condemned individualism ("self-government is a heresy") and adhered to the ethic "love our neighbour as ourself."[51] Charitable in theory, Levy was dogmatic and pugnacious in practice. It was the "peculiar views & conditions of mind of this excellent man" that "wrecked the unity of his family," Yulee reflected in 1868.[52] Yet despite serious family quarrels dating back to the 1820s, David remained magnetized by Levy and his ideas. He compiled and edited two manuscript collections of Levy's writings after his fa-

[49] David Yulee to Nannie Wickliffe Yulee, July 4, 1848, David Levy Yulee Papers, Small Collections 13329, AJA.

[50] For biographical information, see C. Wickliffe Yulee, "Senator Yulee of Florida: A Biographical Sketch," reprinted from *Florida Historical Magazine*, ca. 1931, Yulee Papers, and Leon Huhner, "David L. Yulee, Florida's First Senator," *Publications of the American Jewish Historical Society* 25 (1917): 1–29. On his purchase of slaves, see "List of Slaves Purchased at Public Sale at St. Augustine November 11, 1845 for $7180.00," Moses Elias Levy Diary, Correspondence, and Miscellaneous, 1830–1852 (hereafter Levy Papers), microfilm 932, AJA. The original documents in this collection are located at the University of Florida, Gainesville. Yulee implied later that he and his brother Elias thought of themselves as Christians as early as the 1830s. His father "knew of his sons having adopted a different faith," Yulee wrote sometime after 1854, in "Diary of Moses Levy," 22, Levy Papers. Yulee's marriage probably more sealed than began his relationship to Christianity.

[51] "Letter Book & Account Book, in Which are Intermixed Many Memoranda of His States of Mind," 44, 48, 64, Levy Papers. The first quotation is a paraphrase of Levy by Yulee; the second two are Levy's own words. Italics in this and subsequent quotations are found in the original texts. This manuscript book was prepared by Yulee after Levy's death and bound together with a similar collection of writings, "Diary of Moses Levy." On Levy, see Joseph Gary Adler, "Moses Elias Levy and Attempts to Colonize Florida," in Samuel Proctor and Louis Schmier, eds., *Jews of the South: Selected Essays from the Southern Jewish Historical Society* (Macon, Ga., 1984), 17–29.

[52] David Levy Yulee, "Narrative of My Administration of My Father's Estate," unpaginated manuscript, ca. 1868, Levy Papers.

ther's death. Carefully recording Levy's thoughts, he then turned bitterly to denounce them. "Can two persons walk together unless they agree," Levy had asked rhetorically, to which Yulee added, "This article shows the cause of his separation from every one [*sic*]."[53] To all appearances a Christian with his Christian wife, Yulee remained tied to Judaism by wrestling with his father's memory.

The opposition to mixed marriage of American Jewry, the force of anti-Semitism, and the bonds of Jewish tradition suspended intermarried Jews between Jewish and Christian worlds. Jewish spouses stood back from the Christianity of their families, drifted toward religious inactivity, yet retained a small but certain loyalty to Judaism. Thus Isaac Mayer Wise summed up the life of Benjamin Gratz (1792–1884) after his funeral: "He had very little intercourse with Jews" during sixty-six years in Kentucky and "married twice, Christian ladies of course," but occasionally observed "the *Kipper* Day" with friends and asked for "a Jewish minister" to bury him.[54] Gratz lived an ostensibly happy, assimilated life, and one of his daughters married a grandson of Henry Clay. Still, he was aware of himself as a Jew and sensed that this was the grounds of both pride and alienation.

The family histories of all these interfaith couples make it clear that goodwill and mutual respect had not only to mediate private conflicts but also to guide them in their public relations with religious institutions and a society marked by prejudice. Because they did not dismiss Judeo-Christian beliefs or withdraw from organized worship, working out equitable religious solutions was a complex undertaking. They must have felt buffeted by public attitudes. In the end, however, families made their own choices.

Their moral independence strengthened over time. Couples who married near the turn of the twentieth century were less loyal to congregations than interfaith families in the past. Julia and Julian Harris attended a Methodist church after their wedding in Atlanta in 1897. Yet the minister's "bigoted and intolerant sentiments" soon put them off, Julian recalled in 1925. They "attended no church since."[55] Instead, they focused on religion at home. Julia integrated Protestant and Catholic observances for their children. Using standardized baby books to record the experiences of her sons Charles (1899–1903) and Pierre (1901–4), she wrote for each child under the heading "First Prayer" the familiar Protestant lines, "Now

[53] Moses Elias Levy, "Letter Book & Account Book," 37, Levy Papers. Yulee, one should note, took back the name "Yulee" just before his marriage; Levy had dropped "Yulee" when he settled in St. Thomas around 1800 (memorandum, Small Collections 13894, AJA).

[54] Untitled article, *Israelite*, March 28, 1884, 4.

[55] Julian Harris to Edwin Mims, November 14, 1925, box 14, folder 24, Julian Harris Papers. Julian's letter does not make clear whether the minister's prejudice was religious, racial, or both. Although couples married near the turn of the century were less involved with religious institutions than earlier families, my research does not settle whether this trend persisted to the present day.

I lay me down to sleep." In Charles's book she added: "This prayer was said each night as the Catholic bell tolled for six o'clock."[56] Julia made no entry to show that Charles, named after her father, was baptized. For Pierre, whose name honored Julian's Catholic grandfather, she noted under the printed title "Rites and Ceremonies": "the Catholic church." When the boys sadly died within months of each other, the Harrises asked a Methodist minister to come to the house to conduct their funerals.[57]

The loss of their children further loosened Julia and Julian from the religions of their birth, yet without ending their moral commitments. They sampled widely among belief systems. Julia took a correspondence course in sociology offered by the University of Chicago in 1910–11. Covering subjects such as heredity and political economy, her lessons examined human nature and society without reference to religion. After 1920, the Harrises consulted astrologers, numerologists, and chirologists (analysts of hands) to interpret their characters and identify favorable times for action. Julia also read "the 'legends' of the Jews" and reported her browsing to Julian because "I happened to remember how you used to read the *Talmud.*"[58]

This easygoing eclecticism stood side by side with the ethical and personal courage needed to oppose the Georgia Klan in the 1920s. Klansmen paraded outside the offices of the *Enquirer-Sun* in Columbus and tampered with the mail. Esther, Julian's mother, believed that their "fight on intolerance" somehow began in her son's Catholic boyhood. "I knew all the while," she told him in 1924, "that much of it was done on account of your love for me."[59] Julian had described himself in 1913 as a "renegade" Catholic and, as an old man, turned away clergy who wished to reclaim him as an "adornment to the church" in light of his "courageous defense" of Catholic rights.[60] Nonetheless, in one sense Esther was right. Julian, as well as Julia, sustained moral interests, rooted complexly in religious train-

[56] The baby books have been disassembled and are found in box 37, folders 3–10 (Charles) and 11–15 (Pierre), Julian Harris Papers. Charles's "first prayer" was dated February 1902 (folder 3), and Pierre's was October [1903], 57 (folder 11). Only some pages are numbered.

[57] Information on the funerals is found in copies of newspaper clippings in box 37, folders 10 (Charles) and 15 (Pierre), Julian Harris Papers. The phrase "the Catholic church" appears in folder 11, n.p.

[58] [Julia Harris] to Julian Harris, n.d., box 24, folder 20, Julian Harris Papers. Notes from Julia's sociology course are found in box 25, folder 7. Astrological charts and similar kinds of analysis are found in box 26, folder 19. An astrological reading of Julia is tentatively dated 1919. A character interpretation based on the shape of Julian's hand was done in April 1930.

[59] Esther Harris to Julian Harris, November 9, 1924, box 25, folder 21, Julian Harris Papers. Julian described the Klan's threatening actions in his letter to Edwin Mims, November 14, 1925.

[60] He described himself as a "renegade" in a letter to Esther, May 10, 1913, box 25, folder 3, Julian Harris Papers. The phrases praising Julian as a Catholic are those of his brother Evelyn in a letter dated August 11, 1954, box 26, folder 5, Julian Harris Papers.

ing and family affection, through all the intellectual changes and domestic compromises of their adult lives.

The Harrises' liberal ethic was equally indebted to their experience in interfaith families. For the most part, mutual respect remained an unspoken guide to household religious relations. Yet on occasion, family members wrote philosophically about balancing dissimilar convictions with love of kin. When Esther Harris explained her views on family tolerance during Julian's campaign against the Klan, she revealed one source of his respect for personal freedom. "My faith has been handed down to me from generations," she told her son: "I am staunch in it."

> A mother rears her children according to her light, her training, etc [*sic*] but she knows full well that when her children become men & women they have a perfect right to their views & that her responsibility is practically ended when they reach manhood & womanhood. I would not want them to accept my religious belief under protest or by force.[61]

Esther's profession of belief in forbearance was not unique in the writings of American Victorian interfaith families. When Benjamin Gratz married his first Christian wife in 1819, his sister Rebecca told a friend that "in a family connection I have always thought conformity of religious opinions essential and therefore could not approve my brothers [*sic*] election." Yet she came to see that generous feelings might counterbalance diverse opinions. She wrote in 1826 to her sister-in-law Maria:

> I never had any apprehension of the [Christian?] influence over the faith of my brother and I trust my dear sister, when we have passed our lives in love & affection towards each other—good will & charitableness to all men[—]that we shall be reunited in a better world, there to perfect the good gifts of which we have a foretaste here.[62]

In a similar spirit, David Yulee reasoned with his father in 1849 that they need not quarrel about religion. Why should families be exempt from the moral imperative to respect all human beings?

> Do you reject association and attachment with others of your fellow men, because they are variant with yourself in opinion? No, for they are your fellow men, and entitled to your love as such, and to your esteem of their respective

---

[61] Esther Harris to Julian Harris, November 9, 1924, box 25, folder 21, Julian Harris Papers.
[62] Rebecca Gratz to Maria Gist Gratz, July 23, 1826, box 3, folder 2, Rebecca Gratz Papers (MS collection 236), AJA. The earlier letter was addressed to Maria Fenno Hoffman, July 12, 1819, copy in box 4, folder 5, Rebecca Gratz Papers. The original letter is located in the New-York Historical Society.

virtues. And why should your children be less the object of your regard? They are all the children of one God and therefore alike worthy of your love.[63]

All these individuals assumed that religious commitments were meaningful and should persist despite their strain on family harmony. They were no less convinced, however, that generosity and patience might work without a foundation in religious agreement to keep peace among kin.

This moral perspective was less often expressed in words than in the small acts that together make up domestic life. This is not to say that interfaith families were unaffected by major intellectual and spiritual trends of the nineteenth century, both liberal and conservative, or that they were uninvolved with Protestantism, Catholicism, and Judaism as formal religions. But their ethic for living in religiously divided families consisted far more of a practical charity than articulated rules. Thinking for themselves as laypeople, they took an experimental approach to the moral problems of their households. The profound difficulty of reconciling freedom and love meant that conflict coexisted with compromise. Yet the ethical challenge of respecting family members unlike oneself also deepened the potential gratifications. Ralph Barton Perry eloquently described love in a lecture in 1937 as "essentially a duality; an exchange of gifts": "The happy miracle lies not in unity alone, but in association of unity with polarity, tension, and surprise."[64] This, at its best, was the reward of interfaith marriage in Victorian America.

---

[63] David Yulee to Moses Levy, December 7, 184[9?], Yulee Papers.
[64] *In the Spirit of William James* (New Haven, 1938), 43.

Appendix American Victorian Interfaith Couples (arranged chronologically by date of marriage)

Names	Faiths	Date of Marriage [a]	Residence(s)
Benjamin Gratz–Maria Gist	Jewish–Protestant	1819	Kentucky
–Ann Shelby	Jewish–Protestant	1843	Kentucky
Thomas Ewing–Maria Boyle	Protestant–Catholic	1820	Ohio
Isaac Lea–Frances Carey	Protestant–Catholic	1821	Pennsylvania
George Ripley–Sophia Dana	Protestant–Catholic	1827	Massachusetts, New York
Judah Benjamin–Natalie St. Martin	Jewish–Catholic	1833	Louisiana, London, Paris
Samuel Ward–Anna Barker	Protestant–Catholic	1840	Massachusetts, New York
David Levy Yulee–Nannie Wickliffe	Jewish–Protestant	1846	Florida
William Tecumseh Sherman– Ellen Ewing Sherman	Protestant–Catholic	1850	Ohio, Washington, D.C., Missouri, New York
William Russell Smith–Wilhelmine Easby	Protestant–Catholic	1854	Alabama, Washington, D.C.
Stephen A. Douglas–Adele Cutts	Protestant–Catholic	1856	Washington, D.C.
Joel Chandler Harris–Esther LaRose	Protestant–Catholic	1873	Georgia
James Molony–Helen Wise	Protestant–Jewish	1878	Ohio
Zebulon Vance–Florence Martin	Protestant–Catholic	1880	North Carolina
Julian LaRose Harris–Julia Collier	Catholic–Protestant	1897	Georgia
Ralph Barton Perry–Rachel Berenson	Protestant–Jewish	1905	Massachusetts
Graham Stokes–Rose Pastor	Protestant–Jewish	1905	New York

[a] Three families became interfaith homes following the conversion to Catholicism of these wives: Sophia Dana Ripley in 1847 or 1848, Anna Barker Ward in 1858, and Wilhelmine Easby-Smith in 1862.

Chaplain Willard W. Bartlett gives a lecture on native religions to MAG-15 Marines in Vietnam. Courtesy National Archives, neg. no. 127-N-A187119.

CHAPTER ELEVEN

Prophetic Ministry and the Military Chaplaincy during the Vietnam Era

ANNE C. LOVELAND

In the theological ferment of the 1960s, few religious institutions escaped moral scrutiny. In particular, the new "radical" or "secular theology" of that decade—what Harvey Cox called "a theology of social change"—raised questions about the proper role of the clergy in the church and in society. Echoing the German theologian Dietrich Bonhoeffer, the secular theologians argued for a "religionless Christianity" stripped of otherworldliness and the preoccupation with personal salvation and focused on the needs of this world. In place of the traditional priestly/pastoral role, they advocated a "prophetic" role for the clergy, challenging the myths, ideologies, and institutions of society in the light of biblical faith. Thus Harvey Cox, in *The Secular City,* one of the key works of the period, taught that the mission of the church was to be found "in events of social change" and in the midst of social problems. As the secular theology gained currency, it propelled a "new breed" of activist, politically conscious clergy into "the freedom revolution" of the 1960s—marching for civil rights in Selma, joining striking grape pickers in California, organizing welfare unions and tenants councils in Buffalo and Chicago, and, eventually, protesting against the Vietnam War.[1]

[1] Harvey Cox, *The Secular City: Secularization and Urbanization in Theological Perspective,* rev. ed. (New York, 1966), 228–29, 91. On the theological ferment of the 1960s, the "secular theology" and the "new breed" of clergy, see Sydney E. Ahlstrom, *A Religious History of the American People,* 2 vols. (Garden City, N. Y., 1975), 2:599–601; Sydney E. Ahlstrom, "The Radical Turn in Theology and Ethics: Why It Occurred in the 1960's," and Richard Henry Luecke, "Protestant Clergy: New Forms of Ministry, New Forms of Training," in *Annals of the American Academy of Political and Social Science* 387 (January 1970): 1–13 and 87–95, respectively; and Langdon Gilkey, "Social and Intellectual Sources of Contemporary Protestant Theology in

Not surprisingly, the secular theology generated considerable criticism of chaplains serving in the armed forces of the United States. Initially, in the early 1960s, critics focused attention on the conflict chaplains allegedly experienced between their roles as military officers and ministers and argued that they tended to resolve it, consciously or unconsciously, in favor of the military. In November 1966, William Robert Miller summarized the critics' line of thinking in an article in the *Christian Century*. As a member of a "kept" clergy, "beholden to the state," it was impossible for the chaplain to perform a "prophetic ministry," Miller contended. "And if the possibility of a prophetic ministry is ruled out by the conditions of his employment, how can he be a Christian minister at all?" he asked. In Miller's view, for a chaplain "to harmonize his beliefs and what they imply with the objectives of a secular enterprise, particularly one predicated on unswerving loyalty to the state," was to give up the minister's pledge "to a higher loyalty than any government of men" and "the right of disobedience to all authority but God's."[2]

Time magazine captured the fundamental moral problem posed by Miller and other critics with regard to chaplains in its headline "Honest to God—or Faithful to the Pentagon?"[3] On the one hand, chaplains were members of the "profession of arms" (though they carried no weapons), officers in the armed forces bound by an oath to "support and defend the Constitution of the United States against all enemies, foreign and domestic" and to "bear true faith and allegiance to the same," and they had dedicated themselves to a military ministry. On the other hand, they were ministers of God, clergy endorsed by their faith groups or denominations whose tenets they promised to uphold. What complicated the moral problem confronting chaplains was that the Judeo-Christian tradition and the teachings of the Bible, which the great majority of them followed, were ambiguous on the subject of war and military service. They could be, and had been, invoked to justify pacifism, just war, even holy war.

When the chaplaincy issue became caught up in the controversy over U.S. military intervention in Southeast Asia, it received even more attention. A number of voluntary interfaith organizations and religious denominations protested the war, basing their opposition, as James H. Smylie has pointed out, on traditional just war doctrine. They questioned not only the morality of U.S. intervention in Vietnam but also the conduct of the war.[4]

America," and Harvey G. Cox, "The 'New Breed' in American Churches: Sources of Social Activism in American Religion," *Daedalus* 96 (Winter 1967), 69–98 and 135–50, respectively.

[2] William Robert Miller, "Chaplaincy vs. Mission in a Secular Age," *Christian Century,* November 2, 1966, 1336.

[3] "Honest to God—or Faithful to the Pentagon?" *Time,* May 30, 1969, 49.

[4] James H. Smylie, "American Religious Bodies, Just War, and Vietnam," *Journal of Church and State* 11 (Autumn 1969): 383–408.

Groups such as Clergy and Laymen Concerned about the War in Vietnam (CALCAV) were especially outraged by the high level of civilian casualties, the commonplace use of napalm and white phosphorous, the forced evacuation of towns and villages, the defoliation of crops, and the torture of prisoners to secure information.[5]

As the controversy over the war in Vietnam escalated, the debate over the chaplaincy narrowed to a concern with chaplains' alleged complicity in an immoral, unjust war. In the 1969 article "The Scandal of the Military Chaplaincy" published in *Judaism*, Gordon C. Zahn accused chaplains of *"skandalon"*—"leading others into immorality or, at least, blinding them to the immorality of acts in which they are, or may become, engaged." Like Miller, Zahn believed that chaplains should engage in a prophetic ministry, that they should seek to awaken and instruct the consciences of soldiers to deter them from performing "immoral acts of war." However, most chaplains were "quite unwilling to see themselves as bearing any moral guidance responsibilities with respect to the nature of a given war or of acts performed in that war," he observed. Zahn charged that in abdicating their responsibility, chaplains lent support to an unjust war. Even those who did not expressly urge men to fight and kill suggested by their presence "spiritual compatibility, if not . . . outright endorsement," he declared.[6]

In the wake of revelations of the 1968 My Lai massacre and other war crimes and atrocities, the indictment of the chaplains in Vietnam took on additional sharpness. "Where were the chaplains?" asked Robert McAfee Brown. "On an issue of the greatest moral sensitivity, on which the representatives of the churches could have been expected to speak forthrightly and prophetically, why were the chaplains so silent? . . . [I]n this instance a special prophetic responsibility was not exercised. . . . We ought . . . to expect a military chaplain to be leading the outcry when murder is committed in the name of freedom." The American bombing of Cambodia during the spring of 1973 also triggered a reaction against military chaplains. Over Memorial Day weekend, CALCAV sent a letter to more than one hundred command chaplains on air bases in the United States and Asia. The letter, signed by fourteen eminent church leaders, appealed to the chaplains to demonstrate "the courage of those who are determined to be men of God before they are servants of state." It urged them to carry out their prophetic responsibility by supporting pilots and crew members who had refused to participate in the bombing and by confronting other service personnel "with their personal and inescapable accountability to history and to history's Lord." If the chaplains believed, as CALCAV and

---

[5] See, for example, Mitchell K. Hall, *Because of Their Faith: CALCAV and Religious Opposition to the Vietnam War* (New York, 1990), 34–35, 65, 79, 126.

[6] Gordon C. Zahn, "The Scandal of the Military Chaplaincy," *Judaism* 18 (Summer 1969): 313, 314, 415.

the signers did, that the war was "without moral warrant," they should communicate that belief "boldly and without wavering." The letter also exhorted the chaplains to "set forth the alternatives emerging from that conviction, including leaving the Air Force, resisting, and disobeying orders."[7]

Although they received little publicity at the time, some chaplains did agonize over the Vietnam War and their ministerial responsibilities. Some came to see the war as morally ambiguous; others viewed it as morally indefensible. But they apparently did not believe they had a prophetic responsibility regarding the war. Most remained silent; only a few made their views known in a public forum. Even those who spoke out publicly seem to have done so to ease a troubled conscience, not to challenge or change military or government policy. Moreover, when they served in Vietnam, those who questioned U.S. involvement in the war refrained from expressing doubts about the morality of intervention or the overall conduct of the war. Their overriding concern while in Vietnam was for their men. They seem to have agreed with the argument Chaplain Galen Meyer made in his end-of-tour report to the chief of Navy chaplains. Citing chaplains who were troubled by the moral ambiguity of the war, Meyer asked, "Should the ambiguity of the war deter an involvement for the sake of the men?" His answer: "No. . . . God did not let the moral ambiguities of the world deter him entering our world in human flesh for our sakes. For the sake of the men here, we must be involved as we are. Our absence would be harder to justify than our presence now is." When Chaplain William J. Hughes went to Vietnam, he was already opposed to U.S. involvement in Southeast Asia, and he became more opposed during his tour of duty. Nevertheless, he wrote, "I have been silent on this issue in my preaching. I have done this deliberately because I genuinely felt that I and my men should not, indeed could not, oppose this war from within the area of conflict. I have honored our dead, comforted our wounded, and admonished, encouraged, or consoled." Hughes believed that the chaplain had "a necessary place" in the military and especially in a combat environment where his own moral agonizing might help him in counseling soldiers. "Our men need pastors who can feel, taste, and see the moral issues of our day and who can struggle with them to find a way to live with meaning in a bewilderingly complex situation," he added.[8]

[7] Robert McAfee Brown, "Military Chaplaincy as Ministry," in Harvey G. Cox, ed., *Military Chaplains: From Religious Military to a Military Religion* (New York, 1971), 144–45; Clergy and Laity Concerned, "An Appeal to Air Force Chaplains," *American Report*, June 4, 1973, 9; Steering Committee Meeting Minutes, May 3, 1973, typescript in Clergy and Laity Concerned Papers, Swarthmore College Peace Collection, Swarthmore, Pa.; *New York Times*, May 26, 1973, 4, May 27, 1973, sec. E, p. 5.

[8] Meyer quoted in Herbert L. Bergsma, *Chaplains with Marines in Vietnam, 1962–1971* (Washington, D.C., 1985), 175–76; William J. Hughes, "A Chaplain's Dilemma about Viet Nam," *Christian Advocate*, September 30, 1971. See also Billy W. Libby, "The Chaplain's Allegiance to His Church," *Military Chaplains' Review* (Fall 1983): 32–36; William P. Mahedy, *Out*

The great majority of chaplains supported the Vietnam War.[9] Stung by the attacks on their integrity, they not only defended the war but also their vocation. Specifically, they disputed the notion that they had a prophetic responsibility with regard to the war. Some, like U.S. Army chaplain William Wells, argued that for a military chaplain to criticize the war would increase "the tendency toward a 'politicized' army" and violate the principle of civilian control of the military. Air Force chief of chaplains Roy M. Terry flatly dismissed the CALCAV Memorial Day letter to his chaplains as a "request for disloyalty and disobedience." Most chaplains, even those who questioned U.S. involvement in Vietnam, contended that the prophetic role was inappropriate in a combat situation. Clarence Reaser of the Army Chaplain School, unlike Wells, saw nothing wrong with chaplains protesting the war by speaking to civilian communities or legislators, "people . . . who have the means to take the action he recommends." But, he argued, "when one speaks to military personnel (particularly to those in Vietnam), who do not make policy nor have the influence substantially to change it, it is questionable judgment to speak on the evils of the Vietnam war even if one feels deeply that the war is evil."[10]

In contrast to their critics, most chaplains insisted that their primary role in Vietnam was pastoral. They saw themselves as engaged in "a ministry of presence," which meant being with soldiers in all their activities, including combat operations, and providing "comfort and reassurance" when needed.[11] Moreover, they stressed the extent to which being an "insider" aided them in performing such a ministry. "Only when a minister is a trained soldier, sailor, marine or air man can he understand and identify with his men so as to serve them effectively," Navy chaplain Albert Ledebuhr wrote.[12] Indeed, many chaplains insisted that their willingness and ability

---

of the Night: The Spiritual Journey of Vietnam Vets (New York, 1986), 9; Martin H. Scharlemann, *Air Force Chaplains, 1961–1970* (n.p., n.d.), 125; *New York Times,* January 30, 1972, sec. 4, p. 6; and Rosemary Sawyer, "The BDU-Pulpit: Ministering to the Military," *Stars and Stripes,* July 26, 1989, 16.

[9] See, for example, *New York Times,* June 22, 1971, 37, 70; Rodger R. Venzke, *Confidence in Battle, Inspiration in Peace: The United States Army Chaplaincy, 1945–1975* (Washington, D. C., 1977), 127; *Washington Post,* September 2, 1969, 1, 6; *Time,* May 30, 1969, 49; Bergsma, *Chaplains with Marines,* 88; "The New Breed . . . ," *Army Digest* 23 (December 1966): 39–41; and, for a book-length defense of the Vietnam War by a Navy chaplain, John J. O'Connor, *A Chaplain Looks at Vietnam* (Cleveland, 1968).

[10] "More on the Military Chaplaincy," *Christian Century,* April 14, 1971, 467; John E. Groh, *Air Force Chaplains, 1971–1980* (Washington, D.C., 1986), 28; Clarence L. Reaser, "The Military Chaplain: God's Man or the Government's?" *Princeton Seminary Bulletin* 62 (Autumn 1969): 72–73.

[11] [A. Ray Appelquist], "Editor's Notes: Dissent over Vietnam," *Chaplain* 25 (May–June, 1968): 1; Bergsma, *Chaplains with Marines,* 5, 157; Henry F. Ackermann, *He Was Always There: The U.S. Army Chaplain Ministry in the Vietnam Conflict* (Washington, D.C., 1989), 226, and see also 5, 15.

[12] Albert Ledebuhr, "Military Chaplaincy: An Apologia," *Christian Century,* November 2, 1966, 1335.

to identify with the men constituted their most important contribution to the spiritual and moral welfare of the troops.[13] Another Navy chaplain, Richard G. Hutcheson Jr., responding directly to criticism of the chaplaincy by various religious groups, invoked some of the themes of the secular theology in defending the chaplain's "ministry of presence." "Is there a theology of involvement in the world?" he asked. "Is there a place in the church's mission for Christian professionals within the secular structures, sharing the lives of those served, participating in the ambiguities and contradictions of their existence, seeking to minister to and even sometimes to modify the structures of which they are a part? Or does the mission of the church require its professionals to sit above the social and institutional structures of the world as 'come-outers,' unsullied by participation, free to urge disobedience, passing judgment as outsiders?"[14] Just as the secular theologians discovered the mission of the church in the secular city, Hutcheson and other chaplains seemed to be saying that it could also be found in the equally secular environment of the armed forces and the Vietnam War.

Like the debate over the Vietnam War, the controversy over the military chaplaincy quickly became polarized. Critics of the chaplaincy reached the point of contending that chaplains in Vietnam failed their vocation as ministers of God unless they spoke out or resigned in protest against the war. Some carried the argument to its logical conclusion, calling for the "demilitarization" and civilianization of the chaplaincy.[15] On the other side, supporters of the chaplaincy—most of them chaplains—continued to insist on a strictly pastoral role. The debate ended in stalemate.

If anything, the criticism that chaplains received from antiwar individuals and groups confirmed rather than undermined their attachment to the pastoral role. Nevertheless, during the 1960s and early 1970s, the chaplaincies of each of the three branches of the armed forces developed a new ministry that represented a significant departure from the traditional pastoral role. What came to be known as an "institutional ministry" was a ministry to the military as an institution or system rather than to individuals in it. Chaplain Hutcheson hinted at such an approach in his description of the "theology of involvement" when he spoke of "Christian professionals . . . seeking to minister to and even sometimes to modify

[13] New York Times, June 22, 1971, 70.

[14] Richard G. Hutcheson Jr., "Should the Military Chaplaincy Be Civilianized?" Christian Century, October 31, 1973, 1075.

[15] See, for example, U.S. Army Office of the Chief of Chaplains, Historical Review, 1 July 1969 to 30 June 1970 (Washington, D.C., 1971), 51; Charles P. Lutz, "What Now for the Military Chaplaincy?" Christian Century, February 28, 1973, 257–58 ; New York Times, June 22, 1971, 37; and William J. Byron, "Religious Concern and the Indochina War," America, February 5, 1972, 116.

the structures of which they are a part." Chief of Chaplains Gerhardt W. Hyatt, who developed the institutional ministry for the U.S. Army, described it as "a dynamic ministry to the system" and a way of bringing the chaplaincy "up to date" in order to confront the momentous changes taking place inside and outside the armed forces. The influence of the secular theology on Hyatt's thinking is clear. The challenge facing chaplains in the 1970s, he declared, was to move beyond the traditional pastoral role of ministering to individuals to the admittedly difficult role of "transform[ing] the society in which we live." He envisioned chaplains as "agents of change," exerting influence not only on the members of their congregations but on the U.S. Army as a system—"on its institutions, its policies, its practices and its way of life."[16]

An early example of the institutional ministry, which illustrates how it functioned in a combat situation, was the Personal Response program devised by chaplains with the Marines Corps in Vietnam in the mid to late 1960s. It originated in the summer of 1965, when Lieutenant General Victor Krulak, commanding general of the Fleet Marine Force, Pacific, and his staff chaplain, Allen B. Craven, authorized Chaplain Robert L. Mole to begin work on the "Southeast Asia Religious Research Project." He developed an orientation program on the religions and customs of Vietnam, which chaplains began presenting to newly arriving troops in all commands of the III Marine Amphibious Force. In July 1966, when Chaplain Richard A. McGonigal relieved Chaplain Mole as the project officer, he was charged with revising and refining the materials and methods developed by Mole, paying particular attention to "the personal response of our military personnel as they work with the Vietnamese people in achieving victory over the enemy and establishing a strong and stable government for themselves." One result was a new name for the project—Personal Response (the two words used in McGonigal's charter letter). It indicated a significant shift of emphasis, from providing marines with information about Vietnamese customs and religious traditions to changing their attitudes toward the Vietnamese people. Attitude surveys McGonigal administered among the marines of I Corps had shown the need for the new emphasis, for they indicated that a significantly large percentage of marines disliked Vietnamese, especially those in the military. Personal Response sought to eliminate the Americans' negative attitudes and prevent problems and violent incidents growing out of them. The Chaplain Corps Planning Group, which

---

[16] Gerhardt W. Hyatt, "The Army Chaplaincy, Today and Tomorrow," *Chaplain* 31 (Fall Quarter, 1974): 3; U.S. Army Military History Institute (USAMHI), "Senior Officers Debriefing Program: Interview with Major General Gerhardt W. Hyatt (U.S. Army Chief of Chaplains, Ret.) by Chaplain Colonel J. H. Ellens, 19 July 1976," typescript in Archives Branch, USAMHI, Carlisle Barracks, Pa., 2, 13–14, 55.

supervised the development of the program, defined it as "a systematic effort" to:

a. Understand the Vietnamese culture by learning about its people, why they believe and act as they do, their religious principles and ethical value systems, in order to,

b. Modify and eventually eliminate unfavorable attitudes and offensive behavior patterns toward indigenous citizens,

c. Promote constructive relationships and appropriate mutual assistance between military personnel and the Vietnamese, and

d. Increase in some degree trust and confidence between American military personnel and indigenous citizens.

To accomplish these objectives, McGonigal developed a training program consisting of lectures, discussion, and role-playing in simulated village settings and also prepared the *Unit Leader's Personal Response Handbook*. The handbook employed a teaching method known as the "critical incident technique," which isolated specific behaviors promoting or undermining cross-cultural understanding and cooperation.[17]

Personal Response training conducted by chaplains, and by line officers and noncommissioned officers they had trained, began late in 1966 with the initial focus on noncommissioned officers (NCOs) and marines in the Combined Action Platoons (CAPs). The CAPs were small detachments of marines and navy corpsmen assigned to live for extended periods in Vietnamese hamlets, with and among the villagers. Teamed up with South Vietnamese Popular Forces (PF) militia, the CAPs constituted a major element of Marine Corps pacification efforts, for their mission was to win the allegiance and sympathy of the local populace by defending them against the Viet Cong (VC), providing medical treatment, implementing various civic action projects, and, by precept and example, developing civic cohesion among the villagers. Winning allegiance and sympathy was no abstract objective. As Michael E. Peterson observed in his study of the CAPs, "the need for cultural sensitivity by the marines . . . extended beyond mere civic action or even a moral imperative: it was tactically vital." The safety, even the very survival, of CAP marines in remote, isolated hamlets depended on establishing a unity of interest between them and the Vietnamese—the basic objective of Personal Response. "We wanted to increase their identification with the people in the hamlets, to be able to see that old lady with the betel nut juice as a grandmother, not as a gook," McGonigal observed. "If the Marine could start talking about that old lady as a grandmother . . . and his role now was to protect her and keep both the ARVN [Army of the Republic of Vietnam] and the VC off her back, it

[17] Bergsma, *Chaplains with Marines,* 104–6; Commander Richard A. McGonigal, United States Marine Corps, interview, October 12, 1984, San Francisco, cassette tape in Oral History Collection, Marine Corps Historical Center, Washington, D.C.

was a different ball game." Seeing a Vietnamese as a "full-fledged human being," the marine would become more careful in his use of firepower and generally more sensitive in dealing with Vietnamese civilians.[18]

Throughout its operation in Vietnam, into the early 1970s, Personal Response proved to be a valuable aid to marines in the field. Numerous lifesaving incidents were attributed to its success in improving intercultural attitudes. As Herbert L. Bergsma observed, "It was easier to patrol when the people liked you." McGonigal, who admitted to having been concerned about "unnecessary killing" and a large number of civilian casualties, also believed Personal Response was effective. "I think we saved some lives," he said. "I do think it made a big difference in the CAP units." In his opinion, it was a realistic and successful attempt to "limit the carnage, and save a few Marine lives and a few Vietnamese lives."[19]

In the 1970s, the military chaplaincies utilized the institutional ministry in a variety of ways. Under U.S. Army Chief of Chaplains Hyatt, for example, it was used to address drug and alcohol abuse, racism, marriage and family problems, and various disciplinary issues. To provide chaplains with the expertise they needed, programs such as Clinical Pastoral Education (CPE) and Organizational Development (OD) offered training in the behavioral sciences and taught such things as pastoral counseling, chapel program development, and interpersonal, communication, conflict-resolution, and decision-making skills. The annual reports of the Office of the Chief of Chaplains for 1973–74 and 1974–75 described OD as "designed for the purpose of facilitating innovative ministries" and to "aid in the emergence of a proactive, rather than a reactive, chaplaincy, capable of providing an influential, prophetic ministry to the military institution." Describing the goals of the institutional ministry as a whole, Chief of Chaplains Hyatt declared that it embraced "the whole range of human relations issues." Elaborating, he observed, "We are in business to help replace social injury with personal wholeness, schism with harmony and dysfunctional behaviors with positive life styles. The OD program, CPE, alcohol and drug abuse prevention, family counseling and value clarification classes all contribute to this ministry."[20]

---

[18] Michael E. Peterson, *The Combined Action Platoons: The U.S. Marines' Other War in Vietnam* (New York, 1989), 43; McGonigal, interview; McGonigal quoted in Jack Shulimson, *U.S. Marines in Vietnam: An Expanding War, 1966* (Washington, D.C., 1982), 244. See also Richard G. Hutcheson Jr., *The Churches and the Chaplaincy* (Atlanta, 1975), 164–65.

[19] Bergsma, *Chaplains with Marines*, 106–7; McGonigal, interview. Richard Hutcheson, *Churches and the Chaplaincy*, 165, says that chaplains in the army developed a program similar to Personal Response.

[20] Office of the Chief of Chaplains (OCCH), *Annual Report of Major Activities: Historical Review 1 July 1973 to 30 June 1974* (Washington, D.C., [1974], typescript at U.S. Army Center of Military History, Washington, D.C.), 41; OCCH, *Annual Report of Major Activities: Historical Review 1 July 1974–30 June 1975* (Washington, D.C., [1975], typescript at U.S. Army Center of Military History, Washington, D.C.), 41; Hyatt, "Army Chaplaincy," 6. OD had been developed in the 1950s by industrial psychologists working in the civilian sector. In the 1970s, to

Two chaplains programs that grew out of OD and implemented the concept of ministering to the Army as a system were the Ministry of Human Relations and Personal Effectiveness Training (PET). Hyatt instituted the Ministry of Human Relations in November 1973 to help improve race relations by eliminating institutional as well as personal racism and promoting equal opportunity and affirmative action. Along with efforts to increase recruitment of minority group clergy, aid chaplains in incorporating elements of black religion and liturgy into their chapel programs, and counsel commanders on race relations issues, the Ministry of Human Relations sponsored numerous workshops to train chaplains. One series of workshops conducted under contract with the National Training Laboratories provided sensitivity training to some 900 chaplains and 350 line officers in the early 1970s. Chaplains with special training in turn held race relations seminars within their chapels or as part of their installation's race relations program. Hyatt described the chaplains' Ministry of Human Relations as a way of sharing in "the humanization of organizations and in the process of social change."[21]

The Personal Effectiveness Training program, which became a part of all Combat Army Primary and Basic NCO Courses by the mid-1970s, was designed by chaplains to improve the leadership effectiveness of junior officers and NCOs, particularly in dealing with alcohol and drug abuse, racial tensions, and various disciplinary problems among unit soldiers. A typical PET program consisted of sixteen hours of instruction broken down into weekly or sometimes daily segments of two to four hours. Chaplains taught small groups of between twelve and twenty-four individuals, using a combination of lectures, discussion, dramatization and role-playing, and other participant interaction exercises. Initial sessions encouraged self-awareness and openness on the part of the participants as a means of supplanting indifference or hostility with a "caring" attitude toward the troops. Later sessions focused on the specific day-to-day problems the participants confronted, in order to train them in communication, problem-solving, and counseling skills.[22]

In promoting the institutional ministry to the U.S. Army, Hyatt emphasized that he was not asking chaplains to abandon their traditional pastoral role. For him the ultimate goal of chaplains remained spiritual—the "spir-

implement OD within the U.S. Army chaplaincy, Hyatt contracted with the National Training Laboratories, an independent research and training organization.

[21] OCCH, *Annual Report of Major Activities: Historical Review of the Office of Chief of Chaplains 1 July 1972 to 30 June 1973* (Washington, D.C., [1973], typescript at U.S. Army Center of Military History, Washington, D.C.), 66; OCCH, *Annual Report . . . 1 July 1973 to 30 June 1974*, 39.

[22] OCCH, *Historical Review 1 October 1976–30 September 1977* (Washington, D.C., [1977], typescript at U.S. Army Center of Military History, Washington, D.C.), 27; OCCH, *Annual Report . . . 1 July 1974–30 June 1975*, 29; OCCH, *Annual Report . . . 1 July 1973 to 30 June 1974*, 45–48.

itual good" of the military community. He believed, however, that to confront the secular problems of a secular institution, chaplains needed secular tools or means. He conceded that programs such as OD, CPE, and PET were "humanistic and devoid of spiritual content," as some critics charged. "That's right," he declared, "OD *is* devoid of spiritual content simply because it is not an end or goal. It is a *process* . . . whereby you take the power of your personal faiths and together build powerful collegiality which can challenge and change the world and build the city of God." The same argument applied to the behavioral sciences. They, too, were "tools" to be utilized by chaplains to enhance their own skills or address the problems of the U.S. Army as an institution. "We are not leaving religion for CPE, OD or any other behavioral science approach," Hyatt reassured chaplains in a 1976 information letter. "We use these tools, when appropriate, but never as a substitute for God or His power, or in rejection of our high calling as ministers, priests and rabbis." In equipping themselves with "people skills," Hyatt insisted, chaplains were extending their "basic clergy role" rather than developing a substitute for it.[23]

The Navy Chaplain Corps and the U.S. Air Force chaplaincy also developed institutional ministries, which included various human relations programs similar to those of the Army. Under the guidance of Roy Terry, the Air Force chaplaincy placed a great deal of emphasis on chaplains' use of sociological, psychological, and humanistic skills and on their role as an "agent of change" and a "bridge builder" within the Air Force. Describing that new role, the chief of chaplains noted the chaplain's "unique function as a humanizing and personalizing influence in a necessarily mission-centered and often impersonal military structure. He is a sensor, interpreter, enabler, moral presence—a bridge between such sources of division as age, sex, rank, race, religion, or military function." The chief commended the chaplain as "a resource available to every commander who desires to reduce the causes of tension by increasing genuine communication, understanding, and acceptance." Besides developing their own ministry to the Air Force as an institution, chaplains helped to organize the Social Actions (SA) agency in 1971 under the Directorate of Personnel and contributed advice and staffing to assist SA programs in drug and alcohol abuse education, race and human relations, equal opportunity, and sexual abuse and other family issues.[24]

The institutional ministry apparently escaped the notice of the critics of the chaplaincy. One suspects it would not have alleviated their concerns.

[23] USAMHI, "Senior Officers Debriefing Program," 4, 5; OCCH, Department of the Army, *1 July 1975 to 30 September 1976* ([Washington, D.C., 1976], typescript at U.S. Army Center of Military History, Washington, D.C.), 60.

[24] Groh, *Air Force Chaplains*, 94, 96, 126, 454–60, 621–24. On the institutional ministry in the Navy, see Hutcheson, *Churches and the Chaplaincy*, 165, 174–79.

Although Hyatt and other chaplains insisted on its prophetic nature, it seems unlikely the critics would have agreed.[25] Chaplains performing the prophetic role did not, after all, advance the kind of radical critique of the Vietnam War and the military that had become a sine qua non for many of the critics. Indeed, the effects of the institutional ministry are somewhat ambiguous. On the one hand, it did represent an effort to reform the military system. Personal Response, for example, was designed, at least in part, to prevent atrocities like the My Lai massacre; and the institutional ministries of the early 1970s meshed with the "people-oriented" programs instituted by the armed forces leadership in its effort to "humanize" the military environment, first in the experimental "liberalization program" of the early 1970s and then in the All Volunteer Force instituted in 1973.[26] And Hyatt's concern to enable chaplains "to assume a more influential role in the development of command policies and decisions" marked the beginning of a process that led, in the late 1970s, to formal recognition of the chaplain's responsibility to advise the commander on matters of ethics and morality.[27] "Army chaplains demonstrate a prophetic presence," declared the 1979 "Chaplain Professional Development Plan" for the Army. It continued:

> They are so in touch with their own value system and those of their churches that they boldly confront both the Army as an institution and individuals within it with the consequences of their actions. . . . They are knowledgeable, able and willing to confront both individuals and the Army with the ethical aspects of decision-making, policies and leadership, and the extent to which these, in both war and peace, reflect on [sic] basic Judeo-Christian ethical framework.[28]

[25] Hutcheson, *Churches and the Chaplaincy,* 183–84, insists that "ministry to the institution itself (as distinguished from the pastoral ministry to persons who make up the institution) is inherently a prophetic function." During the early and mid-1970s, reports issued by the Army Office of the Chief of Chaplains consistently used the adjective "prophetic" in describing programs such as OD. See, for example, OCCH, *Annual Report . . . 1 July 1973 to 30 June 1974,* 41; OCCH, *Annual Report . . . 1 July 1974–30 June 1975,* 41; and also Neil M. Stevenson, "Chaplains in the Marginal Role," *Navy Chaplains Bulletin* (Spring 1971): 4, and Holland Hope, Earl S. Bloxham, William V. O'Connor, and Francis X. Wallace, "A Look at the Chaplaincy: Yesterday and Today," *Military Chaplains' Review* (Spring 1975): 8.

[26] See, for example, "Humanizing the U.S. Military," *Time,* December 21, 1970, 16, 19–22; *New York Times,* February 17, 1971, 21; and *The Chaplain and the Modern Volunteer Army: Lesson 2 of FY72 Chaplain Training Packet* ([Washington, D.C.], August 1971).

[27] Hyatt, "Army Chaplaincy," 4.

[28] "Chaplain Professional Development Plan" quoted in Robert Vickers, "The Military Chaplaincy: A Study in Role Conflict," *Military Chaplains' Review* (Spring 1986), 83. For later assertions of a prophetic role for chaplains, see, for example, Headquarters, Department of the Army, *The Chaplain and Chaplain Assistant in Combat Operations,* FM 16-5 (Washington, D.C., December, 1984), 21–23, and Headquarters, Department of the Army, *Religious Support Doctrine: The Chaplain and Chaplain Assistant,* FM 16-1 (Washington, D.C., April 1989), 3-8–3-10.

On the other hand, the intent and, in many cases, the effect of Personal Response and the institutional ministries was to strengthen, not undermine, the military system, including its war-making function. Personal Response had a tactical as well as a moral purpose. The institutional ministry's concern to promote harmony, efficient administration, and what Hyatt called "positive life styles" made it as much an effort at social control as reform.

Criticism of the institutional ministry came not from the chaplains' critics but from chaplains themselves. In the case of the Personal Response program, the secular emphasis on cross-cultural understanding and behavior disturbed some chaplains who thought it represented a departure from the chaplain's primary mission of offering a spiritual ministry to American service personnel. Increased command implementation of Personal Response prompted other chaplains to object that commanders were using the program for purely military purposes, as a form of psychological or ideological warfare or as a means of gathering military intelligence, rather than improving cultural understanding. While such an enterprise was perfectly legitimate from a military standpoint, one chaplain observed in his end-of-tour report, it was "questionable in ministry."[29]

In the 1970s, the development of an institutional ministry and a prophetic role for U.S. Army chaplains, along with the introduction of programs such as CPE, OD, and PET and increasing reliance on the behavioral sciences, alienated many chaplains who held to the more traditional concept of ministry. A study done in 1976 showed that, overall, Army chaplains ranked the "classic clergy role" of preacher and counselor as most satisfying and placed recently developed roles such as PET instructor or OD specialist in the least satisfying category. Even after Hyatt left the Office of Chief of Chaplains, his innovations continued to incite debate among chaplains.[30] In the Navy, the institutional ministry provoked some tension between chaplains regarded as "specialists" (meaning those educated or trained in the behavioral sciences and placed in specialized assignments) and more traditional-minded chaplains who had little enthusiasm for the new, secular, people-oriented programs—and who constituted the majority of the Chaplain Corps. Similarly, in the Air Force, the chaplaincy's emphasis on "people-helping skills" and programs in the early 1970s precipitated considerable tension—sometimes a visible struggle—between "skill-oriented" chaplains who utilized behavioral and social sci-

[29] Bergsma, *Chaplains with Marines,* 103–4, 183–84 (Chaplain Neil M. Stevenson quoted on p. 184); Hutcheson, *Churches and the Chaplaincy,* 164–65; McGonigal, interview.

[30] Kermit D. Johnson, "How Army Chaplains View Themselves, Their Work, and Their Organization," *Chaplain* 34 (Second Quarter 1977): 30. For the debate over the prophetic ministry and ministering to institutions, see the *Military Chaplains' Review* for Spring 1978 and Winter 1979.

ence approaches and "pastoral-oriented" chaplains who felt more comfortable performing traditional functions such as preaching, teaching, and leading worship.[31]

As the chaplains who resisted it recognized, the institutional ministry constituted a significant innovation within the military chaplaincy. Certainly the critics of the chaplaincy played a role in bringing about such change, but their criticism was not the only or even the most important factor. Chaplaincy leaders such as Gerhardt Hyatt seem to have been influenced by the same secular theology that inspired the critics, and many younger chaplains no doubt became apprised of the secular theology and the relevance of the behavioral sciences while attending seminary in the 1960s. Nevertheless, allegiance to the pastoral role was so entrenched in the military chaplaincy that neither the critics nor the secular theology was sufficient to provoke the kind of change the institutional ministry represented. It took the problems raised by the war in Southeast Asia and the moral and social issues confronting the armed forces during the Vietnam era to jolt the chaplaincies into fashioning a new prophetic role for chaplains. Rather than a response to a challenge issuing from the civilian sector, the institutional ministry was primarily an effort on the part of the chaplaincies to address problems within the armed forces of the 1960s and 1970s.

[31] Hutcheson, *Churches and the Chaplaincy*, 165–66, 175, 176; Groh, *Air Force Chaplains*, 462–66 and see also 616–19.

REDRAWING MORAL BOUNDARIES
IN MODERN AMERICA

The original caption read: "'The Courtship of Miles Standish.' *Note inscription on back of boy's hand*"—which contains initials and the word "LOVE." New York City Board of Education Archives, Milbank Memorial Library, Teachers College, Columbia University.

CHAPTER TWELVE

Listen, My Children: Modes and Functions of Poetry Reading in American Schools, 1880–1950

JOAN SHELLEY RUBIN

The reading of poetry may seem a subject unlikely to shed much light on the moral underpinnings of American life. Insofar as the activity prompts associations with spiritual interludes or lovers' tête-à-têtes, it evokes a private world, an ethereal realm remote from the pressing national problems that have engendered ethical debate. Yet poetry also possesses a significant public dimension. Between 1880 and 1950, for example, Americans encountered the genre in speaking choirs, around Girl Scout campfires, at civic ceremonies and church services, in celebrity performances, on the radio, and in the schoolroom. The recitation of poems at those sites transmitted not only sound and sense but also ideologies of reading. As it turns out, to examine the values attending the dissemination of verse is to become aware that Americans endowed exposure even to the most unworldly poetic sentiments with moral and social utility. Specifically, an exploration of the teaching of poetry in school reveals the way in which educators during the Progressive period both sustained and recast the moral functions their predecessors had assigned to poetry instruction by adopting reading practices at once innovative and conservative.

Perhaps more important, an investigation of poetry in public highlights the moral implications of the cultural hierarchies that have shaped conventional accounts of American literature's development. Those accounts reflect the outlooks of writers and scholars who have esteemed experimentation, thought of literary history as a succession of movements to "make it new," and prided themselves on membership in an intellectual elite. In particular, the belief in what a 1905 forum in the *Critic* called

"The Slump in Poetry"[1] was essential to the self-definition of the so-called "new poets" who came to prominence in the 1910s. These figures—Amy Lowell, Robert Frost, Edward Arlington Robinson, Edgar Lee Masters, and Edna St. Vincent Millay, to name a few—depended for their identity on their sense that they were reinvigorating a moribund art. Although distinct from the "high modernists" of the 1920s, the "new poets" were self-consciously "modern," in behavior if not always in literary craft; to varying degrees, and in tension with their drive for an audience, they rebelled against idealism and sentimentality. The more avant-garde figures within the group succeeded in reconceiving poetic diction and form, often adopting a vernacular idiom or free verse. They also failed, in that poetry remained a tiny fraction of the book market.

Yet concealed within this scenario of decline, renaissance, and rarefaction are clues that the "slump" was in part an artifact of poets' and critics' desire to define their own roles in contradistinction to certain popular reading and writing practices. Moreover, William Dean Howells made a crucial observation in 1902 when, after voicing his dismay at the passing of the "lords of rhyme," he added hopefully, "The really interesting and important thing to find out would be whether the love of poetry shares the apparent decline of poetry itself." His query underscored the difference between reading and writing, between the fate of the classics and that of new works.[2]

Many participants in the *Critic*'s forum corroborated that possibility. Decrying the scientific, antiromantic tendencies of the age, the poet Madison Cawein, for example, pointed out that if "the world does feel a crying necessity for something in the way of serious poetry, it seldom turns to the poets of the present, but to those of the past, who seem to be able to satisfy all its requirements in this respect." The remarks of Richard Badger, head of Houghton Mifflin, bore out Cawein's statement. Badger recognized no "slump." Rather, he contended, the very growth of the book market, by permitting sales over many years of older writers, placed younger ones at an inevitable disadvantage. "Edition after edition is called for, of all great poetry," Badger asserted, "and that so far from the demand decreasing, it increases with enormous strides, and in direct proportion to the education of a cultivated opinion among the body of the people." Other voices in the *Critic*'s pages substantiated poetry's vitality not by identifying a "niche market" for high culture but by shifting the spotlight to agencies of popularization. What school or municipal library, one writer asked, could function without the collected works of Longfellow, Lowell, and Whittier? The most instructive contribution in this regard came from

---

[1] "The Slump in Poetry," *Critic*, March–April 1905, 263–77, 347–50.
[2] William Dean Howells, "The Editor's Easy Chair," *Harper's*, March 1902, 674.

the poet Paul Lawrence Dunbar: "It may be the consensus of opinion that the love for poetry is declining, but I for one don't believe it. . . . Go into any school on a Friday afternoon, in our Middle West, and I think after you have gotten through listening to the 'Friday afternoon exercises,' you will agree with me. Perhaps New York, Chicago, Philadelphia, and Boston are too busy for it, but I do not believe that we of the great Middle West, and the people of the old New England towns, and the old dramatic Southerners have yet gotten past it."[3]

Such comments thus made visible continuities in consumption that persisted despite the vicissitudes of production. In addition to traditions of reading, moreover, another set of continuities belied poetry's demise: traditions of memory and meaning. "In a hot laundry, where the girls stood ironing collars by the thousand through the August days," the educator Vida Scudder reported, "one girl, chanting Wordsworth's dew-pure poems on Lucy to a little tune of her own, set all her mates to follow. 'It makes it seem cooler in there,' was the comment of one of them." Scudder's observations signal the diverse settings of, and uses for, the remembrance of verse—uses independent of whether an individual currently read any poems at all.[4]

The speculations about a silent audience, the chronological lag between production and consumption, the existence of multiple sites for dissemination, and the functions of remembered texts that surface in the turn-of-the-century debate over the status of poetry may or may not undermine the claim of a "slump." In any event, the question may be artificial: "What age," Francis B. Gummere asked, "has not thought itself at the death-bed of poetry?"[5] Still, the controversy over the decline of poetry contains a message of more general significance: it suggests the need to differentiate literary history, always written as an account of the new, from the history of reading, and in turn to depict the culture of a given era in terms of readers' encounters with an eclectic mixture of steady sellers and innovative forms, domestic products and foreign imports, "serious" writing and "lighter" works, remembered texts and imputed meanings.

The remainder of this essay will begin heeding that message by exploring the institution Dunbar named as a key agency of dissemination: the public school. Here, despite changes in the readership of the "outside world," poetry's audience remained total and constant: everybody learned it every year. Here traditions of reading generated traditions of memory. It might be objected that most of the materials related to poetry reading in school—courses of study, essays on pedagogy—are merely prescriptive,

[3] "The Slump in Poetry," 265, 267–68, 269, 271, 347–50.
[4] Vida Scudder, "Democracy and Education," *Atlantic Monthly,* June 1902, 821.
[5] Francis B. Gummere, *Democracy and Poetry* (Boston, 1911), 305.

that they do not capture classroom realities. In fact, this was not always the case; many do indicate how instructors implemented lesson plans. Some also reveal how pupils responded, although the subject of students as readers is beyond the scope of this discussion.[6] A more serious limitation is that the authors of curricular materials tended to be innovators and hence atypical teachers. Nevertheless it is important to remember that the educators who intoned, with Longfellow, "Listen, my children" were themselves a population of readers. They have as much to teach historians as they did their pupils.

In the late nineteenth and early twentieth centuries, learning poetry in the American school entailed both reading and recitation. Much of the former consisted in acquiring "a body of facts" about authors and literary movements. Reading a poem also meant studying it: deciphering unfamiliar vocabulary, attending to technicalities of meter and rhyme, mastering the spelling and grammar lessons the text provided. Writing in 1925, for example, the progressive educator Hughes Mearns observed: "For a half century *The Lady of the Lake* . . . has been almost a sacred book. . . . For the whole of the eighth school year it was studied word by word, memorized, scanned, and parsed." After 1890, high schools preparing students for college entrance requirements also routinely subjected to intensive scrutiny Bryant's "Thanatopsis," Gray's "Elegy," Lowell's "The Vision of Sir Launfal," Longfellow's *Evangeline,* Coleridge's *The Rime of the Ancient Mariner,* and the poems of Milton. At the same time, students read for the purpose of oral performance. The tradition of the declamation, while no longer in vogue, survived in other practices that incorporated spoken verse: exercises at the start of each school day, weekly programs (often on Friday afternoon) at which students delivered poems "by heart," elocution contests, and holiday observances considered incomplete without the presentation of thematically appropriate "pieces."[7]

A number of sources supplied teachers with poetic texts. The latter volumes of the famous McGuffey and Hillard readers reprinted brief poems like Leigh Hunt's "Abou Ben Adhem" and the shorter works of Whittier and Longfellow. Anthologies such as Palgrave's *Golden Treasury* made lengthier verse available. Early surveys like Julian Hawthorne and Leonard Lemmon's *American Literature* (1891) scattered poems among lit-

---

[6] I have discussed student responses in "'They Flash upon That Inward Eye': Poetry Recitation and American Readers," *Proceedings of the American Antiquarian Society* 106, pt. 2 (1997): 273–300.

[7] Arthur H. R. Fairchild, *The Teaching of Poetry in the High School* (Boston, 1914), 84–85; Hughes Mearns, *Creative Youth* (Garden City, N.J., 1925), 118–19; Donald E. Stahl, *A History of the English Curriculum in American High Schools* (Chicago, 1965), 14–15, 88–89. For purposes of this essay, I have separated Shakespearean drama—a standard feature of the high school curriculum—from the category of "poetry."

erary commentary. Universities published editions of the works applicants needed to know. Along with those forms of print, beginning in the late 1870s educators relied on one that compensated for deficiencies in school libraries: the "memory gem" collection. These were predominantly excerpts from poetry, together with some prose selections, ranging from two to fifteen lines in length and usually classified by grade or subject. Many teachers in both elementary and high schools devoted ten minutes a day to individual or group recitation of an assigned quotation.[8]

Underlying the use of memory gems lay assumptions about the role of reading in child development. The term in one sense referred to the fact that the quoted lines represented the essence of a longer work. Yet the phrase, with its connotations of preciousness and rarity, also suggested that the mind could function as a repository of "riches" acquired in youth that would remain stable in value. The title page of one volume contained this injunction from the British essayist Sir Arthur Helps: "We should lay up in our minds a store of goodly thoughts in well-wrought words, which should be a living treasure of knowledge, always with us, and from which, at various times, and amidst all the shifting of circumstances, we might be sure of drawing some comfort, guidance, and sympathy."[9] Such language locates memory gems in the tradition of the commonplace book, into which readers copied beloved passages so as to preserve them for future reminiscence or inspiration.[10] It reflects as well the influence of faculty psychology—the view, popular among humanistic educators by the early nineteenth century, that memory and other components of the mind, although inborn, were expanded and perfected only through active learning. At the same time, Helps's imagery elaborates the connection between reading poetry and acquiring capital. (Helps's own books included *Essays Written in the Intervals of Business*.) In particular, the phrase "goodly thoughts" encompasses both the idea of "the best" literature and a reference to commodities or "goods." In a society where the fluctuating fortunes of the nouveaux riches and the influx of immigrant "strangers" enhanced the need for stability, the figure of the reader as prudent banker could be particularly appealing. Yet that analogy (one thinks as well of the phrase "memory bank") also conveys the enticements of the marketplace about which Jackson Lears has written, as if the mind, rightly furnished, could become a dazzling Ali Baba's cave.[11]

[8] Ruth Miller Elson, *Guardians of Tradition: American Schoolbooks of the Nineteenth Century* (Lincoln, 1964), 211–42; Stahl, *English Curriculum in American High Schools*, 88.

[9] W. H. Lambert, *Memory Gems: Graded Selections in Prose and Verse for the Use of Schools* (Boston, 1883).

[10] On the commonplace book, see, for example, Mary Thomas Crane, *Framing Authority: Sayings, Self, and Society in Sixteenth-Century England* (Princeton, 1993).

[11] Herbert M. Kliebard, *Forging the American Curriculum* (New York, 1992), 8–9; Barbara Sicherman, "Reading and Middle-Class Identity in Victorian America: Cultural Consump-

At the same time, memory gem collections reflected the widely shared belief that the reading of poetry, even more than other literary genres, promoted the creation of a "higher" self. While the proponents of memory gems perceived no contradiction between that goal and the storehouse conceit, the latter trope nevertheless coexisted with another vocabulary diametrically opposed to it: the language of cultivation. Untroubled by the mixed metaphor, the authors of the prefatory material in a 1907 collection explained that memory gems were "seed-thoughts" which were "gleaned from the fields of literature." Like the term "culture" itself, this organic imagery drew its force from traditional notions of agrarian virtue. In the garden of the mind, a space tamed yet free from the corruptions of society, the "higher self" could flourish.[12]

Both these understandings of the mind—as storehouse and garden— connected the reading and memorization of poetry to the development of specific mental qualities. The first of these was moral sense. The student, Joseph C. Sindelar explained, needed "the culture side of education" in order to "stimulate his moral energies." To that end, Sindelar interspersed aphoristic "lessons in ethics" between the prose and verse selections he assembled. Under the heading "Too great stress cannot be laid on the early forming of good habits," for example, he introduced these lines from Longfellow: "Let us, then, be up and doing, / With a heart for any fate; / Still achieving, still pursuing, / Learn to labor and to wait." The repetitive nature of the daily exercise, instead of boring students, ostensibly made such lessons more effective. Compilers invoked another, less prominent metaphor—that of fabric—to underscore the value of drill in strengthening "the warp and woof of character": "The pupil should not only be able to say the selection, but he should repeat it so often that it becomes inwoven with the very fibre of his mind." Moreover, the oral nature of the recitation enhanced its putative moral benefits; teachers associated vocal training with producing an eloquent citizenry possessed of high principle and judgment.[13]

The idea of buttressing morality by memorizing and reciting poetry affiliated those activities with traditions of religious instruction, notably the recitation of Bible verses in Sunday schools.[14] In addition, the expectation that even poetry memorized in the public school could, as Helps

---

tion, Conspicuous and Otherwise," unpublished paper in my possession; T. J. Jackson Lears, *Fables of Abundance: A Cultural History of Advertising in America* (New York, 1994).

[12] W. H. Williams, *Memory Gems for School and Home* (New York, 1907), v–vii.

[13] Joseph C. Sindelar, *Best Memory Gems* (Chicago, 1915), 3, 8; F. T. Oldt, *Memory Gems Graded for Use in School* (Lanark, Ill., 1891), 2; Williams, *Memory Gems*, v; Nan Johnson, "The Popularization of Nineteenth-Century Rhetoric: Elocution and the Private Learner," in Gregory Clark and S. Michael Halloran, eds., *Oratorical Culture in Nineteenth-Century America: Transformations in the Theory and Practice of Rhetoric* (Carbondale, Ill., 1993), 157.

[14] Anne M. Boylan, *Sunday School* (New Haven, 1988), 44.

put it, furnish "comfort, guidance, and sympathy" endowed reading non-biblical texts with the consolations of faith. It is tempting, of course, to view that assumption solely as evidence of the waning of religious orthodoxy. The British romantic poets whose work loomed so large in the curriculum were partly responsible for the conflation of the sacred and the secular. In attempting to reconcile belief and doubt, Wordsworth, Tennyson, Browning, and others had blurred the boundary between God and man. Emphasizing the divine nature of human love, such figures, as Hoxie Neale Fairchild argued, diminished the importance of "penitence and penance, the way of the Cross." In the context of this "Christianity without tears," literature that explored mankind's goodness assumed a standing equal to actual Bible study. Readers undergoing their own crisis of faith were relieved to learn, from critics, teachers, and ministers alike, that poetry could substitute for prayer and that the poet could serve as spiritual guide. Yet, granted that the practice rested on a liberalized theology, the congruence of the form of the recitation in both church and public schools should alert us that, from the student's perspective, poetry reading might strengthen rather than weaken religious authority. To stand before a hushed class and speak edifying lines on Sunday and to do the same thing on Monday could make both experiences seem forms of devotion. Moreover, as romantic poets, with ministerial sanction, emphasized the function of Christian belief as an antidote to psychic turmoil or ethical confusion, the cultivation of moral sense through the study of "inspirational" verse could seem an extension of, rather than a replacement for, religious teaching. As the educational reformer Charles A. McMurray explained in 1899, "To drink in . . . potent truths through poetry and song . . . is more than culture, more than morality; it is the portal and sanctuary of religious thought; and children may enter here."[15] It is questionable whether the term "secularization" is adequate to encompass these practices.

In any case, the ability of poetry to serve religious purposes by shaping moral sense was only part of the rationale for its study. Educators attached a second aim to reading verse: cultivating aesthetic sensitivity. For some, of course, this goal was inseparable from morality. As the Reverend Noah Porter observed, possessing a "poetic sensibility" did not insure "poetic taste"; an appreciation of beauty resulted only from training in the recognition of "choice and pure words" (as opposed to "the sewerage of modern poetry"). Yet within that framework Porter made ample room for poetry as a delight to the ear. Most memory gem compilers likewise mingled moral didacticism and aesthetic pleasure. "These gems," one editor ex-

[15] Hoxie Neale Fairchild, *Religious Trends in English Poetry* (New York, 1949), 3:3–18, 505 (quoted), (1957), 4:3–17, 61–167, 528–46; Charles A. McMurray, *Special Method in the Reading of Complete English Classics in the Grades of the Common School* (Bloomington, Ill., 1899), 55–56.

plained, "are presented with the hope that good may result to the children from the mastery of such a range of strong and beautiful quotations." In some cases, however, the stress on beauty overshadowed moral objectives—or obliterated them entirely. One prolific Indiana textbook author confined the rationale for his 1889 compilation to the goal that pupils would "gradually learn to love the beautiful in language, and to discriminate between classic and mediocre writing."[16]

A third objective of poetry reading in the American classroom of 1890 or 1910 was to instill patriotism. Before each holiday, students recited appropriate commemorative verse, such as Oliver Wendell Holmes's "Washington's Birthday." Sir Walter Scott's lines "Breathes there a man with soul so dead, / who never to himself hath said, / This is my own, my native land?" appeared in virtually every memory gem collection. Like the goal of fostering appreciation for beauty, the enhancement of patriotic fervor was not entirely separable from moral instruction, because patriotism was a subset of "love for that which is good and ennobling." When L. C. Foster and Sherman Williams assembled *Selections for Memorizing* (1892), however, they gave poems that "teach patriotism" a standing equal to those that "are good literature" and "inculcate good morals." In addition, as teachers knew, rousing stanzas praising national heroes made verse more palatable to boys who thought it feminine.[17]

In short, in the years roughly between 1880 and 1910 prescriptive pronouncements about the reading of poetry in school exemplified the educator William Torrey Harris's vision of humanistic study as a whole: students would thereby acquire "knowledge of truth, a love of the beautiful, a habit of doing the good," particularly for one's country. These benefits derived from line-by-line reading, the drill of the recitation, and attention to form as well as theme. The structure of the memorization exercise itself reinforced the virtues of diligence, hard work, and thoroughness. Concomitantly, such analysis discouraged emphasis on the reader's "personal affinities, likings, and circumstances," which, in Matthew Arnold's words, had "great power to sway our estimate of this or that poet's work, and to make us attach more importance to it . . . than in itself it really possesses."[18]

To be sure, the romantic, religiously inflected dimension of the nineteenth-century poetry curriculum in this period worked against the ideal of self-discipline, encouraging instead the outpouring or even indulgence of feeling. In that respect, it mirrored the assumption Ruth Miller Elson

[16] Noah Porter, *Books and Reading* (New York, 1871), 252, 256; Williams, *Memory Gems*, vi; Will P. Hart, *Memory Gems of Poetry and Prose* (Indianapolis, 1889), 5.

[17] Hart, *Memory Gems*, 9; L. C. Foster and Sherman Williams, *Selections for Memorizing* (Boston, 1892), iv.

[18] Harris is quoted in Herbert M. Kliebard, *The Struggle for the American Curriculum, 1893–1958* (Boston, 1986), 37; Matthew Arnold, "The Study of Poetry," *Essays in Criticism*, 2d ser. (New York, 1924), 7.

detected in nineteenth-century schoolbooks generally: that moral virtue arose from training the heart more than the intellect.[19] Moreover, the parsing and so on tended to fragment the text and could actually obscure its moral message. As a set of abridgments, the memory gem anthology may even be said to have involved a kind of cheating on discipline.

Yet, despite these crosscurrents, the structure, content, and ideology of schoolroom poetry reading remained strikingly stable as the twentieth century unfolded. First, while the term "memory gem" began fading between 1910 and 1920, the memorized recitation and its accompanying rationale did not. In his influential *The Teaching of Poetry in the High School* (1914), Arthur H. R. Fairchild reiterated that "to store the mind with the noble thoughts and the lofty sentiments of great poetry is to repel vulgar and commonplace views," as well as to provide consolation in later life. The report *Reorganization of English in Secondary Schools* (1917), which the National Council of Teachers of English (NCTE) and the National Education Association (NEA) issued jointly, agreed. Courses of study for the next three decades reflect the persistence of the practice: fifty lines a year memorized in Kansas (1927) and at least one hundred lines a year in Rochester, New York (1929); selections by "popular vote" of the class in Des Moines (1931); one poem for each tenth grade unit in Chicago (1933); passages for "sheer beauty of thought and imagery, or for expression of universal truth" in New Orleans (1946).[20]

Second, the poetry curriculum in the interwar period displayed notable continuities in prescribed texts. Juxtaposing Melvin Hix's *Approved Selections for Supplementary Reading and Memorizing* (1905, 1908), which anthologized the poetry taught through grade eight in New York, Philadelphia, Chicago, New Orleans, and "other cities," and *Required Poetry for Memorization in New York City Public Schools* (1925)—a comparison spanning the period of the "new poetry"'s emergence—reveals that approximately two-thirds of the works on the later list appeared on the earlier one (with some grade levels varying more than others). Both collections relied for the primary grades on poems expressly for children, with even more Robert Louis Stevenson and Christina Rosetti selections in the 1925 curriculum. Both contained, for grades five through eight, the following: Longfellow's "The Arrow and the Song" and "The Builders"; Bryant's "To the Fringed Gentian" and "To a Waterfowl"; "Abou Ben Adhem"; Browning's "The Year's at the Spring"; Ben Jonson's "It Is Not Growing Like a Tree"; Emerson's "The Rhodora"; Wordsworth's "The Daffodils"; Tenny-

[19] Elson, *Guardians of Tradition*, 226–27.

[20] In the Library of Congress, the latest use of the phrase "memory gem" as a title is 1924, but it is the only example from that decade. Arthur H. R. Fairchild, *Teaching of Poetry*, 92. James Fleming Hosic, comp., *Reorganization of English in Secondary Schools* (Washington, D.C., 1917). The courses of study cited are organized alphabetically by place in Special Collections, Milbank Memorial Library, Teachers College, Columbia University, New York City.

son's "The Charge of the Light Brigade"; and Shelley's "To a Skylark." Moreover, aside from the inclusion of Joyce Kilmer's "Trees," Henry Van Dyke's "Work," one poem by the popular American poet Edgar Guest, and a few more British works, the changes to the later requirements (for example, the addition of numerous patriotic poems) seem more the product of World War I and the Progressive "Americanization" movement than of innovations in poetic technique.

Furthermore, Nebraska schoolchildren in the lower grades during the mid-1920s learned almost the same works as their counterparts in New York. The Nebraska syllabus differed in including verse by midwestern "favorite sons" James Whitcomb Riley and Eugene Field (although these appeared in abundance on a 1924 Connecticut list of suggestions for memorization). The New York and Nebraska curricula also varied in some individual titles (for example, different choices from Longfellow and Lowell) but not in the character of the poems. All but one of the works "to be memorized" in the Nebraska syllabus had appeared in Hix's *Approved Selections* twenty years earlier, the exception being Oliver Wendell Holmes's "Union and Liberty." This picture of standardization modifies the historian's conventional portrait of the rift between rural and urban America in the 1920s. "Everyone knows," Mearns complained, "that [the best poetry] for the fifth year of school life is Longfellow; for the sixth year, Bryant; for the seventh year, Whittier . . . ; for the eighth year, Poe and Holmes"[21]— everyone, that is, irrespective of where they lived.

The state and local courses of study for high school English that proliferated beginning in the late 1920s reveal similar continuities over time and place. In the thirty curricula sampled, the titles for reading prescribed most frequently throughout the period 1917–39 indicate the tenacity of nineteenth-century culture: the top choices included Arnold's "Sohrab and Rustum," Whittier's "Snowbound," and *The Rime of the Ancient Mariner* (still prominent on college entrance examinations in 1935), as well as *Evangeline* and Bryant's "To a Waterfowl," with "Sir Launfal" and "Thanatopsis" close behind. Students also still regularly read—and universities demanded—Scott's "The Lady of the Lake" (often in ninth or tenth grade rather than eighth) and excerpts from Tennyson's "Idylls of the King." More recent favorites were Masefield's "Sea Fever" and Noyes's "The Highwayman," while Browning loomed large for college-bound students. Of contemporary American verse, however, only Frost's "Birches" (treated as a description of New England) appeared as often as the most widely assigned older works.

Apart from noting the deeper anxieties about changing values that permeated the interwar period,[22] one might explain those continuities, at

[21] Mearns, *Creative Youth*, 124.
[22] I have discussed those anxieties in *The Making of Middlebrow Culture* (Chapel Hill, 1992).

least for the elementary grades, by citing the difficulty of recent verse. A striking feature of the required selections prior to 1925, however, is that, by the standards of the 1990s, many are hard to read. Nevertheless, the belief that younger children should build a basis for broad study did make the presecondary classroom a less logical place for the introduction of new writing than the high school. Another constraint, presumably, was that the perception of recent poetry as amoral or crude made it less likely to win school board approval at any grade level than tried-and-true nineteenth-century vehicles for moral uplift, although the failure of most readers to detect an underside of despair (as in the case of Frost) might have counteracted that concern. The educators' assumption that students would find narrative poems most engrossing also biased their selections toward classic epics. A more tangible factor sustaining the status quo was the cost for school districts of newer teaching materials. Finally, the dissemination of recent verse depended partly on the success of publishers in securing permission to reprint copyrighted work.[23]

In any event, the "steady assignments" these various lists document constitute a graphic illustration of the discrepancy between literary production and consumption at any one time: despite the ferment created by the "new poetry" and the self-image of its practitioners, it did not much infiltrate American classrooms for two decades. In many classrooms the moral and aesthetic framework of the earlier era held as well. Charles and Frank McMurray's 1921 lesson plan for Longfellow's "Excelsior" (still required for memorization in Nebraska in 1925) remained committed to fostering "enjoyment" and "appreciation of a certain moral idea." The dominant techniques for achieving those ends were repetition, concern with meaning, and structured extraction of an ethical principle. Deciphering "difficult words and phrases" and retelling "the story" preceded a "figurative" reading: "Since the story is not to be taken literally, let us see how it should be interpreted." Although that strategy of distinguishing symbol from fact would become a sine qua non of reading modernist poetry, the latent content it here unearthed "pointed" the moral that persons with "high ideals" must show "unselfishness, courage, determination, energy." In some parts of the country, poetry also continued explicitly to augment religious instruction. Fort Worth high school students in 1939 read Longfellow (as well as some Sandburg and Frost) to develop "awe for Him who is the creator of inanimate wonders and of human beings."[24] In that case, pedagogues not only perpetuated nineteenth-century texts and outlooks but also appropriated "new poetry" for older purposes. Put another

[23] On copyright constraints, see "Course of Study in English for Rochester Senior High Schools," vol. 2, "Literature," Rochester, 1929, 219.

[24] Charles A. McMurray and Frank McMurray, *The Method of the Recitation* (New York, 1921), 329–32; "A Tentative Course of Study for Literature for the Senior High School, Fort Worth, 1939," 00.

way, the culture of the genteel tradition remained an integral part of the culture of modern America.

Nonetheless, continuity is not the whole story. Diffusion of the new occurred readily in sporadic locales. In the late 1920s, English teachers in Rochester high schools actively advocated modern poetry. So did progressive private institutions, such as Mearns's Lincoln School, affiliated with Columbia's Teachers College. In the 1930s, many high school juniors and seniors spent a week on contemporary poets. "Tracking" made a difference: the 1933 "enriched" course of study for Chicago tenth-graders incorporated four of Pound's poems and three of Eliot's along with numerous examples of early modernism. Twelfth-grade elective courses covered recent verse, supported by a section on the "new poetry" in the fourth volume of the textbook *Literature and Life*.[25] Although older verse decidedly predominated, by 1940 limited eclecticism within the bounds of standardization was the hallmark of the poetry unit in places scattered from Norfolk to Fresno.

Moreover, even the longevity of the nineteenth-century curriculum concealed a process of change. To explore poetry reading in the American school is to see, first, that literary canons do not evolve within only the "high-culture" circles of New York literary critics or elite universities. Second, however, it is to perceive the susceptibility of canonized works to multiple uses. While generations of students recited *Evangeline,* pedagogical experts, swayed by discomfiting social trends, were (however unevenly) altering the rationale for doing so.

One such theorist was Johann Friedrich Herbart. Beginning in the 1890s, Herbart's American followers popularized his belief that the elementary school should embody the "culture-epochs" through which the developing child passed. That outlook coincided with wider trends in anthropology; it infiltrated poetry instruction in the form of an emphasis on verse that either described primitive behavior or dated from a supposedly less advanced civilization. Thus it strengthened the justification for reading English ballads during the first year of high school, as well as for certain staples such as "Hiawatha."[26]

The most important American educator to come under Herbart's influence was, of course, John Dewey. Dewey shared the view that schoolwork should derive from children's natural interests but cautioned against filtering developmental stages through literary representation. Instead, he advocated a curriculum based on two general principles: fidelity to the child's experience and organization of subject matter around the needs of

[25] Edwin Greenlaw and Dudley Miles, *Literature and Life,* bk. 4 (Chicago, 1932), 743–76.
[26] Kliebard, *Struggle,* 18–20, 34, 44–49, 67–68.

a democracy. The first of these tenets, the focus of much that went under the name of progressive education in the early 1900s, implicitly rejected the concept of the mind as a storehouse. As Dewey's disciple William Heard Kilpatrick phrased it, education should be "considered as life itself and not as a mere preparation for later living." At the same time, however, other reformers advanced their own version of the connection between education and democracy by arguing that schooling should transmit practical skills geared to producing a society of efficient adults.[27]

These competing outlooks both emboldened advocates of poetry in the classroom and threw them on the defensive. The tensions informing the resulting pedagogical materials nicely illustrate that, at the level of application, discrete developments in educational theory disintegrated into approaches as eclectic as the poetry reading lists themselves. But the matter was not merely philosophical. By the eve of World War I, American high school enrollment and graduation rates had entered a period of expansion, with even sharper growth between 1920 and 1935. Although their relative importance is a subject of some debate, several factors account for the increase: the collapse of the demand for youth in manufacturing; the assimilation of the foreign-born after immigration restriction; high agricultural income per capita (outside the North); and both the proliferation of white-collar occupations and, during the depression, the disappearance of work opportunities. Whatever its sources, this burgeoning high school population created anxieties for teachers accustomed to instructing the children of educated parents. As one writer lamented, "Great numbers of students now come to the classroom without a single tendency favorable to a literary interpretation of life; and they go forth to a commercial and industrial existence which is devoid of poetic feeling." Moreover, the "soda-fountain or moving picture show" tempted both working- and middle-class students to seek easy amusement rather than the "higher pleasure" of books. Those developments made such terms as "preparation," "experience," "citizenship"—and poetry reading—part of a politics of culture inseparable from theories of learning or art.[28]

Although they evinced little engagement with pedagogical controversy, several educators writing in the second decade of the twentieth century registered the changing climate by simultaneously moderating and reiterating poetry's traditional moral functions. For instance, Arthur H. R.

---

[27] Ibid., 67, 69–122. Kilpatrick is cited in ibid., 162. On Dewey, see Robert B. Westbrook, *John Dewey and American Democracy* (Ithaca, 1992).

[28] Henry Suzallo, introduction to Arthur H. R. Fairchild, *Teaching of Poetry*, viii; Arthur H. R. Fairchild, *Teaching of Poetry*, 163. See also Lawrence A. Cremin, *American Education: The Metropolitan Experience, 1876–1980* (New York, 1988), 212–42; James Bryant Conant, *The American High School Today* (New York, 1959), 6–8; and Claudia Goldin, "How America Graduated From High School: 1910 to 1960," *Journal of Economic History*, forthcoming 1998.

Fairchild and the Harvard professor of education Charles Swain Thomas, aware of the drawbacks of rote learning, urged English teachers to nurture a child's emotional as well as intellectual understanding of a poem. Yet Fairchild claimed that great poetry stimulated only "elevated and refined" feelings, rather than a "weak sensuousness." Christianity went unmentioned, but the purpose of reading verse remained the realization of life's "eternal laws and of its enduring ideals." Fairchild's advice for tackling the words of a text paralleled his repudiation of weakness: "The true enjoyment of poetry demands effort, steadiness of purpose, sometimes even pain, to achieve it." Similarly, Thomas insisted on intensive interrogation of texts in order to elucidate a poet's message; he told students to "check every word that was not perfectly clear, master every obscure reference, and determine the grammatical relationship of each word, phrase, and clause to its neighbors."[29]

Another contemporary figure involved in teacher training, Roger Henwood Motten, initially made the case for verse in vitalist, almost mystical terms: it should be taught, he wrote in 1916, because "it is life." In the same essay, however, Motten both appeased the proponents of efficiency and upheld poetry's older moral function, pronouncing literature at once "cultural" and "practical." Motten's argument was a pedagogical juggling act, executed on the backs of the same texts as those in Hix's *Approved Selections*. In a parallel development, by World War I speech professionals had begun rejecting elocutionists' preoccupation with gesture and display. Their goal was less moral cultivation than the stimulation of speakers' minds and emotions. Yet advocates of "expression" and "oral interpretation" retained a belief in the values of discipline and control, both of which, in their view, the recitation enforced with special effectiveness.[30]

The aforementioned 1917 NCTE-NEA report performed still another balance. Its authors' three "fundamental reasons" for studying literature renamed the moral, aesthetic, and patriotic justifications of the nineteenth century but did not depart very far from them: now the goals were social and ethical, cultural, and vocational. Cognizant of the transformed high school population, the authors declared hopefully that reading was "still the chief recreation of many people." Especially for the new "vocational pupils," literature might "be of great assistance in building character and may provide a good antidote for the harmful pleasures that invite the weary workers in our cities." Fears of deteriorating taste and behavior

[29] Arthur H. R. Fairchild, *Teaching of Poetry*, 12, 101, 127, 135–37, 164; Charles Swain Thomas, *The Teaching of English in the Secondary School* (Boston, 1927), 28–32, 224.

[30] Roger Henwood Motten, "The Value of Poetry in the Schools," *Colorado College Publication*, General Series no. 88, vol. 2, no. 31 (June 1916): 239–74; Paul C. Edwards, "The Rise of Expression," in David W. Thompson, ed., *Performance of Literature in Historical Perspectives* (Lanham, Md., 1983), 529–48.

skewed the list of recommended poems in the 1917 curriculum toward nineteenth-century verse free of "the morbidly introspective, the vicious, the mentally abnormal." Yet the NCTE-NEA report, in part the result of a movement to broaden the curriculum beyond college entrance requirements, conceded that "the admission of a large foreign element into our schools" justified including some "modern" books about daily life because they would more easily sustain pupils' attention.[31]

If many educators in the years 1910–19 thus cautiously distanced themselves from their predecessors while affirming much of past practice, the curricular discussions of the 1920s and 1930s reveal the full effects of pedagogical reform and social change on prescriptions for poetry instruction. By that time, poetry's advocates knew they were fighting a rearguard action. Not only did the numbers of high school students continue to swell, but something had "come between poetry and boys and girls." A Minneapolis document mournfully reported that "a class of girls of higher than average intelligence when asked to tell which they would rather be, Gertrude Ederle, who swam the English Channel, or Edna St. Vincent Millay, voted almost unanimously in favor the champion swimmer. In their eyes hers was a more notable achievement than to have written The King's Henchman [*sic*]."[32]

To one cohort of progressive educators, Dewey and Kilpatrick's outlook promised to repel that trend. A representative figure, Sterling Andrus Leonard, declared in 1922 that the goal of reading was "not arousing appreciation of literature itself" but "an achievement of realized, true, and significant experience." Imbued with the greater psychological sophistication of the mid-1930s, the professor of education Howard Francis Seely announced a similar creed, redefining appreciation as both the cause and the consequence of "active integration of one's selfhood." From this starting point, both authors rejected memory gems, recommended only materials of "immediate interest to children," and suggested the inclusion of modern poetry to help students respond "freely, spontaneously, honestly." This subjectivity (against which Arnold had warned) eradicated the overtly moral aspect of poetry instruction. As Leonard declared, "It can hardly be stated too often that no conventional and formal 'pointing of moral' is for a moment considered here as a function of literature. Insistence on the final quatrain of *The Ancient Mariner* rather than its amazing, varied pictures, or on the tacked-on last lines of *Thanatopsis* . . . cannot be too strongly condemned." Seely likewise dissociated poetry reading from "the search for 'lessons' or 'morals'": "Personally, I wish that every En-

[31] Hosic, *Reorganization of English*, 32, 63–65, 97.
[32] Howard Francis Seely, *Enjoying Poetry in School* (Richmond, 1931), viii; "Course of Study in Literature for Junior High School," Minneapolis, 1931.

JOAN SHELLEY RUBIN

glish teacher would bury these two words 'deeper than did ever plummet sound.'"³³

These progressives also endorsed the "'demolition of teacher supremacy.'" Citing a standardized test of the capacity to judge poetic quality (a stunning, if ludicrous, example of the view of E. L. Thorndike's followers that educators could measure anything), Leonard observed that only the exceptional teacher would "fail to discover in his class pupils with distinctly better judgment than his own in matters of literary appreciation." That position led to a flurry of Columbia Teachers College doctoral dissertations designed to determine what children "liked" in poetry in order to adapt the curriculum accordingly. "We teachers are hosts," Seely explained. "The poet and pupils are our guests. As we introduce our guests to each other we shall linger with them a moment to help them get acquainted before we leave them to develop their relationship alone." In that role, teachers not only relinquished the burden of ethical instruction but also the obligation to foster the "technical" command of form or even full comprehension of meaning. Quoting the efficiency proponent Franklin Bobbitt, Leonard averred, "'One of the most mischievous superstitions of education has been that when a thing is presented it must be completely understood.'"³⁴

This perspective in turn implied teaching students an alternative approach to the printed page: instead of decoding a text, the reader was to embrace it. As Leonard phrased it, "'The literature of power' is rarely to be 'chewed and digested,' in grades [*sic*] and high school at least it is mainly to be 'apprehended'—taken hold of, that is, as genuine and living experience." Similarly, the pedagogue John Hooper condemned teachers who, when they "emphasize the element of comprehension, and fail to recognize the existence of apprehension ... preclude any possibility of encouraging feeling without knowledge." A concomitant of this view was that there was "nothing inherently hard" about poetry. Paradoxically, submission to the text—"revel[ing]" in its "music," "idea," or "artistry"—was the key to the appreciation associated with the integrated self. Mearns approvingly reported that a student editor, reading a classmate's poem, had commented that the author was "'too fine for thinking; she is great when she's herself.'" Forced memorization and "drill," or even reports, were banished from the procedure.³⁵

³³ Sterling Andrus Leonard, *Essential Principles of Teaching Reading and Literature* (Philadelphia, 1922), 49, 52, 102, 209, 226, 370–437; Seely, *Enjoying Poetry*, 28, 65, 91. See also John Hooper, *Poetry in the New Curriculum* (Brattleboro, Vt., 1932).
³⁴ Leonard, *Teaching Reading and Literature*, 56, 212; Seely, *Enjoying Poetry*, 145.
³⁵ Leonard, *Teaching Reading and Literature*, 201–2; Hooper, *Poetry*, 38; Mearns, *Creative Youth*, 19.

If this method weakened the teacher's moral authority, however, it had its own moral implications, because in the long run the emphasis on ease had the prospect of boosting readership. Hence the "experience" curriculum promised to stabilize high culture despite students who came from homes without "somebody reading beside the lamp." Licensing the substitution of less demanding texts to give "boys of coarse fiber" reading they would "like" might also be regarded as an early example of "dumbing down" the curriculum in the name of relevance to students' lives. In addition, Mearns and others specifically yoked poetry instruction to defending or promoting the purity of American young people. (This was true despite or, arguably, because of the sexual implications of surrending to "experience"; one might hypothesize that casting poetry in those terms promised to idealize and hence contain the sexual impulses of adolescents.) Thus, by entitling his account of his poetry classes at the Lincoln School *Creative Youth* (1925), Mearns implicitly refuted the scandalous portrait Samuel Hopkins Adams had drawn in *Flaming Youth* two years earlier. Less confidently, another group of teachers placed both Whittier's "Snowbound" and Frost's "The Death of the Hired Man" under the heading "The Happiness of Home-Keeping Hearts"—as if to ensure that students stayed by the fireside.[36]

In 1935 the "experience" model became the basis for another NCTE-sponsored project, *An Experience Curriculum in English*. "The class," its authors recommended, "should be a rather informal literary club in which the teacher is simply the most experienced member." Sharing "moral sentiments" (as in both "Abou Ben Adhem" and Sandburg's "Prayers of Steel") and "worthy expressions of patriotism" (Emerson's "Concord Hymn") remained objectives, as did the appreciation of technique and rhythm ("Sea Fever"), but all reading experiences that fostered the "enlargement of the individual" carried equal weight. Throughout the interwar period, this curriculum also filtered into state and local courses of study in a number of ways. Thirteen years after Fairchild's paean to hard work, Kansas educators—still assigning in high school "The Lady of the Lake," *Evangeline*, "The Vision of Sir Launfal," "Sohrab and Rustum," *The Ancient Mariner*, and "Snowbound"—recommended that "nothing hard or technical should be attempted" and "nothing should be burdensome." The course of study for Kansas City elementary schools in 1932 likewise condemned past practice: "Too often we have selected poems unrelated to the experiences of children and thus beyond their comprehension. We have also tried to explain the meaning of difficult phrases, allusions, and finally have asked

---

[36] Leonard, *Teaching Reading and Literature,* 125, 248; "A Tentative Course of Study for Literature for the Senior High School," Fort Worth, 1939, 24.

the children to state the poem in their own words, thus killing all love for the poem." The Rochester innovators warned against concluding that "even the selecting of certain words or phrases for comment in some way violates the spirit of the poem" but sought to have pupils "experience the quickening and intensity of the emotions" from a "surrender" to the "mood" of a poet. The most florid formulation came from Montgomery County, Maryland, in 1939: "Literature is not the written expression in the form of the essay, novel, poetry, or drama, but rather is the living growth experienced by a person as he cooperates with the realities of life. . . . It is the expanding living made possible for him through the symbolized representation (words)." By 1946 the Florida state curriculum declared succinctly that "the old analytical process . . . seems to be gone."[37]

Nonetheless there were ties between the "experience" curriculum and the approaches that both preceded and survived alongside it. Given the similarity between conversion and submission to feeling, the religious dimension was not entirely absent despite the erosion of moral instruction. Moreover, the method of "apprehension" magnified the sensual delight buried in the conceit of "gems." To go further, these elements signal the persistence in American culture of tendencies antithetical to the tough-mindedness or "terrible honesty" that Ann Douglass has recently attributed to the 1920s. Outside the classroom, this romantic mode of reading informed the public performances of Edna St. Vincent Millay, who conveyed, in addition, the sexual component of surrender to the text. It also surfaced in the counsel that Carl and Mark Van Doren offered general audiences faced with modernist poems: for example, regarding Stevens, "His poems are most to be enjoyed by one who does not, at any rate in the beginning, worry about what they say." Other aspects of the "experience" curriculum suggest larger cultural connections as well. First, the abandonment of "storage" and preparation was perfectly adapted to a society in which spending was replacing delayed gratification. Similarly, the premium on ease of apprehension may measure the pervasiveness of Americans' expectations about the ability to assimilate sound and images quickly and effortlessly that movies and radio left in their wake. Anyone who has ever formally studied—or taught—literature can appreciate the point that overanalysis can kill the joy of reading, yet that position rests on an *assumption*, an animus against difficulty. As such, it throws into relief Eliot's countervailing view that "poetry in our civilization . . . must be difficult"; it

[37] National Council of Teachers of English, *An Experience Curriculum in English* (New York, 1935), 20, 22, 55–59; "Course of Study for High Schools, Part II, English" (1921), State of Kansas, 1927, 14; "Course of Study in English for Grades I–VI," Kansas City, 1932, 36; "Course of Study," Rochester, 210; "Design Bulletin, Junior and Senior High School English," Montgomery County, Md., September 1939, 1; "A Brief Guide to Teaching English in the Secondary School," Florida State Department of Education, 1946, 41.

argues that teachers abetted the modernist pose of distance from ordinary readers by failing to convey how to read for complexity; and it supplies a neglected context for the emergence of the New Criticism, which made detailed explication into another kind of religion.[38]

In addition, the progressives' curriculum further illuminates the extent to which the pursuit of intense experience gripped middle-class Americans contending with a bureaucratized, impersonal society. The attachment of that quest to poetry reading is fraught with irony, because it was the distance of the printed page from "real life" that so troubled figures such as Randolph Bourne and Jane Addams. No less (but no more) than other manifestations of the search for experience, "reveling" in a text as a means of "self-integration" might deflect attention from social change. The progressives' deliberate avoidance of moral instruction was in a sense the first step down a road that dead-ended in self-absorbed individualism. It was on just this score, in fact, that Dewey and others eventually challenged the Progressive Education Association, arguing in the 1930s that the preoccupation with personal liberation obstructed genuine reform.

That critique, however, should not lead to the conclusion that conceiving poetry reading as experience was the brainchild of an elite bent on social control. For one thing, submission to the text could subvert not only reform impulses but also the discipline necessary to sustain a capitalist economy. (In any event, escape was not the progressive educators' primary vocabulary; connection to immediate life was.) For another thing, despite the heavy component of individualism, community and democracy had a place in the "experience" framework. Seely, for example, specified that discovering through reading "kinship with the lives of others" would enable students to "grow" not only as "individuals" but also "as members of the social group." Mearns, invoking Dewey, went further, pleading that the "spiritualization of public education" was the "hope of civilization." In fact, by appropriating some "new poetry" (Lowell, Robinson, the early Pound) to those social purposes, Mearns arguably stripped it of what Williams Carlos Williams, writing to Monroe, identified as part of modernist poetry's essence: its "tincture of disestablishment."[39]

The vision of poetry reading's social functions accounts for a second practice that coexisted with the "experience" approach, that is, the reduc-

[38] Ann Douglass, *Terrible Honesty* (New York, 1995), 191–93; Carl Van Doren and Mark Van Doren, *American and British Literature since 1890*, rev. ed. (New York, 1939), 51. Eliot is quoted in Robert E. Spiller et al., *Literary History of the United States*, 3d ed. (New York, 1963), 1342. See also Craig S. Abbott, "Modern American Poetry: Anthologies, Classrooms, and Canons," *College Literature* 17 (1990): 209–21.

[39] Seely, *Enjoying Poetry*, 113, 137; Mearns, *Creative Youth*, 28, 128; Harriet Monroe, *A Poet's Life: Seventy Years in a Changing World* (New York, 1938), 270. For the class argument, see Cary Nelson, *Repression and Recovery: Modern American Poetry and the Politics of Cultural Memory, 1910–1945* (Madison, 1989).

tion of a poem to instrumental content and the construction of categories along thematic lines: not only "The Happiness of Home-Keeping Hearts" but also, for example, "Extending our Experience with Respect to Community Living," under which the 1939 Montgomery County curriculum placed both "Paul Revere's Ride" and *Evangeline*. Although it slighted feelings, this strategy was not entirely incompatible with giving oneself over to poetic emotion, because educators reasoned that experiencing poetry aided students in grasping its theme. As the United States faced the rise of fascism and, later, the cold war, however, these thematic rubrics conveyed more pointed messages. "America may be in danger of becoming smug and gullible and materialistic," the 1939 Fort Worth course of study declared by way of introduction to a section entitled "Spirit of the Western World," but "there is as yet within her the leaven of democratic and religious principles which will protect her from the various 'isms' that threaten the world." The same curriculum listed "Abu Ben Adhem" as an example of "World Fellowship," whereas "Sea Fever" served to inculcate the lesson that "England has been the democratic leader—meeting the challenge of the sea."[40] These uses resuscitated the patriotism prominent in nineteenth- and early-twentieth-century poetry instruction but reinforced the progressives' disregard for analyzing form and language. Another result of the stress on theme was, again, a distortion of some poets' avant-garde or alienated stance: for example, the 1932 Indiana secondary English syllabus listed Amy Lowell's "Patterns" under "Poems That Tell a Story," precisely the opposite of what she and other Imagists intended; likewise, the Chicago 1933 course of study grouped all its examples of early modernism under "Developing a Feeling of Pride and Appreciation for the Nation of Today."[41] The postwar assumption that most American children required schooling for "life adjustment" further strengthened the reduction to content, because, with the humanities under siege, linking literature to "knowledge of, practice in, and zeal for democratic processes" provided the justification for teaching it at all.[42]

Long before reader-response theory gained currency, American teachers were telling students that poetry took shape in an "active" process of "creative reading" that involved both author and audience.[43] To see the way teachers themselves participated in that process over time is to discern

[40] The section contained both Sandburg's "Prayers of Steel" and excerpts from "The Bay Psalm Book." "A Tentative Course of Study for Literature for the Senior High School, Fort Worth, 1939," 52–60, 93–116.

[41] "Tentative Course of Study for Secondary Schools in Indiana, Grades 7–12," 1932, 254; "A Course of Study in Literature—10B," Chicago Public Schools, 1933, 8.

[42] Kliebard, *Struggle*, 251.

[43] The term "creative reading" became popular in the 1920s. See, for example, Edwin Greenlaw and Clarence Stratton, *Literature and Life*, bk. 2 (Chicago, 1922), iv. 4–6.

the importance of determining not only what was published and canonized but also how it was used. An even fuller picture of poetry at school, including its shifting moral functions, necessitates a closer look at textbooks,
anthologies, and reminiscences; understanding poetry's wider status depends as well on exploring other institutions that disseminated it. By distinguishing the history of reading from literary history, that investigation
would itself be a moral enterprise, producing the inclusive record of cultural life a democratic society requires.

CHAPTER THIRTEEN

Talking about Sex: Early-Twentieth-Century Radicals and Moral Confessions

CHRISTINE STANSELL

When Hutchins Hapgood looked back on the heyday of bohemian radicalism in the years 1910 to 1919, it was the New Women he saw as the movers of history: "When the world began to change, the restlessness of women was the main cause."[1] "Restlessness" alluded to the sexual liberalism widely ascribed to bohemian women, who were known for sleeping with men to whom they weren't married, living with their lovers, and eschewing marriage for multiple love affairs. Even in the first decade of the century, such behavior would have rendered any respectable woman an outcast. But by the second decade, late-Victorian sexual mores were giving way to an erotic ethos that celebrated women's sexual desire for men and legitimated youthful experience before marriage for both sexes.

The radicals were leaders in this transformation of a nineteenth-century moral framework that condemned extramarital sexuality for both men and women (although in practice allowing men some latitude) to a modern, contextual understanding of sex, both inside and outside marriage, as an expression of a developing self. The change did not affect everyone— in the early twentieth century (as well as today) many Americans continued to hold to the precepts of the older tradition. But it did shape notions of modernity so thoroughly that, over time, the contextualist ethic came to dominate American culture. In the shift, the sources of moral legitimation for sex also changed from religious and institutional to social and psychological. Nineteenth-century, middle-class Americans understood sex to be permissible when it was embedded in marriage—God's will as

---

[1] Hutchins Hapgood, *Victorian in the Modern World* (New York, 1939), 152.

ordained in holy matrimony. The early-twentieth-century radicals abandoned marriage as the locus of morality and upheld instead a principle of honesty among equals: the acknowledgment of sexual interests among a community of freely participating men and women. Truth telling and equality became the means to distinguish a desirable and permissible sexuality, whomever the parties and whatever the context.

Across the Left intelligentsia, the sexually emancipated Woman moved to the center of a program of modernist transformation, the protagonist of a deep-seated historical movement that would equalize the vexed relations between the sexes. Freely expressed sexuality, inside but especially outside marriage, would be the means of achieving a Whitmanian democratic sociability and reciprocity between men and women. Restless women were seen as leaders in a program of cultural regeneration, an avant-garde who could bridge outmoded Victorian divisions between the sexes. Free love became a precept of revolution, a virtual synonym for the equality of men and women. Earlier generations of women's rights and socialist thinkers had found such associations abhorrent to their goals of improving the situations of women and working people. But for the new radicals, free love was, purportedly, a way of enacting a feminism shared by both sexes. Bohemian radicals such as Hapgood saw themselves as an admiring audience for and coconspirators of the heroines of the day. They enunciated fond expectations of the benefits that would accrue to all from women's eventual triumph.[2] Free love was the democratic solvent that could remove the barriers between the sexes.

The contribution of early-twentieth-century moderns was to create for free love a moral basis in honesty and to tie sexual freedom to an emerging cultural concern with psychological depth and personal authenticity. Among artists, political activists, and intellectuals in Chicago and New York, free-love feminism produced a stream of sexual conversation and revelation. In books, salon discussions, letters, and plays, the radical intelligentsia made their attempts to create free-love arrangements the subject of intense "free expression," a political watchword of the day that affiliated the free-speech battles of the Industrial Workers of the World (IWW) with censorship litigation and the heterodox speech of salons. Talking about sexual matters—erotic exchanges, configurations of partners, the attendant emotions of passion, jealousy, humiliation, rapture—became seen as a political program in itself.

There were nineteenth-century antecedents on which the radicals drew, particularly a tradition of Romantic confession, mostly male. And middle-class Victorian culture had been rife with sex talk in its own peculiar, deflected ways: in the reform literature about prostitution, for example.

---

[2] Mari Jo Buhle, *Women and American Socialism, 1870–1920* (Urbana, Ill., 1981), 262–63.

Women were essentially banned from Romantic confession but not from reform writing, because reform language allowed them to frame sexual discussion in a melodramatic language of female sexual victimization. The garrulous exponents of modern free love broke with this asymmetrical pattern by transforming the male Romantic confessional soliloquy into a conversation between the sexes that ostensibly accorded women an erotic voice. The transformation of sexual mores was thus linked to the emergence of a literary and conversational space for dialogue. Sex became entangled with communication: a matter for talk, understanding, and disclosure. It became the prism through which a central problem of modern social life, the troubled relations of men and women, was revised and rearticulated, under the aegis of bohemian feminism.

Considered from our own vantage point, the suppositions of free love are now woven through so much of American life that it is difficult to appreciate its shock value for earlier generations. But in the early twentieth century, the assault on sexual respectability was in the "nature of a crusade," as one Greenwich Village artist put it. The "spirit of revolt," of unimpeded expressiveness between the sexes, was even strong in the dancing at the Liberal Club: "as you clutched your feminine partner and led her through the crowded dance floor at the Club, you felt you were doing something for the progress of humanity, as well as for yourself and, in some cases, for her."[3] Love without marriage was seen, the writer Floyd Dell remarked wryly, as infinitely superior to conventional partnerships—"its immediate indulgence brought the world, night by night, a little nearer to freedom and Utopia."[4] This was so much the case that a friend of the lovers John Reed and Louise Bryant joked after their quiet wedding in 1916 that they needed to hush up the matter lest they lose face in the Village: "it's a terrible *'scandal'* and is bound to get out."[5]

The elevation of sex outside of marriage to a political principle derived from a long political/intellectual tradition. Free-love doctrine originated among utopian socialists in France and England in the early nineteenth century—most notably Charles Fourier—and gained currency among labor radicals in antebellum America. Disciples maintained that erotic love was a sacred human capacity that, by its very nature, stemmed from voluntary attachment. To circumscribe it with the sanctions of church and state—which is what legal marriage did—stifled, indeed desecrated it. For men, the loss of personal liberty in legal marriage spawned possessiveness

---

[3] Lawrence Langner, *The Magic Curtain* (New York, 1951), 68. Langner was the impresario of the new downtown New York theater.

[4] Floyd Dell, *Homecoming* (New York, 1933), 289.

[5] Bryant to Reed, December 9, 1916, John Reed Collection, Houghton Library, Harvard University.

and tyranny, and for women, subjection and enslavement. From the beginning, then, free love was allied through its critique of marriage with women's rights. Free-love doctrine stressed sexual responsibility and a higher, nobler monogamy unfettered by legal or ecclesiastical authority. Mostly, adherents took care to distance themselves from "varietism," the condoning of multiple partnerships. Their radicalism, in Victorian terms, lay not in advocating promiscuity but in insisting on women's sexuality, the reciprocal nature of sexual attraction, the importance of eros to social well-being, and the moral claims of sex outside marriage.[6]

There was a distinct and unbroken thread of free-love thought in the United States from the 1830s through the turn of the century, intertwined with other kinds of iconoclasm, especially "free thought," or religious disbelief. But free love was a marginal movement, hardly worth noticing in terms of its historical effect (except for free-lovers' contributions to the birth control movement). Mostly free-lovers clustered in little knots of true believers, sectarian, distinctly odd, and, by 1900, quite old, with the leading practitioners in their seventies. At the turn of the century, the movement was concentrated in the Pacific Northwest, with an anarchist/free-love commune on an island in Puget Sound—Emma Goldman dubbed it the anarchist graveyard—and a newspaper published in Vancouver. The devotees, who were also adherents of nudism and vegetarianism (one resident of the Puget Sound Commune lived year-round in a stump) were mostly working-class, native-born radicals, along with a few Russian Jews and middle-class eccentrics. Outside the Northwest, the most important center of the tradition was New York City, where a few free-thinking physicians openly championed contraception and sexual indulgence as health measures.[7]

But while free-lovers were a tiny minority at the turn of the century, they were also great talkers and inveterate proselytizers. Scattered throughout the country and upheld in their fervor by subscriptions to free-love newspapers, various village atheists in the late nineteenth century impressed their opinions on others , especially on the inquiring young. Some of the later radicals had encountered free love in their youths in the persons of

[6] Ellen Carol Dubois, "Feminism and Free Love," unpublished paper in my possession; Linda Gordon, *Woman's Body, Woman's Right: A Social History of Birth Control in America* (New York, 1974), chap. 5. The most important exceptions who did advocate "varietism" were the residents of John Humphrey Noyes's Oneida Colony, who practiced "complex marriage."

[7] Patricia Brandt, "Organized Free Thought in Oregon: the Oregon State Secular Union," *Oregon Historical Quarterly* 87 (Summer 1986): 176; Charles Pierce Le Warne, *Utopias on Puget Sound, 1885–1915* (Seattle, 1975), 175–76, 189; Carlos A. Schwantes, "Free Love and Free Speech on the Pacific Northwest Frontier," *Oregon Historical Society Quarterly* 82 (Spring 1981): 271–93; Taylor Stoehr, introduction to *Free Love in America* (New York, 1979); Lawrence R. Veysey, *The Communal Experience: Anarchist and Mystical Counter-Cultures in America* (New York, 1973), 39–43 and passim.

admired and charismatic older rebels: an openly adulterous aunt who was a devotee of Victoria Woodhull (the most famed free-lover the nineteenth century produced); a cross-dressing neighbor lady; a physician who was a free-love publicist for contraceptive techniques.[8] The most common encounters were probably between a wide-eyed young person, male or female, and a free-thinking man of society, prone to dark philosophical reflections on marriage and love within the privacy of his study. Such was the meeting, for example, of the teenager Floyd Dell with George Cram Cook in Davenport, Iowa, in the early 1900s. Cook was a Harvard graduate who had returned to his hometown to live on the land as an American Tolstoy; his sex radicalism was part of his assault on provincial convention. As he held forth to his young friend on Nietzsche and monism, he also lectured about the oppressions of marriage and the sacredness of eros and plotted aloud about seducing a young anarchist actress in Chicago.[9]

For such free-thinking men of education and standing, free-love thought at the turn of the century tinged social rebellion and transformed a Victorian rakishness into an intellectually justified revolt against bourgeois life. The romantic involvements of Charles Erskine Scott Wood show how a man of social position could graft free love's critique of monogamy onto the long-standing privilege of a Victorian gentleman to engage covertly in extramarital sexual affairs. Wood was another well-heeled philosophical anarchist, a lawyer in Portland, Oregon, with a lucrative law practice, a grand house, a well-born and devoted wife, and many children. But through the 1890s, as he became a city father, he also crafted a counter-persona, the lonely rebel. He dressed in bohemian garb—a long, flowing cape and broad-brimmed hat—and turned his wife's sedate gatherings into masques and poetry readings with just a touch of aestheticism and decadence.[10]

Wood's proximity to the Puget Sound colony put him in touch with an active free-love tradition. After 1900, as he began to defend labor radicals, he became friendly with Emma Goldman and other working-class free-

[8] The follower of Woodhull was the brazenly adulterous aunt of Charmian London, Bay Area radical and wife of Jack London; see Clarice Stasz, *American Dreamers: Charmian and Jack London* (New York, 1984), 14, 94. Mabel Dodge Luhan was seduced as an adolescent, so she claimed, by a neighbor woman dressed as a man; see Christopher Lasch, "Mabel Dodge Luhan: Sex as Politics," in *The New Radicalism in America, 1889–1963* (New York, 1965), 114. Elizabeth Gurley Flynn's high school sweetheart was the son of Dr. William Robinson, leading free-love exponent of birth control. Rosalyn Fraad Baxandall, *Words on Fire: The Life and Writing of Elizabeth Gurley Flynn* (New Brunswick, N.J., 1987), 6.

[9] Cook and Dell's relationship can be traced in the Cook Papers in the Berg Collection at the New York Public Library.

[10] Edwin R. Bingham, "Experiment in Launching a Biography: Three Vignettes of Charles Erskine Scott Wood," *Huntington Library Quarterly* 35 (May 1972): 221–39; Erskine Wood, *Life of C. E. S. Wood* (N. P. 1978). The latter is available at the Huntington Library, San Marino, California.

lovers. The audience for his free-love views were local women he converted in the course of seducing them. A long line of lovers winds forlornly through the Wood papers: his secretary; fellow members of the local branch of the Socialist Party; a young New Womanish physician; his wife; and the feminist Sara Bard Field, his longest-lasting, longest-suffering, most obsessively devoted lover (she outlasted all the competition and eventually became his second wife).

For Wood, free love justified his excursions outside marriage and at the same time allowed him to hold on to marriage's safeties. In a peculiarly fin-de-siècle manner, he melded anarchist tenets of personal liberty, Romantic sonorities about Truth and Beauty, and a lyrical celebration of female sexual power (Field was "Circe" to his "Ulysses") to embellish his seductions and betrayals with a higher morality. Free-love principles prompted him to avow honesty about his involvements with all the women, but in fact, principles usually failed at the mark. Sara Bard Field and his wife, Nannie Wood, continually made dreadful discoveries, slopping through great puddles of indiscretion into which his "great love"—the measure of "the pulsing thought of modern man"—had overflowed.[11]

Such stories indicate that the familiar demarcation between Victorian prudery and modern sexual freedom was very much a retrospective creation of the twentieth century. Although Wood's polygamous career certainly gained support and momentum after the turn of the century, he began his extramarital forays in the 1890s and experienced no difficulty in finding partners. Memoirs of the fin de siècle often hint at a vast moral wreckage beneath the surface of late-Victorian bourgeois family life, sexual secrets that involved covert revisions and subversions of the reigning code of marriage. This was especially true of the men—polygamous fathers, philandering uncles—but the women, too, could carry on: lesbian aunts, adulterous mothers. As children, the early moderns encountered Victorians who under the cover of high-sounding ideals had woven free love into the comfortable fabric of bourgeois life.

At the turn of the century, eastern European immigrants began to infuse new life into this fading, even genteel American free love tradition and to reinvigorate the opposition to bourgeois sexual hypocrisy. Russian anarchists introduced free love into the ferment of the immigrant intelligentsia and the syndicalist movement, eschewing the socialists' conservatism on sexual matters by insisting on a connection between revolution and erotic emancipation. This was mostly an intellectuals' phenomenon:

[11] C. E. S. Wood to John Reed, March 2, 1910, John Reed Collection, Houghton Library, Harvard University. The convoluted saga of Wood's entanglements and his relations with Field can be followed in the C. E. S. Wood Collection, Huntington Library, San Marino, California.

the masses of immigrants never shared the free-love views advanced by spectacled New Women and bookish male zealots in the cafés of New York and Chicago. But the result of the immigrant intellectuals' interest was, nonetheless, to make available to the broader radical intelligentsia a charged association between working-class militance and free love. In many quarters of the Left, sexual emancipation came to seem an attribute of a newly ennobled and politically farseeing people.

In Russia, notions of free love dated back to the 1860s, when Chernyshevsky's Nihilist tract on the relations of women and men, *What Is to Be Done*, had electrified the radical intelligentsia. Chernyshevsky celebrated the joys of voluntary union; he judged women's subjection in legal marriage to be the basis of other social tyrannies. The ideas commanded the allegiance of Russian radicals through the 1890s and circulated throughout eastern Europe as well, following the paths of exiles and expatriates.[12] Politicized young men and women who emigrated, whether to London, Paris, New York, or Chicago, carried free love in their ideological baggage.[13]

Living out of wedlock was not for the pious or faint hearted, but neither was it flatly ostracized, at least by the immigrant Left. The emigré Jewish press affirmed at least some precepts of the free-love critique. Poets warned young women to beware the funereal dirge of the wedding march, journalists translated the sensational works of European sexual emancipation—Ibsen, Strindberg—even before they were available in English.[14] In a broader immigrant youth culture, free-love discussion was folded into a more general rebellion against traditional family restrictions. Shorn of its overt politics, the affirmation of voluntary love may have appealed, if only for a moment, to daughters who were both flirting with radicalism and kicking up their heels as high rollers in the dance halls and nickelodeons in the face of their parents' dismay.

But whatever the impact of the politicos' free-love enthusiasms in working-class communities, the link they created between proletarian life and sexual freedom was arresting to middle-class radicals. While nineteenth-century socialists had represented workers as virtuous upholders of sexual morality and monogamy who struggled valiantly against the debasing effects of capitalism, twentieth-century radicals often imagined working people to be blessed with the rich emancipatory benefits of a prescient sexual experimentation that the timid American middle class was only beginning to venture on its own. Emma Goldman, who was seen as a voice of the "people," played a critical role in developing the association between

---

[12] Richard Stites, *The Women's Liberation Movement in Russia: Feminism, Nihilism, and Bolshevism, 1860–1939* (Princeton, 1978), chap. 4.

[13] See, for example, Konrad Bercovici, *It's the Gypsy in Me* (New York, 1941), 25–32; Alice Wexler, *Emma Goldman: An Intimate Life* (New York, 1984), 57.

[14] Buhle, *Women and American Socialism*, 261.

class and sexual liberation. As Goldman expanded her political provenance after 1905 beyond the immigrant and labor Left, she became the chief Americanizer of immigrant free love, popularizing the fundamentals to heterogeneous audiences in lectures such as "Marriage and Love," "Free Love," and "Sex Problems."

In the hands of the intelligentsia, the contemptible "Puritanism" of the culture—a key term of the moment—thus had both a critical and an affirmative thrust: critical of the supposedly tepid American middle class, celebratory of the purportedly life-embracing revolutionary workers. In part this duality was structured by an old tradition of erotic voyeurism across class lines. Victorians had also believed the laboring classes to be inured to bourgeois sexual morality, although they judged them harshly for this. The departure of the radical moderns lay in their image of a supposed working-class libertinism as a political ideal that might inspire and invigorate middle-class private life and undo the pernicious effects of sexual hypocrisy.

Hutchins Hapgood, Harvard graduate, newspaper writer, philosophical anarchist, and man-about-town, played a leading role in putting the idealization of plebeian free love into play among native-born radicals. Hapgood began his journalistic career in New York in the 1890s. Along with other democratic realists of the moment—like his friend and newspaper colleague Abraham Cahan, the Russian Jewish immigrant writer—he helped transform the abstract moral schemas of the sunlight-and-shadows genre of urban observation into a more particularized ethnography of working-class life. Hapgood was one of the first New York writers to become fascinated with the Lower East Side as a place of rich culture and teeming "human interest." After 1900 he published two books of his rambles about the neighborhood, *Spirit of the Ghetto,* a philo-Semitic account of Jewish American urban culture, and *Autobiography of a Thief,* a "human document" of a pickpocket. By 1905, Hapgood was married to Neith Boyce, a serious and ambitious novelist of New Woman sensibility, and had two small children. Always under financial pressure to publish, Hapgood found himself at a loss for new material in New York and set off to Chicago to locate fresh deposits of human interest, leaving Boyce and his children at home in Westchester County. At that moment Chicago was a city brimming with literary potentiality: lots of "bully material," he wrote Boyce, sure to yield the "original and corking point of view." [15]

[15] For biographical details, see Hapgood's autobiography *Victorian in the Modern World* and Ellen Kay Trimberger's introductions in her edited collection of letters written by Hapgood and Boyce to each other, *Intimate Warriors: Portraits of a Modern Marriage, 1899–1944* (New York, 1991). The phrases about his writing come from Hapgood's letter to Neith Boyce, September 28, 1905, Hapgood Family Papers, Beinecke Library, Yale University.

Hapgood was looking to escape the limits of the genre of the urban picturesque he had tapped so successfully in New York by turning to a full-length study of a representative American workingman. It was a promising moment to make the move. The year 1905 signaled the emergence of Chicago as the capital of the revolutionary labor movement when the founding congress of the IWW met there that summer. The city was, to Hapgood's mind, more radical in its plebeian aspirations than New York: "the hot-bed of the Middle West, the place where labor is most riotous, most expressive, where the workingman abounds in his own sense and has formed an atmosphere of democracy extending far beyond his own class."[16] The months in Chicago he spent with working-class anarchists and liberal sympathizers of labor at Hull House and the University of Chicago were a political turning point, he felt, changing him from a genial man-about-town into a seasoned supporter of the labor movement. The sojourn resulted in two books. *The Spirit of Labor* was a depiction of Anton Johanssen, an anarchist trade unionist. *An Anarchist Woman* was an account of a free-love affair between two leading figures in Johanssen's circle: Terry Carlin, a working-class bohemian and anarchist (later to be Eugene O'Neill's companion and drinking partner) and his companion Marie, a former prostitute.

Hapgood's subject was, supposedly, the spirit of labor, which he attributed to the syndicalist militants who challenged the old guard in the Chicago Federation of Labor. But the writing would slip into sex talk, despite his assurances to a fretting Boyce back home that he had resisted the temptation to write a "sex novel," since the anarchists turned out to be committed free-lovers with no compunctions about "varietism." They changed partners and living arrangements at will. Married women tolerated their spouses' affairs because, as a cheerful Margaret Johanssen tactfully put it of her husband, Anton, "the need to work and love and have pleasure among many men and women"—his sexual adventures afield—brought interest and life into their marriage.[17] While the book managed to establish Johanssen's intellectual and political trajectory as the defining axis, the sexual plot often threatened to derail the affair, enticing readers with references to the hero's picaresque sexual adventures and the titillating, shifting combinations of brothers and sisters in the movement.

Much of Hapgood's exposition of life among the "other half" was well known from magazine fiction and social investigation, but in the discovery of plebeian free love he had undoubtedly hit on an "original and corking point of view." *The Spirit of Labor* eroticized the subject of labor and the figure of the radical workingman, affirming a connection between working-class life and erotic license that sympathizers had always before denied.

---

[16] Hutchins Hapgood, *The Spirit of Labor* (New York, 1907), 12.
[17] Ibid., 168.

Hapgood had set out to describe the "expressiveness" of the American worker; it turned out to be, in good measure, a superabundance of eros. The atmosphere of democracy that beckoned across class lines was sexual as well as industrial, a liberalized regime of heterosexual love.

Profligate workers, once the depraved others of the Victorian literature of poverty, figured in this framework as positive points of reference. Although free love also had currency among intellectuals, Hapgood noted approvingly that revolutionary workers were the avant-garde. "Very anarchistic ideas about all have their birthplace in the laboring class," he lectured Boyce.[18] Hapgood was quite a sexual adventurer himself; he suspended his affairs for only the briefest time after he married. Yet the sophisticated New Yorker sometimes felt himself something of a naïf in the fast-paced Chicago working-class set. The psychoanalytic vocabulary of repression was not yet available to him to articulate his own timidities, but notions of Comstockery and Puritanism were.

In *An Anarchist Woman,* the sexual interests that were muted in the Johanssen book moved to center stage. Purportedly an investigation of the social conditions of working-class women's lives, the book turned out to be the "sex novel" that Boyce feared was in the works. The sexual narrative subsumed the material on poverty and working conditions to join a Victorian story of women's sexual redemption with a modern exploration of the extremities of heterosexual feeling. Hapgood's Marie was a working-class innocent, forced as an adolescent into exploitative work that made her vulnerable to the temptations of the fast life of the dance halls and streets. There were many fictionalized versions of such accounts in circulation in the early twentieth century, novels and progressives' philanthropic testimonials about needy women who fell prey to sexual vice and were rescued by noble benefactors, tender suitors, and settlement house workers.[19]

Hapgood, however, was an ambitious literary man, not a hack, who was interested in escaping formulas rather than recycling them. *An Anarchist Woman* pulled the rescue tale out of its persistently Victorian preoccupations and placed it within a different moral register by posing free love rather than marriage as the agent of redemption. Terry Carlin, wild-eyed

[18] Hapgood to Boyce, October 9, 1905, Hapgood Family Papers.

[19] Whatever the actualities of the biography, Hapgood's rendering of his heroine's coming-of-age partook of the highly sexualized understanding of workingwomen current in liberal social investigation at the time that saw promiscuity as a major social problem but attributed it to environmental rather than moral causes. Hardship, not innate depravity, produced in young girls an understandable "desire to taste pleasures, to escape into a world of congenial companionship," which usually ended disastrously, as Jane Addams succinctly put the common view of reformers. Rescue required the intervention of sympathetic friends, be they settlement workers or decent, loving men, who provided hapless women with healthful pleasures and affinities: social clubs, decent work, marriage, and family life. Jane Addams, *Twenty Years at Hull House* (New York, 1910), 245.

proletarian and reader of Nietzsche, rescued Marie from the streets and took her to reign over his bohemian ménage, reading philosophy and po- etry, smoking incessantly, and, in the evenings, entertaining an anarchist salon in their "three little slummy rooms."[20] Both had love affairs with oth- ers in the course of Hapgood's narrative, shifting arrangements that at once reclaimed Marie from a life of debased passions and served, through the extreme emotional turmoil they engendered in her, to turn her into an anguished modern heroine living on the sexual edge.

Hapgood's experience as a man-about-town in New York had taught him the literary benefits of crossing the lines that separated him from his material, the piquance the writer might create in the text from reminding readers of his own proximity to the strange life he described. He became something of a free-lover himself, on equal footing with the others in mix- ing and matching bed partners, drawn into an affair with Marie (quite pos- sibly with Terry Carlin's collaboration).[21] A habit of womanizing that he had once, when he was wooing Boyce in the 1890s, deplored in himself acquired a wholly new meaning as a political strategy. For a literary radical in 1905, sex was the means to escape his "leisure class" psychology and propel him out of the voyeurism of the slumming journalist into a politi- cally and emotionally potent identification with working-class aspirations. "These last two months have meant a great deal to me," he informed Boyce, who was ever more lonely and anxious as the Chicago experiment devel- oped. "They have made me see the real sadness of things more deeply than I ever did before and they have removed almost the last vestige of snobbishness of the 'class' feeling that I had. My relations in past years with thieves, vaudevillists etc., etc., seem now to me quite unimportant, socially. But these working people and the radical atmosphere in which the thought of the working class results—this seems significant to me in a tremendous almost terrible way, and the personalities—many of them— fascinate, please sadden and excite me."[22] The lofty rhetoric concealed a code of sexual involvement—the key words "fascinate," "please," and "excite"—discernible to a practiced eye, that of a fearful wife.

And as his embrace of the erotic spirit of labor allowed Hapgood, so he believed, to replace class prejudice and voyeurism with democratic sym- pathies, so it also opened him, he thought, to an understanding of women's psychology that transcended convention and masculine prejudice and brought him closer to his wife. Having lived with the complicated, pas- sionate, New Womanish Boyce for some years, Hapgood puzzled in his

[20] Hapgood, *An Anarchist Woman* (New York, 1909), 153.
[21] The onset of the affair with Marie can be gleaned from Hapgood's letters to Boyce in the late months of 1905.
[22] Hapgood to Boyce, December 6, 1905, Hapgood Family Papers.

own way over the question of the day: What does Woman want? Working-class free love provided him with what he saw as the means to ally himself with modern women's desire.

To do Hapgood justice, in 1905 such equanimity with the subject of female sexual desire was rare, among men or women. The image of the erotically restless New Woman that would be disseminated by radicals in the years 1910–1919 was not yet available in political discussions, and advocates of women's rights viewed with abhorrence any association with free love. So in his delineation of Marie, Hapgood drew not on women's rights ideology but rather on the loose psychological formulations of the New Woman novels, a genre in which he had never worked but which was Boyce's métier. His story of a heroine given to extreme emotional states born of living at the outer edges of gender convention echoes Boyce's writings, a literary act of affiliation that, he believed, drew him closer to his wife.

An Anarchist Woman was a tricky book to publish in 1909, only six years after the suppression of *Sister Carrie* under the threat of the Comstock obscenity law. In the text, Hapgood protected himself against objections by claiming the familiar position of the realist writer, whose effort simply to illustrate social conditions should forestall any suspicions of indecency. Yet in his private relations, he was feeling his way toward another role, that of champion, male sponsor of his amoral, plebeian heroine and, by extension, of the eroticized modern womanhood she represented. It was not that Hapgood abandoned the superior stance from which previous novelists had viewed their abandoned heroines but rather that moral rescue was bound up for him with literary rather than philanthropic activity and, indeed, with becoming his subject's lover himself. He urged Marie to write a memoir, he confided to Boyce, who pressed him to disclose the exact nature of his Chicago "entanglements," but Terry Carlin discouraged her. As the authoritative literary man on the scene, he thought he might force Terry Carlin to move over.[23]

But while Hapgood set in motion a competition between himself and the dark, magnetic Carlin, who figured in his mind as a sort of Nietzchean superman of the working class, the more significant triangle he conjured into being was between himself, Marie, and Neith Boyce. Throughout these months, Boyce mostly maintained a jaunty, devil-may-care tone about Hapgood's relationships, although occasionally it cracked with anxiety or admonition. "Varietism," she ventured, was so "crude & unlovely—and besides it takes all the zest out of sinning!!"[24] Hapgood's response was to assure his wife of her primacy by turning Marie into a literary subject they

[23] Ibid., November 25, [1904 or 1905].
[24] Boyce to Hapgood, undated letter [1905], ibid.

held in common. As sex became writing for Hapgood and writing became sex, he construed it as a gift of comradely generosity to share his material with Boyce, a fellow writer who was working on New Woman themes. Hapgood apportioned to Boyce some of his "bully material," the letters Marie had written to him. The epistolary revelations amounted to an aphrodisiac; the exchange elicited a shiver of sexual feeling in both. Boyce imagined herself as Hapgood's mistress—in effect, as another Marie; Hapgood envisioned himself in Boyce's arms. Thus he adopted the Chicago free-lovers' habit of sexual honesty—"every event, untoward or favorable, gave them food for expressed thought"—to his own middle-class marriage of two professionals.[25]

What had begun as an exercise in human-interest writing, then, ended as an eroticized triangle with Hapgood, the liberal-minded commentator on free love and radical women, serving as the mediator between women of different classes. Preparing to leave Chicago, he bubbled over with exuberance to his wife about the generative relationship between loving her and his enriched knowledge of other women. "What haven't I got to say to you! But the important thing is that I love you! And I know it all the better. . . . I see values in things you think are low and contemptible—but yet somehow . . . I shall make an effort . . . to make you see my recent experience and what it has taught me."[26] As with the Chicago anarchists, free love promoted a superabundance of mutually enriching talk.

For Hapgood, then, the public discussion of sexual life and private erotic exchanges became enmeshed. The radical ethos of open discussion and sexual frankness wound through his intimate correspondence with Boyce, injecting their marriage with the excitement of free-love transgression and erotic triangles.

Love letters are, admittedly, difficult historical documents to use. They seem to issue from wellsprings of ancient emotion and to exist in a timeless realm of attachment and need. The world exists only at their margins: indeed, love letters belong to those moments when lovers create, in the writing, a world of their own. There was scant mention of current events in the voluminous correspondence of Hapgood and Boyce. Rather, they used the letters to enact a sexual connection, turning aside momentarily for practical matters about children's shoes and doctor's bills, publisher's advances and repairs on the house. But in that private conversation about sexual desire and attachment, idiosyncrasies and perversities took shape from historical materials at work in the world at large.

[25] Hapgood, *Spirit of Labor,* 168.
[26] Hapgood to Boyce, undated letter [1905], Hapgood Family Papers.

Although Hapgood had never been one for sentimental effusions, even when he was zealously courting Boyce in the 1890s, his encounter with working-class sexuality in 1905 provoked him into an epistolary language that flaunted what still must have been the reigning romantic imagery of hearts and flowers. A few years later, the socialist writer Mary Heaton Vorse rhapsodized to her new lover Joe O'Brien, a labor journalist, that "you come into an inner piece of my spirit that I have kept closed always." The two moved in the same sophisticated circles in New York that Hapgood and Boyce frequented, but their letters recur to images exalted not by modern, erotically laden heterosexuality but by Victorian virtues of domesticity and sentiment. "I pray to the god inside me," replied O'Brien, "to make me work very hard and always be kind, so that my Mary will put up her folding-up rose-leaf of a hand in mine and go with me to the edge of life and find contentment and singing things."[27]

Compare this to Hapgood's scribblings from his room late at night, which reproduced in writing the verbal exhortations and imprecations of sex. "I am naughty tonight." "Why are you not here? I'd try to give you a good time. Did I every give you a good time? Did any other man ever do as well? better? Do you love me? will you always love me? Well, why don't you say so? Kiss me. Hug me. Closer, closer. ah! ah! ah! I'm quite wild. I don't dare go to bed." There is a dash of conventional epistolary longing— "Do you love me?" Otherwise the phrasing is colloquial, with just a hint of the verbal play with which a man might whip up a "good time" with a prostitute—"Did any other man ever do as well?"—or at least an easygoing workingwoman similar to those who had intrigued Hapgood in Chicago. The letters reenacted the rhythms of desire and the conversation of the bedroom, recalling sometimes the strategies of pornography: the sly proposition, the naughty wink. "I wish you could be with me now! I want to sleep with you tonight! Is it allowed."[28]

Hapgood's favored means of erotically thickening the atmosphere between himself and the absent Neith Boyce was the free-love triangle he had first mobilized with Marie. As his free-love relations expanded beyond his literary tasks in the years after 1905, which the two spent living in Europe and back in Chicago until they returned to New York in 1914, the circulation of letters and stories about his affairs became more frankly erotic, a delicious frisson of transgression. "Tell me you love me and also tell me about the flirtations you are having," he teased. "Have you been unfaithful? Have you sinned? Did you like it. . . . Do you like me better than ever? What shall we do when we meet so as to take another step?" "Come and

[27] Dee Garrison, *Mary Heaton Vorse: The Life of an American Insurgent* (Philadelphia, 1989), 57.

[28] Hapgood to Boyce, undated letter, "Later, Saturday night" [1905], Hapgood Family Papers.

hug me and confess it all," he begged. Disclosure was the aphrodisiac. "I am full of lust and love and desire to talk and hear you talk."[29]

Conversations about sex were reported on both sides; letters careened about among the partners and other sexual talkers. In Chicago, Hapgood chatted with Emma Goldman about her sex life with Ben Reitman and with Reitman about a prostitute he had known; Reitman, who was himself in a heavy-breathing epistolary relation with Emma Goldman, gave Hapgood the letters of the prostitute, which Hapgood then sent on to Boyce.[30] Hapgood invited the confidences of Mrs. Darrow, a woman embittered by Clarence Darrow's years-long affair with a West Coast labor radical, and implicitly contrasted her morose devotion to his own wife's alluring willingness to venture outside the marriage. "You say you are sensitive to the interest and attraction of other men," he commended Boyce. "I think that this is true, and I am very glad of it. You would not be the interesting woman you are, if you were not."[31]

Boyce sportingly tried to keep up, although her heavy responsibilities for their children and the difficulties of doing her own writing frequently overwhelmed her. In gay moments, however, she did talk about sex, although more euphemistically and allusively than her husband. But her determined gallantry sometimes failed her; of Hapgood's lover of the moment in Paris, for instance, she declared flat-footedly that "she is the one person in the world I hate."[32] Mostly, however, she abided by the principle that their sexual entanglements were common property, erotic equity for the marriage. She had few affairs in comparison with her husband's many— only one, we will see, was serious—but after some resistance she agreed to make the letters available to her husband in exchange for the documentation of his own contemporaneous amour.

For Hapgood and, to a lesser degree, Boyce, sexual talk emerged from free-love conversation. But if in its loftier aspirations free love aimed to subvert the marriage system, in its more earthbound aspect it edged closer to a modulated pornography. The infusion of erotic confession lifted middle-class marriage out of its old context of economic practicability, kinship relations, and morality and refashioned it as a modern relation authorized by an avant-garde politics that allowed the "free expression" of authentic sexual selves. The circulation of letters and the disclosure of

[29] Ibid.

[30] On the Reitman/Goldman correspondence, see Candace Falk, *Love, Anarchy, and Emma Goldman* (New York, 1984), and Alice Wexler, "Emma Goldman in Love," *Raritan* 1 (Summer 1982): 116–45. For Reitman's loan of the letters to Hapgood, see another undated letter to Boyce [1912].

[31] Hapgood to Boyce, undated letter, "Tuesday night," 1904, Hapgood Family Papers. Darrow's relationship with Mary Field Parton is mentioned throughout Sara Bard Field's letters in the Wood Collection.

[32] Boyce to Hapgood, September 10, 1907, Hapgood Family Papers.

sexualized relations with others created keyholes through which each partner in turn might peek. The idealistic, feminist imprimatur of free love sanitized these "low" elements, removing sex talk and writing from the precincts of the brothel and the leather-bound volumes of Victorian pornography and making the explicit discussion of adultery, for example, fit stuff for such a woman of letters as Neith Boyce.

Acts of disclosure, confined to conversations and letters à deux, could also take place in public and semipublic. Sexual revelations—gossip about others, admissions about oneself—were self-conscious acts whereby the radicals stretched their faculties for friendship, tolerance, free expression, and political enlightenment. Secrecy, the painful mysteries of extramarital sex, hypocrisy, the sexual double standard: these were relics of a Victorian past. To be modern was to talk. The sensation of being bohemian, at the leading edge of modern life, no longer necessarily emanated from artistic aspiration, as it had in the nineteenth century, but rather from sexual tale-telling: "the relief of telling the story . . . [of the] last unhappy love affair to a sympathetic listener," Floyd Dell, soon to be a pundit of American sexual mores (in the 1920s he published a series of books on the problems and joys of modern marriage) described confessionalism.[33] Dorothy Day took a less benign view of Village sex talk, especially as practiced by Dell. His love affairs "should have taken place on the stage of the Hippodrome before a packed house," she commented caustically.[34]

Day was responding to the ways in which, as we have seen with Hapgood, sexual conversations could function as a theater of potency for men. Women might play a leading role in their own intimate erotic dramas with partners, but they seldom projected themselves onto a wider stage. Rather, they flung the net of disclosure wide to create supports for themselves. Talking helped adjudicate and control sexual complications and salve hurts. Often the impulse to socialize a sexual situation served the requirements of the heterosexual couple, but occasionally opening up a conversation could also subvert the erotic operations of a free-loving man. Thus imperious Mabel Dodge, one of the few women who excelled at free-love tactics, took matters in hand conversationally in 1913 when she sensed warmth between her then-lover John Reed and a sexy hanger-on in Greenwich Village. Dodge didn't bother to negotiate with Reed but went straight to Babette. "I immediately wrote her a note and told her I wouldn't have it, and that my instinct and my nervous system had told me all about her

[33] Dell, *Homecoming*, 26.

[34] On modernity and confessionalism in the psychiatric context, see Elizabeth Lunbeck, *The Psychiatric Persuasion* (Princeton, N.J., 1994). Day is quoted in Steven Watson, *Strange Bedfellows: The First American Avant-Garde* (New York, 1991), 158.

intention and that she could stop right there." The love affair was aborted. "Oh, how we were all intertwined!" she marveled.[35]

The feminist Sara Bard Field negotiated her way for years through C. E. S. Wood's multiple involvements by weaving conversational relations with other women. Field's sister, Mary Parton, was involved in the long-running free-love affair with Clarence Darrow, who refused to divorce his unhappy but devoted wife. Margaret Johanssen, the willing wifely heroine of *The Spirit of Labor*, was also a close friend. In San Francisco in these years, the women shared with one another the travails of loving promiscuous men. Field also spoke with and wrote to as many of Wood's other lovers as would reciprocate, although the circle was always widening and she never quite kept up. New candidates appeared whom she failed to rope into her circle of disclosure but she did manage to develop confessional relationships with a few. Wood was another who circulated love letters written to him, but Field accomplished something of a flanking action around his control of sexual information by developing her own relationships, actual and epistolary, with some of the senders. A mutual accord with Kitty, Wood's long-suffering, Portland-based, anarchist lover and secretary, pleased her greatly. To their mutual lover, she preened herself on the achievement their intimacy represented: "Two women who love *one* man . . . not a speck of that jealousy with which the story books teem."[36]

These women turned sexual talk to therapeutic rather than provocative uses. Female conversation helped Field cling to the high ground of her "soul affinity" for Wood while externalizing what were, in the emotional scheme of free love, base reactions of jealousy and rage, the monstrous evils Field detested herself for entertaining. She reported back to Wood other women's criticisms and condemnations of his actions, taking care to present herself as his defender. Field had been raised in a rigid midwestern Baptist home, and despite her adult agnosticism, her defiance of convention exacted a high price in self-esteem. She sometimes felt "smutty." She held herself aloof in her sacralized passion for Wood from bohemian promiscuity, "not lovely to me even if done by good looking intelligent people who call it high sounding."[37] As she situated herself in a coterie of unorthodox women, she comforted herself with the knowledge of what they shared but also with the conviction that she differed.

The old dichotomy between good and bad women had crumbled, but still, she drew distinctions. Florence Deshon, a stunning Hungarian actress who had taken up in the Village with Max Eastman, came in for a gibe when Field visited New York in 1917; "a bit shop-worn, I fear, sexually

[35] Mabel Dodge Luhan, *Movers and Shakers* (New York, 1936), 261.
[36] Field to Wood, undated letter, box 7, folder 266, Wood Collection.
[37] Field to Wood, July 7, 1917, ibid.

speaking," she wrote Wood pityingly, "having been handed about among a number of men in Washington Square."[38] The confiding Kitty, who admitted to Field a "sex hunger" that had led into other affairs besides the one with Wood, served as a foil for Field's single-minded devotion. "I cannot conceive of such a thing *for myself*," she declared primly, "as divorcing my physical love from my soul affinity."[39] In an erotic game of King-of-the-Hill, she clambered to the top where she might know all, elbowing aside rivals. There, at the pinnacle, she might have a power which could rival that of Wood, the person who really knew all. Or did he? Women's sex talk might illuminate corners where even he hadn't visited. Had he known before Field mentioned it, for example, that Kitty had other lovers?

This was not the sustaining, diffusely sensuous "female world of love and ritual" whose idealized womanly tenderness permeated Victorian middle-class culture. It was rather an adjunct to heterosexual relations, a combination of training post and retreat for recuperation. But haven't women always complained about men to one another? Yes, surely the confessions of Bard and her friends echoed ancient women's plaints. But the terms of disclosure were quite new, partly in the women's compulsion to distance themselves from that old tradition of female sadness. The modern touch came in their intense effort, expressed through words, not prayer or magic, to transcend jealousy and hurt, to repudiate an emotional vulnerability they associated with Victorian female weakness and to forge, teeth gritted, a determined alliance with male sexual adventurism. Confessions to friends, then, enacted a stringent self-discipline—not unlike religious confession. Expressing their grievances to one another, women drew off some of the power of disabling anger, reminded themselves of the ethical system to which they owed fealty, and discovered sources of psychological authority for themselves. They fortified themselves for the next round.

When sexual talk was so widespread, self-dramatizing, and sensational, it was easy for the theatrically inclined to imagine it onstage. Heterosexual exchanges, pitched to angst and discord, would become a dramatic fund for experiments in the "new theater," culminating in the "depth" drama of the Provincetown Players. The partners in sexual dialogue, negotiating with each other or with a third party in a triangle, would move onstage. These "he said/she said," one-act plays, structured around psychological action with virtually no plot and performed on a bare stage, were the genesis of modern, "serious" theater in New York, the earliest alternative to the light musicales and melodramas of Broadway. There is a direct connection

[38] Ibid., October 6, 1917.
[39] Ibid., undated letter, box 7, folder 277.

between the Provincetown Players and Eugene O'Neill, who produced his first plays with them and whose dramas of psychodramatic authenticity came to define modern theater in America in the 1920s. Through the new theater, the radicals' heterosexual dialogue and disclosure would become implicated in more general aesthetic and cultural notions of psychological realism.[40]

In 1913 Floyd Dell formed the Liberal Club Players. The Liberal Club was an institution for Greenwich Village bohemia, conceived as a free-spirited alternative to the stodgy gentlemen's clubs. Newly arrived from Chicago and brimming with bohemian energy, Dell gathered together a group of ambitious amateurs and established professionals and set about staging monthly one-act plays. He envisioned a theater that would emerge from the living material around its players, a community enacting itself, rather than presenting the European avant-garde to high-minded American audiences as arty "little theaters" did. So Dell took lovers' quarrels, men's promiscuity, women's resentments, and the impossibilities of marriages and staged them, mostly as farce. Some of the plays were thematic and ideological, fleshed out with set pieces on the inevitable failure of monogamy and the death of love in marriage—not that different from an Emma Goldman lecture. Others were lightly confessional, self-ironizing treatments of what Dell cheerfully admitted was "the behavior of myself and various of my friends, who in our search for 'eternal love' went from one wife and sweetheart to another."[41]

The "he said/she said" format of the plays replicated the openness and ideological symmetry of the modern love dialogue. Two actors performed on a stage created as a psychological space with only minimal scenery and props. But the plays also spoofed free-love's self-dramatizing pretensions to high-mindedness and honesty. A man and woman, each believing mistakenly the other is married, fall into a free-love passion, but eros fizzles when they discover that there are no third parties to make up a sexy triangle. The self-dramatics of free love turn out to be as flimsy as the Liberal Club productions: a bohemian tells his new lover in the Village he is fleeing a stultifying bourgeois marriage back in Chicago, but he turns out to be a compulsive liar and womanizer who uses the story on every woman he picks up. Heterosexual honesty, the great shibboleth of bohemia, becomes in its feints and evasions the force that drives the psychological plot. "Enigma," one of the few dramatic "depth" plays that Dell wrote (dedicated to one of the troupe's stars, the glamorous Chicago actress Kirah Markham,

---

[40] Joel Pfister, *Staging Depth: Eugene O'Neill and the Politics of Psychological Discourse* (Chapel Hill, N.C., 1995).

[41] Dell quoted in Keith Norton Richwine, "The Liberal Club: Bohemia and the Resurgence in Greenwich Village, 1912–1918," (Ph.D. diss., University of Pennsylvania, 1968), 133.

and her notoriously promiscuous lover Theodore Dreiser) circles around lovers' lies for its duration, never achieving a resolution. The stark confrontations of the heterosexual dialogue have turned in on themselves; honesty creates its own baroque circumlocutions.[42]

On Cape Cod in the summer of 1916, a group of Liberal Club players summering among the Portuguese fishermen in Provincetown agreed to replicate the community theater but with a greater degree of seriousness. The higher purpose had something to do with the presence of George Cram Cook, Dell's free-love mentor from back in Iowa, who was devoted to the Greek drama and believed something of equal import could be done for the modern age, and with the dissolute but undeniably talented Eugene O'Neill, who was lurking about and was known from the Village bars. Free-love theatrics and conversation were booming in Provincetown itself, which was packed that summer with lovers, former lovers, ménages, and spouses in varying states of separation. In such an atmosphere, with the European war raging in the background and American intervention imminent, light bohemian banter passed into the modernist register of psychological depth.

One of the first plays to be staged by the group in an old fish house was Boyce and Hapgood's "Enemies." The piece was created from the Liberal Club formula of he said/she said, but with heterosexual dialogue that reached for painful confession and honesty. The characters were the nameless, allegorical figures of He and She, speaking to each other from across the great gender divide. No one in the audience could fail to recognize, however, the authors' own conflicts from the references to Her bad housekeeping and His drinking, His affairs and Her aloofness. Although both names are credited with authorship, textual evidence indicates that "Enemies" was primarily Boyce's work. The dialogue is firmly disciplined in its symmetry—my point of view, your point of view, give and take, tit for tat— but it is Her speech that is indisputably the crowning accusation. "You, on account of your love for me, have tyrannized over me, bothered me, badgered me, nagged me, for fifteen years. You have interfered with me, taken my time and strength, and prevented me from accomplishing great works for the good of humanity. You have crushed my soul, which longs for serenity and peace, with your perpetual complaining." Boyce's pent-up energies were at work here, an alternative understanding of the marriage and her own role in it that had long been suppressed by the sheer volume of Hapgood's talk and the prolixity of his relations. The historian who has fol-

[42] "Enigma" is published in Floyd Dell, *King Arthur's Socks* (New York, 1922). See his other collections of Liberal Club plays: *The Angel Intrudes* (New York, 1918) and *Sweet and Twenty: A Comedy in One Act* (Cincinnati, 1921).

lowed the long saga of their marriage inwardly cheers. At last! Did anyone in the audience at the fish house feel the same way?[43]

At the same time, the enterprise of reconciling free-love arrangements with his marriage to a complicated New Woman and the psychological and erotic drama that it entailed came increasingly to figure as literary material for Hapgood, "corking" and "bully" in its own right. While politicized free-love talk bred high excitation in his marriage, his marriage in turn provided him a footing in an emerging literature of male expertise on modern love. Politics provoked sex, and sex garnered publishers' advances. In 1919, Hapgood published under his own name a first-person narrative of his marriage with Boyce—who went unnamed, denoted simply "she" in the manner of "Enemies." The book, *Story of a Lover,* followed the births of their first three children and climaxed with Boyce's one serious affair with an old Harvard friend of Hapgood's, which took place shortly after Hapgood had been in Chicago.

Written in 1914 at the zenith of feminist esprit and free-love experimentation (Hapgood's and others') in the Village, *Story* is purportedly a sympathetic tale of the psychological and sexual development of a New Woman, a fond and admiring tale of a cultural heroine in which the husband ostentatiously takes a back seat. But the book is in fact a complicated, unremitting testament to a relentless masculine resentment, its feminist trappings serving to embellish the narrator's own enlightened tolerance and to heighten readers' sympathies for his grievances. Articulated antifeminism was altogether absent; indeed, the narrator insists on his adherence to principles of sexual equality—women's work, their economic independence, their sexual freedom. *Story of a Lover* thus represents an important departure from an ideological critique of militant womanhood; rather, it is an early entry—perhaps the first—in a lively, twentieth-century tradition of male grievance, founded on psychological wounds rather than political objections.

Although Hapgood's grievances culminated in Boyce's affair with another man, her adultery was only a chapter in his story of a deeper betrayal of his sexual and emotional needs that began with her first pregnancy and continued with her preoccupations with more babies, domestic cares, and her own writing. The wife of *Story* is an allegorical figure of female mystery, aloof, remote and mystical, a fin-de-siècle presence of undulating emotional curves and twists through which a modern woman peeks out occasionally. "I said she had no soul. . . . Sometimes in her hinting way, she

[43] Ellen Kay Trimberger has established the context for the authorship of "Enemies" in *Intimate Warriors.*

would quietly suggest that if she should try to express herself to me I would run away . . . call attention to the vanity and egotism in me that demanded above everything else a sympathetic listener." In such formulations a contradictory psychological plot creeps into Hapgood's "realistic" account: material with which one can read a counternarrative sympathetic to Boyce. But that reading is mostly subdued, in fact smothered, under the weight of Hapgood's fulsome emotional testimony to his own marital commitment and good intentions. The book is extraordinary chiefly in its feat of endlessly describing a depressed woman without ever acknowledging she is depressed. Boyce's debilitating state after the birth of their first child, "a time of weeping sensibility," is enfolded into the mysteries of her nature; her difficult second pregnancy, which took place in a small New York walk-up apartment, elicits memories of how "beautifully exhausted she was," billowing after a climb up four flights with such a "wonderful sufficiency" that all she wanted to do was read in bed.

Hapgood's challenge in the book was to justify his own massive grievance against Boyce for her one affair despite his own professions of free-love equality and his career of nonstop, chipper womanizing. He solved it by fashioning himself as a supplicant at the shrine of the New Woman's emotional fecundity and Boyce as withholding, uncaring, and self-involved. The problem with heterosexual relations thus became his commitment and her lack of it, despite the fact that he was a compulsive womanizer continually absent from home and she had primary responsibility for their children and professed only need and love for him. Her affair wounded him not because of jealousy or possessiveness, those artifacts of a bygone age of masculine domination, but because she refused to talk about it with him. The book ends with an ambiguous reconciliation. "She" suffers a nervous breakdown and emerges chastened and subdued.[44] Having forgone free love in life, the wife allows her spouse to rekindle his interest in her through free-love fantasies; the two meet in a French restaurant and imagine themselves to be adulterous lovers, retiring to a back room to make love as zestful participants in linked triangles.

Hapgood's was a sleight of hand possible only in the twentieth century, when a comparatively broad-based feminist consensus in the intelligentsia required new bases for men's resentments of women beyond the well-worn channels of nineteenth-century antifeminism. The liberal man of egalitarian principles formulated his complaints within an ostensibly reciprocal conversation, gesturing toward the female voice at the same time that he found it wanting. *Story of a Lover* represented a reinforcement of male

---

[44] Although she also emerges as still surprisingly (to the narrator) angry that he has gone on with his affairs. But she accepts, more or less, his "sexual straining towards the universe's oblivion," and although he remains "passionately unsatisfied" with her aloofness—still she doesn't love him in the right way—the two achieve some implicit accord, at least in the text.

authority over the character of the New Woman, an assertion of the narrator's power to describe her, criticize her, tell her how she was bearing up and where she was falling short. He applauded his fictive feminist wife and blamed himself for his traditional expectations of her, even as he formulated those expectations as normative and unobjectionable. In elevating her to a position of spiritual potency and cultural allure, he managed to claim vulnerability for himself, thus ignoring the very real differences in power and status between the two. Talking about sex, for all its purported equality of disclosure, ended up in the hands of a male pundit as a genre we might call "male feminism with a vengeance."

The destiny of sexual talk as a middlebrow form, accommodating men's complaints about noncompliant New Women, followed the trajectory of free love in the culture at large over the next twenty years. Talking about sex originated in the second decade of the twentieth century as an amalgam of a militant cultural feminism, a cross-class fascination with working-class mores and a belief in the utopian promises of conversational disclosure between the sexes. In the twenties, the political aura dissolved. The sexual liberalism that had flourished in the cities during the previous decade passed into the realm of commercialized eros, denuded of feminism: flappers replaced New Women, youth culture took the place of bohemia, and explicit sexual come-ons were utilized to sell consumer goods, not working-class revolution. Romance magazines, with their true confessions, brought to popular culture a version of the intellectuals' fascination with honesty and disclosure.

Yet the narrative of declension misses what was problematic in talking about sex all along: the optative character of the supposed equal exchange of views. Bohemian sex talk can be seen as an early contribution to the annals of "men talk, women listen," a chronicle that has played a large part in our understanding and experience of sexual modernism. With New Women assigned such a heavily laden symbolic role in modernist culture, it was left for them to display their spiritual and erotic riches and for others—men—to speak for them. The positive outlook and the supposed towering self-confidence of the free-loving woman became a seductive model of action, will, individualism, and sexual identification in the modern world, but those ascribed powers left women little room to address their own actual vulnerabilities. The symbolic burden of modernism, so attractive to women deprived of the traditional idealizations—as well as oppressions—of Victorian culture, in fact interfered with their ability to speak for themselves, except in private places.

The modernization of the patriarchal critique did something to liberalize sexual relations, but it still gave women scant ability to articulate their own interests, grievances, or even skeptics. It was rare for women to give back as good as they got in sex talk. Emma Goldman's feisty friend Almeda Sperry, a working-class lesbian, described putting the salacious and foul-mouthed Ben Reitman, Goldman's lover, in his place with blunt repartee, but Sperry was fortified by the rough plebeian sexual politics she had learned on the streets as a prostitute. There were a few other lesbian skeptics on the margins of bohemia who voiced a cynicism about the promises of heterosexual free love. The avant-garde editor Margaret Anderson, a veteran of both Chicago and New York bohemias, dryly mocked the propensity of radical men to use their wives and lovers as theater managers to set the men up onstage. In a more serious vein, the Portland physician—and lesbian—Marie Equi was the one radical who threatened to blow the whistle on C. E. S. Wood by going to the papers after two of his lovers committed suicide within a year of each other in the early 1920s.[45]

The lyrical promise of the years 1910–19 has often been seen as an off-shoot of European ideas newly imported to America, especially the radical insights of psychoanalysis. But no one has explained satisfactorily how the New York and Chicago Left managed to reconcile the dark precepts of Freud's work with their bounding good faith in heterosexual amity. In fact, Freud's ideas played only a minor role in the radical intelligentsia. They worked, rather, from homegrown materials in fashioning their ethic of honesty as a central and necessary element of modern sexuality. Talking about sex was inflected not so much with Freudian tragedy as with a vision of feminist equality, the pleasures of plebeian esprit, and the heightening of heterosexual excitement.

That dose of bounding good spirits gave much to feminism in the early years of the century. It nourished women's and men's sensibility of optative equality, or willed reciprocity—the deep-seated conviction that people of good faith, with the aid of particular forms of interpersonal communication, could rectify ancient injustices between men and women, whatever the political and institutional context. Talking about sex was, in its early days, an American sensation, creating a conviction of history making and theatrical revolutionism for the participants. Yet its antecedents in a rich and heavy tradition of male sexual discussion and privilege always threatened to overwhelm its innovative promise for women, at least between heterosexual lovers. Between women, sex talk sometimes opened out into

---

[45] Sperry's letter of 1912 is quoted in Falk, *Love, Anarchy, and Emma Goldman*, 173. Anderson rolled her eyes rhetorically at the way Margery Currey, herself a lively feminist, made Dell's pontifications the centerpiece of her Jackson Park salon evenings. Margaret Anderson, *My Thirty Years' War* (New York, 1969), 37. Marie Equi was an IWW sympathizer; she may have been Margaret Sanger's lover and would later live for many years with Elizabeth Gurley Flynn. The suicides were Kitty and Janina Klecken, the physician. There are alarmed allusions to Equi's anger and threats to go public with Wood's private life in the letters of Field and Wood in the early 1920s in the Wood Collection.

something broader, when touching on desire, vulnerability, and hurt could embolden and strengthen.

My account here joins those of other feminist scholars in investigating the ambivalent legacy of the first sexual revolution. The intention is not to disparage sexual liberation as a positive element of modern feminism, for the ability to enjoy the full range of the body's pleasures is, I believe, an absolute requirement for the integrity of self on which feminism depends. It is rather to call attention to how truth telling, therapeutic confession, and theoretically egalitarian exchanges in print and conversation could not become the moral forces necessary to right imbalances between even well-meaning men and women when speech itself was so entwined with structures of male privilege and female disability.

Homage to Fortuna on the margins of mid-nineteenth-century American society: George Caleb Bingham, *Raftsmen Playing Cards* (1847), reprinted by permission of St. Louis Art Museum, St. Louis, Missouri.

CHAPTER FOURTEEN

"What If History Was a Gambler?"

T. J. JACKSON LEARS

"The bullets have your names on them," said Safet Somo, a fifteen-year-old boy in Sarajevo. He hoped the North Atlantic Treaty Organization (NATO) planes, which had just begun to bomb the Bosnian Serbs, would destroy the bullet meant for him. But his attitude was fatalistic and stoic. "I am not afraid," he said. "When my destiny day comes, my bullet will find me wherever I am hiding. You can't escape destiny."[1]

The words conjure up an archaic world ruled by blind Fortuna, haunted by visions of dark enchantment, filled with folk cursed or blessed by forces they neither control nor understand. The idea that "you can't escape destiny" poses a direct challenge to the fundamental dogma of Western liberal thought: the belief that the individual can master fate through will and choice. This faith in human autonomy has rarely been more fervently promoted than in the contemporary United States. Insistence on the individual's capacity to control his or her fate has not been as politically potent since before the Great Depression.

Yet outside the more fortunate classes, one senses a deep distrust of any ideology that requires a naïve faith in people's capacity to chart their own destinies. This distrust is nothing new. For centuries, a popular culture of luck has played counterpoint to the dominant ideal of human control over fate. The long lines at the lottery machines and the revival of casino gam-

I want to thank Rachel Lears for the best research assistance I have ever had, Karen Parker Lears and Adin Lears for astute advice and encouragement, and the members of my 1996 NEH Summer seminar for helping me to clarify fundamental issues.

[1] Kit R. Roane, "For a Change, Crash of Shells Heartens Sarajevo Residents," *New York Times*, August 31, 1995, sec. A, p. 17.

bling from New Jersey to Mississippi give testimony that this culture is still very much alive—particularly in an era when deindustrialization and contracting real wages make celebrations of individual mastery more problematic than ever. The worldview of Safet Somo, despite its apparent strangeness, may be more common than it seems on first inspection.

Believing that life is governed by "the breaks" can induce resignation, passivity, even pathology—the helpless addiction of the chronic, losing gambler. In less extreme versions it can still promote a kind of resignation that paralyzes ambition, undermines a sense of personal responsibility, and promotes political quiescence. Neither Rotarians nor radical feminists find much to admire in this worldview. "It shamed me that the only thing my family wholeheartedly believed in was luck and the waywardness of fate," writes the novelist Dorothy Allison, recalling her white-trash origins in piedmont South Carolina. "They held the dogged conviction that the admirable and wise thing to do was keep a sense of humor, never whine or cower, and trust that luck might someday turn as good as it had been bad— and with just as much reason."[2] This attitude possesses its own dignity and even wisdom (as Allison comes to realize), but it also embodies the docile "underclass" behavior that annoys the achieving classes whatever their political stripe.

Yet acceptance of fate could also energize risk taking. As early as the 1820s, Tocqueville noted Americans' propensity for taking chances: "Those who live in the midst of democratic fluctuations have always before their eyes the image of chance; and they end by liking all undertakings in which chance takes a part." American commerce was a "vast lottery," Tocqueville wrote; individuals undertook business "not only for the sake of the profit it holds out to them, but for the love of the constant excitement occasioned by that pursuit." Amid the feverish fluctuation of fortune, the life of an average American "passed like a game of chance." Tocqueville was referring mostly to men, but it is important to remember how often women were required to take risks as well, in childbirth as well as in their mates' entrepreneurial schemes. Capricious turns of fate were part of life.[3]

This was especially true in an expansive commercial society, where the pervasiveness of risk blurred the line between legitimate and illegitimate gambling—most apparently in stock and commodity trading.[4] Many businesspeople knew, though few publicly acknowledged, that hard work was not always the key to success; good fortune made a crucial difference too. Even Horatio Alger realized that pluck depended partly on luck, and vice

[2] Dorothy Allison, *Skin: Talking about Sex, Class, and Literature* (Ithaca, 1994), 25.

[3] Alexis de Tocqueville, *Democracy in America*, ed. Phillips Bradley, 2 vols. (1835; New York, 1945), 1:305, 2:165, 248–49.

[4] For sensitive discussion of this and other related issues, see Ann Fabian, *Card Sharps, Dream Books, and Bucket Shops: Gambling in Nineteenth-Century America* (Ithaca, 1990).

versa. Certainly this was true for Safet Somo. Embracing his inescapable destiny, he went fearlessly into the streets of Sarajevo to sell candy and cigarettes, making ten dollars a day to help support his family.

American attitudes toward luck have a long and revealing history. At least since Tocqueville's time, creators of conventional wisdom attributed material or moral success to free will and free choice, exercised in accordance with the unfolding plan of God (or later Science or Evolution). The contradictions in this scheme only fitfully became apparent. Belief in luck and the magical power to grasp it was confined to the margins of respectable society: African Americans, Irish, German, or Italian immigrants, superstitious farmers—not to mention amateur and professional gamblers—all of whom tended to lack the characteristically Protestant commitment to disciplined achievement.

Yet it was not simply a case of the dominant culture of will *versus* the popular culture of luck. Cultural divisions were various; they could be linked with philosophical debates, new directions in art and science, and ancient and modern religious thinking. Luck had many faces. This was especially true in the twentieth century, after the gradual, halting shift from mechanical to probabilistic ideas of causality resurrected chance as a legitimate category of thought. From William James to Ralph Ellison, from avant-garde art to academic philosophy, American thinkers tolerated and even sometimes embraced the importance of chance in human affairs. Their speculations had broad ethical and religious significance and perhaps some hidden affinities with the popular culture of luck.

The early English settlers in North America included many devotees of luck. Gambling on horse races, cockfights, or the turn of a card was a popular way of reaffirming insouciant masculinity; the gambler could pose as a hell of a fellow who cared not a fig for money matters. New England Puritans were less tolerant of gambling than were southern Anglicans, but even the righteous leaders of Massachusetts fought a losing battle against the amusements of the alehouse.[5]

But by the early nineteenth century a coherent critique of gambling had begun to emerge. For Mason Locke Weems, writing in 1816, gambling was "DIAMETRICALLY OPPOSITE TO THE VERY END OF OUR CREATION!" He

[5] For useful background on colonial attitudes toward gambling, see Increase Mather, *A Testimony against Several Prophane and Superstitious Customs Now Practiced in New England* (London, 1687), quoted in John Samuel Ezell, *Fortune's Merry Wheel: The Lottery in America* (Cambridge, Mass., 1960), 12–13. See also Perry Miller, *The New England Mind: The Seventeenth Century* (Cambridge, Mass., 1954), 15–16; John M. Findlay, *People of Chance: Gambling in American Society from Jamestown to Las Vegas* (New York, 1986), 20; David Hackett Fischer, *Albion's Seed: Four British Folkways in America* (New York, 1989), 126–27, 148–49, 250–51, 340–43; Timothy Breen, "Horses and Gentlemen: The Cultural Significance of Gambling among the Gentry of Virginia," *William and Mary Quarterly*, 3d ser., 34 (April 1977): 239–57.

was sure that "God created the human family to be as one great *social body*," joined in interdependent harmony. Weems thought gamblers' self-absorption embodied "a shameful discordance from the universal harmony." He underwrote republican notions of the public good with William Paley's commonsense philosophy—in particular Paley's "argument from design" for the existence of God: the grand design of nature requires a grand designer.[6]

Yet Weems's pamphlet also contained what would become the evangelical and Victorian critiques of gambling. He told stories of young men brought low by cards and dice, driven to drunkenness and finally suicide. Weems's narratives were an early sign of the characteristic nineteenth-century tendency to link gambling with alcohol, prostitution, violence, and loss of self-control generally—and to treat those vices as failures of individual will. Moralists in this tradition redefined the eighteenth-century relationship between gambling and masculinity; instead of cocky masculinity, the gambler embodied pathetic dependency. He was an antiself; small wonder his career ended so often in suicide. Throughout the early and middle decades of the nineteenth century, evangelical reformers linked gambling to fashion, luxury, and sybaritic leisure. In most tracts, the gambler's attitude of "something for nothing" showed contempt for labor and selfish disregard for domestic responsibility; gone was Weems's emphasis on the gambler's broader betrayal of community. The privatization of public virtue was under way in earnest.[7]

A focus on the individual soul of the gambler led to a melding of religion and psychology. The tendency to list gambling as one among several uncontrollable passions introduced a language of bodily and emotional experience into ministerial critiques. "THE APPETITE [for gambling] IS INSATIABLE," the Congregational Rev. John Richards told Dartmouth College students in 1852. For decades moralists emphasized that the gambler's chief characteristic was overexcitability, which manifested itself in dramatic physical symptoms. "When the breath comes fast and hard; when the heart pulses painfully, as the tug for victory comes; when the eyes strain, the hands are clenched, the teeth set, and the whole body is rigid, and the quick words leap, and the odds grow more fearful, and are dared to the brink of ruin, then you see the awful end to which with rapid stride this 'harmless thing' [gambling] hurries," announced the Reverend John Ware at the Boston Music Hall in 1871. "It fastens like a vampire upon those who yield to it."[8]

---

[6] Mason Locke Weems, *Anecdotes of Gamblers, Extracted from a Work on Gambling* (Philadelphia, 1816), 2, 5.

[7] For one among many examples of evangelical critiques, see Timothy M. Flint, *The Ruinous Consequences of Gambling* (New York, 1827).

[8] Rev. John Richards, *Discourse on Gambling Delivered at the Congregational Meeting House at Dartmouth College, November 7, 1852* (Hanover, N.H., 1852), n.p.; John F. W. Ware, *The Gambling*

The idea of gambling as a nearly physiological affliction (or addiction) was being explored at about the same time by Fyodor Dostoyevsky, whose protagonist in *The Gambler* (1866) was swept up in feverish forces beyond his control as he squandered several fortunes at the tables of Roulettenberg. The clinical picture of the gambler linked him to the drunkard or the chronic masturbator; like them, he was enfeebled and ultimately enslaved by a single overriding passion. This profile reflected broader redefinitions of male success. During the early nineteenth century, utilitarian, liberal, and evangelical strains of thought converged to redefine economic achievement as rational accumulation rather than rash expenditure and risk. Especially outside the South, the devotee of fortune was increasingly deemed a failure.[9]

For Victorian reformers, gambling became a sign of lost manhood. The Connecticut Congregationalist Anthony Comstock, writing of offtrack betting parlors (then called "horse-pools") in 1883, asserted that "a clerk who frequents these places, and is brought under these seductive influences, is not to be trusted in office or store. The wild excitement that fires his brain will unman him. The things he would not do he will do."[10] If manliness was defined as self-mastery, submission to chance was emasculating. Yet Comstock's choice of occupational examples suggested a haunting possibility: was the creed of calculating diligence merely a morality for clerks?

Nietzsche posed the question most pointedly, but even High-Victorian moralists such as Ware wondered if the issues were more complex than Comstock imagined. "The gambling element in life," according to Ware, was not confined to the fetid gambling hells of the urban slums or the opulent casinos at fashionable resorts. It was a near universal tendency to take chances for the excitement of it—for the hell of it, Ware might have said, as he held the propensity toward risk taking to be a kind of primordial, volcanic energy. The stakes were spiritual as well as social. To resist Christianity was to take the ultimate risk, to submit to blind, unpredictable fate; to live a Christian life was to live in accordance with the immutable divine Law of Providence.[11]

All this was conventional enough, but Ware veered in a new direction when he asserted toward the end of his sermon that "this gambling element in itself is no unmitigated evil." Because God made it universal, there

---

Element in Life: Sermon Preached in the Music Hall, Boston, Sunday, October 29, 1871 (Boston, 1871), 3, 5. For the persistence of this view, see Henry Ward Beecher, *Gamblers and Gambling* (Philadelphia, 1896).

[9] Fyodor Dostoyevsky, *The Gambler and Other Stories*, trans. Constance Garnett (New York, 1917). For two among many examples of the critique of fortune, see "The True System: Every Man the Architect of His Own Fortune," *Genesee Farmer*, December 20, 1834, 103, and "Good and Bad Luck," *Michigan Farmer*, November 15, 1849, 340.

[10] Anthony Comstock, *Traps for the Young*, John Harvard Library Edition (1883; Cambridge, Mass., 1968), 126.

[11] Ware, *Gambling Element*, 3, 7, 9.

must be some use for it; indeed, it might well be "the secret instinct and impulse which suggest and carry on great enterprises, which give tenacity in presence of difficulties, and prevent defeats from growing into despairs. It is this spirit which spurs us when flagging, and supplies new hope when old hopes fail." It brought Columbus to the New World, cheered Washington at Valley Forge, subdued a wild continent, and built a great American nation. Risk taking, for Ware, was an essential force that had to be harnessed but should never be suppressed. This subterranean stream of vitalism eventually spilled over the boundaries of Comstock's pinched and dour version of Christianity. But most commentators on luck (including Ware himself) continued to emphasize the centrality of control rather than the possibilities of chance.[12]

To be sure, there were changes in emphasis. The spread of a Social Gospel among liberal Protestants occasionally worked to recast and broaden the critique of gambling. Washington Gladden and his colleagues revived the communitarian emphasis of Weems, targeting the practice of selling stocks or commodities on margin as well as playing cards or throwing dice. Social Gospelers highlighted the difficulty of distinguishing between legitimate and illegitimate gambling in a speculative capitalist society—a difficulty most antigambling moralists ignored.[13]

As Progressive reform spread, so did the revival of communitarian arguments against gambling. By 1907, Frank N. Freeman, a Yale philosophy professor, observed that "gambling . . . in the nature of the case causes a loosening of social ties. It sets each man's hand against his brother and thus is of the very essence of immoral action." But this remained a minor strand of thought, even among critics of gambling.[14]

More commonly, antigambling reform resurrected familiar ideals of domesticity and labor. One clerical contributor to an *Arena* magazine symposium on "gambling and speculation" in 1891 observed that female gamblers could be saved more easily than men because women were more susceptible to sentiment: "At a gathering of these young women several were compelled to leave the room when 'Home, Sweet Home' was played on the piano." A storekeeper in northern Arizona in 1908, "six months after the gambling curse had been lifted" from his town by legislation, said with satisfaction: "Well—things ain't just the same. I don't sell so many silk vests and giddy neckties as I used to; but I figure out I sell a whaling sight more pork and beans,—and get paid for them." For most critics, the per-

---

[12] Ibid., 18–21. For the vitalist strain, see Walter Houghton, *The Victorian Frame of Mind* (New Haven, 1957), 263–304.

[13] For a characteristic Social Gospel critique, see Washington Gladden, "Three Dangers," *Century* 6 (August 1884): 620–27.

[14] Frank N. Freeman, "The Ethics of Gambling," *International Journal of Ethics* 18 (October 1907): 76–91.

sistent patterns of bourgeois morality remained in place; pork and beans and "Home, Sweet Home" triumphed over the vanities of fashion.[15]

By the 1880s, though, some liberal religious thinkers were tying their arguments against gambling to evolutionary models of the ascent of man. From this view the gambler failed to see "the divine import of money as a sign of man's supremacy over the lower spheres of nature," as the Unitarian Octavius Brooks Frothingham announced in 1882. "He is animal and passionate through and through." The idea that gambling signified regression to animality was consistent with the progressive assumptions of an age when, as Henry Adams dryly noted, "evolution from lower to higher raged like an epidemic." There was no warrant, in Darwin or elsewhere, for granting evolution any purpose or direction—let alone a benevolent or linear one. Yet the grant served a profound cultural need by keeping the forces of chance at bay.[16]

Throughout the early and mid-nineteenth century, liberal apologists for Christianity had invoked Science and Providence as allies against Fortuna. Paley's argument from design melded religious and secular ideas of order. In theory, Darwin's *Origin of Species* (1859) destroyed Paley's static, harmonious universe, enthroning random mutation where the hand of God had been. Neither ministers nor scientists confronted the element of randomness in Darwinian thought during the early years of controversy over evolution. Ministers were wedded to a providential order, and scientists, to a mechanistic universe where every cause had an effect and vice versa. Religious and secular thinkers alike evaded difficulties by asserting that natural selection moved in a purposeful, progressive direction. The phrase "survival of the fittest" allowed Evolution to become another word for Progress, or even for Providence—a bizarre non sequitur that has persisted, in some circles, down to the present.[17]

The specter of chance was effectively exorcised, at least for the moment. Ministers and scientists alike could agree with T. H. Huxley's dictum (1873) that "chance and luck are merely aliases for ignorance." Chance is "only a negation—the denial of intelligence or design," announced a Presbyterian journal called *Hours at Home* in 1870. "Every advance from ignorance to intelligence in all the departments of science, disproves, by the most

[15] Rev. H. C. Vrooman, "Gambling and Speculation: A Symposium," *Arena*, April 1891, 421; Barton Wood Currie, "The Transformation of the Southwest through the Legal Abolition of Gambling," *Century* 89 (April 1908): 905–10.

[16] Octavius Brooks Frothingham, "The Ethics of Gambling," *North American Review* 135 (August 1882); 168; Henry Adams, *The Education of Henry Adams* (1907; New York, 1931), 284. See also Robert Bannister, *Social Darwinism: Science and Myth in Anglo-American Social Thought* (Philadelphia, 1979), chap. 1.

[17] On the evasion of chance in Darwinian thought, see Bannister, *Social Darwinism*, esp. chaps. 1–3, and George Levine, *Darwin and the Novelists: Patterns of Science in Victorian Fiction* (Cambridge, Mass., 1988), 19, 89–94, 141.

positive evidence, the doctrine of chance and asserts an overruling Providence." For a few decades during the second half of the century, mechanistic ideas of causality continued to run parallel with Calvinistic traditions of Providence.[18]

The twinning of Providence and Progress allowed moralists to resist what to them seemed the master trend of the age. As John Bigelow wrote in *Harper's* in 1895, "The propensity to treat the events of human life as accidental or the sport of chance was never more nearly universal than it is to-day." The "heathen goddess" Fortuna presided over the boards of trade and the stock exchanges as well as the casinos and horse-pool parlors; the true gamblers in these places were those who aimed to get their adversaries' money without presenting any equivalent for it. Under the sway of his passion, Bigelow's gambler was "reduced to the level of a beast of prey" and ultimately to suicide.[19]

Yet there was a way out. According to Bigelow, it required the recognition that "there is no such thing as chance. What we commonly term chance or luck is simply a mode of expressing our ignorance of the cause or series of causes of which any given event is the inevitable sequence." If the gambler were brought to see his philosophical mistake, moral reform might follow. The gaming table could be "as effective a means of grace as the communion table." It could bring home the great truth of Providence and the necessity of trusting in God rather than fate or fortune. A stable cosmology could reinforce a stable morality.[20]

Rejection of chance required a belief in the centrality and superiority of Homo sapiens. Even if those who considered themselves Darwinians did not fully grasp the subversive implications of natural selection, they did realize that they had to distinguish men from monkeys. To maintain familiar moorings, human beings had to be elevated above the rest of biological life, either on religious or on secular grounds. The Harvard biologist Nathaniel S. Shaler, among others, revived the Paleyite argument from design and tried to reconcile it with Darwin by showing that human intelligence was too complex to be merely a product of chance. For Shaler as for his contemporaries, the choice between design and chance was between meaning and meaninglessness.[21]

Whatever idiom the writer used to pose this conflict, the stakes were high. Well into the twentieth century, belief in luck evoked condemnation from Christian moralists and militant atheists alike. Childhood supersti-

---

[18] Thomas Henry Huxley, *Introductory Science Primer* (London, 1873), 27; "Chance," *Hours at Home* 11 (October 1870): 522–24.

[19] John Bigelow, "What Is Gambling?" *Harper's Monthly,* February 1895, 470–80.

[20] Ibid., 473, 478.

[21] Nathaniel S. Shaler, "Chance or Design," *Andover Review* 12 (August 1889): 117–33.

tions, apparently harmless, were more sinister than they seemed. "The bud may be picturesque sometimes, but the blossom is always noxious," warned an *Outlook* contributor in 1895. Superstition was rooted in "a puerile conception of God and his providence, an inadequate appreciation of the correspondences between cause and effect." Progressive Protestant faith could yoke mechanical causality and Providence.[22]

But science and God could also be sundered. In *The Theory of the Leisure Class* (1899), Thorstein Veblen lumped belief in luck with "devout observances" and other "archaic traits" that would soon be rendered obsolete by the relentlessly advancing "discipline of the machine." A relic of primitive animism, belief in luck was sand in the gears of industrial progress. The key to efficiency was a workforce with heads uncluttered by superstition and filled instead with a matter-of-fact understanding of cause and effect. Nongamblers, all. Often Veblen sounded like a late-twentieth century social scientist discussing "obstacles to modernization in the Third World"— for example, when he wrote, "This lowering of efficiency through a penchant for animistic methods of apprehending facts is especially apparent when taken in the mass—when a given population with an animistic turn is viewed as a whole." Veblen did not specify which given populations in the United States might be so afflicted, but he gave a hint of how widespread he thought the problem was when he noted that "the gambling spirit which pervades the sporting element shades off by insensible gradations into that frame of mind which finds gratification in devout observances." For Veblen, though, the industrialization of consciousness proceeded inexorably; values would evolve to meet the new industrial conditions. Meanwhile, we would live with what a later generation of technological determinists would call "cultural lag."[23]

Despite their mutual hostility, Veblen and the church ladies shared a belief in a huge, relentlessly unfolding plan of progress—directed by science alone or by science and God in tandem. This was the substitute for Providence devised by devotees of "social evolution," who channeled the chaotic implications of Darwinism into a linear stream of thought. On the banks were believers in luck, superstitious folk, mostly of "backward" classes or races, and children. Children who failed to shed their infantile belief in luck would end up poorly, always making excuses, refusing to take responsibility for their actions, never standing on their own two feet—so the

[22] Lily Rice Foxcroft, "Superstition in the Bud," *Outlook*, September 1895, 466–67. For comparable views, see Willam H. Kimball, "Fate and Freedom," *Journal of Speculative Philosophy* 16 (October 1882): 337–42, and Kimball, "Gambling for the Sake of Christ," *Unitarian Review* 21 (January 1884): 65–67.

[23] Thorstein Veblen, *The Theory of the Leisure Class* (1899; New York, 1959), 183, 187. For a comparable view, see M. J. Gorton, "Premonitions, Coincidences, and Superstitions," *Scientific American*, April 4, 1891, 212.

Century suggested in "A Divergence of Views concerning Luck" (1911). The piece presented a young man at college who complained to his uncle of "hard luck" after he had run his motorcar into a cow, failed at his lessons, and lost his credit at the shops. His uncle had no patience with this complaint. "We have outgrown the use of charms and amulets," he said. "The civilized world has ceased to believe in the evil eye or 'controls.' It is time that we also outgrew the belief in luck."[24]

Yet even before the turn of the century, faith in human mastery was becoming threadbare. Amid widening inequalities and fire-breathing denunciations of social injustice, the slogans of self-reliance began to sound hollow, especially to sensitive souls. In *The World of Chance,* published in the panic year of 1893, William Dean Howells recounted the fortunes of an aspiring young writer, S. N. Ray, to underscore the centrality of caprice in the courtship of business success. Ray's publisher Brandreth tells him that "there are no laws of business. There is nothing but chances, and no amount of wisdom can forecast them or control them."[25] Howells realized that luck was threaded throughout the fabric of entrepreneurial society, rendering it more interesting but less just than a perfectly planned utopia.

Howells's own passion for justice led him toward the bland yet admirable utopian vision embodied in *A Traveller from Altruria* (1894). But many of his contemporaries, who shared his skeptical attitude toward the formulaic creed of success, took their discontent in different directions. Recovering the vitalist strain in Victorian thought, they returned to the theme articulated by Tocqueville and Ware, the importance of risk taking in the creation of national and personal greatness.[26] The idea was especially resonant in the 1890s, as upper-class male observers fretted that American men, under the influence of Victorian propriety, were growing effete.

A resurgent discourse of manliness returned the gambling spirit (though usually not gambling itself) to comparative respectability. "Gambling is reprehensible, but the spirit that underlies it is noble," wrote a *Forum* contributor in 1891. "A genuine gambler is a great man gone wrong, and gambling is a misdirection of courage and energy and enterprise—of all those attributes that make man most manly." Some games of chance required the coolness under fire that we prized in our fighting men. Poker was the best example: "What a school of control it is!" announced the author of a poker manual in 1900. "Officers in the army and navy are always capital players because they are taught to restrain their tempers and emotions in the line of duty until it becomes second nature to them. Look at Admiral

---

[24] "A Divergence of Views concerning Luck," *Century* 82 (September 1911): 785–86.

[25] William Dean Howells, *The World of Chance* (New York, 1893), 339.

[26] Walter Houghton discusses this vitalist strain under the heading "Enthusiasm" in his *The Victorian Frame of Mind, 1830–1870* (New Haven, 1957), 263–304. For Howells's utopian vision, see William Dean Howells, *The Altrurian Romances* (Bloomington, 1968).

Dewey's face and see a crack poker player." This was far from "Home, Sweet Home." Real men took risks with a poker face.[27]

Even as Progressive reformers placed unprecedented restrictions on literal gambling, metaphorical gambling acquired new luster. The cultural rehabilitation of the gambler was part of (but not reducible to) a revitalization of bourgeois manhood at the turn of the century. It was embodied in ideals as witless as Theodore Roosevelt's "strenuous life" and as serious as William James's "moral equivalent of war." A common longing to recapture some spontaneous, pulsating energy from the prison of Victorian convention, a common vitalist undercurrent, energized impulses as different as Rooseveltian militarism and Jamesian pragmatism. In James's case, the desire for revitalization led him on a search for supernatural meaning (or at least the *possibility* of it) in what he feared was a meaningless universe. This apparently modern, existential quest was nonetheless conducted under Victorian Protestant auspices: the effort to vindicate ethical action in the world.

At a crucial point in James's development, his entire philosophical and moral project pivoted on the concept of chance. Unlike many of his contemporaries, James had been unable to ignore the great contradiction in late-Victorian intellectual life: between free will and determinism. How could one reconcile familiar ideas of individual moral efficacy (not to mention religious belief) with the various mechanistic determinisms that were acquiring legitimacy as traditional ideas of Providence waned? James addressed this question directly in two classic essays: "The Dilemma of Determinism" (1884) and "The Will to Believe" (1896). The first presented chance as a portal of escape from a mechanistic universe; the second resuscitated Pascal's wager, adducing a new, pragmatic set of reasons for gambling on God.[28]

In "Dilemma," James made his ethical concerns central from the outset. He told the Harvard Divinity students that he would "disclaim openly on the threshold all pretension to prove to you that the freedom of the will is true. The most I hope is to induce some of you to follow my own example in assuming it true, and acting as if it were true." His first move was to observe that ideas of order in the world were rooted in the need for subjective

[27] W. B. Curtis, "The Increase of Gambling and Its Forms," *Forum* 12 (October 1891): 281–92; Eugene Edwards, *Jack Pots* (Chicago, 1900), 16. See also Lawrence Irwell, "Gambling as It Was, and Is," *New Century Review* 4 (July 1899): 33–38. For a spirited but idiosyncratic defense of gambling, based on cultural relativism, hereditarian psychology, and libertarian politics, see James Harold Romain, *Gambling, or Fortuna, Her Temple and Shrine* (Chicago, 1891).

[28] For useful background on how issues of chance became central to James's consciousness, see Paul Jerome Croce, "From History of Science to Intellectual History: The Probabilistic Revolution and the Chance-Filled Universe of William James," *Intellectual History Newsletter* 13 (1991): 11–32, and Croce, *Science and Religion in the Era of William James*, vol. 1, *The Eclipse of Certainty* (Chapel Hill, 1995).

satisfaction—what James would call, in another context, "the sentiment of rationality." He took aim at the most hallowed principle of mechanistic determinism: "The principle of causality, for example, what is it but a postulate, an empty name covering simply a demand that the sequence of events shall some day manifest a deeper kind of belonging of one thing with another than the mere arbitrary juxtaposition which now phenomenally appears? It is as much an altar to an unknown god as the one St. Paul found at Athens."[29]

James sought to dissolve the chains of determinism by resurrecting the claims of chance. This was a daring move, one that James was sure would run afoul of responsible opinion—especially the opinions of determinists, who believed that "chance is something the notion of which no sane mind can for an instant tolerate in the world. What is it, they ask, but barefaced crazy unreason, the negation of intelligibility and law?" But there was nothing "intrinsically irrational or preposterous" about chance, James insisted; we had merely gotten used to seeing it censoriously. Chance in itself was neither good nor bad. Indeed, "it may be lucidity, transparency, fitness incarnate, matching the whole system of other things, when it once has befallen, in an unimaginably perfect way. All that you mean by calling it 'chance' is this is not guaranteed, that it may also fall out otherwise." James was astonished that "so empty and gratuitous a hubbub as this outcry against chance should have found so great an echo in the hearts of men." But perhaps he began to glimpse an explanation when he observed that "the idea of chance is, at bottom, exactly the same thing as the idea of gift,—the one simply being a disparaging, and the other a eulogistic, name for anything on which we have no effective *claim*."[30]

James had hit on an extraordinary insight here, though he did not develop it. The uncertain, unclaimable quality of chance was what made it so offensive to the late-Victorian imagination—an imagination that, despite its tendency to determinism, had fostered more faith in human mastery over fate than any previous body of Western thought. Preoccupied with controlling both inner and outer environments, the late-Victorian bourgeoisie made claims on everyone and everything. Chance was a stench in the nostrils of the disciplined achiever.

James's resurrection of chance, however challenging to conventional wisdom, was done for good, Victorian reasons. He wanted to salvage some intellectually sound basis for ethical action. He found it in the idea of a pluralistic universe, a universe of "indeterminate future volitions" where we could still act as if moral conduct mattered. For James, this conclusion was

[29] William James, "The Dilemma of Determinism" (1884), in John J. McDermott, ed., *The Writings of William James* (New York, 1968), 589.
[30] Ibid., 592–93.

more satisfying than the evasions of the "soft determinists" who claimed to find free will in conformity to universal law. But the pluralistic universe did pose a fundamental challenge to traditional ideas of Providence. If Providence existed in James's universe, he admitted, it would have to be a little less than omniscient, a little more like a chess master facing an amateur opponent: the master knows how the game will come out (he will win), but he doesn't know all the moves.

In "The Dilemma of Determinism," James had created an escape hatch from the iron cage of necessity, religious or secular. Twelve years later, he made a similar argument, for similar reasons, in "The Will to Believe." Here again, chance played a key role in vindicating a morally meaningful universe. The essay was a Protestant resuscitation of Pascal's wager, which in its original Catholic form struck James and his audience alike as laughably unpersuasive. Belief that masses and holy water brought salvation was simply not a live option for late-Victorian, liberal Protestants; it lacked "the inner soul of faith's reality." But pose the possibility that faith might satisfy our deepest passions, unleash ethical energies, revitalize our very being—then the odds shifted dramatically. James was willing to accept Pascal's wager if the benefit to be gained from religion was a renewed sense of moral engagement with the world. Otherworldly salvation was secondary. To the lamentation of Dostoyevsky's Alyosha that without God, everything is permitted, James had replied yes, but we can still act *as if* some things are required of us, and we will live life more intensely if we do.[31]

James's yearning for ethical intensity led him to revalue risk and chance; comparable impulses led his contemporaries in similar directions. John Burroughs defended a Bergsonian vitalist conception of evolution in 1915; the center of his argument was the pervasiveness of chance in organic life. Revitalized respect for belief in luck came from a variety of sources. While most commentators continued to ascribe superstition to the backward and ignorant, a few, such as the psychiatrist H. Addington Bruce, recognized that "in the light of modern discoveries regarding the influence of the mind on bodily states," it was not surprising that lucky charms or good- and bad-luck rituals sometimes actually worked, even among the educated. The body, the unconscious, the child, the primitive, the whole palpitating vastness of organic life—all seemed to be coming into their own after the turn of the century, commanding new respect as causal forces or repositories of wisdom, evoking new interest and even admiration from an intelligentsia that felt cut off from spontaneous experience.[32]

[31] William James, "The Will to Believe" (1896), in McDermott, *Writings,* 717–35, quotation at 720; Fyodor Dostoyevsky, *Brothers Karamazov,* trans. Constance Garnett (1880; New York, 1931), 69, 72.
[32] John Burroughs, "Life and Chance," *North American Review* 202 (August 1915): 230; H. Addington Bruce, "Our Superstitions," *Outlook,* August 26, 1911, 998–1006. For a gen-

Even the Victorian obsession with work seemed to be loosening. The work ethic had always been honored as much in the breach as in the observance, but injunctions to plodding diligence had nonetheless been a major component of officially sanctioned norms throughout the nineteenth century. After the turn of the century, those norms seemed to be growing a little more supple, as youth workers such as Luther Gulick and G. Stanley Hall groped toward a new appreciation of the ways that play could foster a coherent cosmos and a satisfying sense of self. These were the sort of insights that would be fully developed by Johan Huizinga in his classic *Homo Ludens* (1938).[33]

The tendency to question accepted hierarchies of work and play, adulthood and childhood, bestowed new intellectual legitimacy on luck. Childlike spontaneity could be linked with the acceptance of arbitrary fate. An *Atlantic* editorial of 1917, "Io Fortuna!" revealed some of the connections. Dismissing all the bluff and bluster about mastery of fate and captaincy of soul, the author recommended the wisdom of the child, who lived in the immediate present, in accordance with the whims of Fortuna: "And his deepest secret is this, that he looks on all fortune as adventure. For it is not for nothing that upon one stem have grown the two words *Happen* and *Happiness*." It would be hard to find a more explicit repudiation of "manly" self-command.[34]

Homage to Fortuna like the *Atlantic* writer's—or William James's—remained a marginal point of view. Well into the twentieth century, moralists still blasted believers in luck for their absence of backbone; by 1910, legalized gambling had entered a long period of decline—one that would not end until the 1970s. But at the highest intellectual levels a quiet revolution was under way.

European and American thinkers alike—including James's friend and sometime mentor Charles Peirce—were challenging mechanistic determinism on scientific rather than religious grounds, posing instead a probabilistic notion of causality and a statistical idea of law. The shift from a mechanical to a probabilistic concept of causality made chance more than an alias for ignorance. The consequences were immediately apparent in discussions of evolutionary theory: biologists and, later, geneticists could openly confront the element of randomness in Darwinian theory instead of concealing it behind schemes of linear progress, as mechanistic thinkers

eral discussion of this theme, see T. J. Jackson Lears, *No Place of Grace: Antimodernism and the Transformation of American Culture, 1880–1920*, 2d ed. (1981; Chicago, 1994).

[33] G. Stanley Hall, *Adolescence* (Boston, 1904); Luther Gulick, *The Philosophy of Play* (New York, 1920); Johan Huizinga, *Homo Ludens: A Study of the Play-Element in Culture* (1938; Boston, 1955). For a subtle reading of this awakening interest in play, see Donal Mrozek, "The Natural Limits of Unstructured Play, 1880–1914," in Kathryn Grover, ed., *Hard at Play: Leisure in America, 1840–1940* (Amherst, 1992), 210–26.

[34] "Io Fortuna!" *Atlantic Monthly*, January 1917, 141–42.

had done. According to Peirce, to see natural laws or uniformities in nature as the result of evolution was to see them "not to be absolute, not to be obeyed precisely. It makes an element of indeterminacy, spontaneity, or absolute chance in nature," he wrote in 1891. We had to expect "a certain swerving of the facts from any formula."[35]

For anyone who demanded certainty, this could be disturbing news if one thought hard enough about it. It suggested, as Ian Hacking has written, that there are no constants in nature, "over and above those numbers upon which we increasingly settle." "Natural law" was a statistical construction of regularity amid the chaotic unpredictability of the universe. "Chance pours itself in at every avenue of sense," Peirce wrote. "It is of all things the most obtrusive." Statistical concepts of regularity allowed scientists to continue formulating orderly explanations while they acknowledged the obtrusiveness of contingency. Even as James was composing his philosophical defense of chance in "The Dilemma of Determinism," statisticians were making it a legitimate category of scientific thought.[36]

But often the intellectual rehabilitation of chance robbed the concept of its power. By acknowledging indeterminism, statistical thinking tamed chance, as Hacking makes clear. Chance became little more than the predictably unpredictable occurrence, the standard deviation. In the actuarial tables of insurance companies, the risk assessment studies of government planners, or the market research of major corporations, a new conception of the cosmos emerged—one that was all the more orderly because it acknowledged and aimed to manage the occasional eruption of disorder. The taming of chance underwrote the rise of sorting and categorizing institutions in both the private and public sectors of advanced industrial society. The face of modern authority has worn a variety of expressions, ranging from the bland impassivity of the party bureaucrat to the frenetic bonhomie of the marketing executive. The managerial agenda common to all has depended on statistically based norms, which reduced chance to the exception that proved the rule.[37]

The managerial scheme of things emerged alongside the drive to recover primitive masculinity and childish play. The two developments were closely related. The language of management provided a new idiom for

[35] Charles S. Peirce, "The Architecture of Theories," *Monist* (January 1891): 161–76, reprinted in Philip Wiener, ed., *Values in a Universe of Chance: Selected Writings of Charles S. Peirce* (Stanford, Calif., 1958), 142–59, quotation on 148.

[36] Ian Hacking, *The Taming of Chance* (Cambridge, 1990), 200. Peirce quoted in Hacking, *Taming of Chance,* 200.

[37] On risk assessment, see Mary Douglass and Aaron Wildavsky, *Risk and Culture: An Essay on the Selection of Technical and Environmental Dangers* (Berkeley, 1982); Mary Douglass, *Risk Acceptability according to the Social Sciences* (New York, 1985). On actuarial use of statistics, see Viviana Zelizer, *Morals and Markets: The Development of Life Insurance in the United States* (New York, 1979). On market research and the worldview behind it, see Jackson Lears, *Fables of Abundance: A Cultural History of Advertising in America* (New York, 1994), pt. 2.

orchestrating the recapture of lost spontaneity. Sometimes that idiom was studded with Darwinian metaphors, which had entered social science and given even gambling some legitimacy. In 1900, the sociologist W. I. Thomas identified "the gaming instinct" as one of several "instincts developed in the struggle for food and rivalry for mates." It was "born in all normal persons. It is one expression of a powerful reflex fixed far back in animal experience." Powerful animal instincts were "normal" (and normality itself was a new, statistical construction), but those instincts were in need of appropriate outlets. Antigambling reformers under the sway of this argument admitted that gambling could not be merely prohibited; wholesome alternatives had to be found.[38]

The search for substitute gratifications reduced play to recreation—something satisfying but fundamentally unserious, a sport or hobby that would re-create the player's capacity to perform in the workplace where it counted. Gambling, however instinctual its origins, did not fall into this category. During the 1920s and 1930s, the spread of managerial thought provided a new and more supple language of personal efficiency. Legalized gambling became more restricted than ever before in American history, as casinos were confined to exotic locales such as Las Vegas or Havana. In the relatively stable and prosperous consumer culture that emerged after World War II, carnivalesque impulses were contained in a dynamic equilibrium of production and consumption; gambling came to be seen as abnormal.[39]

In the midcentury critique of gambling, clinical idioms reinforced moral language. A psychology of adjustment identified gambling with neurotic compulsion. "I submit that the gambler is not simply a rational though 'weak' individual who is willing to run the risk of failure and moral censure in order to get money the easy way, but a *neurotic with an unconscious wish to lose,*" wrote the psychoanalyst Edmund Bergler in *The Psychology of Gambling* (1958). The gambler remained an antiself, but on grounds of pathology rather than immorality. Though gambling survived and even flourished on the margins of a suburbanizing society, the gambler could be defined as a deviant by social scientists who envisioned American society as a smoothly functioning system.[40]

Yet the managerial vision provoked widespread skepticism and resistance. The emergence of quantum physics in the 1920s and 1930s pushed the probabilistic revolution into uncharted realms of uncertainty. Few nonspecialists understood the full significance of Werner Heisenberg's inde-

[38] W. I. Thomas, "The Gaming Instinct," *American Journal of Sociology* 6 (1900): 760.

[39] On the restriction of legalized gambling, see Findlay, *People of Chance,* chaps. 5–7; for a fuller exploration of the containment of carnival in twentieth-century consumer culture, see Lears, *Fables of Abundance,* esp. pt. 2.

[40] Edmund Bergler, *The Psychology of Gambling* (New York, 1958), 12.

terminacy principle, but many embraced it as a means of escape from a perfectly managed universe. Dreams of chaotic freedom inspired a continuing flight to the disorderly fringes of society and thought, where gamblers, artists, writers, and philosophers could freely indulge their fascination with untamed chance. Surrealists and dadaists used chance imagery in their work as a way of tapping into the "inexhaustible, uncontrollable" unconscious and erasing the false boundaries between art and life. As Tristan Tzara wrote: "Art is not the most precious manifestation of life. Art has not the celestial and universal value that people like to attribute to it. Life is far more interesting."[41]

And life was fortuitous contingency. Marcel Duchamp dropped threads on canvas and glued them in the configurations they formed when they fell; Max Ernst created what he called "the decalcomania of chance" by spreading ink between two sheets of paper, then pulling them apart; Tzara composed poems by drawing words from a hat. Later in the century, during and after World War II, the composer John Cage ruled a staff on a sheet of paper, then placed notes on the staff at the points on the paper where certain minute imperfections occurred; the painter George Brecht rolled inked marbles over an irregular surface, then rebounded several off one another. And Jackson Pollock dripped paint on canvases, floors, walls, wherever it fell.[42] Was this all simply highjinks *pour épater le bourgeois?* Sometimes it seemed so, as in the happenings that Cage and friends began to stage during the mid-1960s. Or was there more going on?

There was, first of all, a departure from familiar notions of craft and control. Automatism, Brecht wrote, required "that we accept its product as something which it really is not," that we read into dreams, hallucinations, and fantasies "characteristics which they do not possess in an absolute way. Duchamp called this 'irony' ('a playful way of accepting something')." Acceptance of chance required a playful sense of irony, which subverted literalist demands for certainty.[43]

But devotees of chance imagery were not simply subversive. "Chance opened up perceptions to me, immediate spiritual insights," said Hans Arp. "Intuition led me to revere the law of chance as the highest and deepest of laws, the law that rises from the fundament. An insignificant word might become a deadly thunderbolt. One little sound might destroy the earth.

---

[41] Tristan Tzara, "Lecture on Dada" (1922), in Robert Motherwell, ed., *The Dada Painters and Poets: An Anthology* (New York, 1951), 248. The influence of twentieth-century physics on ideas about chance and necessity is a huge subject, one far beyond the scope of my inquiry here. For useful overviews, see I. J. Good, "Changing Concepts of Chance," *Nature*, March 31, 1988, 405–6; Werner Heisenberg, *Physics and Philosophy* (New York, 1956); P. C. Davies, *The Ghost in the Atom* (New York, 1989); and E. Lorenz, *The Essence of Chaos* (New York, 1993).

[42] George Brecht, *Chance Imagery* (New York, 1965), 5–7, 14.

[43] Ibid., 4.

One little sound might create a new universe." Behind dada lay "an almost Buddhist religion of indifference" and at-oneness with the cosmos, so Tzara claimed, cryptically. For Brecht, the reason for using the term "chance imagery" was "to place the painter's, musician's, poet's, dancer's chance images in the same category as natural chance images (the configuration of meadow grasses, the arrangement of stones on a brook-bottom), and to get away from the idea that the artist makes something 'special' and beyond the world of ordinary things." The world of ordinary things was a world of chance. The logic of indeterminism, which Brecht found in twentieth-century physics as well as statistics, provided him and other chance imagists with a rationale for breaking down barriers between art and life.[44]

Why did they want to break them down? The motives no doubt varied with each artist; nearly all involved some protest against the traditional authority of high art: a familiar avant-garde reflex. But nearly all, as well, involved some gesture toward a more playful connection with the material world—more playful, at least, than the impulse toward technological mastery. And few artists during these midcentury decades were indifferent toward the development of modern managerial authority.

The issues surrounding chance remained political and ethical as well as aesthetic. Untamed chance grew more appealing as Nazi storm troopers goose-stepped across Europe and Stalin conducted his show trials. Huizinga composed his paean to serendipitous play in the shadow of totalitarian dictatorships. By the 1930s, the specter of statistically based social control offered cold comfort to refugees from mechanistic determinism. Recovering William James (and taking comfort from Heisenberg), philosophers and religious thinkers found contingency more attractive. The popularity of Christian existentialism during and after World War II was one expression of this feeling. Some existentialist theologians (Paul Tillich, Simone Weil) sought to restore an element of spontaneity, even randomness to their descriptions of the experience of grace that had become so routinized in both the Protestant and Catholic traditions. Like chance (for James), grace could be a kind of spiritual gift.[45]

Most of these intellectual projects paid little attention to the popular culture of luck—the dense cloud of signs and portents, omens and premonitions and coincidences, that lay beneath the abstract realm of theologians and philosophers. Ordinary believers in luck were instinctively

---

[44] Jean [Hans] Arp, "Dada Was Not a Farce" (1949), in Motherwell, *Dada Painters and Poets*, 294; Tzara, "Lecture on Dada," 247; Brecht, *Chance Imagery*, 5. For a surrealist theory that justifies chance imagery (and possibly gambling as well), see Georges Bataille on the notions of "expenditure" and "formlessness" in his *Visions of Excess* (Minneapolis, 1985), esp. 31, 128–29.

[45] Paul Tillich, *The New Being* (New York, 1955), esp. chaps. 6, 7; Simone Weil, *Gravity and Grace* (New York, 1953), 3–6. For the influence of Heisenberg, see William Barrett, *Irrational Man: A Study in Existential Philosophy*, Anchor Books Edition (New York, 1958), 38–40.

more at ease with contingency and irrationality, more doubtful that diligence was the only path to success, than the increasingly professionalized intelligentsia could be. The avant-garde artists and writers, the philosophers of play, the theologians of grace—nearly all, despite their reverence for chance, lived in a universe apart from the gamblers on the street.

Ralph Ellison was one of the few American modernists to bridge the gap between numbers running and philosophical debate. In *Invisible Man* (1952), Ellison caught some of the largest significance of the popular culture of luck. The narrator has moved from the rural South to Harlem in the 1930s; it is a world where little old ladies keep their dream books next to their Bibles, so they will know what number to play, where street corner crapshooters affect a grand insouciance even as they bend their knees to Fortune. For most of the novel the narrator resists this world, as he works his way through two philosophies of history that emphasize human mastery over fate: first liberal individualism, then Soviet-style collectivism. Both eventually seem hollow, fundamentally flawed in their dependence on a notion of history as linear progress.

The narrator's deconversion from the communist "Brotherhood" involves a repudiation of its "scientific" worldview and a reconnection with his own vernacular vision. Gradually the strains between ideology and experience begin to show. Within weeks after he has become a spellbinding street organizer, the narrator receives an anonymous note warning him to go slowly, to avoid arousing the racial anxiety of the white leadership. He begins haltingly to recover some of his cultural past: Brother Tarp, the old janitor in his Harlem office, had years ago filed through a section of leg-iron to escape a chain gang down South. The old man gives it to the narrator as "a kind of lucky piece," and the narrator keeps it on his desk, even though the Brotherhood's leadership disapproves.[46]

The narrator also begins to discover alternatives to the Brotherhood in the present. One is ultimately embodied in Tod Clifton, a brilliant, charismatic organizer, "a hipster, a zoot suiter, a sharpie—except his head of Persian lamb's wool had never known a straightener." Together they confront the black nationalist, Ras the Exhorter; Clifton comes away strangely disturbed—maybe Ras is "unscientific," as the Brotherhood claims, but "sometimes a man *has* to plunge outside history," he says. For the narrator the alternative to purposeful, linear history is chaos, but he is haunted by Clifton's words even as he gives thanks for Brotherhood. When he is removed from Harlem at the height of his success, his anger flares: "For a moment I had almost allowed an old southern backwardness which I had thought dead to wreck my career." Meanwhile Clifton disappears, resurfacing as a street vendor, selling dancing Sambo dolls, working without a

[46] Ralph Ellison, *Invisible Man* (1952; New York, 1992), 381.

license, one step ahead of the police. The narrator is enraged, then appalled as he sees Clifton gunned down in a pointless confrontation with a pursuing cop.[47]

"Why should a man deliberately plunge outside of history and peddle an obscenity?"—a dancing Sambo, an emblem of black degradation—the narrator wonders.[48] Why should Clifton abandon the orderly, progressive world picture provided by the Brotherhood? Maybe for some of the same reasons William James rejected the "block universe" of mechanical determinism. And maybe for some different ones.

The complexity of Ellison's philosophical position becomes apparent as the narrator descends underground to the subway. As he watches a group of black boys, recently arrived in Harlem from the deep South, standing stiffly in their suits on a subway platform, the narrator feels an odd but fundamental kinship with them. They look like him. They remind him of what one of his teachers said to him: "'You're like one of those African sculptures, distorted in the interests of design.' Well, what design and whose?" What was their common bond with him, their common role in history? How could these "birds of passage who were too obscure for learned classification" fit into any linear scheme of progress?

> What if history was a gambler, instead of a force in a laboratory experiment, and the boys his ace in the hole? What if history was not a reasonable citizen, but a madman full of paranoid guile, and these boys his agents, his big surprise! His own revenge? For they were outside, in the dark with Sambo, the dancing paper doll; taking it on the lambo with my fallen brother Tod Clifton (Tod, Tod) running and dodging the forces of history instead of making a dominating stand.[49]

The passage suggests a wide range of interpretations. It is part of a plea to include the historically voiceless in history—a task taken up by historians in the decades since Ellison published *Invisible Man*. It could also be construed as a warning that the forgotten people of the world, the exploited and colonized, are beginning to stir. But far more challenging are the philosophical and ethical textures in the passage. History is unmanageable, it suggests; the dream of technical mastery is an illusion. The acceptance of arbitrary fate is the beginning of wisdom.

This outlook is not mere passivity. It is a different way of inhabiting the world, outside the triumphalist blarings of will and choice. But it is not a prescription for ethical or even political quiescence. It could be the way of the trickster, exercising the powers of the powerless, or of the artist, em-

[47] Ibid., 359, 371, 425–27.
[48] Ibid., 431.
[49] Ibid., 433–34.

bracing what Joyce called "silence, exile, and cunning."[50] It is the way of Ellison's narrator, who retreats to his brightly lit underground lair and embraces invisibility as a liberation rather than a curse. And it is the way of Safet Somo, darting about the streets of Sarajevo, "running and dodging the forces of history instead of making a dominating stand," reminding us that chance is less a problem to be solved than a portal of possibility.

[50] James Joyce, *A Portrait of the Artist as a Young Man* (1916; New York, 1964), 247.

David Brion Davis, 1997. Courtesy of David Brion Davis.

David Brion Davis: A Biographical Appreciation

RICHARD WIGHTMAN FOX

I never had the privilege of being David Brion Davis's student, but I came close when as a Stanford graduate student I was hired as his research assistant. He had come to Stanford's Center for Advanced Study in the Behavioral Sciences in 1972, and I spent the year searching out some very far-flung references and citations for his *Problem of Slavery in the Age of Revolution*. Like the other fellows at the center (Eugene Genovese among them), Davis would sit cloistered in his redwood office, a bucolic hideaway nestled among the oak trees of the Stanford hills, and I would deliver photocopies or books, some of them in foreign languages. His command of the literature in a variety of languages was awe inspiring, of course, but I was even more struck by his ability to keep all the note cards subordinate to the "big story"—the interpenetration of moral and material elements in the rise of opposition to slavery. I loved brushing up against the artifacts of Davis's productive process, registering the physical placement of his books, colleagues' manuscripts, note cards, pens and pencils, and his bicycle propped securely against the wall across the room from his desk.

Somehow, I had no idea how, a book was emerging from all this *stuff*. Some mystifying alchemy was going on in his brain as evidence was weighed and ideas congealed. I remember him saying, looking up from his typewriter one day, that scholarship was a lonely vocation; you had to enjoy long periods of solitude. That comment fortified me for months as I went about my own schedule of classes and papers and dreamed of someday having an office and knowing how to fashion a book. I thought of Davis ensconced in his oak trees and transporting himself through extended acts of mind into distant worlds of struggle and aspiration. We became friends during his year at the center. I started right out calling him "David," which I could get away with because this was the West Coast and because at Stanford many of us (at least after orals) called our professors by their first names. Davis liked this casual practice and said he wished it was done that way in the East. I've called him David ever since and will do so here.

In two conversations with me in 1995, David looked back over his life, showing the same fascination with the contingencies and particularities of his personal story that he has always had for those of the historical record. To my mind David's overriding sense of the power of the particular and the contingent is the key to understanding his life as well as his work. Things happen eruptively, not according to plan; history is as unpredictable as life, much more like a narrative of accidents than an unfolding of essences. David's attention to particulars gives his history writing its empirical density and shields him from the temptations of postmodern skepticism. He has never doubted that there are facts out there and that it is our duty to find them and establish their meaning. But he has also never doubted that those "facts" are awash in a sea of "values" and that our goal as scholars is to conduct a moral inquiry as well as a scientific one. The significant facts are always afloat in the brutal, poignant, or redemptive ironies and paradoxes that mark the human condition in all eras. Our historical scholarship should record not just the behavior, but the endeavor of our ancestors. If we tell the story of the past with enough imagination, it will illuminate the deepest moral dilemmas of our own lives. And it will make of our history writing a moral practice, as we judge the achievements and failures of our predecessors with humility rather than condescension. A lifelong student of "progress," David is (as he put it in the preface to *Slavery and Human Progress*) an "agnostic" about actual progress.[1] He shares the double sentiment of William James, who in his lecture of the 1890s called "What Makes a Life Significant" observed first that the "thing of deepest . . . significance in life" was "its character of progress, or that strange union of reality with ideal novelty which it continues from one moment to another to present." But James then concluded:

> Those philosophers are right who contend that the world is a standing thing, with no progress, no real history. The changing conditions of history touch only the surface of the show. The altered equilibriums and redistributions only diversify our opportunities and open chances to us for new ideals. But, with each new ideal that comes into life, the chance for a life based on some old ideal will vanish; and he would needs be a presumptuous calculator who should with confidence say that the total sum of significances is positively and absolutely greater at any one epoch than at any other of the world.[2]

[1] David Brion Davis, *Slavery and Human Progress* (New York, 1984), xvi.
[2] John J. McDermott, ed., *The Writings of William James* (Chicago, 1977), 657, 660.

In the same 1984 preface in which he confessed to his agnosticism on the subject of progress, David declared himself an agnostic on the question of God. He was then a member of a Conservative Jewish synagogue, since his second wife, Toni, is Jewish, and they were raising their two sons, now grown, in the Jewish faith. But in 1987, as he turned sixty, David's moral and intellectual instincts drew him into a yearlong formal conversion to the Jewish faith, and here too the theme of historical particularity is paramount. The significant contingencies of personal and public history are not only surrounded by values, they *are* values. God is in the details. The path to faith is mysterious, but many who come to believe in God speak, as David does, of a dawning wonder at creation, at the proliferating web of human and natural dramas, and of a welcome seeding of gratitude in one's heart. "God created man because he loves stories," Elie Wiesel has said, and that observation captures for me the pitch and tone of David's religious belief and historical practice.[3]

It started with a proliferation of stories. An only child, born in Denver in 1927, he lived with his parents and his paternal grandmother, Isabel Minerva Brion Davis, who was "almost an older sibling." She was "an omniverous reader," he remembers, who showered him with tales of her own and the nation's past. She had been born in 1861 and remembered hearing on her porch of Lincoln's assassination. As a teenager in rural New York, she was a schoolteacher and kept a revolver in her desk for protection. Still a teenager, she moved to Nebraska, where one day, she told David, a group of Indians in war paint broke into her home and stole a blanket. Isabel filled his head with history, and gave him companionship that lasted until her death in 1953, a year after the death of David's mother.

Martha Wirt Davis was born in 1905 into a family with German Lutheran roots, but she was raised a Christian Scientist, a faith she later rejected. She became a painter and a writer, publishing how-to articles in women's and family magazines and, under her pen name, Wirt Van Arsdale, a mystery novel titled *The Professor Knits a Shroud,* which became a "Crime Club" selection. She was forty-six years old when she died suddenly of a heart attack, during David's first year as a graduate student at Harvard. Her writing and painting had been an important inspiration for him. But equally significant for his formation was her attention to the details of his education, which took place under the stresses of the relentless geographical displacement imposed by his father's up-and-down literary career.

Clyde Brion Davis was born in 1894 and raised in the denomination named the Christian Church. He left school in the ninth grade, but his education continued on his own as he read history, philosophy (he loved Spinoza and Kant), and literature (Anatole France was a favorite). Like Martha Wirt he rebelled against his parents' faith. Both of them continued

---

[3] Elie Wiesel, *The Gates of the Forest,* trans. Frances Frenaye (New York, 1966), n.p. (epigram).

to believe in some sort of divine force but thought it might well be a force indifferent to human beings. Clyde considered himself, in adulthood, an agnostic.

His writing took his family from one place to another over the entire course of David's childhood: Seattle, Buffalo, Denver, Carmel, and Beverly Hills, to name the major stops. They never owned a house before David went away to college. He went to five high schools in four years and never lived in a single house longer than three years, a pattern that played havoc with his youthful social life and drove him deeply into books and the life of the mind, a course his parents encouraged by reading to him often. They were, in fact, concerned that he was reading too much as a child, for he complained of headaches, which they attributed to eye strain. Of course, their constant reading to him made him crave books all the more. Later his father gave him a list of choice authors, including Mark Twain and Anatole France. And David acquired his own catalogue of favorites: Robert Louis Stevenson's *Kidnapped,* Dos Passos's *USA* trilogy, anything by Hemingway.

Clyde Brion Davis was a journalist working his way up during the depression from newspaper to newspaper. He left the *Seattle Post-Intelligencer* in 1930 to become a columnist at the *Buffalo Times,* and David remembers the drive eastward that summer on the mostly dirt roads across the northern states. Several years in grammar schools around Buffalo were followed by the fifth grade in Denver and sixth grade in Carmel, California, which David thought was "paradise." Unfortunately for this edenic life, his father was becoming a well-known novelist. The success of *The Anointed* (a Book-of-the-Month-Club selection in 1937) was followed by the even bigger splash of *"The Great American Novel — —"* (a full club selection in 1938), and Clyde decided to give up journalism and write fiction full-time. The family headed back to Buffalo so that he could be closer to the literary life of Manhattan. David cried inconsolably on leaving Carmel.

"Small things can change your life," Clyde Brion Davis wrote in the third sentence of *"The Great American Novel — —"* and his son picked up this same sense of the weight of particulars—and of luck.[4] At the junior high school in Hamburg, New York, a general science teacher named Ed Martelle spotted David in the crowd. His attentiveness helped build up David's self-confidence and persuaded him he wanted to be a scientist. Much later, as a first-year professor at Cornell, David located Martelle, by then a principal in Binghamton, and paid him a visit.

On September 1, 1939, David was in a restaurant eating Italian food with his mother when a newsboy burst in the door brandishing a paper with "WAR" spread across the top. Martha and Clyde had been isolationists, du-

---

[4] Clyde Brion Davis, *"The Great American Novel — —"* (New York, 1938), 3.

bious about Franklin Roosevelt's foreign policy. Once the United States entered the war, however, Clyde attempted to become a war correspondent for *PM*. He made it as far as Lisbon but was unable to get to any other part of Europe and had to return home. His fiction writing also was going nowhere, although David believes his father's manuscript *Shadow of a Tiger* (which David had published posthumously in 1963) may be his best book. Reunited in 1942, the family headed for Hollywood so that Clyde could try writing for the screen. As a tenth-grader David received another dose of his beloved California in the form of Beverly Hills High School. Despite having no social life, he enjoyed the school and did well (he loved German in particular). He wished he could stay, but his father had little success in Hollywood, and they returned to New York, this time to Manhattan.

His eleventh-grade school year there was a disaster. His parents put him in the Straubenmueller Textile High School so he could keep up with his German, but the teachers quickly discovered they were unequipped to teach him either science or literature at the level he needed. They stuck him in the library where he read Dreiser's *American Tragedy* and other books. Things got worse when his parents took him right out of Straubenmueller, and he passed the exam to enter the Bronx High School of Science. Arriving after the start of the school year, he found all the seats in his classroom occupied, so he had to sit on the radiator. He was left in the dust by the mostly Jewish pupils, who ran circles around him in both science and German (where their Yiddish gave them a large advantage). On a particular Jewish holiday David was one of the few students to show up for school. He had never heard of "Jewish holidays," and noting the empty halls he innocently remarked to one of the (Jewish) teachers, "There sure are a lot of Jews in this school," to which the teacher responded with a smile, "There sure are." Had he remained at the school, he is convinced he would have failed his courses.

This moment was one of the lowest in David's life, and his mother fortunately stepped forward to push for his admission to the McBurney School, a private day school run by the YMCA. His three semesters there halted his slide into academic disrepute, a descent that he feels might easily have continued and thrust his life into an entirely different course. Benjamin Chamberlain, his English teacher, took charge of teaching him to write. ("I can see you've been reading Dos Passos," he wrote on one of his papers.) David thrived and won all the top medals, not only in creative writing but in debate and extempore speaking. Still, he had no social life. There were no dates in high school. He corresponded with a girl in Hamburg, five hundred miles away, whom he had seen twice. He liked skiing and hiking, but with the exception of a spirited stint on McBurney's champion swimming team, he was never much drawn to team sports, either as player or spectator. He was a de facto seminarian of the intellectual life.

Through high school David persisted in the idea that he would become a scientist. He remembers being especially fascinated by a Museum of Natural History exhibit on atomic energy. But in the war years he changed his mind. After graduation in the spring of 1945 he became an infantry private and was sent to Georgia to train for the invasion of Japan. On maneuvers one day in August, his unit got word of Hiroshima. With the visit to the Natural History exhibit fresh in his mind, David explained to his fellow GI's that the war would be over before they could be shipped out for the invasion that would have cost many of them their lives. Instead of Japan he was sent to Germany, on a segregated troop ship. In mid-Atlantic some superior officer gave him a billy club and told him to go down to the hold to prevent the black troops from gambling. That was David's first knowledge of the two thousand African Americans on board. "I found myself, in effect, on board a slave ship," David wrote of this experience. "Gazing through the flickering light at dozens of crap games," the eighteen-year-old enforcer of the law "was greeted by some amused, half-naked black soldiers who asked, 'What yo doin' down here, white boy?'"[5]

David's letters home from Germany, which he cites in the same published memoir, reveal not only a preoccupation with the racism rampant in the American army but also a deep interest in literary expression. There is a lot of Hemingway and Dos Passos in them, and a lot of the teenager making contact with his two literary parents. When he went on his "R and R" vacation in February 1946, he had the time to think about his future. The GIs in Germany could choose trips to a number of destinations, and all of them except David avoided the sign-up sheet for the Riviera because they had no idea what it was. David found himself alone at the Hotel Ruhl in a tourist-free Nice, lounging on a balcony overlooking the Mediterranean. There it first dawned on him that he might want to be a college teacher and a historian. He knew it was too early to make a firm career choice, but in a remarkable letter home on October 9, 1946 (a letter now in his possession), he announced some of the central concerns that would later animate his scholarly work.

I believe that the problems that surround us today are not to be blamed on individuals or even groups of individuals, but on the human race as a whole, its collective lack of perspective and knowledge of itself. That is where history comes in. There has been a lot of hokum concerning psychoanalysis, but I think the basic principle of probing into the past, especially the hidden and subconscious past, for truths which govern and influence present actions, is fairly sound. Teaching history, I think, should be a similiar process. An unearthing of truths long buried beneath superficial facts and propaganda; a

[5] David Brion Davis, "World War II and Memory," *Journal of American History* 77 (September 1990): 581.

presentation of perspective and an overall, comprehensive view of what people did and thought and why they did it.

Teaching that sort of history, David told his family, might "make us understand ourselves. It would show the present conflicts to be as silly as they are. And above all it would make people stop and think before blindly following some bigoted group to make the world safe for Aryans or democrats or Mississippians."

First he had to go to college. He came back from Germany in November 1946 and started Dartmouth in the spring of 1947. Unfortunately, the history department there was "terrible," he recollects, so he majored in philosophy and took a good deal of psychology. Thanks to his work in psychology he considered for a time becoming a doctor and a psychiatrist, but the idea faded when he learned he would have to retool in biology and chemistry. Creative writing was also on his mind. He enrolled in Martha Foley's writing class at Columbia Summer School, but Foley was ambivalent about his work. So was the *Atlantic,* which rejected one of David's stories that his father had submitted.

On graduating from Dartmouth in 1950, David was still not sure which career to pursue. Newly married, he got a fellowship from Dartmouth to spend the summer interviewing Germans about the Allied occupation and wrote a long report. In the fall he tried finding a job in journalism, but even with his father's assistance he could find nothing, although for a time a post in Denver looked promising. Had the newspaper market been better in that particular year, David thinks he might never have embarked on the path of graduate education. In October 1950 he found employment in Wichita, where the aircraft manufacturer Cessna hired him as a sheet metal worker. When Cessna found out he was a college graduate, however, they redirected him away from the production line and made him a scheduler. From that position David applied to Harvard's American Civilization graduate program. He honestly filled out his financial aid form, acknowledging his then wife's receipt of some stocks from her family, and was admitted, without financial aid, for the fall of 1951.

One might guess that the rest of David's career unfolded naturally from that point on, and a curriculum vitae summary would suggest it did: two years in Cambridge, a year away teaching at Dartmouth, a final year at Harvard researching and writing his thesis under Howard Mumford Jones on the subject of homicide in American fiction, and assistant professor at Cornell beginning in 1955, followed by tenure three years later. But as David looks back at those years he remembers how difficult they were and recollects two points at which he came close to tumbling off the professional historical track. Again, contingency and luck, as he sees it, were decisive.

In eerie anticipation of our own era, the job market for the fall of 1955 was abysmal. Even a candidate, like David, who had published two of his first-year graduate student papers ("The New England Origins of Mormonism" in the *New England Quarterly* in 1953 and "Ten-Gallon Hero" in the *American Quarterly* in 1954), was in no position to expect to be hired. At the American Historical Association convention one of David's Dartmouth mentors, political theorist (and Diderot biographer) Arthur Wilson, introduced him to Cornell history chairman Paul Gates as they passed in a corridor. Months later at spring break, David and his wife left Cambridge for a trip to South Carolina, and Paul Gates chose that moment to call David to offer him a job. Unable to reach him, Gates contacted Clyde Brion Davis and said he would have to give the position to Cornell's second choice if he could not reach David. Knowing the state of the job market, the senior Davis called the South Carolina State Police and informed them that there was a "family emergency." Although the police failed to track him down, David happened to call his father from a pay phone as he started home and then made contact with Gates just in time.

David had one more hurdle to overcome. He had expected his dissertation to gain ready approval at Harvard because his adviser had signed off on it. But as he labored in Ithaca teaching three courses, he found out that Frederick Merk, one of his committee members, was offering some resistance. Faced with the prospect of thesis revisions in addition to course preparations and aware that Cornell would not renew his one-year appointment if his degree was not forthcoming, David feared as the fall darkened that his career was doomed. In a state of angst he flew to Cambridge to talk to Merk, who had fortunately decided in the interim that the manuscript required only slight changes. Cornell published *Homicide in American Fiction* in 1956, and David was awarded tenure in 1958. Merk's change of heart, like the luck of the serendipitous phone call to his frantic father, kept David on the path toward university teaching and research. His "Problem of Slavery" series, one of the most important scholarly endeavors of our time, may appear to us to be the inevitable product of David's skill and will, but it hung historically by the thread of a contingent series of small but decisive events. David Brion Davis would in any case have become a writer and probably, given his parental models, a writer about American culture, but his particular adult trajectory was decisively molded by forces over which he had little or no control.

His overriding sense of historical contingency has imbued David's scholarship with its dense factual array and its appreciation for the unexpected and ultimately inexplicable in the historical record. His interpretive flair rests on the foundation of his wonder at the power of particulars to give shape to culture. His important stock-taking article "Some Recent Directions in American Cultural History" closes with a strong endorsement of biography as a mode of writing especially well equipped to effect "a synthesis of culture and history," for it can show "how cultural tensions and contradictions may be internalized, struggled with, and resolved within actual individuals."[6] David's own biography would prove the point, as cultural forces deposited in him by his family and impinging on him from the outside through the depression, the war, and the postwar years joined with his own native endowment to forge an idiosyncratic self—a man whose intense devotion to ideas, to scholarship, and to friends has caused many of us to shake our heads in gratitude. Those of us whose luck has brought our paths into proximity with his carry him around with us as an exemplar, one we can call on as we confront and struggle with our own "cultural tensions and contradictions." We can have the warm satisfaction of knowing that from his mature vantage point we are all a part of the providential stream of particulars that prompts him to marvel and give thanks.

[6] David Brion Davis, "Some Recent Directions in American Cultural History," *American Historical Review* 73 (February 1968): 705.

Contributors

Edward L. Ayers is the Hugh P. Kelly Professor of History at the University of Virginia. He is the author of *The Promise of the New South: Life after Reconstruction* (Owsley Prize, Southern Historical Association; Rawley Prize, Organization of American Historians) and director of *The Valley of the Shadow: Two Communities in the American Civil War*, a digital history.

Joel Bernard is writing a book on the origins of Anglo-American moral reform. He lives in Portland, Oregon.

William E. Forbath is Professor of Law and History at the University of Texas at Austin and author of *Law and the Shaping of the American Labor Movement* as well as numerous articles on social and constitutional history.

Richard Wightman Fox is Professor of History at Boston University. He is the author of *Reinhold Niebuhr: A Biography* and coeditor of *A Companion to American Thought* and *In the Face of the Facts: Moral Inquiry in American Scholarship*.

Jonathan A. Glickstein is Associate Professor of History at the University of California, Santa Barbara. He is the author of *Concepts of Free Labor in Antebellum America* and, most recent, "Pressures from Below: Pauperism, Chattel Slavery, and the Ideological Construction of Free Market Labor Incentives in Antebellum America," *Radical History Review* (Fall 1997).

Karen Halttunen is Professor of History at the University of California, Davis. She is the author of *Confidence Men and Painted Women: A Study of Middle-Class Culture in America, 1830–1870* and a forthcoming study of murder and the Gothic imagination in American culture.

T. J. Jackson Lears is Board of Governors Professor of History at Rutgers University, New Brunswick. He is the author of *No Place of Grace: Antimodernism and the Transformation of American Culture, 1880–1920* and *Fables of Abundance: A Cultural History of Advertising in America.*

Anne C. Loveland is T. Harry Williams Professor of American History at Louisiana State University. She is the author of *American Evangelicals and the U.S. Military, 1942–1993, Lillian Smith: A Southerner Confronting the South* (Willie Lee Rose Publication Prize), and *Southern Evangelicals and the Social Order, 1800–1860.*

Lewis Perry is Andrew Jackson Professor of History at Vanderbilt University. His books include *Intellectual Life in America: A History* and *Boats against the Current: American Culture between Revolution and Modernity, 1820–1860.*

Anne C. Rose is Associate Professor of History and Religious Studies at Pennsylvania State University and the author of *Transcendentalism as a Social Movement, 1830–1850* (Best Book of 1981, Society for Historians of the Early American Republic), *Victorian America and the Civil War*, and *Voices of the Marketplace: American Thought and Culture, 1830–1860.*

Joan Shelley Rubin is Professor of History at the University of Rochester and author of *The Making of Middlebrow Culture*. Her work-in-progress includes the collaborative *A History of the Book in America* and a study of poetry and the reading public.

Jonathan D. Sarna is the Joseph H. and Belle R. Braun Professor of American Jewish History at Brandeis University and the author, editor, or co-editor of thirteen books including *Jacksonian Jew: The Two Worlds of Mordecai Noah, Minority Faiths and the American Jewish Mainstream*, and *Religion and State in the American Jewish Experience*. He is currently working on a new history of American Judaism.

Amy Dru Stanley is Assistant Professor of History at the University of Chicago. She is the author of *From Bondage to Contract: Wage Labor, Marriage, and the Market in the Age of Slave Emancipation* and articles on ideas of freedom and slavery in the *Journal of American History* and other publications.

Christine Stansell is Professor of History at Princeton University, the author of *City of Women: Sex and Class in New York, 1789–1860*, and coeditor of *Powers of Desire: The Politics of Sexuality*.

Tamara Plakins Thornton is Associate Professor of History at the State University of New York, Buffalo, and the author of *Handwriting in America: A Cultural History* and *Cultivating Gentlemen: The Meaning of Country Life among the Boston Elite, 1785–1860*.

Index

abolitionism, 4, 11
  and the body, 5, 127–33, 138–39
  and civil disobedience, 105
  and feminism, 137–40
  and law, 105–8
  and marriage, 131–35, 139, 141
  and moral reform, 110–11
  and possessive individualism, 125, 136
  and violence, 113–15, 120–21
Ackerman, Bruce, 185–86, 189, 191,
    196–97
aesthetics, and poetry, 267–68, 271, 274
African Americans
  and citizenship, 106–10, 179
  and Civil War, 150, 153, 156–59
  and labor, 60
  and New Deal, 192
  and patriotism, 109–10
  and Populists, 179
  and possessive individualism, 125
  See also abolitionism
ambidexterity. *See* handedness
American exceptionalism, 3–4, 62, 65,
    68–75
American Law Institute (ALI), 190
American Revolution, 6, 205–6
Americanization, of Jewish prayers, 207–8,
    211, 215, 219
Anglican Church, 17, 19, 24, 27, 29–30
antislavery. *See* abolitionism
Arendt, Hannah, 104
Arnold, Matthew, 268
asylums, 3, 42, 48–54

Beard, Charles and Mary, 5, 151–52
Beecher, Henry Ward, 3, 73–75
Birnbaum, Philip, 219
blacks. *See* African Americans
body, 5, 126–30, 132–33, 140, 143. *See*
    also eroticism
Boston, 29–30, 34–36
bourgeoisie
  and labor, 66–67, 69
  and social discipline, 55–56
  See also class; mystery, cult of
Boyce, Neith, 290–97, 302–5
Brandeis, Louis, 182–83
Brecht, George, 325–26
Bromfield, Edward, 30–32, 34–35
Brown, William Wells, 112–13
Burns, Ken, 5, 147–50, 156

Cambodia, 7, 247
Carlin, Terry, 291–92
caste. *See* race
Catholicism, 45–46, 235–36
chance. *See* luck
chaplains, military
  and institutional ministry, 7, 250–58
  moral problem of, 246–47
  pastoral vs. prophetic ministry of, 7–8,
    246–51, 254–58
Charleston Reform Movement, 6, 210–11
citizenship, 4–6
  blacks and, 106–10, 116–17
  and civil disobedience, 103–8, 116–17,
    120–21